# MCSD Visual Basic 6 Distributed

# The Cram Sheet

This Cram Sheet contains the distilled, key facts about the MCSD Visual Basic 6 Distributed exam. Review this information last thing before you enter the test room, paying special attention to those areas where you feel you need the most review. You can transfer any of these facts onto a blank sheet of paper before beginning thc cxam.

## CONFIGURING THE DEVELOPMENT ENVIRONMENT

1. Conditional compilation directives begin with the symbol #, and include **#If**, **#ElseIf**, **#Else**, and **#End If**.

2. **Win32** and **Win16** are known constants used with conditional compilation to determine the system on which the compiling is occurring.

3. Compile code before checking in VSS to ensure maintenance of a functional project.

## CREATING WEB-BASED CLIENTS

4. IIS can be used for creating thin-client applications requiring little support.

5. Use the **URLFor** method to determine runtime URLs for Webitems.

## CREATING AN ACTIVEX DOCUMENT

6. Navigate to the location of the VBD file to load an ActiveX document.

7. Use the **NavigateTo** method to move from document to document within code.

## CREATING BUSINESS SERVICES

8. Unattended Execution does not allow user interface elements; therefore, they are not allowed.

9. **LogPath** and **LogMode** properties are used with COM servers set to Unattended Execution to determine the file location for error logging.

10. Unique properties of objects, such as ID numbers, are best modeled as properties.

11. Setting **MTSTransactionMode** to the following values has the listed effect:
    - **NotAnMTSObject** Ignores MTS; does not participate in any way.
    - **NoTransactions** Does not participate in transactions.
    - **UsesTransactions** Will use client transaction, but will not generate its own.
    - **Requires Transactions** Will use client transaction or create its own.

12. Out-of-process ActiveX EXEs with the **Instancing** property set to **MultiUse** allow many clients to create many objects from a single component.

13. The following **ObjectContext** object methods perform the listed functions:
    - **SetAbort** Method results unacceptable for completing transaction.
    - **SetComplete** Method results acceptable for completing transaction.
    - **IsCallerInRole** Check participation of component caller in the given or specified role.

50. Recordsets can be created using different types of cursors (**adOpenForwardOnly**, **adOpenStatic**, **adOpenDynamic**, and **adOpenKeyset**). Know when to use each type.

51. Benefits of using disconnected recordsets in ADO include:
    - They can be scrolled and modified without maintaining a persistent connection.
    - They free up data service components to be recycled within MTS.

52. Disconnected recordsets require that the **LockType** property be set to **adLockBatchOptimistic** and the **CursorLocation** be set to **adUseClient**.

53. Server-side cursors are best for applications that do not access all the records in a recordset or that need to see the changes made by other users.

54. Joining tables using the **INNER JOIN** syntax of the **SELECT** statement is recommended.

55. Data modifications are typically more efficient when using the **Execute** method of the **Connection** object and passing it the SQL.

56. Multiple errors can be returned in the **Errors** collection of the **Connection** object. The first error is also returned in the VB **Error** object.

57. Know how to create an RDO recordset asynchronously.

58. Use the **BeginTrans**, **CommitTrans**, and **RollbackTrans** methods of the ADO **Connection** object to create logical units of work.

### DISTRIBUTING APPLICATIONS

59. The Package and Deployment Wizard can be used to create standard, Internet, and dependency packages.

60. When creating an Internet setup package the **CODEBASE** attribute of the **<OBJECT>** tag contains source and version information.

61. Remember to increment the version number in VB before compiling your application if you want existing clients to upgrade to the newer version.

62. Package and Deployment Wizard Setup packages can be deployed using the network, a floppy disk, or the Internet.

63. The server on which a COM component will be instantiated can be set using the DCOMCNFG utility.

64. The DCOM software is installed with Windows NT Service Pack 3 and must be installed separately on Windows 95 and 98.

65. MTS contains a package export utility that creates an executable for configuring client computers.

66. To configure a distributed application using the Package and Deployment Wizard you must generate and include a VBR file in the setup package.

67. In order to use DCOM, a COM object must have a reference in the HKEY_CLASSES_ROOT\AppID of the client computer.

### MAINTAINING DISTRIBUTED APPLICATIONS

68. MTS does not implement load balancing as of version 2.0.

69. Checking the Project Compatibility option upon compilation does not allow the component to be compatible with existing clients.

70. Binary Compatibility should only be used when method and property signatures remain the same between versions.

71. Your code can create a COM object on a specific server using the **CreateObject** statement.

72. Dynamic load balancing can be implemented using a referral component and algorithms to dynamically select the appropriate server.

73. Static load balancing always instantiates components on specific servers for specific users.

**Certification Insider**™ Press

37. Know how to create a Property page for an ActiveX control and use these events:
   - **SelectionChanged** Indicates that a property page element has changed.
   - **ApplyChanges** Saves information changes within the control's property page.
38. Know the following **UserControl** events:
   - **WriteProperties** Used to save persisted component data to the **PropertyBag** object.
   - **ReadProperties** Used to read in persisted component data after having been previously saved in the **WriteProperties** event.
   - **InitProperties** Used when no persisted data exists. Initializes component data prior to any saving to persistent storage (**PropertyBag** object).
39. **Extender** properties are referenced inside an ActiveX control using the *Extender.propertyname* syntax.
40. Testing an ActiveX control is most efficiently done using a project group.
41. Make a control data bound by setting the **DataBindingBehavior** property of the **UserControl** object.
42. Choose Project|Components to add third-party controls to your toolbox

**IMPLEMENTING DATA SERVICES**

43. Review the three methods for creating an ADO recordset (using the **Open** method of the **Recordset** or the **Execute** method of the **Command** or **Connection** objects). In the following, assume **cnSQL** represents an ADO **Connection** object.
   - **Recordset** object **Open** method:

```
rsAuthors.Open _
    "SELECT * FROM authors", cnSQL
```

   - **Connection** object **Execute** method:

```
Set rsAuthors = _
    cnSQL.Execute _
    ("SELECT * FROM authors")
```

   - **Command** object **Exccute** method:

```
With cmSQL
    .ActiveConnection = cnSQL
    .CommandText = _
        "SELECT * FROM authors"
    .CommandType = adCmdText
    .CommandTimeout = 10
End With

Set rsAuthors = cmSQL.Execute
```

44. ADO recordsets can be persisted to disk using the **Save** method.
45. Calling a stored procedure using an ADO **Command** object differs from a generic SQL statement by altering the value assigned to the **CommandType** property:

```
cmSQL.CommandType = adCmdStoredProc
```

46. Passing parameters to an ADO **Command** object is performed with the **CreateParameter** method of the **Command** object and the **Append** method of the **Parameters** collection:

```
Set prmSSN = _
    cmSQL.CreateParameter("@au_id", _
    adChar, adParamInput, _
    Len(strSSN), strSSN)
cmSQL.Parameters.Append prmSSN
```

47. Using the **Refresh** method of the **Parameters** collection and directly assigning values to indexed members of the **Parameters** collection can also be used for passing parameters to a stored procedure.
48. Executing a prepared statement using ADO is accomplished by setting the **Prepared** property of the **Command** object to **True** prior to executing. Subsequent uses of the **Command** object will utilize the prepared statement.
49. The **rdExecDirect** RDO option is used to bypass the creation of temporary stored procedures on the SQL database when executing statements.

- **IsSecurityEnabled** Check if authorization checking is invoked for component.

14. The <out of context> value for Watch variables indicates the value is currently out of the variables' defined scope.

15. The difference between the behavior of Break When Value Is True and Break When Value Changes requires an explicit Boolean statement as the variable definition. If the given expression is like **Name="Lizzy"**, Break When Value Is True should be used to ID a specific application variable value.

16. Watch variable expressions can be simple variable names, Boolean expressions, or any value expression. Simple Boolean statements, such as **Developer="Linda"**, are most commonly used with Break When Value Is True.

17. Specific variable values, object properties, or method results can be printed within the Immediate window.

18. The Local window provides the ability to view properties of the current form and all its constituent controls.

### DISTRIBUTED APPLICATION DESIGN

19. Distributed applications can be logically divided into services (User, Business, and Data).

20. The Visual Component Manager is used to publish information about components and other data so that it can be shared by multiple developers.

21. Security can be implemented at the business object or data services layers in Windows NT.

22. The conceptual design identifies the requirements of the application, whereas the physical design determines how the solution will be deployed.

23. To reuse the interface of an existing component, use the **Implements** keyword when creating a class module.

24. Populate elements in different tiers with data by filtering through the layers in order to maintain proper n-tier architecture.

### IMPLEMENTING USER SERVICES

25. The **CausesValidation** property triggers the **Validate** event on the control that is about to receive focus.

26. The **ConnectionString** and **RecordSource** properties of the ADO Data Control are necessary to allow the control to retrieve records.

27. A data environment can reference a stored procedure using a command.

28. The **AddressOf** operator is used to pass the address of a callback procedure to a Win32 API function.

29. Invoking the following error handlers will have the listed effect:
    - **On Error Goto** Followed by a line indicator, such as **ValidateError**, this causes the application to jump to that named line upon encountering an error.
    - **On Error Resume Next** Errors result in immediate execution of the next line of code.
    - **On Error Resume** Errors result in re-execution of the same line. Error is completely ignored.

30. When a procedure does not contain an error handler, errors are handled by either passing the error up to a calling procedure, if it exists, or issuing an application runtime error.

31. DispID and vtable interfaces are both forms of early binding.

32. The **HelpContextID** property of controls and the **HelpFile** property of the **App** object are used to implement user assistance.

33. You can use the **Add** method of the **Controls** collection to create controls dynamically.

### CREATING ACTIVEX CONTROLS

34. **Property Get** procedures are used to provide read access to an object property.

35. **Property Let** or **Set** procedures are used to provide write access to an object property. Eliminating these property functions leaves a property read-only.

36. Events in class modules are defined using the **Event** keyword and fired using the **RaiseEvent** statement.

# Microsoft
# Visual Basic 6
# Distributed

Microsoft
Certified
Solution
Developer

Michael Lane Thomas
and Dan Fox

**MCSD Visual Basic 6 Distributed Exam Cram**

**Limits Of Liability And Disclaimer Of Warranty**

The author and publisher of this book have used their best efforts in preparing the book and the programs contained in it. These efforts include the development, research, and testing of the theories and programs to determine their effectiveness. The author and publisher make no warranty of any kind, expressed or implied, with regard to these programs or the documentation contained in this book.

The author and publisher shall not be liable in the event of incidental or consequential damages in connection with, or arising out of, the furnishing, performance, or use of the programs, associated instructions, and/or claims of productivity gains.

**Trademarks**

Trademarked names appear throughout this book. Rather than list the names and entities that own the trademarks or insert a trademark symbol with each mention of the trademarked name, the publisher states that it is using the names for editorial purposes only and to the benefit of the trademark owner, with no intention of infringing upon that trademark.

The Coriolis Group, LLC
14455 N. Hayden Road, Suite 220
Scottsdale, Arizona 85260

602/483-0192
FAX 602/483-0193
http://www.coriolis.com

Library of Congress Cataloging-in-Publication Data
Thomas, Michael Lane.
  MCSD Visual Basic 6 distributed exam cram / by Michael Lane Thomas
and Dan Fox
      p.   cm.
  Includes index.
  ISBN 1-57610-375-7
  1. Electronic data processing personnel--Certification.   2. Microsoft
software--Examinations--Study guides.   3. Microsoft Visual
BASIC   I. Fox, Dan (Dan L.).   II. Title.   III. Title: MCSD Visual Basic
six distributed exam cram.
QA76.3.T53   1999
005.26'8--dc21                                                    98-52821
                                                                    CIP

Printed in the United States of America
10 9 8 7 6 5 4 3 2 1

**Publisher**
Keith Weiskamp

**Acquisitions Editor**
Shari Jo Hehr

**Marketing Specialist**
Cynthia Caldwell

**Project Editor**
Toni Zuccarini

**Technical Reviewer**
John Lueders

**Production Coordinator**
Meg E. Turecek

**Cover Design**
Jody Winkler

**Layout Design**
April Nielsen

14455   North   Hayden,   Suite   220   •   Scottsdale,   Arizona   85260

## *The Smartest Way To Get Certified* ™

Thank you for purchasing one of our innovative certification study guides, just one of the many members of the Coriolis family of certification products.

Certification Insider Press™ was created in late 1997 by The Coriolis Group to help professionals like you obtain certification and advance your career. Achieving certification involves a major commitment and a great deal of hard work. To help you reach your goals, we've listened to others like you, and we've designed our entire product line around you and the way you like to study, learn, and master challenging subjects. Our approach is *The Smartest Way To Get Certified.*

In less than a year, Coriolis has published over one million copies of our highly popular *Exam Cram, Exam Prep*, and *On Site* guides. Our *Exam Cram* books, specifically written to help you pass an exam, are the number one certification self-study guides in the industry. They are the perfect complement to any study plan you have, as well as to the rest of the Certification Insider Press series: *Exam Prep*, comprehensive study guides designed to help you thoroughly learn and master certification topics, and *On Site*, guides that really show you how to apply your skills and knowledge on the job.

Our commitment to you is to ensure that all of the certification study guides we develop help you save time and frustration. Each one provides unique study tips and techniques, memory joggers, custom quizzes, insight about test taking, practical problems to solve, real-world examples, and much more.

We'd like to hear from you. Help us continue to provide the very best certification study materials possible. Write us or email us at **craminfo@coriolis.com** and let us know how our books have helped you study, or tell us about new features that you'd like us to add. If you send us a story about how an *Exam Cram, Exam Prep*, or *On Site* book has helped you, and we use it in one of our books, we'll send you an official Coriolis shirt for your efforts.

Good luck with your certification exam and your career. Thank you for allowing us to help you achieve your goals.

Keith Weiskamp
Publisher, Certification Insider Press

*I dedicate this book to my wife, Jennifer, who withstood all the difficulties I imposed on her in enduring the last two to three months. I know these projects have been incredibly taxing on you. Thank you sweetie for hanging in there. Also to my father, Larry, for believing in me and being close enough to let some of his drive rub off on me. And finally, to the Lord Jesus Christ, who seems to replace every closed door with a ballroom of opportunity just down the hall...time and time again.*

*—Michael Lane Thomas*


*Without the support and encouragement of my wife, Beth, and daughter, Laura, I could not have completed this project. They were both patient and understanding despite the long hours and "mental distance." I love you both.*

*—Dan Fox*

# About The Authors

**Michael Lane Thomas** is a computer industry consultant and technical trainer who also spends his free time writing and speaking. He has spoken publicly on some of the hottest technologies to hit the industry, such as XML, SQL, and Y2K issues, and has been heard at Microsoft-sponsored national technical conferences, special interest groups, and on Kansas City's airwaves on 980KMBZ radio.

As an MCT, he currently teaches Microsoft Official Curriculum (MOC) courses, ranging from all the BackOffice products to the full range of Microsoft development and language technologies. Michael is certified to teach approximately 40 Microsoft courses, with more on the horizon, but he prefers to focus on the most recent development courses because "that's where the fun stuff is!"

When not teaching, Michael spends his time consulting as a SQL DBA, application developer, and general mentor. He prefers the challenge of designing, building, and developing complex intranet, three-tier Web applications, and advanced Web-based solutions. Michael currently holds the titles of MCP, MCP+I, MCSE, MCSE+I, MCT, MCSD, MCP+SB, MSS, and A+.

After graduating from the University of Kansas with a B.A. and B.S. in Mathematics, Michael has continued his traditional academic pursuits with a slow but steady climb towards his M.S. in Engineering Management from the University of Kansas. Michael is a former contributor and technical editor for the *Microsoft Certified Professional Magazine*, and author, contributor, and/or technical editor for six books to date.

Michael lives with his loving wife Jennifer, affectionately known by his nieces and nephew as "Racecar Jenny," for her sporty little blue ZX2. Residing in the western end of southern Johnson County, he occasionally longs for his days traveling around the world, but the smile of his wife Jennifer quickly reminds him why he is so lucky he finally came home.

**Dan Fox** is a consultant and instructor for Solutech, Inc. in Overland Park, Kansas. In addition to his consulting and teaching work with Visual Basic, Visual InterDev, SQL Server, and Powerbuilder, Dan is also the Database Line of Business Manager for Solutech. In his role at Solutech he also mentors consultants and designs intranet and client/server solutions.

After graduating from Iowa State University with a B.S. in Computer Science, Dan worked for Chevron in Houston, Texas, and the National Association of Insurance Commissioners in Kansas City before joining Solutech in 1995. A Microsoft Certified Solution Developer, Systems Engineer, and Trainer, Dan is a frequent contributor to the *Visual Basic Programmer's Journal* and has spoken at several Developer Days conferences.

Dan lives with his wife Beth and daughter Laura in Overland Park where they root for the Cubs and dream of a trip to the World Series at Wrigley Field.

# Acknowledgments

Without a doubt, I would like to offer the greatest of thanks to Shari Jo and Toni. To Shari Jo, thanks for turning around and walking back up those stairs in San Jose. To Toni, thanks for the patience. I am sure you were convinced I was taking you for granted—nothing could be further from the truth. Thanks also to Ellen Strader, the copy editor, whose job it was to point out the spots in the manuscript where I was more apt to have been sleeping than writing consciously. I would be amiss not to thank the book designers April Nielsen and Jody Winkler for giving a little pizzazz to the project and also big thanks to my Production Coordinator Meg Turecek for providing the all important layout of the book. Thanks to my co-author, Dan Fox, for his help, input, and contribution, without which I would have been a great deal more stressed in getting the project completed.

—*Michael Lane Thomas*


I would like to say thanks to several of the great people at The Coriolis Group, including Shari Jo Hehr, the acquisitions editor; Toni Zuccarini, the project editor; Ellen Strader, the copy editor; designers April Nielsen and Jody Winkler; and the Production Coordinator Meg Turecek, who was responsible for the layout of the book. Each of them provided invaluable help throughout the entire process. My thanks to Toni especially, as she deserves much of the credit for keeping everything together and making the process go smoothly. I'd also like to thank Michael Lane Thomas for bringing me in on the project and for his contribution to making the book a success.

—*Dan Fox*

# Contents At A Glance

# Table Of Contents

# Introduction

Welcome to the *MCSD Visual Basic 6 Distributed Exam Cram*! This book aims to help you get ready to take—and pass—the Microsoft certification test numbered 70-175, "Designing and Implementing Distributed Applications with Microsoft Visual Basic 6.0." This introduction explains Microsoft's certification programs in general and talks about how the *Exam Cram* series can help you prepare for Microsoft's certification exams.

*Exam Cram* books help you understand and appreciate the subjects and materials you need to pass Microsoft certification exams. *Exam Cram* books are aimed strictly at test preparation and review. They do not teach you everything you need to know about a topic (such as all the trade-offs involved in using Active Server Pages or DHTML or the nitty-gritty technical details of the calling mechanisms used by DCOM). Instead, we (the authors) present and dissect the questions and problems we've found that you're likely to encounter on a test. We've worked from Microsoft's own training materials, preparation guides, and tests, as well as from actual experience implementing distributed applications. Our aim is to bring together as much information as possible about Microsoft certification exams.

Nevertheless, to completely prepare yourself for any Microsoft test, we recommend that you begin your studies with some classroom training, or that you pick up and read one of the many study guides available. We also strongly recommend that you install, configure, and fool around with the software or environment that you'll be tested on, because nothing beats hands-on experience and familiarity when it comes to understanding the questions you're likely to encounter on a certification test. Book learning is essential, but hands-on experience is the best teacher of all.

## The Microsoft Certified Professional (MCP) Program

The MCP program currently includes eight separate tracks, each of which boasts its own special acronym (as a would-be certificant, you need to have a high tolerance for alphabet soup of all kinds).

➤ **MCP (Microsoft Certified Professional)** This is the least prestigious of all the certification tracks from Microsoft. Passing any of the major Microsoft exams (except the Networking Essentials exam) qualifies an individual for MCP credentials. Individuals can demonstrate proficiency with additional Microsoft products by passing additional certification exams.

➤ **MCP+I (Microsoft Certified Professional + Internet)** This midlevel certification is attained by completing three core exams: Windows NT Server 4, TCP/IP, and Internet Information Server (3 or 4).

➤ **MCP+SB (Microsoft Certified Professional + Site Building)** This certification program is designed for individuals who are planning, building, managing, and maintaining Web sites. Individuals with the MCP+SB credential will have demonstrated the ability to develop Web sites that include multimedia and searchable content and Web sites that connect to and communicate with a back-end database. It requires passing two of the following three exams: "Designing and Implementing Commerce Solutions with Microsoft Site Server 3.0, Commerce Edition," "Designing and Implementing Web Sites with Microsoft FrontPage 98," and "Designing and Implementing Web Solutions with Microsoft Visual InterDev 6.0."

➤ **MCSD (Microsoft Certified Solution Developer)** The MCSD credential reflects the skills required to create multitier, distributed, and COM-based solutions, in addition to desktop and Internet applications, using new technologies. To obtain an MCSD, an individual must demonstrate the ability to analyze and interpret user requirements; select and integrate products, platforms, tools, and technologies; design and implement code and customize applications; and perform necessary software tests and quality assurance operations.

To become an MCSD, you must pass a total of four exams: three core exams and one elective exam. The required core exam is "Analyzing Requirements and Defining Solution Architectures." Each candidate must also choose one of these two desktop application exams—"Designing and Implementing Desktop Applications with Microsoft Visual C++ 6.0" or "Designing and Implementing Desktop Applications with Visual Basic 6.0"—plus one of these two distributed application exams— "Designing and Implementing Distributed Applications with Microsoft Visual C++ 6.0" or "Designing and Implementing Distributed Applications with Microsoft Visual Basic 6.0." This book is devoted to the Visual Basic 6 Distributed exam, the last in that list.

# Table 1    MCSD Requirements*

## Core

| Choose 1 from the desktop applications development group | |
|---|---|
| **Exam 70-016** | Designing and Implementing Desktop Applications with Microsoft Visual C++ 6.0 |
| **Exam 70-176** | Designing and Implementing Desktop Applications with Microsoft Visual Basic 6.0 |
| **Choose 1 from the distributed applications development group** | |
| **Exam 70-015** | Designing and Implementing Distributed Applications with Microsoft Visual C++ 6.0 |
| **Exam 70-175** | Designing and Implementing Distributed Applications with Microsoft Visual Basic 6.0 |
| **This solution architecture exam is required** | |
| **Exam 70-100** | Analyzing Requirements and Defining Solution Architectures |

## Elective

| Choose 1 from this group | |
|---|---|
| **Exam 70-015** | Designing and Implementing Distributed Applications with Microsoft Visual C++ 6.0 |
| **Exam 70-016** | Designing and Implementing Desktop Applications with Microsoft Visual C++ 6.0 |
| **Exam 70-029** | Designing and Implementing Databases with Microsoft SQL Server 7.0 |
| **Exam 70-024** | Developing Applications with C++ Using the Microsoft Foundation Class Library |
| **Exam 70-025** | Implementing OLE in Microsoft Foundation Class Applications |
| **Exam 70-055** | Designing and Implementing Web Sites with Microsoft FrontPage 98 |
| **Exam 70-057** | Designing and Implementing Commerce Solutions with Microsoft Site Server 3.0, Commerce Edition |
| **Exam 70-165** | Developing Applications with Microsoft Visual Basic 5.0 |
| | OR |
| **Exam 70-175** | Designing and Implementing Distributed Applications with Microsoft Visual Basic 6.0 |
| | OR |
| **Exam 70-176** | Designing and Implementing Desktop Applications with Microsoft Visual Basic 6.0 |
| **Exam 70-069** | Application Development with Microsoft Access for Windows 95 and the Microsoft Access Developer's Toolkit |
| **Exam 70-091** | Designing and Implementing Solutions with Microsoft Office 2000 and Microsoft Visual Basic for Applications |
| **Exam 70-152** | Designing and Implementing Web Solutions with Microsoft Visual InterDev 6.0 |

\* This is not a complete listing—you can still be tested on some earlier versions of these products. However, we have tried to include the most recent versions so that you may test on these versions and thus be certified longer. We have not included any tests that are scheduled to be retired.

The MCSD program is being expanded to include FoxPro and Visual J++. However, these tests are not yet available and no test numbers have been assigned.

Core exams that can also be used as elective exams can be counted only once toward certification. The same test cannot be used as both a core and elective exam.

Elective exams cover specific Microsoft applications and languages, including Visual Basic, C++, the Microsoft Foundation Classes, Access, SQL Server, Excel, and more. If you're on your way to becoming an MCSD and have already taken some exams, visit **www.microsoft.com/ train_cert/** for information about how to proceed with your MCSD certification under this new track. Table 1 shows the requirements for the MCSD certification.

➤ **MCSE (Microsoft Certified Systems Engineer)** Anyone who has a current MCSE is warranted to possess a high level of expertise with Windows NT (version 3.51 or 4) and other Microsoft operating systems and products. This credential is designed to prepare individuals to plan, implement, maintain, and support information systems and networks built around Microsoft Windows NT and its BackOffice family of products.

To obtain an MCSE, an individual must pass four core operating system exams, plus two elective exams. The operating system exams require individuals to demonstrate competence with desktop and server operating systems and with networking components.

You must pass at least two Windows NT-related exams to obtain an MCSE: "Implementing and Supporting Microsoft Windows NT Server" (version 3.51 or 4) and "Implementing and Supporting Microsoft Windows NT Server in the Enterprise" (version 3.51 or 4). These tests are intended to indicate an individual's knowledge of Windows NT in smaller, simpler networks and in larger, more complex, and heterogeneous networks, respectively.

You must pass two additional tests as well. These tests relate to networking and desktop operating systems. At present, the networking requirement can be satisfied only by passing the Networking Essentials test. The desktop operating system test can be satisfied by passing a Windows 95, Windows NT Workstation (the version must match whichever core NT curriculum you are pursuing), or Windows 98 test.

The two remaining exams are elective exams. An elective exam may fall in any number of subject or product areas, primarily BackOffice components. These include tests on Internet Explorer 4, SQL Server, IIS, SNA Server, Exchange Server, Systems Management Server, and the like. However, it's also possible to test out on electives by taking advanced networking tests such as "Internetworking with Microsoft TCP/IP on Microsoft Windows NT" (but here again, the version of Windows NT involved must match the version for the core requirements taken).

Whatever mix of tests is completed toward MCSE certification, individuals must pass six tests to meet the MCSE requirements. It's not uncommon for the entire process to take a year or so, and many individuals find that they must take a test more than once to pass. Our primary goal with the *Exam Cram* series is to make it possible, given proper study and preparation, to pass all Microsoft certification tests on the first try.

➤ **MCSE+Internet (Microsoft Certified Systems Engineer + Internet)** This is a newer Microsoft certification and focuses not just on Microsoft operating systems, but also on Microsoft's Internet servers and TCP/IP.

To obtain this certification, an individual must pass seven core exams, plus two elective exams. The core exams include not only the server operating systems (NT Server and Server in the Enterprise) and a desktop operating system (Windows 95, Windows 98, or Windows NT Workstation), but also include Networking Essentials, TCP/IP, Internet Information Server, and the Internet Explorer Administration Kit (IEAK).

The two remaining exams are electives. These elective exams can be in any of four product areas: SQL Server, SNA Server, Exchange Server, and Proxy Server.

➤ **MCDBA (Microsoft Certified Database Administrator)** The MCDBA credential reflects the skills required to implement and administer Microsoft SQL Server databases. To obtain an MCDBA, an individual must demonstrate the ability to derive physical database designs, develop logical data models, create physical databases, create data services by using Transact-SQL, manage and maintain databases, configure and manage security, monitor and optimize databases, and install and configure Microsoft SQL Server.

To become an MCDBA, you must pass a total of five exams: four core exams and one elective exam. The required core exams are "Administering Microsoft SQL Server 7.0," "Designing and Implementing Databases with Microsoft SQL Server 7.0," "Implementing and Supporting Microsoft Windows NT Server 4.0," and "Implementing and Supporting Microsoft Windows NT Server 4.0 in the Enterprise."

The elective exams that you can choose from cover specific uses of SQL Server and include "Designing and Implementing Distributed Applications with Visual Basic 6.0," "Designing and Implementing Distributed Applications with Visual C++ 6.0," "Designing and Implementing Data Warehouses with Microsoft SQL Server 7.0 and Microsoft Decision Support Services 1.0," and two exams that relate to NT "Internetworking

## Table 2  MCDBA Requirements

### Core

| All 4 of these are required | |
|---|---|
| **Exam 70-028** | Administering Microsoft SQL Server 7.0 |
| **Exam 70-029** | Designing and Implementing Databases with Microsoft SQL Server 7.0 |
| **Exam 70-067** | Implementing and Supporting Microsoft Windows NT Server 4.0 |
| **Exam 70-068** | Implementing and Supporting Microsoft Windows NT Server 4.0 in the Enterprise |

### Elective

| Choose 1 from this group | |
|---|---|
| **Exam 70-015** | Designing and Implementing Distributed Applications with Microsoft Visual C++ 6.0 |
| **Exam 70-019** | Designing and Implementing Data Warehouses with Microsoft SQL Server 7.0 and Microsoft Decision Support Services 1.0 |
| **Exam 70-059** | Internetworking with Microsoft TCP/IP on Microsoft Windows NT 4.0 |
| **Exam 70-087** | Implementing and Supporting Microsoft Internet Information Server 4.0 |
| ▶ **Exam 70-175** | Designing and Implementing Distributed Applications with Microsoft Visual Basic 6.0 |

with Microsoft TCP/IP on Microsoft Windows NT 4.0" and "Implementing and Supporting Microsoft Internet Information Server 4.0."

Note that the exam covered by this book can be used as the elective for the MCDBA certification. Table 2 shows the requirements for the MCDBA certification.

➤ **MCT (Microsoft Certified Trainer)**  Microsoft Certified Trainers are individuals deemed able to deliver elements of the official Microsoft curriculum based on technical knowledge and instructional ability. Therefore, it's necessary for an individual seeking MCT credentials (which are granted on a course-by-course basis) to pass the related certification exam for a course and to take the official Microsoft training on the subject, as well as to demonstrate an ability to teach.

This latter criterion may be satisfied by proving that one has already attained training certification from Novell, Banyan, Lotus, the Santa Cruz Operation, or Cisco, or by taking a Microsoft-sanctioned workshop on instruction. Microsoft makes it clear that MCTs are important cogs in the Microsoft training channels. Instructors must be MCTs before Microsoft will allow them to teach in any of its official training channels, including Microsoft's affiliated Authorized Technical Education Centers (ATECs), Authorized Academic Training Programs (AATPs), and the Microsoft Online Institute (MOLI).

Certification is an ongoing activity. Once a Microsoft product becomes obsolete, MCPs typically have 12 to 18 months in which to recertify on current product versions. (If individuals do not recertify within the specified time period, their certification becomes invalid.) Because technology keeps changing and new products continually supplant old ones, this should come as no surprise.

The best place to keep tabs on the MCP program and its various certifications is on the Microsoft Web site. The current root URL for the MCP program is at **www.microsoft.com/mcp/**. However, Microsoft's Web site changes frequently, so if this URL doesn't work, try using the search tool on Microsoft's site with either "MCP" or the quoted phrase "Microsoft Certified Professional program" as the search string. This will help you find the latest and most accurate information about the company's certification programs.

# Taking A Certification Exam

Alas, testing is not free. Each computer-based MCP exam costs $100, and if you do not pass, you may retest for an additional $100 for each additional try. In the United States and Canada, tests are administered by Sylvan Prometric and Virtual University Enterprises (VUE). Here's how you can contact them:

➤ **Sylvan Prometric** You can sign up for a test through the company's Web site at **www.slspro.com**. You can also register by phone at 800-755-3926 (within the United States or Canada) or at 410-843-8000 (outside the United States and Canada).

➤ **Virtual University Enterprises** You can sign up for a test or get the phone numbers for local testing centers through the Web page at **www.microsoft.com/train_cert/mcp/vue_info.htm**.

To sign up for a test, you must possess a valid credit card or contact either company for mailing instructions to send it a check (in the United States). Only when payment is verified, or a check has cleared, can you actually register for a test.

To schedule an exam, call Sylvan or VUE, or sign up online at least one day in advance. To cancel or reschedule an exam, you must call by 7 P.M. (Pacific time) the day before the scheduled test (or you may be charged, even if you don't appear to take the test). When you want to schedule a test, have the following information ready:

➤ Your name, organization, and mailing address.

➤ Your Microsoft test ID. (Inside the United States, this is your Social Security number; citizens of other nations should call ahead to find out what type of identification number is required to register for a test.)

➤ The name and number of the exam you wish to take.

➤ A method of payment. (As we've already mentioned, a credit card is the most convenient method, but alternate means can be arranged in advance, if necessary.)

Once you sign up for a test, you'll be informed as to when and where the test is scheduled. Try to arrive at least 15 minutes early. You must supply two forms of identification to be admitted into the testing room—one of which must be a photo ID.

All exams are completely "closed book." In fact, you will not be permitted to take anything with you into the testing area. However, you will be furnished with a blank sheet of paper and a pen. We suggest that you immediately write down on that sheet of paper all the information you've memorized for the test.

In *Exam Cram* books, this information appears on The Cram Sheet inside the front of each book. You'll have some time to compose yourself, record this information, and even take a sample orientation exam before you must begin the real thing. We suggest you take the orientation test before taking your first exam, but because they're all more or less identical in layout, behavior, and controls, you probably won't need to do this more than once.

When you complete a Microsoft certification exam, the software will tell you whether you've passed or failed. All tests are scored on a basis of 1,000 points, and results are broken into several topic areas. Even if you fail, we suggest you ask for—and keep—the detailed report that the test administrator should print for you. You can use this report to help you prepare for another go-around, if needed.

If you need to retake an exam, you'll have to call Sylvan Prometric or VUE, schedule a new test date, and pay another $100. Microsoft has the following policy regarding failed tests: The first time you fail a test, you are able to retake the test the next day. However, if you fail a second time, you must wait 14 days before retaking that test.

# Tracking MCP Status

As soon as you pass any Microsoft exam (other than Networking Essentials), you'll attain Microsoft Certified Professional (MCP) status. Microsoft also generates transcripts that indicate which exams you have passed and your corresponding test scores. You can order a transcript by email at any time by sending an email addressed to **mcp@msprograms.com**. You can also obtain a copy of your transcript by downloading the latest version of the MCT guide from the Web site and consulting the section titled "Key Contacts" for a list of telephone numbers and related contacts.

Once you pass the necessary set of exams (one for MCP, four for MCSD, five for MCDBA), you'll be certified. Official certification normally takes anywhere from four to six weeks, so don't expect to get your credentials overnight. When the package for a qualified certification arrives, it includes a Welcome Kit that contains a number of elements:

➤ An MCP, MCSD, or MCDBA certificate, suitable for framing, along with a Professional Program Membership card and lapel pin.

➤ A license to use the MCP logo, thereby allowing you to use the logo in advertisements, promotions, and documents, as well as on letterhead, business cards, and so on. Along with the license comes an MCP logo sheet, which includes camera-ready artwork. (Note that before using any of the artwork, individuals must sign and return a licensing agreement that indicates they'll abide by its terms and conditions.)

➤ A subscription to *Microsoft Certified Professional Magazine*, which provides ongoing data about testing and certification activities, requirements, and changes to the program.

➤ A one-year subscription to the Microsoft Beta Evaluation program. This subscription will get you all beta products from Microsoft for the next year. (This does not include developer products. You must join the MSDN program or become an MCSD to qualify for developer beta products. To join the MSDN program, go to **msdn.microsoft.com/ developer/join/**.)

Many people believe that the benefits of MCP certification go well beyond the perks that Microsoft provides to newly anointed members of this elite group. We're starting to see more job listings that request or require applicants to have an MCP, MCSD, MCDBA, and so on, and many individuals who complete the program can qualify for increases in pay and/or responsibility. As an official recognition of hard work and broad knowledge, one of the MCP credentials is a badge of honor in many IT organizations.

# How To Prepare For An Exam

Preparing for any Microsoft product-related test (including Visual Basic 6.0 Distributed) requires that you obtain and study materials designed to provide comprehensive information about the product and its capabilities that will appear on the specific exam for which you are preparing. The following list of materials will help you study and prepare:

➤ The Visual Studio 6.0 product CD-ROMs include comprehensive online documentation and related materials; it should be a primary resource when you are preparing for the test.

➤ The Microsoft Developer Network (MSDN) online at **msdn.microsoft.com** provides a wealth of information on all the development products and includes the reference materials shipped with Visual Studio. You should use and search this site exhaustively for insights on all the topics discussed on the exam.

➤ Microsoft Press offers titles on Visual Basic. Visit **mspress.microsoft.com/findabook/list/subject_L3.htm** for a complete list of its offerings. The more advanced titles will help you learn the ins and outs of distributed applications.

➤ The Microsoft TechNet CD-ROM delivers numerous electronic titles on Visual Basic. Its offerings include Product Information, Product Facts, Technical Notes, Tips and Techniques, and Tools and Utilities. A subscription to TechNet costs $299 per year but is well worth the price. Visit **www.microsoft.com/technet/** and check out the information under the "TechNet Subscription" menu entry for more details.

➤ Find, download, and use the exam prep materials, practice tests, and self-assessment exams on the Microsoft Training And Certification Download page (**www.microsoft.com/train_cert/download/downld.htm**).

In addition, you'll probably find any or all of the following materials useful in your quest for Visual Basic 6.0 expertise:

➤ **Microsoft Training Kits**  Although there's no training kit currently available from Microsoft Press for Visual Basic 6.0, many other topics have such kits. It's worthwhile to check to see if Microsoft has come out with anything by the time you need this information at **mspress.microsoft.com/sections/train.asp**.

➤ **Study Guides**  Several publishers—including Certification Insider Press—offer learning materials necessary to pass the tests. The Certification Insider Press series includes:

>   ➤ **The *Exam Cram* series**  These books give you information about the material you need to know to pass the tests.

>   ➤ **The *Exam Prep* series**  These books provide a greater level of detail than the *Exam Cram* books.

>   *Note: There currently is an Exam Prep book for the Visual Basic 6.0 desktop exam but not for the distributed exam.*

➤ **Classroom Training** CTECs, AATPs, MOLI, and unlicensed third-party training companies (such as Wave Technologies, American Research Group, Learning Tree, Data-Tech, and others) all offer classroom training on Visual Basic 6.0. These companies aim to help prepare developers to build great applications with these tools to pass the certification tests. In particular the official Microsoft curriculum courses 1013, 1016, and 1298 will prepare you well for the exam. Although such training runs upward of $350 per day in class, most of the individuals lucky enough to partake (including your humble authors, who've even taught such courses) find them to be quite worthwhile.

➤ **Other Publications** You'll find direct references to other publications and resources in this text, but there's no shortage of materials available about Visual Basic. To help you sift through some of the publications out there, we end each chapter with a "Need To Know More?" section that provides pointers to more complete and exhaustive resources covering the chapter's information. This should give you an idea of where we think you should look for further discussion.

By far, this set of required and recommended materials represents a nonpareil collection of sources and resources for Visual Basic and related topics. We anticipate that you'll find that this book belongs in this company. In the section that follows, we explain how this book works, and we give you some good reasons why this book counts as a member of the required and recommended materials list.

# About This Book

Each topical *Exam Cram* chapter follows a regular structure, along with graphical cues about important or useful information. Here's the structure of a typical chapter:

➤ **Opening Hotlists** Each chapter begins with a list of the terms, tools, and techniques that you must learn and understand before you can be fully conversant with that chapter's subject matter. We follow the hotlists with one or two introductory paragraphs to set the stage for the rest of the chapter.

➤ **Topical Coverage** After the opening hotlists, each chapter covers a series of topics related to the chapter's subject title. Throughout this section, we highlight topics or concepts likely to appear on a test using a special Study Alert layout, like this:

This is what a Study Alert looks like. Normally, a Study Alert stresses concepts, terms, software, or activities that are likely to relate to one or more certification test questions. For that reason, we think any information found offset in Study Alert format is worthy of unusual attentiveness on your part. Indeed, most of the information that appears on The Cram Sheet appears as Study Alerts within the text.

Pay close attention to material flagged as a Study Alert; although all the information in this book pertains to what you need to know to pass the exam, we flag certain items that are really important. You'll find what appears in the meat of each chapter to be worth knowing, too, when preparing for the test. Because this book's material is very condensed, we recommend that you use this book along with other resources to achieve the maximum benefit.

In addition to the Study Alerts, we have provided tips that will help you build a better foundation for Visual Basic knowledge. Although the information may not be on the exam, it's certainly related and will help you become a better test-taker.

This is how tips are formatted. Keep your eyes open for these, and you'll become a Visual Basic guru in no time!

➤ **Practice Questions** Although we talk about test questions and topics throughout each chapter, this section presents a series of mock test questions and explanations of both correct and incorrect answers. We also try to point out especially tricky questions by using a special icon, like this:

Ordinarily, this icon flags the presence of a particularly devious inquiry, if not an outright trick question. Trick questions are calculated to be answered incorrectly if not read more than once—and carefully at that. Although they're not ubiquitous, such questions make regular appearances on the Microsoft exams. That's why we say exam questions are as much about reading comprehension as they are about knowing your material inside out and backwards.

➤ **Details And Resources** Every chapter ends with a section titled "Need To Know More?". These sections provide direct pointers to Microsoft and third-party resources offering more details on the chapter's subject. In addition, these sections try to rank or at least rate the quality and thoroughness of the topic's coverage by each resource. If you find a resource you like in this collection, use it, but don't feel compelled to use all the resources. On the other hand, we recommend only resources we use on a regular basis, so none of our recommendations will be a waste of your time or money (but purchasing them all at once probably represents an expense that many developers and would-be MCSDs and MCDBAs might find hard to justify).

The bulk of the book follows this chapter structure slavishly, but there are a few other elements we'd like to point out. Chapter 13 is a sample test that provides a good review of the material presented throughout the book to ensure you're ready for the exam. Chapter 14 is an answer key to the sample test that appears in Chapter 13. Additionally, you'll find a glossary that explains terms and an index that you can use to track down terms as they appear in the text.

Finally, the tear-out Cram Sheet attached next to the inside front cover of this *Exam Cram* book represents a condensed and compiled collection of facts, figures, and tips that we think you should memorize before taking the test. Because you can dump this information out of your head onto a piece of paper before taking the exam, you can master this information by brute force—you need to remember it only long enough to write it down when you walk into the test room. You might even want to look at it in the car or in the lobby of the testing center just before you walk in to take the test.

# How To Use This Book

If you're prepping for a first-time test, we've structured the topics in this book to build on one another. Therefore, some topics in later chapters make more sense after you've read earlier chapters. That's why we suggest you read this book from front to back for your initial test preparation. If you need to brush up on a topic or you have to bone up for a second try, use the index or table of contents to go straight to the topics and questions that you need to study. Beyond helping you prepare for the tests, we think you'll find this book useful as a tightly focused reference to some of the most important aspects of distributed applications with Visual Basic 6.0.

Given all the book's elements and its specialized focus, we've tried to create a tool that will help you prepare for—and pass—Microsoft Exam 70-175,

"Designing and Implementing Distributed Applications with Microsoft Visual Basic 6.0." Although this book covers distributed aspects of VB6, you may encounter desktop questions on the exam. If this is a concern to you, you may want to prepare for both exams before you take either. Please share your feedback on the book with us, especially if you have ideas about how we can improve it for future test-takers. We'll consider everything you say carefully, and we'll respond to all suggestions.

Please send your questions or comments to us at **craminfo@coriolis.com**. Please remember to include the title of the book in your message; otherwise, we'll be forced to guess which book you're writing about. Also, be sure to check out our Web page at **www.certificationinsider.com**, where you'll find information updates, commentary, and certification information.

Thanks, and enjoy the book!

# Microsoft Certification Exams

## Terms you'll need to understand:

√ Radio button

√ Checkbox

√ Exhibit

√ Multiple-choice question formats

√ Careful reading

√ Process of elimination

√ Adaptive tests

√ Fixed-length tests

√ Simulations

## Techniques you'll need to master:

√ Preparing to take a certification exam

√ Practicing (to make perfect)

√ Making the best use of the testing software

√ Budgeting your time

√ Saving the hardest questions until last

√ Guessing (as a last resort)

Exam taking is not something that most people anticipate eagerly, no matter how well prepared they may be. In most cases, familiarity helps offset test anxiety. In plain English, this means you probably won't be as nervous when you take your fourth or fifth Microsoft certification exam as you'll be when you take your first one.

Whether it's your first exam or your tenth, understanding the details of exam taking (how much time to spend on questions, the environment you'll be in, and so on) and the exam software will help you concentrate on the material rather than on the setting. Likewise, mastering a few basic exam-taking skills should help you recognize—and perhaps even outfox—some of the tricks and snares you're bound to find in some of the exam questions.

This chapter, besides explaining the exam environment and software, describes some proven exam-taking strategies that you should be able to use to your advantage.

# The Exam Situation

When you arrive at the testing center where you scheduled your exam, you'll need to sign in with an exam coordinator. He or she will ask you to show two forms of identification, one of which must be a photo ID. After you've signed in and your time slot arrives, you'll be asked to deposit any books, bags, or other items you brought with you. Then, you'll be escorted into a closed room. Typically, the room will be furnished with anywhere from one to half a dozen computers, and each workstation will be separated from the others by dividers designed to keep you from seeing what's happening on someone else's computer.

You'll be furnished with a pen or pencil and a blank sheet of paper, or, in some cases, an erasable plastic sheet and an erasable pen. You're allowed to write down anything you want on both sides of this sheet. Before the exam, you should memorize as much of the material that appears on The Cram Sheet (in the front of this book) as you can, so you can write that information on the blank sheet as soon as you are seated in front of the computer. You can refer to your rendition of The Cram Sheet anytime you like during the test, but you'll have to surrender the sheet when you leave the room.

Most test rooms feature a wall with a large picture window. This permits the exam coordinator to monitor the room, to prevent exam-takers from talking to one another, and to observe anything out of the ordinary that might go on. The exam coordinator will have preloaded the appropriate Microsoft certification exam—for this book, that's Exam 70-175—and you'll be permitted to start as soon as you're seated in front of the computer.

All Microsoft certification exams allow a certain maximum amount of time in which to complete your work (this time is indicated on the exam by an on-screen counter/clock, so you can check the time remaining whenever you like). The fixed-length Visual Basic Distributed exam consists of 71 randomly selected questions. You may take up to 90 minutes to complete the exam.

All Microsoft certification exams are computer generated and use a multiple-choice format. Although this may sound quite simple, the questions are constructed not only to check your mastery of basic facts and concepts of Visual Basic and distributed application technologies, but they also require you to evaluate one or more sets of circumstances or requirements. Often, you'll be asked to give more than one answer to a question. Likewise, you might be asked to select the best or most effective solution to a problem from a range of choices, all of which technically are correct. Taking an exam is quite an adventure, and it involves real thinking. This book shows you what to expect and how to deal with the potential problems, puzzles, and predicaments.

Some Microsoft exams employ more advanced testing capabilities than might immediately meet the eye. Although the questions that appear are still multiple choice, the logic that drives them is more complex than older Microsoft tests, which use a fixed sequence of questions (called a *fixed-length* computerized exam). Other exams employ a sophisticated user interface (which Microsoft calls a *simulation*) to test your knowledge of the software and systems under consideration in a more or less "live" environment that behaves just like the original.

For upcoming exams, Microsoft is turning to a well-known technique, called *adaptive testing*, to establish a test-taker's level of knowledge and product competence. These exams look the same as fixed-length exams, but an adaptive exam discovers the level of difficulty at and below which an individual test-taker can correctly answer questions. At the same time, Microsoft is in the process of converting all its older fixed-length exams into adaptive exams as well.

Test-takers with differing levels of knowledge or ability therefore see different sets of questions; individuals with high levels of knowledge or ability are presented with a smaller set of more difficult questions, whereas individuals with lower levels of knowledge are presented with a larger set of easier questions. Both individuals may answer the same percentage of questions correctly, but the test-taker with a higher knowledge or ability level will score higher because his or her questions are worth more.

Also, the lower-level test-taker will probably answer more questions than his or her more knowledgeable colleague. This explains why adaptive tests use ranges of values to define the number of questions and the amount of time it takes to complete the test.

Adaptive tests work by evaluating the test-taker's most recent answer. A correct answer leads to a more difficult question (and the test software's estimate of the test-taker's knowledge and ability level is raised). An incorrect answer leads to a less difficult question (and the test software's estimate of the test-taker's knowledge and ability level is lowered). This process continues until the test targets the test-taker's true ability level. The exam ends when the test-taker's level of accuracy meets a statistically acceptable value (in other words, when his or her performance demonstrates an acceptable level of knowledge and ability) or when the maximum number of items has been presented (in which case, the test-taker is almost certain to fail).

Microsoft tests come in one form or the other—either they're fixed-length or they're adaptive. Therefore, you must take the test in whichever form it appears—you can't choose one form over another. However, if anything, it pays off even more to prepare thoroughly for an adaptive exam than for a fixed-length one: The penalties for answering incorrectly are built into the test itself on an adaptive exam, whereas the layout remains the same for a fixed-length test, no matter how many questions you answer incorrectly.

 The biggest difference between an adaptive test and a fixed-length test is that on a fixed-length test, you can revisit questions after you've read them over one or more times. On an adaptive test, you must answer the question when it's presented, and you'll have no opportunities to revisit that question thereafter. As of this writing, the Visual Basic Distributed exam is a fixed-length exam, but this can change at any time. Therefore, you must prepare as if it were an adaptive exam to ensure the best possible results.

In the section that follows, you'll learn more about what Microsoft test questions look like and how they must be answered.

# Exam Layout And Design

Some exam questions require you to select a single answer, whereas others ask you to select multiple correct answers. The following multiple-choice question requires you to select a single correct answer. Following the question is a brief summary of each potential answer and why it is either right or wrong.

## Question 1

To maintain compatibility with existing clients when compiling an ActiveX component in Visual Basic, you need to select which of the following options on the Project Properties dialog box?

○ a. No Compatibility

○ b. Project Compatibility

○ c. Binary Compatibility

○ d. None of the above. Components are always version compatible.

Answer c is correct. By selecting Binary Compatibility you ensure that the compiler will reuse the same unique identifiers generated when the component was first compiled if possible. This allows existing client applications, with those identifiers compiled into their binary image, to use the new version of the component. Answer a is incorrect because No Compatibility instructs the compiler to generate new identifiers for the component. Answer b is incorrect because Project Compatibility holds some identifiers constant, but changes others, and as a result is only useful during testing.

This sample question format corresponds closely to the Microsoft certification exam format—the only difference on the exam is that questions are not followed by answer keys. To select an answer, position the cursor over the radio button next to the answer. Then, click the mouse button to select the answer.

Let's examine a question that requires choosing multiple answers. This type of question provides checkboxes rather than radio buttons for marking all appropriate selections.

## Question 2

Which are valid intrinsic Active Server Page (ASP) objects? [Check all correct answers]

❑ a. **Response**

❑ b. **Request**

❑ c. **Server**

❑ d. **Browser**

The correct answers to this question are a, b, and c. The **Response** object is used in ASP to format an HTTP response message that is sent to the browser and includes methods such as **Redirect** and **Write**. The **Request** object is used to read the values coming back from the browser such as the form values and query string. The **Server** object is primarily used to instantiate COM objects through ASP. Answer d is wrong because no **Browser** object exists, although a COM object that provides information about the user's browser is installed with ASP.

For this type of question, more than one answer may be required. As far as the authors can tell (and Microsoft won't comment), such questions are scored as wrong unless all the required selections are chosen. In other words, a partially correct answer does not result in partial credit when the test is scored. For Question 2, you have to check the boxes next to items a, b, and c to obtain credit for a correct answer. Notice that picking the right answers also means knowing why the other answers are wrong.

Although these two basic types of questions can appear in many forms, they constitute the foundation on which all the Microsoft certification exam questions rest. More complex questions include so-called *exhibits*, which are usually screen shots of various Visual Basic tools or utilities. For some of these questions, you'll be asked to make a selection by clicking on a checkbox or radio button on the screen shot itself. For others, you'll be expected to use the information displayed therein to guide your answer to the question. Familiarity with the underlying tool or utility is your key to choosing the correct answer(s).

Other questions involving exhibits use charts or network diagrams to help document a workplace scenario that you'll be asked to troubleshoot or configure. Careful attention to such exhibits is the key to success. Be prepared to toggle frequently between the exhibit and the question as you work.

# Recognizing Your Test Type: Fixed-Length Or Adaptive

When you begin your exam, the software will tell you the test is adaptive, if in fact the version you're taking is presented as an adaptive test. If your introductory materials fail to mention this, you're probably taking a fixed-length test. However, when you look at your first question, you'll be able to tell for sure: If it includes a checkbox that lets you mark the question (for later return and review) you'll know you're taking a fixed-length test, because adaptive test questions can only be visited (and answered) once, and they include no such checkbox.

## The Fixed-Length Test-Taking Strategy

A well-known principle when taking fixed-length exams is to first read over the entire exam from start to finish while answering only those questions you feel absolutely sure of. On subsequent passes, you can dive into more complex questions more deeply, knowing how many such questions you have left. On adaptive tests, you get only one shot at the question, which is why preparation is so crucial for such tests.

Fortunately, the Microsoft exam software for fixed-length tests makes the multiple-visit approach easy to implement. At the top-left corner of each question is a checkbox that permits you to mark that question for a later visit. (Note that marking questions makes review easier, but you can return to any question if you're willing to click the Forward or Back buttons repeatedly.) As you read each question, if you answer only those you're sure of and mark for review those that you're not sure of, you can keep working through a decreasing list of questions as you answer the trickier ones in order.

There's at least one potential benefit to reading the exam over completely before answering the trickier questions: Sometimes, information supplied in later questions will shed more light on earlier questions. Other times, information you read in later questions might jog your memory about Visual Basic facts, figures, or behavior that also will help with earlier questions. Either way, you'll come out ahead if you defer those questions about which you're not absolutely sure.

Here are some question-handling strategies that apply only to fixed-length tests. Use them if you have the chance:

➤ When returning to a question after your initial read-through, read every word again—otherwise, your mind can fall quickly into a rut. Sometimes, revisiting a question after turning your attention elsewhere lets you see something you missed, but the strong tendency is to see what you've seen before. Try to avoid that tendency at all costs.

➤ If you return to a question more than twice, try to articulate to yourself what you don't understand about the question, why the answers don't appear to make sense, or what appears to be missing. If you chew on the subject for awhile, your subconscious might provide the details that are lacking, or you might notice a "trick" that will point to the right answer.

As you work your way through the exam, another counter that Microsoft thankfully provides will come in handy—the number of questions completed and questions outstanding. For fixed-length tests, it's wise to budget your time by making sure that you've completed one-quarter of the questions one-quarter of the way through the exam period (or the first 18 questions in the first 23 minutes) and three-quarters of the questions three-quarters of the way through (53 questions in the first 68 minutes).

If you're not finished when 85 minutes have elapsed, use the last 5 minutes to guess your way through the remaining questions. Remember, guessing is potentially more valuable than not answering, because blank answers are always wrong, but a guess may turn out to be right. If you don't have a clue about any of the remaining questions, pick answers at random, or choose all a's, b's, and so on. The important thing is to submit an exam for scoring that has an answer for every question.

At the very end of your exam period, you're better off guessing than leaving questions unanswered.

## The Adaptive Test-Taking Strategy

If there's one principle that applies to taking an adaptive test, it could be summed up as "Get it right the first time." You cannot elect to skip a question and move on to the next one when taking an adaptive test, because the testing software uses your answer to the current question to select whatever question it plans to present to you next. Also, you cannot return to a question once you've moved on, because the software only gives you one chance to answer the question.

When you answer a question correctly, you are presented with a more difficult question next to help the software gauge your level of skill and ability. When you answer a question incorrectly, you are presented with a less difficult question, and the software lowers its current estimate of your skill and ability. This continues until the program settles into a reasonably accurate estimate of what you know and can do, and it takes you through somewhere between 25 and 35 questions, on average, as you complete the test.

The good news is that if you know your stuff, you'll probably finish most adaptive tests in 30 minutes or so. The bad news is that you must really, really know your stuff to do your best on an adaptive test. That's because some questions are so convoluted, complex, or hard to follow that you're bound to miss one or two, at a minimum, even if you do know your stuff. Therefore, the more you know, the better you'll do on an adaptive test, even accounting for the occasionally weird or unfathomable question that appears on these exams.

As of this writing, Microsoft has not advertised which tests are strictly adaptive. You'll be best served by preparing for the exam as if it were adaptive. That way, you should be prepared to pass no matter what kind of test you take (that is, fixed-length or adaptive). If you do end up taking a fixed-length test, remember our tips from the preceding section. They should help you improve on what you could do on an adaptive test.

If you encounter a question on an adaptive test that you can't answer, you must guess an answer. Because of the way the software works, you may have to suffer for your guess on the next question if you guess right because you'll get a more difficult question next.

# Exam-Taking Basics

The most important advice about taking any exam is this: Read each question carefully. Some questions are deliberately ambiguous, some use double negatives, and others use terminology in incredibly precise ways. The authors have taken numerous exams—both practice and live—and in nearly every one have missed at least one question because they didn't read it closely or carefully enough.

Here are some suggestions on how to deal with the tendency to jump to an answer too quickly:

➤ Make sure you read every word in the question. If you find yourself jumping ahead impatiently, go back and start over.

➤ As you read, try to restate the question in your own terms. If you can do this, you should be able to pick the correct answer(s) much more easily.

Above all, try to deal with each question by thinking through what you know about Visual Basic and distributed applications—the characteristics, behaviors, facts, and figures involved. By reviewing what you know (and what you've written down on your information sheet), you'll often recall or understand things sufficiently to determine the answer to the question.

# Question-Handling Strategies

Based on exams we have taken, some interesting trends have become apparent. For those questions that take only a single answer, usually two or three of the answers will be obviously incorrect, and two of the answers will be plausible—of course, only one can be correct. Unless the answer leaps out at you (if it does, reread the question to look for a trick; sometimes those are the ones you're most likely to get wrong), begin the process of answering by eliminating those answers that are most obviously wrong.

Things to look for in obviously wrong answers include spurious menu choices or utility names, nonexistent software options, and terminology you've never seen. If you've done your homework for an exam, no valid information should be completely new to you. In that case, unfamiliar or bizarre terminology probably indicates a totally bogus answer.

Numerous questions assume that the default behavior of a particular utility is in effect. If you know the defaults and understand what they mean, this knowledge will help you cut through many Gordian knots.

# Mastering The Inner Game

In the final analysis, knowledge breeds confidence, and confidence breeds success. If you study the materials in this book carefully and review all the practice questions at the end of each chapter, you should become aware of those areas where additional learning and study are required.

Next, follow up by reading some or all of the materials recommended in the "Need To Know More?" section at the end of each chapter. The idea is to become familiar enough with the concepts and situations you find in the sample questions that you can reason your way through similar situations on a real exam. If you know the material, you have every right to be confident that you can pass the exam.

After you've worked your way through the book, take the practice exam in Chapter 13. This will provide a reality check and help you identify areas to study further. Make sure you follow up and review materials related to questions you miss on the practice exam before scheduling a real exam. Only when you've covered all the ground and feel comfortable with the whole scope of the practice exam should you take a real one.

If you take the practice exam and don't score at least 75 percent correct, you'll want to practice further. Though one is not available for Visual Basic Distributed yet, Microsoft usually provides free Personal Exam Prep (PEP) exams and the self-assessment exams from the Microsoft Certified Professional Web site's download page (its location appears in the next section). If you're more ambitious or better funded, you might want to purchase a practice exam from a third-party vendor.

Armed with the information in this book and with the determination to augment your knowledge, you should be able to pass the certification exam. However, you need to work at it, or you'll spend the exam fee more than once before you finally pass. If you prepare seriously, you should do well. Good luck!

# Additional Resources

A good source of information about Microsoft certification exams comes from Microsoft itself. Because its products and technologies—and the exams that go with them—change frequently, the best place to go for exam-related information is online.

If you haven't already visited the Microsoft Certified Professional site, do so right now. The MCP home page resides at **www.microsoft.com/mcp** (see Figure 1.1).

> *Note: This page might not be there by the time you read this, or it might have been replaced by something new and different, because things change regularly on the Microsoft site. Should this happen, please read the sidebar titled "Coping With Change On The Web."*

The menu options in the left column of this site point to the most important sources of information in the MCP pages. Here's what to check out:

➤ **Certifications** Use this menu entry to pick whichever certification program you want to read about.

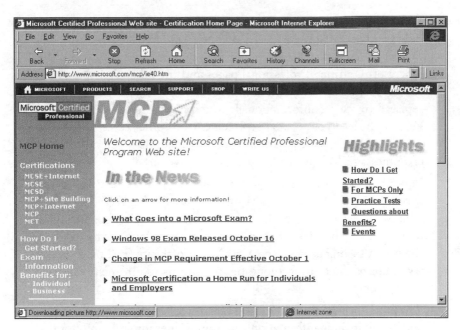

**Figure 1.1**    The Microsoft Certified Professional Web site.

➤ **Find Exam**  Use this menu entry to pull up a search tool that lets you list all Microsoft exams and locate all exams relevant to any Microsoft certification (MCP, MCDBA, MCSD, and so on) or those exams that cover a particular product. This tool is quite useful not only to examine the options but also to obtain specific exam preparation information, because each exam has its own associated preparation guide.

➤ **Downloads**  Use this menu entry to find a list of the files and practice exams that Microsoft makes available to the public. These include several items worth downloading, especially the Certification Update, the Personal Exam Prep (PEP) exams, various assessment exams, and a general exam study guide. Try to make time to peruse these materials before taking your first exam.

These are just the high points of what's available in the Microsoft Certified Professional pages. As you browse through them—and we strongly recommend that you do—you'll probably find other informational tidbits mentioned that are every bit as interesting and compelling.

## Coping With Change On The Web

Sooner or later, all the information we've shared with you about the Microsoft Certified Professional pages and the other Web-based resources mentioned throughout the rest of this book will go stale or be replaced by newer information. In some cases, the URLs you find here might lead you to their replacements; in other cases, the URLs will go nowhere, leaving you with the dreaded "404 File not found" error message. When that happens, don't give up.

You can always find what you want on the Web if you're willing to invest some time and energy. Most large or complex Web sites—and Microsoft's qualifies on both counts—offer a search engine. On all of Microsoft's Web pages, a Search button appears along the top edge of the page. As long as you can get to Microsoft's site (it should stay at **www.microsoft.com** for a long time), use this tool to help you find what you need.

The more focused you can make a search request, the more likely the results will include information you want. For example, search for the string "training and certification" to produce a lot of data about the subject in general, but if you're looking for a preparation guide for Exam 70-175, "Designing and Implementing Distributed Applications with Microsoft Visual Basic 6.0," you'll be more likely to get there quickly if you use a search string similar to the following:

```
"Exam 70-175" AND "preparation guide"
```

Likewise, if you want to find the Training and Certification downloads, try a search string such as this:

```
"training and certification" AND "download page"
```

Finally, feel free to use general search tools—such as **www.search.com**, **www.altavista.com**, and **www.excite.com**—to look for related information. Although Microsoft offers great information about its certification exams online, plenty of third-party sources of information and assistance are available that need not follow Microsoft's party line. Therefore, if you can't find something where the book says it lives, start looking around. If worse comes to worst, you can email us. We just might have a clue.

# Distributed Application Design

**Terms you'll need to understand:**

√ Conceptual design

√ Logical design

√ Physical design

√ Data services

√ User services

√ Business services

√ Visual Component Manager

**Techniques you'll need to master:**

√ Identifying the stages of application design

√ Deriving the components and services of the logical design, given a conceptual design

√ Assessing the potential impact of the design on performance, maintainability, extensibility, scalability, availability, and security

# Design Issues

Designing a distributed application can be a difficult and time-consuming process. As with any creative effort, numerous trade-offs and decisions will be made that affect the outcome of the finished product. Making these decisions intelligently so that the application is functionally complete, while still satisfying performance, extensibility, scalability, and related goals, is the reason this topic is included on the exam.

The particular technique discussed for designing a distributed application is based on a portion of the *Microsoft Solutions Framework (MSF)*. MSF defines team, process, and application development models that Microsoft both uses internally and promotes through its consulting services organization (Microsoft Consulting Services) and its certified partners. This chapter will focus on the application development model, which defines three progressively detailed stages of design: conceptual, logical, and physical.

## Conceptual Design

The *conceptual design* defines the fundamental business problem that the software will solve. This involves activities such as interviewing users, creating and documenting usage scenarios, and communicating clearly to both end users and management the functionality that the new software will embody. The conceptual design does not specify which individual components or interfaces will be created or how they will be structured, but focuses only on the function of the software.

## Logical Design

The *logical design* describes the architecture of the software in terms that the developers and other participants on the development team can understand. This includes breaking down the conceptual design into its constituent parts and identifying both the functional subsystems and the services that make up the software. The logical design should also be independent of how the software will be implemented physically from both a development tools and a hardware perspective.

## Physical Design

The *physical design* is the lowest level of design and includes specifics as to how the software will be implemented in terms of technology and hardware. Essentially, the physical design is concerned with issues such as where the software will be executed, which technologies will be used, and how the software will be distributed.

# Creating A Conceptual Design

The conceptual design process identifies the requirements of the software and documents them through a series of *usage scenarios*. These provide a written and perhaps graphical view of one aspect of the business problem. Often the usage scenario will be documented using a specific notation and termed a *use case*.

Although specific notations are out of the scope of this book, the actual notation used should be consistent throughout the process. The usage scenarios should be developed by talking with and observing end users of the software.

For example, a high-level usage scenario for an order processing system might be:

"A customer views our Web site and orders a product from a list of the available products. We check the customer's credit and balance in addition to collecting shipping information if the customer is new. We ship the product to the customer and update our inventory count after checking the inventory level. A low inventory count triggers a restocking of the product from our supplier. After the order is shipped, we create an invoice and send it to the customer."

# Creating A Logical Design

The logical design addresses the application architecture that will be used. The MSF approach uses a layered model of services to represent the interactions between pieces of the software to be developed. This services model is comprised of user services, business services, and data services and is shown in Figure 2.1.

**User** — Provides the visual and programmatic interfaces to the end user of the software.

**Business** — Encapsulates the business tasks and business rules to carry out the requirements of the software.

**Data** — Maintains the data needed by the business services and promotes maintainability through abstraction.

**Figure 2.1**   The services model of application development.

The fundamental concept to grasp from the figure is that the services provide well-defined boundaries between parts of the system. For example, the user services layer does not communicate directly with the data services layer, but rather communicates through the business services layer. In addition, the layers communicate through documented interfaces that make it easy to change the underlying functionality as long as the interface remains constant. During development, this approach allows the layers to be built in parallel by different groups of developers. This increases the ability to maintain and reuse the software that eventually will comprise the layers.

 Be sure to understand which layers in the model communicate directly and which do not.

## User Services

*User services* provide the interface to the end user of the software. This can include both a visual and a programmatic interface. In applications written with VB, the visual user interface may consist of a traditional VB executable, an ActiveX control, an ActiveX document, an IIS application, or a DHTML application. Chapters 4 through 7 will cover the details for implementing these services.

*Programmatic user services* take the form of applications that incorporate a scripting language such as *Visual Basic for Applications (VBA)*. Excel is a prototypical example of an application that provides a visual user interface, as well as a programmatic user interface through Automation that allows users to manipulate the application.

## Business Services

*Business services* carry out the business tasks that were captured during the conceptual design. A business task is defined by the requirements of the application and can include both algorithms that are independent of the application (business rules) and application-specific requests for business data.

In a distributed application, these services most commonly are implemented as COM components running in Microsoft Transaction Server (MTS) and are discussed in Chapter 8. Keep in mind that security can be applied at this level through the concept of user roles supplied by MTS.

## Data Services

*Data services* provide the capability and security required to retrieve, insert, update, and delete data required by the business services. To the degree feasible, the data services should be both independent of the business service that calls them, and independent of the actual data provider that stores and maintains the data. In this way the data services shield the rest of the application from changes in the mechanism used to interact with and store data.

Chapter 9 will focus on the technologies used in implementing the data services layer of a distributed application.

# Deriving The Services

Different techniques and notations can be used to derive the logical design from the conceptual design. One simple technique is to analyze the usage scenarios for nouns and verbs to extract the services, placing each in its appropriate layer.

For example, using the general usage scenario defined previously, the nouns are:

➤ Customer

➤ Web site

➤ Product

➤ Inventory

➤ Supplier

➤ Invoice

The verbs are:

➤ Visit

➤ Orders

➤ Check

➤ Collect

➤ Ships

➤ Update

➤ Create

➤ Send

➤ Restock

The resulting nouns can then be placed in the service layers; the verbs define the interfaces between the services and can be implemented as methods. Attributes of the nouns such as name, address, and phone number can be modeled as properties of the business objects. Note, however, that not all columns in the resulting table will be necessary to implement as properties. For example, a column that tracks the last update date for the record or the user who updated it are not necessary for most business processing but are tracked for auditing purposes. Microsoft ships its *Visual Modeler* tool with Visual Studio, which you can use to create the logical design.

> *Note: The full functionality of Visual Modeler is out of the scope of this book and the exam, but you can get more information about it in the "Need To Know More?" section at the end of the chapter.*

Figure 2.2 shows a simplified model created in Visual Modeler for the order processing system.

The end result is a logical view of the system architecture. This allows the development team to concretely define the interfaces between the services and begin to consider the physical implementation and logistics of the application.

# Creating A Physical Design

The physical design of an application addresses the actual components that will be developed and where they will be deployed. In a distributed application the software will be split into multiple tiers.

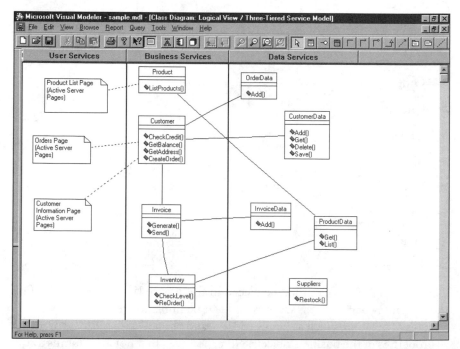

**Figure 2.2**    The logical design of the order processing system.

# Multi-Tier Development

Keep in mind that the concept of service layers defined by the logical design has no connection to where the finished application will actually reside or even the technology used to build it.

 You can, however, use Visual Modeler to generate VB code that will jumpstart the implementation of the application.

The physical design implements the concept of *tiers* and refers to physical machines on which the application will run. For example, the three most common multi-tier architectures are shown in Figure 2.3.

Which physical architecture—or variant thereof—you choose depends on the needs of the application and should address the concepts of:

➤ Performance

➤ Maintainability

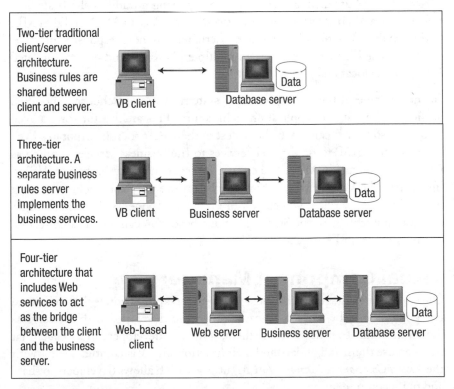

**Figure 2.3**  Common multi-tier architectures.

➤ Extensibility

➤ Scalability

➤ Availability

➤ Security

For example, using an architecture that deploys the business services on a separate physical server increases maintainability and extensibility, because the business rules need to be changed in only one place for all the users to be affected. More specifically, using MTS to implement the business services may also increase scalability, because of the ability to pool database connections and provide components to clients only as they are needed.

However, using a middle-tier server may involve some trade-offs: It may decrease availability and performance, because that server must be running for the application to function correctly and the calls to the server will add overhead (for applications with small user loads). In addition, the middle-tier server requires security that must be enforced.

Another example that developers frequently confront is the trade-off between performance, maintainability, and extensibility using a traditional VB application versus a Web interface using Active Server Pages (ASP) or DHTML. Although the VB application can contain a richer and more responsive interface, the Web-based interface may run on multiple platforms and is easily updated from a single location.

In the example of the order processing system, we might choose a modified version of the four-tier application architecture. This architecture uses a Web front end so that it can reach the widest audience. It then incorporates Web services using ASP to tie the user services to the business services running as COM components in MTS. You can use Internet Information Server (IIS) to implement the Web services, which coexist on the physical machine running MTS. The data services will consist of COM components that run in MTS and communicate with the SQL Server database. You can see the architecture of this solution in Figure 2.4.

# Visual Component Manager

Once of the advantages of creating a multi-tiered application is that individual components may be reusable, because they were developed with the services model in mind. In order to reuse them, however, developers must *know* that they can use them and understand their functionality. Visual Studio ships with the *Visual Component Manager (VCM)* utility, which allows developers to share and reuse components.

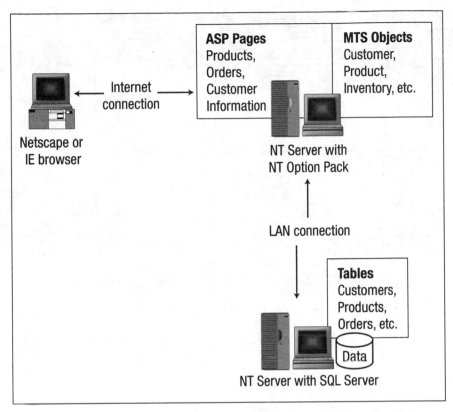

**Figure 2.4**   Modified four-tier application architecture for the order processing system.

The VCM is built on the Microsoft Repository technology that provides a flexible data store for many different kinds of data using either an Access or SQL Server database. For example, using the VCM you can publish source code, components, models, documents, and ASP pages, among other reusable objects.

To access a published component, VB provides the Project|Visual Component Manager menu item that loads the VCM utility. The developer can then select a database and navigate a set of folders to drill down to the type of component that is required. The developer can also search keywords associated with each component. When the component is found, information is displayed (shown in Figure 2.5) and the developer can right-click on the component to add it to the current project and register it on their machine.

Using the VCM, developers throughout the company can share commonly used components, thereby reducing development time and effort.

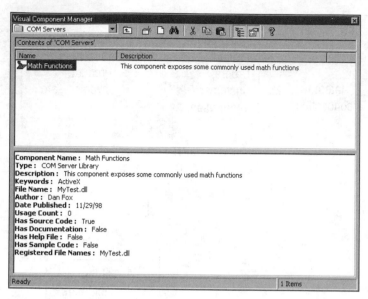

**Figure 2.5** The Visual Component Manager interface.

*Note: You can find more information on publishing components in the "Need To Know More?" section at the end of the chapter.*

# Practice Questions

## Question 1

> At which stage of design are service layers defined?
>
> ○ a.  Conceptual design
>
> ○ b.  Physical design
>
> ○ c.  Logical design
>
> ○ d.  Database design

The correct answer is c. During the logical design phase, the application development model of service layers is used to break up the functionality discovered during conceptual design. As just mentioned, answer a is incorrect because conceptual design is used to gather requirements. Answer b is incorrect because the physical design deals with the location or tiers of the application; answer d is incorrect because database design is a separate process that spans the design stages.

## Question 2

> You can use the Visual Component Manager to do which of the following? [Check all that apply]
>
> ❑ a.  Publish reusable components.
>
> ❑ b.  Build a services diagram.
>
> ❑ c.  Find components published by other developers.
>
> ❑ d.  Generate VB template code.

The correct answers are a and c. The VCM is used to publish components so that developers within the company can find and use reusable components. The VCM uses the Microsoft Repository to store information about the components in a local Access database or a SQL Server database on the network. Answers b and d are incorrect because the Visual Modeler tool is used to build service diagrams and generate template VB code to implement the services.

## Question 3

> Which service layer would a VB form communicate with to invoke a credit validation process implemented as a COM object?
>
> ○ a.  Data services
>
> ○ b.  User services
>
> ○ c.  Business services
>
> ○ d.  Web services

The correct answer is c. Because the VB form is a part of the user services layer (making answer b incorrect), it should communicate with business services implemented as COM objects. Keep in mind that the business services may or may not be physically on the same machine as the user services.

Answer a is incorrect because the data services are not directly called by the user services. Answer d is incorrect because the Web services are used to communicate with business services using a Web front end.

## Question 4

> Which is not a characteristic of services in the MSF Application Model?
>
> ○ a.  Services define boundaries between parts of the solution.
>
> ○ b.  Services define which technology will be used to implement services.
>
> ○ c.  Services are a logical, not a physical construct.
>
> ○ d.  Services are broken down into user, business, and data.

The correct answer is b. Because services are defined during logical design, they are not concerned with which technologies are used to implement the services. Answer a is incorrect because services do define boundaries between the services that assist in a modular development effort. Answer c is incorrect because services are logical and not physical. Answer d is incorrect because it correctly lists the three categories of services in the model.

## Question 5

> Which physical design technique can best be used to increase maintainability and scalability?
>
> O a.  Implement business services in stored procedures
>
> O b.  Implement user services using a VB user interface
>
> O c.  Implement business services in COM components running in MTS
>
> O d.  Implement data services in COM components running on a client computer

The correct answer is c. If one of your design goals is to increase maintainability, then placing your business logic inside COM components and running those components remotely from the clients is a good idea. In this way you can easily change the logic of components without affecting the client applications. In applications with large user loads you can also increase scalability because MTS can efficiently provide object instances to clients. Chapter 12 will also discuss how you can distribute COM objects across multiple servers to increase scalability.

Answer a is the trick answer because implementing business rules in stored procedures does increase maintainability and scalability, but not as much as using the approach in answer c. Answer b is incorrect because a VB user interface may increase client-side performance, but at the cost of maintainability because the VB code must be recompiled and redistributed when changes are required. Answer d is incorrect because implementing COM objects on the client to run business logic will make the application more difficult to maintain as changes are required.

# Need To Know More?

 Lhotka, Rocky: *Professional VB 6 Business Objects*. Wrox Press, Inc., 1998. ISBN: 186100107X. This book addresses many of the issues surrounding designing and building business objects in Visual Basic and is, at the time of this writing, the most referenced guide to the topic.

 McConnell, Steve: *Rapid Development: Taming Wild Software Schedules*. Microsoft Press, 1996. ISBN: 1556159005. Although related more to managing projects than designing applications, every software developer should have this book in their library. It addresses fundamental issues, such as project estimation and milestone-based development.

 Pattison, Ted: *Programming Distributed Applications With COM and Microsoft Visual Basic 6.0*. Microsoft Press, November 1998. ISBN: 1572319615. This is from an author who has a deep understanding of COM and uses it to explain the intricacies of MTS. It also contains some good information on the upcoming release of COM, COM+, and how to prepare for it today.

 For more information on the Visual Component Manager and its uses, search the MSDN online help for the topics "Visual Component Manager Concepts" and "Visual Component Manager Common Tasks."

 For an online white paper on Visual Modeler that describes its major features and functions, see **msdn.microsoft.com/vbasic/ technical/articles/vmodeler/default.asp**.

 A good technical white paper entitled "Re-engineering Application Development" that was jointly developed by Microsoft and Texas Instruments is located online at **msdn.microsoft.com/ repository/techmat/whitepapers/reengad1.htm**. This paper does a good job of defining a service-based architecture and laying the groundwork for moving to component-based development.

 The bulk of the material that documents the Microsoft Solutions Framework (MSF) is available online at **www.microsoft.com/ msf**. Microsoft also provides courses on the framework that are taught by highly competent instructors.

# Configuring
# A Development
# Environment

**3**

**Terms you'll need to understand:**

✓ Reverse-delta storage

✓ Administrative tasks

✓ Parent project

✓ **IsCallerInRole**

✓ **IsSecurityEnabled**

✓ Role membership folder

**Techniques you'll need to master:**

✓ Moving projects

✓ Moving files

✓ Archiving projects

✓ Restoring projects

✓ Limiting archived files

✓ Assigning users to roles

✓ Checking security programmatically

✓ Applying declarative security

# Establishing Source Code Control

*Microsoft Visual SourceSafe* provides a much-needed functionality for team-based development projects. As distributed enterprise-level applications grow in size, complexity, and functionality, the development teams formed to design and program these applications will also grow. With this growth comes the necessity for developers to collaborate on different aspects of the development process. Despite applications' increasing use of component- and object-based designs, which allow for more clearly defined development roles and responsibilities for developers and project team members, the need for synchronizing collaborative efforts still exists. Control of source code is the prime functionality of Visual SourceSafe.

Visual SourceSafe assists teams in managing development projects by storing all project files, both text-based and binary, in a central database. This includes a storage method referred to as *reverse-delta storage* that stores the entire current version of each file plus any changes to the files. To maintain revertability to previous versions of the files, only the bytes that have changed between versions are stored in reversion. So for each byte that changes in a file, the corresponding byte in the previous version of the file is then extracted and stored in the database. This provides for a highly efficient form of storage, while maintaining quick and efficient reversion capabilities.

Visual SourceSafe provides for organized version maintenance in a team development environment by following a basic library check-in/out metaphor. This method streamlines project organization and integrates it into developer design environments. It also provides functionality such as concurrent checkouts, merging, and change reconciliations.

## Installing Visual SourceSafe

Installing Visual SourceSafe for use by the development team involves two separate installs: server and client. You should perform a server installation onto a network-accessible location, allowing access by all developer workstations. To accomplish a server installation:

1. Insert the Visual SourceSafe CD into the server CD-ROM or a LAN-accessible system.

2. Run Setup.exe from the CD.

3. Follow the install wizard, choosing Server when prompted for the type of installation.

A server installation is the only installation that is required to provide source code control to the development project, although performing a client install on each developer workstation will significantly reduce network traffic. When trying to integrate Visual SourceSafe with the Visual Basic IDE, you must do a client installation as follows:

1. Perform a server installation as described previously.

2. Install Visual Basic onto the development system.

3. Perform an installation from the CD by running Setup.exe, or use Netsetup.exe to perform a client installation over the network.

## Performing VSS Administration Tasks

The role of the VSS administrator includes the initial setup of a VSS database. Additional administrator tasks generally include increasing the usefulness of the VSS database through proper configuration. VSS administrator tasks include:

➤ Creating a new database

➤ Designating a project as a Web site project

➤ Creating shadow folders

➤ Customizing the VSS environment

➤ Enabling keyword expansion

➤ Enabling multiple checkouts

➤ Opening a database

➤ Setting default file types

## Moving Projects Within SourceSafe

Within a VSS database, a collection of files known as a *project* is used as an organizational unit to combine all files that are needed to build a single program. A project is similar to a folder, except support for file merging, reverse-delta storage, multiple file versioning, and assorted additional team development capabilities is provided. Subprojects are allowed to be created, up to 15 deep, with each project or subproject supporting up to 8,000 files each.

Occasionally, the need arises to move files or projects from either project to project or database to database. Moving files from project to project, moving subprojects from project to project, and moving projects from database to database are all performed in slightly different ways.

## Moving A File From Project To Project

Moving a file from project to project is performed in a roundabout method. In order to move a file, it must be shared with the new target parent project and then deleted from the original project. This effectively moves a copy of the file into the new project, maintaining the file's history and removing it from the original project location.

> *Note: In order to move a file from one parent project to another parent project, the administrator must give the appropriate rights to the user moving the file. The Add access right is required on the destination parent, and the Destroy access right is required on the original parent project.*

## Moving A Subproject From Project To Project

To move a subproject from a parent project to a different parent project, click on File|Move Project in the VSS Explorer. The Move Project dialog box allows you to choose a new path for the selected subproject and defines a new path for the subproject in the database. This not only redefines a new path for a subproject, it also moves the project to a new parent project. This results in an inability to re-create previous versions of the subproject's parent project.

## Moving Projects From Database To Database

In order to move a project from database to database, a VSS administrator must use the Archive and Restore operations. Generally, the Archive procedure is used to increase the efficiency of the VSS database and to save disk space, but it is also required for moving projects among databases. The basic procedure for archiving a project includes these five steps:

1. Open the database to be archived.

2. Choose Archive|Archive Projects.

   > *Note: Previous versions of Microsoft Visual SourceSafe only exposed the Archive and Restore functions from the command line.*

3. Select the project to archive.

4. Choose the archive method, such as Save Data To File.

5. Provide the version, label, or date information to limit the archived information.

An archive can be limited to file versions, label strings, or even date. To limit archival by version, simply enter the desired version number, such as 3. To limit by label or date, precede the label string or date value with an L or D, respectively, with no space in the version box provided by the Archive Wizard.

Restoring the project into a different database effectively copies the project among databases. If Save Data To File, then Delete From Database To Save Space is chosen as the archive method, the project will be effectively moved from database to database, after a successful restoration. The basic procedure for restoring a database involves five steps:

1. Open the database into which the project will be restored.

2. From the Archive menu, choose Restore Projects.

3. Browse to the archival file.

4. Select the project to restore.

5. Choose the project to serve as the parent project and location for restoration.

Using the Archive and Restore methods, you can successfully move a project from one VSS database to another VSS database.

# Using Visual Basic For Developing Distributed Applications

With the release of Visual Basic 6, several new project types have become available to the Visual Basic programmer. Two of these project types, the IIS and DHTML applications seen in Figure 3.1, provide avenues for developing distributed applications. Both project types produce applications similar in nature to existing solutions, but with numerous benefits over current technologies.

IIS applications and DHTML applications are available with either the professional or enterprise editions of Visual Basic. If you install the standard or learning editions of VB, these project types will not be available.

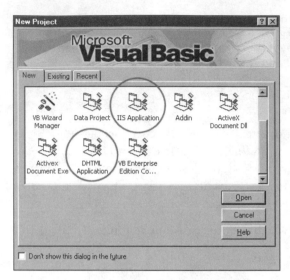

**Figure 3.1**  Visual Basic provides two new projects for developing distributed applications.

# IIS Applications

An IIS application produces a server-side application solution for responding to user HTTP requests. IIS applications are designed to use compiled Visual Basic code to process user requests and respond to HTML element events that occur within the browser, due to user interaction and standard event definitions. The code used to respond to event and user interaction is compiled into a DLL that runs on the Web server. This DLL contains one or more **WebClass** objects that provide the response mechanisms when an instance of the **WebClass** is created on the server. The **WebClass** is hosted by an ASP file, as shown in Figure 3.2, that is generated automatically when the project is compiled. By hosting the **WebClass**, this file serves as the opening to the IIS application, much like the startup **Form** object within a Win32 VB application. IIS applications use HTML as the presentation or user interface by incorporating HTML templates that reside on the server and are dynamically altered and sent to the client browser for rendering.

The basic components of a compiled IIS application include:

➤ HTML template files

➤ Project DLL, containing the source code and **WebClass** object, that is accessed by the Visual Basic **WebClass** runtime component MSWCRUN.DLL

➤ The ASP page used to host the **WebClass** object within Internet Information Server

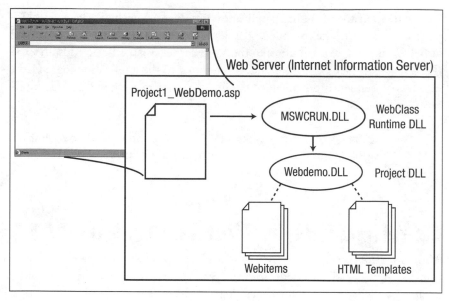

**Figure 3.2**   The Project DLL is loaded on the Web server, hosted within the appropriate ASP page created automatically during the compile process.

The Project DLL and required support files are packaged into a CAB file for distribution to the Web server indicated during use of the Package and Deployment Wizard. The HTML files are not packaged in the CAB file, but are copied to the same Web server as the CAB file.

# DHTML Applications

DHTML applications provide Visual Basic compiled code in the form of a DLL for downloading to the client system. This provides processing of the application logic on the client system. DHTML applications are designed to leverage the power of the Dynamic HTML object model in accessing and responding to events generated by the user interface elements exposed by a DHTML page. By providing the application logic in the form of an in-process DLL downloaded to the client browser processing space, response time to user-initiated actions can be reduced significantly. DHTML applications are designed primarily for use in developing applications to run on intranets.

The basic components of a compiled DHTML application include:

➤ DHTML pages and assorted image files

➤ A compiled project DLL file containing the application logic

Deployment of the DHTML application involves using the Package and Deployment Wizard. The compiled DLL and required support files are packaged into a CAB file for distribution to the Web server. Visual Basic adds an **OBJECT** tag into each page to provide a reference to the application logic DLL, which is subsequently downloaded the first time a page in the DHTML application is loaded.

 CAB files generated for a DHTML application should be digitally signed prior to deployment to ensure client confidence in the origin of the application DLL.

# Configuring A System To Run MTS

*Microsoft Transaction Server (MTS)* is a server product designed to provide transaction processing support and to create an environment for developing reliable, scalable, high performance distributed enterprise-level applications. Visual Basic provides support for creating Component Object Model in-process components that run within an MTS runtime environment. MTS defines an application programming model to support distributed, component-based applications while providing a runtime infrastructure for managing these components. Additional information regarding MTS can be found in Chapter 8.

## Installing MTS

You install Microsoft Transaction Server on a system by using the Windows NT Option Pack installation wizard. You can install MTS on Windows 95/98, Windows NT Workstation, or Windows NT Server. When installing MTS on a Windows 95/98 system, Distributed COM (DCOM) support is required.

> *Note: Internet Information Server 4 uses several aspects of MTS functionality, thus MTS is automatically installed when installing IIS 4 as a part of the Windows NT Option Pack installation wizard. When configuring a system to create and compile IIS applications using Visual Basic, IIS is required, thus MTS will already be installed as a part of the configuration.*

Here are a few additional recommendations to ensure proper performance and operation when you install MTS:

➤ For Windows NT systems, installation of NT Service Pack 3 is required. Service Pack 4 is also recommended.

➤ SQL Server Service Pack 3 is strongly recommended for computers running MTS.

➤ When installing SQL Server 6.5 or earlier on the same system as MTS, you must install MTS last.

# System Package Security

MTS provides organizational and process boundary unit definition in the form of component packages. Packages contain COM components that are written as class modules within a Visual Basic ActiveX DLL project. An MTS package is primarily a *trust boundary* that defines a boundary across which security credentials are verified prior to allowing access to a component from another component or a client process. Packages also serve as deployment units for components running within MTS to be installed onto client systems or additional MTS servers.

The security mechanism provided by MTS is in the form of role-based security. A *role*, in the MTS security model context, is an abstract concept that equates to a logical collection of users. The users are either valid Windows NT users or groups local to the system on which MTS is installed and running. By defining roles, permission to access a component can be limited to a set group of valid NT users, combining component access with NT user authentication mechanisms.

Once roles have been defined within the MTS environment and the appropriate users or groups have been assigned to the roles as desired, you can assign security using two methods: declarative security or programmatic security.

## *Declarative Security*

*Declarative security* involves limiting access to a given component or package to members of a chosen role or roles by explicit assignment through the MTS Explorer. You can assign declarative security at the package or component level by adding the defined roles to the Role Membership folder of the desired component. Any attempt to access a component within a package, except by other components within the same package, will be checked prior to allowing access.

MTS includes a System package used to control access to administrative functions within MTS. By default, the System package has both an Administrator role and a Reader role. Prior to setting up declarative security for the System package, you must map at least one NT account to the Administrator role. Failure to do so prior to enabling System package security will result in a lack of access to configuration-modifying functions within MTS Explorer. Any NT account mapped to the Reader role can view any object in MTS, but cannot create, install, or delete objects within MTS or export packages.

*Note: You cannot set up declarative security for a package running on a Windows 95/98 system because Windows NT accounts are required for authentication.*

## Programmatic Security

*Programmatic security* within the MTS runtime environment relies on the existence of the MTS context object. Each time an instance of an MTS object is created, MTS also creates an associated context object. This MTS extensible object provides a runtime reference or context for the execution of an instance of an object. The IObjectContext interface provides two methods that form the foundation of basic programmatic security: **IsCallerInRole** and **IsSecurityEnabled**.

➤ **IsCallerInRole** This method is used to determine if the direct caller, or the identity of the base client calling the object, is included in a given role passed as a parameter of the method. Use of this method within the Visual Basic code can effectively provide programmatic control based on the configured MTS roles.

➤ **IsSecurityEnabled** This method is used to determine if security checking is applicable to the calling component or base client.

When components call other components in the same package, the components are running within the same server process. In this situation, **IsCallerInRole** will always return True. Use of **IsSecurityEnabled**, which would return False when the direct caller is a component within the same package, can help distinguish this fact, allowing accurate indications of the role membership of the direct caller. An extended explanation of these methods can be found in Chapter 8.

## Disallow Administration Privileges

MTS is installed with a built-in package known as the *System package*. Access to the System package is required for making changes to the MTS configuration, such as adding users to roles, when authorization checking is enabled. MTS will warn users prior to locking out administrators when they attempt to either delete the last user from the Administrator role or enable security on the System package when no users are mapped to the Administrator role.

In order to disallow administrator privileges, you would remove an NT user account or group from the MTS Administrator role, while ensuring that only those accounts for which administrative capability is desired is allowed. It is also recommended that the appropriate Registry keys be switched to read-only by using Regedit.

# Configuring MTS Client Systems

In order for client systems to be able to access a remote server application running within MTS, you must use the export utility within MTS to create a client installation executable. For client computers that have DCOM support installed on the system, running a client executable performs the following steps:

1. Copies the client executable to a temporary directory and extracts the type libraries, proxy stub DLLs, and assorted client-side files.

2. Copies the type libraries and proxy stub DLLs to the Remote Applications subfolder in the Program Files folder.

3. Updates the client system Registry with the entries required by DCOM for accessing the server package remotely.

4. Registers the application in the Add/Remove Programs option in the Control Panel.

When creating a Visual Basic application that uses MTS objects on a remote server, inclusion of the client executable within your general application setup is required to allow your VB application to work properly on a client system.

# Practice Questions

## Question 1

> Microsoft Visual SourceSafe provides the ability to revert to pre-
> vious versions of stored files, known as *versioning*. Storage of
> multiple versions of files can require a large amount of disk space,
> but Visual SourceSafe handles this concern by using a highly effi-
> cient form of storage known as:
>
> ○ a.  Reverse-change storage
>
> ○ b.  Delta byte storage
>
> ○ c.  Reverse-delta storage
>
> ○ d.  Reverse byte change storage
>
> ○ e.  Delta storage

The correct answer is c. Reverse-delta storage is a highly efficient form of
storage that focuses on storing only the bytes that have changed. "Delta" is a
character in the Greek alphabet often used to represent a change in some quan-
tity or numerical value within a mathematical equation. Because VSS stores
changes to files over multiple versions of the file, this method is referred to as
*delta storage*. The methods used by VSS focus on storing only the most recent
complete version of the files, while storing the byte changes necessary to revert
the current version back to a previous version. This method optimizes retrieval
for the most recent version and also represents the most requested version.
Therefore, the storage method is referred to as reverse-delta storage.

## Question 2

---

Microsoft Visual SourceSafe involves two primary types of installation: server and client. Performing which combination of installations is inherently necessary for providing source code control for development projects?

○ a. Client installation on all developer systems involved in project

○ b. Server installation

○ c. Client installation on at least one workstation and server installation

○ d. Server installation and client installation on all developer systems

○ e. Client installation on at least one developer system

---

The correct answer is b. When installing Visual SourceSafe, only a server installation is required to provide source code control, the core functionality of Visual SourceSafe.

Answers a, c, d, and e are incorrect because although client installations are possible and can provide additional benefits, they are not inherently required to set up the core functionality of Visual SourceSafe. A server installation alone will provide the necessary support for creating databases, projects, and performing administrative tasks. Although a client installation *is* required to integrate Visual SourceSafe into the Visual Basic IDE, a client is not inherently required, nor required at all when not using Visual Basic in a development project.

## Question 3

---

What advantage can be obtained when performing a client installation on a developer system?

○ a. Reduced administrative procedures

○ b. More efficient storage

○ c. Less processing overhead

○ d. More available code control options

○ e. Reduced network traffic

---

The correct answer is e. By performing a client installation on a developer system, network traffic can be significantly reduced. Although client installations are not inherently required to provide full Visual SourceSafe functionality, excessive traffic can be generated by using a server-only install.

Answer a is incorrect because the number of administrative procedures typically required do not go down when a client installation is performed. Client installations do not decrease the relative storage requirements, therefore answer b is incorrect. Answer c is not correct because a client installation will actually increase processing overhead in some situations. Full Visual SourceSafe functionality is provided by the server installation, therefore answer d would not be correct.

## Question 4

Part of the administrative tasks involved in using Visual SourceSafe include moving project elements to different locations. What scenario is possible concerning movement of elements?

○ a. Move a subproject to a new parent object by using the **Move Project** command.

○ b. Use the **Move** command to move a file from a parent project for which the Add access right exists to a parent project for which the Destroy access exists.

○ c. Move a file from subproject to another subproject by using the **Move Project** command.

○ d. Use the **Move Project** command to move a subproject from a database to another database.

○ e. Use the **Move** command to move a subproject from a database to another database.

The correct answer is a. The **Move Project** command within the VSS Explorer is used to move a project from one parent project to another parent project. The Move Project dialog box allows a new path to be provided for a given subproject. This process has the primary downside of not allowing for re-creation of a previous version of the project parent from the history.

When using the **Move** command to move a file from project to project, the Add access right is required on the destination parent project, whereas the Destroy access right is required on the origin parent object. These rights are required to perform the activities of sharing the file with the new parent object and deleting the original file from the parent project of origin. Therefore, answer b is incorrect. You cannot use the **Move Project** command to move a single file, therefore answer c is incorrect. You also cannot use either the **Move Project** nor the **Move** commands to move a project from one database to a separate database, so answers d and e are incorrect.

## Question 5

What type of file is considered the entry point to accessing an IIS application running on a Web server?

O a.  HTML template file

O b.  ASP file

O c.  MSWCRUN.DLL

O d.  Project DLL

O e.  CAB file

The correct answer is b. An IIS application compiled in Visual Basic automatically generates an ASP page that is used to host the application. Navigating to this ASP page will cause the **WebClass_Start** event to fire within the compiled DLL:

```
http://www.myserver.com/Project1_WebDemo.asp
```

The ASP page provides a conduit for hosting and initiating the event handlers compiled into the server-side DLL.

HTML template files are used as Webitems to be sent back to the client as responses, not as an entry point to the application, therefore answer a is not correct. The MSWCRUN.DLL file is known as the **WebClass** runtime library, providing management and support services, therefore answer c would not be correct. The project DLL houses the application code and objects that are instantiated or loaded by the ASP page, therefore answer d is incorrect. Answer e is incorrect because the CAB file is merely a compressed compartment for holding the application files.

# Need To Know More?

 Banick, Steve and Chris Denshikoff: *Web Management with Microsoft Visual SourceSafe 5.0*. Que Education and Training, 1997. ISBN: 0789712334. This book isn't just geared for Web developers, as the title implies. The writing style leaves something to be desired, but with very few books on Visual SouceSafe in the marketplace, this one would be a decent introduction.

 An FAQ on VSS can be found at the following **www.pts.com/static/msvss.html**. Click on Frequently Asked Questions on the left-hand-side link.

 A *PC Magazine* Online review of Visual SourceSafe can be found at **www.zdnet.com/pcmag/issues/1605/pcmg0116.htm**.

 A review of several source control products, including Visual SourceSafe 4, can be found at **www.silicom.com/~alobba/no_tables/pc_vc.html**.

# Implementing User Services

**4**

## Terms you'll need to understand:

- √ **LostFocus** event
- √ Stack overflow error
- √ **CausesValidation** property
- √ **Validate** event
- √ **KeyPreview** event
- √ **KeyPress** event
- √ **KeyDown** and **KeyUp** events
- √ **Controls** collection

- √ **VBControlExtender**
- √ Early binding
- √ Late binding
- √ IUnknown
- √ **HelpFile** property
- √ **HelpContextID** property
- √ **Implements** keyword

## Techniques you'll need to master:

- √ Validating input in forms
- √ Creating callback procedures from the Windows API
- √ Implementing asynchronous processing using COM components
- √ Instantiating and invoking a COM component

- √ Using data binding to display data from a data source
- √ Implementing online user assistance
- √ Implementing error handling

# Understanding User Services

In a distributed application, the user services layer directly interacts with the user of the application. This includes both the graphical user interface and the code that implements features such as navigation, error handling, and the validation of data. With the release of Visual Basic 6, the types of user interfaces you can create have been expanded. Not only can you create a traditional compiled executable that uses forms, dialogs, and controls, you can now also create both server-side and client-side Web-based applications. User services also encompass the creation of ActiveX controls and ActiveX documents, techniques both available starting with Visual Basic 5.

In order to cover all the topics you'll need to be familiar with for the exam, this and the next three chapters will focus on user services. In this chapter we'll deal with the issues relating to traditional VB applications. These include validation, calling business services, and interacting with the Win32 API, among others. Although most of these topics should be familiar if you've used VB in the past, you should pay particular attention to some new wrinkles. Chapter 5 will then delve into the new Web-based applications that can be created, covering the basics of IIS and DHTML applications. Finally, Chapters 6 and 7 will complete the discussion of user services by taking a look at ActiveX controls and ActiveX documents.

In total, user services are stressed fairly heavily on the exam. So if you're an experienced VB developer who might be tempted to spend less time studying for this section, thinking that not much is new here, you should rethink your options and definitely take the time to review this material. Who knows, you might even find a few things you didn't already know.

# Validating Data

Perhaps one of the most confusing and error-prone topics when creating the user interface of an application is validating the user input. Distributed applications in particular should at least perform basic validation in the user services layer. Keep in mind that distributed applications communicate across machine boundaries, so by catching errors in the user services layer you eliminate the overhead of discovering those errors only after communicating with backend services.

Traditionally, VB developers have used several techniques for validating user input before submitting it to the backend. In this section we'll cover using the **LostFocus** event, the Masked Edit control, the **Validate** event, a technique for creating a user-defined validation procedure, and keystroke-level validation.

# Using The **LostFocus** Event

In versions of VB before 6.0, the ability to validate user input in a form was not very robust. As a result, developers often attempted to use the standard **LostFocus** event of controls to perform a validation check and required the user to input the data again by keeping the focus on the control. Typically this would take the form of making sure that the user had entered either numeric data or that the data was in the proper range. For example, in a form that requests the user to input their age in the textbox **txtAge**, the code may look like the following:

```
Private Sub txtAge_LostFocus()
    If Not IsNumeric(txtAge.Text) Then
        lblMesssage.Caption = "Please enter a number"
        txtAge.SetFocus
    End If
End Sub
```

Unfortunately, although this code works well for a single input field on a form, it quickly wreaks havoc on the application once other controls are added to the form that use a similar method of validation. To illustrate this, if the form contains another textbox, **txtBirthday**, that uses the **IsDate** function to confirm that a date was entered, the application will spin off into an infinite loop by simply filling in one of the textboxes as the user presses the Tab key. Left to its logical conclusion, this would cause a stack overflow error and kill the application.

 Understanding the sequence of events is definitely covered by the exam. We would recommend adding the **Debug.Print** statement in event handlers to review the order in which events like those mentioned here occur.

The key to why this apparently simple code goes so wrong is in understanding that the **LostFocus** event fires only after focus has already been given to another control. In other words, the sequence of events that takes place when the user presses the Tab key to move from **txtAge** to **txtBirthday** is:

```
txtAge_LostFocus
txtBirthday_GotFocus
txtBirthday_LostFocus
txtAge_GotFocus
txtAge_LostFocus
txtBirthday_GotFocus
txtBirthday_LostFocus
txtAge_GotFocus
txtAge_LostFocus
...ad infinitum
```

As you can see, the **GotFocus** event of **txtBirthday** is already in the queue and will be executed after the **LostFocus** event of **txtAge** occurs, regardless of what action the **LostFocus** event initiates. In this case, because **txtBirthday** received the focus, it will immediately lose the focus when the **txtAge.SetFocus** method executes. Conversely, when the **LostFocus** event of **txtBirthday** fires, it will attempt to change the focus back to itself, thereby causing **txtAge** to once again lose the focus.

To avoid this scenario, you'll need to create a form-level Boolean variable that will be used to bypass the validation if another control is being validated. Then, when a control does receive focus, you would set the validating variable to **False** to allow the control to once again be validated. You can see the code for implementing this in the simple example of **txtAge** and **txtBirthday** in Listing 4.1.

## Listing 4.1 Performing validation using LostFocus and a form-level variable.

```
Option Explicit
Private mflValidating As Boolean

Private Sub txtAge_GotFocus()
    mflValidating = False
End Sub

Private Sub txtAge_LostFocus()

    If mflValidating Then
        Exit Sub
    End If

    If Not IsNumeric(txtAge.Text) Then
        mflValidating = True
        lblMessage.Caption = "Please enter a number"
        txtAge.SetFocus
    End If

End Sub

Private Sub txtBirthday_GotFocus()
    mflValidating = False
End Sub

Private Sub txtBirthday_LostFocus()

    If mflValidating Then
        Exit Sub
    End If
```

```
If Not IsDate(txtBirthday.Text) Then
    mflValidating = True
    lblMessage.Caption = "Please enter a date"
    txtBirthday.SetFocus
End If

End Sub
```

As you'll see shortly, this method can still be used, although VB6 provides a more elegant way of handling validation.

# Using The **Validate** Event And **CausesValidation** Property

The **Validate** event and **CausesValidation** property are new members exposed by all the standard and ActiveX controls that ship with VB6. These two members work in tandem to handle the validation tasks like those discussed in the previous section.

The key to understanding the **Validate** event is that it is fired on the control before the focus has actually left the control. This contrasts with the **LostFocus** event that fires only after focus has already been given to another control. To cause the **Validate** event to fire, you must set the **CausesValidation** property on the control about to receive the focus to trigger the **Validate** event of the control that is losing focus. This may sound confusing, but rewriting the example from the previous section should suffice to explain it.

In the previous example, the **txtAge** textbox needs to be validated for a numeric value and the **txtBirthday** textbox for a date value. The code we used to validate the controls should be placed in the **Validate** event of their respective controls and modified as shown in Listing 4.2.

## Listing 4.2    Using the **Validate** event to validate controls.

```
Private Sub txtAge_Validate(Cancel As Boolean)

    If Not IsNumeric(txtAge.Text) Then
        lblMessage.Caption = "Please enter a number"
        Cancel = True
    End If

End Sub
```

```
Private Sub txtBirthday_Validate(Cancel As Boolean)

    If Not IsDate(txtBirthday.Text) Then
        lblMessasge.Caption = "Please enter a date"
        Cancel = True
    End If

End Sub
```

Note that the **Validate** event takes one argument, **Cancel**, which you can use to leave the focus on the control being validated. By setting **Cancel** to **True**, focus will remain on the control and the **SetFocus** method need not be called. The default is **False**, which allows the focus to change once the code in the event has been executed.

The final piece of the puzzle is to make sure the **CausesValidation** property of both controls is set to **True** (which is the default). If **CausesValidation** is set to **False**, the **Validate** event of the control losing focus will not be fired. For example, by setting **txtAge.CausesValidation** to **False**, the **Validate** event of **txtBirthday** will not fire as the user attempts to change the focus from **txtBirthday** to **txtAge**.

Although the behavior of the **CausesValidation** property may at first glance seem inverted, a good reason lies behind it. Let's say that the user is doing data entry on a form with several textboxes, radio buttons, and checkboxes. By using the **Validate** event and setting the **CausesValidation** property to **True** on all the controls, the user can be alerted to data entry errors and the application can enforce that the focus does not change until the user corrects the value. However, by not allowing the focus to change, you also are restricting the user from clicking on controls that may provide assistance or other information that allows for error resolution. These types of controls, such as a Help button, should have their **CausesValidation** property set to **False** to allow use of the control to help resolve problems.

## Using The Masked Edit Control

One of the underlying principals behind performing validation is to not do any more than you have to. To that end, you should try to employ user interface elements that assist the user in entering the correct data to begin with.

The Masked Edit control is an ActiveX control that you can use to restrict user input to a specific input mask that specifies the type and number of characters entered, as well as the format of the data once the control loses focus. You can see the important properties of the control in Table 4.1.

**Table 4.1    Masked Edit control properties.**

| Property | Description |
|---|---|
| AllowPrompt | Determines whether the prompt character is also a valid input character. |
| AutoTab | When **True**, the focus is automatically moved to the next control in the Tab order once the input mask has been satisfied. |
| ClipText | Returns the text of the control, excluding any literal characters in the **Mask** property. This is useful for getting values such as Social Security numbers to insert into a database. |
| Format | Determines the format of the control once the user moves the focus from the control; this is similar to the **Mask** property. Additionally, it allows for multiple representations of numeric data, depending on whether it is negative, positive, zero, or null. |
| Mask | Sets the input mask of the control. This is a string that is a mix of placeholders and literal characters. For example, a mask for a Social Security number is: ###-##-####. |
| PromptChar | Sets the character used to prompt the user for data. Typically this is set to an underscore. |
| PromptInclude | Determines whether the prompt characters are returned in the **Text** property. |
| Text | Returns what the user input, including the literal characters specified in the **Mask** property. |

The single characteristic event of the Masked Edit control is **ValidationError**. This event will fire when the user enters data that does not conform to the input mask. Its two arguments, **InvalidText** and **StartPosition**, return the entire text of the control, including the literals and prompt characters and the position at which the error occurred, respectively.

An example of using the Masked Edit control to allow the user to enter a date value follows:

```
mskBirthdate.Mask = "##/##/####"
mskBirthdate.Format = "dd-mmm-yyyy"
mskBirthdate.AutoTab = True
mskBirthdate.MaxLength = 10
mskBirthdate.PromptChar = "_"
```

Although the Masked Edit control can restrict user input to numeric values, it cannot validate the content of what is entered. In other words, you may still need to use the **Validate** event to ensure that proper dates or times are entered.

# Creating A Validation Procedure

In some situations, the requirements of the users may dictate that validation does not occur as the user navigates through the form, as with the **Validate** or the **LostFocus** event, but only when the user is ready to save the data. This is typically the case in higher volume data entry applications where the users' rhythm and productivity may be slowed if the user interface is constantly interrupting them.

In order to perform the validation, you can take the approach of creating a form-level validation function procedure that is called once all the controls are populated and a save button or menu item is selected. You can see an example of this function for the form that contains the txtAge and txtBirthday controls in Listing 4.3.

## Listing 4.3    A form-level validation procedure.

```
Private Function ValidateForm() As Boolean

   ValidateForm = False

'Look through the controls and validate them
   If Not IsDate(txtBirthday.Text) Then
       lblMessage.Caption = "Please enter a date"
       txtBirthday.SetFocus
       Exit Function
   End If

   If Not IsNumeric(txtAge.Text) Then
       lblMessage.Caption = "Please enter a number"
       txtAge.SetFocus
       Exit Function
   End If

   ValidateForm = True

End Function
```

Note that the function sets the focus to the first control that does not pass validation and exits. If all the controls are validated, it returns **True**. Obviously, you could spruce up this code to also do things like setting the label of the control to a different color to draw the user's attention to it, or even letting the function process all the controls and return the results in an area of the screen. This would allow the user to see all the errors before proceeding. In either case, the function can be called from a save button or menu item:

```
If ValidateForm Then
   'Save the data
End If
```

The only other issue in creating a form-level validation procedure is making sure that the user does not press a save button or select a save menu item before the required controls are filled in. To do this you can take advantage of the **KeyPreview** property of the form. When set to **True**, this property enables the form to receive all user keystrokes through the **KeyPress** and **KeyDown** events before they are handled by the individual controls. The **KeyPress** event can use the **Controls** collection of the form to check that all the required controls are filled in. It uses a **For Each** loop and references each **Control** object in the **Controls** collection. If all the controls are populated, the save button or menu item can be enabled.

 One of the issues related to forms on the exam is understanding how and when forms are loaded and unloaded. Be sure to understand how the **Load** statement differs from the **Show** method and how forms are unloaded with the **Unload** statement. Also be sure to note what happens when you set the form object to **Nothing**.

The **Controls** collection is simply a collection of **Control** objects that reference all the controls on the form. You can think of a **Control** object as a generic object that can take on the methods and properties of any control on a form. You can use the **TypeName** function to determine which type of control the **Control** object currently represents. You can see the code to enable a save button on a form in Listing 4.4.

## Listing 4.4    Code to automatically enable a save button as the user enters data on a form.

```
Private Sub Form_KeyPress(KeyAscii As Integer)
Dim objControl As Control

For Each objControl In Form1.Controls
    If objControl.Tag = "Required" Then
        If Len(objControl.Text) = 0 Then
            Exit Sub
        End If
    End If
Next objControl
```

```
cmdSave.Enabled = True

End Sub
```

The only wrinkle in the code in Listing 4.4 is the use of the **Tag** property. Because it is rare that all controls on a form are required, you can set the **Tag** properties of the required controls to a string such as "Required" at design time and then check the property at runtime to determine which controls to check. Also keep in mind that the preceding code will generate a runtime error if one of the required controls does not support the **Text** property. For this reason, you may want to use the **TypeName** function to determine the class of the control and perhaps handle it differently.

# Using Keystroke Events

The final topic to cover regarding validation is using the keystroke events to validate and change the data as the user is entering it. The three primary events you'll need to be familiar with are **KeyPress**, **KeyUp**, and **KeyDown**. These events are exposed by all the standard and ActiveX controls that ship with VB and, as we saw earlier, the **Form** object.

## Using *KeyPress*

The **KeyPress** event fires on the control when the user presses and releases one of the ANSI keys. *ANSI keys* are any of the standard printable characters that can be generated on the keyboard, as well as the Enter and Backspace keys.

The event passes in by reference the standard ANSI keycode in a parameter called **KeyAscii**. You can alter this value within the event and thereby alter the output to the application. In addition, by setting **KeyAscii** to 0, you can ignore the keystroke altogether. For example, to ignore all numbers (keycodes 48 through 57) typed in by the user in a textbox called **txtName**, you code the following event:

```
Private Sub txtName_KeyPress(KeyAscii As Integer)
    If KeyAscii >= 48 And KeyAscii <= 57 Then
        KeyAscii = 0
    End If
End Sub
```

A common example of altering the keycode might be to force all the input to uppercase. You can do this by converting the keycode to its ASCII character using the **Chr** function, applying the **UCase** function to convert it to uppercase, and then converting the new character back to the keycode value using the **Asc** function:

```
Private Sub txtAge_KeyPress(KeyAscii As Integer)
    KeyAscii = Asc(UCase(Chr(KeyAscii)))
End Sub
```

Much like the Masked Edit control, the **KeyPress** event is an excellent place to put code that assists the user in entering correctly formatted data before it is sent to the backend services.

## Using *KeyUp* And *KeyDown*

You can think of the **KeyUp** and **KeyDown** events as a superset of the **KeyPress** event. Not only do these events fire when ANSI keys are entered but on every keystroke on the keyboard, including arrows, function keys, numeric keypad, and Page Up and Down keys. Generally you use these events when you need to write code that is specific to when a user presses or releases a key or when you want to trap for these special keys.

Like the **KeyPress** event, the **KeyUp** and **KeyDown** events pass in the keycode of the key that was pressed as an argument. However, you can also use these events to trap for a user pressing the Ctrl, Alt, or Shift keys in combination with another key. This is possible because the events pass in a second argument, **Shift**, which corresponds to the state of the Ctrl, Alt, and Shift keys.

The **Shift** argument can be confusing at first, because in order for it to convey three different values simultaneously (the state of the three special keys), it must be represented as a bit mask. You can see the values of the keys in the bit mask and their corresponding predefined constants in Table 4.2.

Because this is a bit mask, you can determine if multiple keys are pressed by simply adding the two values together. For example, to determine if the Ctrl and Alt keys were both pressed, you would test the **Shift** argument for a value

| Table 4.2 | Bit values of the Shift argument in the KeyUp and KeyDown events. | |
| --- | --- | --- |
| **Constant** | **Value** | **Meaning** |
| **vbShiftMask** | 1 | Shift key was pressed. |
| **vbCtrlMask** | 2 | Ctrl key was pressed. |
| **vbAltMask** | 4 | Alt key was pressed. |

of 6. Eight different combinations of the three keys are actually possible, including when none of the keys are pressed.

An example of using the **KeyDown** event might be to trap whether the user had pressed the F5 key along with the Ctrl key to begin a particular process in your application:

```
Private Sub Text1_KeyDown(KeyCode As Integer, Shift As Integer)

    If KeyCode = vbKeyF5 And Shift = vbCtrlMask Then
        'Start the process
    End If

End Sub
```

> In all the keyboard events, you can use the built-in VB constants to check for individual keys. To find these constants, open the Object Browser and search for **KeyCodeConstants** using the search control. This is also a good place to see which keycodes you can trap for.

The only situations in which **KeyUp** and **KeyDown** do not fire is when you press the Enter or Esc key in a form on which command buttons have their **Default** or **Cancel** properties set to **True**.

# Creating Controls

The user interfaces you create in your applications should be flexible enough to handle and display data returned from the backend services. To this end, VB6 has extended the ability to create and manipulate dynamically created controls on a form. This enables your application to respond to changes in the data or even customize itself to the usage pattern of the user. If done carefully, your user interface may even be able to adapt itself to not require redistribution as other pieces of the distributed application change.

## Adding Standard Controls

You may be aware that in previous versions of VB the **Load** statement was used to add controls to a predefined control array, but it was not possible to completely create controls on the fly. This limitation meant that you could not add controls to the form unless they were included in the toolbox for the project and at least one instance of the control was already present in a control array.

VB6 has lifted this limitation by exposing an **Add** method on the **Controls** collection. This method takes three arguments: the **ProgID** or programmatic identifier of the control class, the name the new control should use, and an optional argument to reference the container of the new control.

For example, to add a new **CommandButton** to the form, you would use the following code:

```
Form1.Controls.Add "VB.CommandButton", "cmdOk"
```

> *Note: You can ascertain the **ProgID** by using the Object Browser and appending the class of the control, in this case **CommandButton**, to the name of the library that is displayed as Member Of in the lower portion of the Object Browser window.*

You can then reference the control immediately by using the **Controls** collection. To set the properties of the newly created control, you can access it using the name of the control or its ordinal number:

```
Form1.Controls("cmdOk").Visible = True
```

Or use the alternate syntax:

```
Form1.Controls!cmdOK.Visible = True
```

For example, the code in Listing 4.5 dynamically creates textboxes and label controls to populate a form for collecting address information. You can see the resulting form in Figure 4.1.

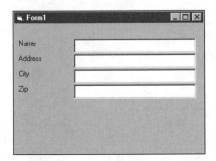

**Figure 4.1**   Dynamically created labels and textboxes.

## Listing 4.5 Dynamically creating controls and placing them on a form.

```
Private Sub Form_Load()
Dim objControl As control
Dim lintTextTop As Integer
Dim lintLabelTop As Integer

'Create the controls
Form1.Controls.Add "VB.Textbox", "txtName"
Form1.Controls.Add "VB.Textbox", "txtAddress"
Form1.Controls.Add "VB.Textbox", "txtCity"
Form1.Controls.Add "VB.Textbox", "txtZip"

Form1.Controls.Add "VB.Label", "lblName"
Form1.Controls("lblName").Caption = "Name"
Form1.Controls.Add "VB.Label", "lblAddress"
Form1.Controls("lblAddress").Caption = "Address"
Form1.Controls.Add "VB.Label", "lblCity"
Form1.Controls("lblCity").Caption = "City"
Form1.Controls.Add "VB.Label", "lblZip"
Form1.Controls("lblZip").Caption = "Zip"

'Set their properties
For Each objControl In Form1.Controls
    objControl.Visible = True
    objControl.Height = 350
    If TypeName(objControl) = "TextBox" Then
        objControl.Width = 3000
        objControl.Left = 1500
        lintTextTop = lintTextTop + 375
        objControl.Top = lintTextTop
    Else
        objControl.Left = 100
        lintLabelTop = lintLabelTop + 375
        objControl.Top = lintLabelTop
    End If
Next

End Sub
```

# Removing Controls

To remove controls that you've added dynamically, you can simply call the **Remove** method of the **Controls** collection:

```
Form1.Controls.Remove "cmdOK"
```

Using this method, you can only remove controls that were added using the **Add** method. You must use the **Unload** statement to remove any controls created using the **Load** statement.

# Handling Events For Dynamically Created Controls

Once you've added the new controls to a form, you may find the need to handle various events that they fire. This is especially true if you want to add dynamic **CommandButtons** or other controls that require an event handler to be useful.

In these cases you must first declare an object variable using the **WithEvents** keyword to refer to the newly created control and then write code in events for that object variable. For example, to create a **CommandButton** and write code for its events, you would first declare a variable of type **CommandButton** in the general declarations section of the form:

```
Private WithEvents cmdOK as CommandButton
```

This creates event handlers for the **cmdOK** button that you can write code in and that will be fired once you've created the button with the **Add** method of the **Controls** collection using the **cmdOK** object variable:

```
Set cmdOK = Form1.Controls.Add("VB.CommandButton", "cmdOK")
```

# Adding ActiveX Controls

The previous examples have dealt with adding controls that are standard or intrinsic to VB, such as **CommandButton**, **TextBox**, and **Label**, or controls that are referenced by every VB project and are always available to be created. Using **Controls.Add** you can also dynamically create ActiveX controls that are referenced in the project (included in the toolbox) or those that are not (referred to as *unreferenced controls*). In both cases the control must already be present on the client machine.

The method for creating ActiveX controls that have been added to the toolbox is almost identical to the steps presented earlier. In order to create a slider control, first add the Windows Common Controls 6 component to the toolbox by right-clicking on the toolbox and selecting Components. Then add the following code to the **Form_Load** event:

```
Form1.Controls.Add "MSComctlLib.Slider", "Slider1"
```

You may encounter an error dialog box that directs you to change the project's Remove Information About Unused ActiveX Controls option in the Project

Properties dialog box. This occurs if no other form in your application contains an instance of the Slider control.

To dynamically create a control that is not already referenced by the project, you must also add the control's license key to the project before creating it. Normally, by referencing the control in the toolbox, VB will retrieve and compile the license keys into the executable. Obviously, with unreferenced controls this is not possible because VB has no way of knowing which controls you might want to create.

The **Licenses** collection contains license key information for all unreferenced controls that require licenses. These may be third-party ActiveX controls or even controls created in VB that were compiled with the Require License Key option set. In most cases, this information is required unless the control was created wholly with intrinsic controls for internal use.

To add the license key, call the **Add** method of the **Licenses** collection, passing it the **ProgID** of the control and the license key as a string. To add an unreferenced Slider control you would use the code:

```
Licenses.Add "MSComctlLib.Slider", strSliderKey
Form1.Controls.Add "MSComctlLib.Slider", "Slider1"
```

You can determine the value of **strSliderKey** at design time by referencing the control (adding it to the toolbox) and then running the code:

```
strSliderKey = Licenses.Add("MSComctlLib.Slider")
```

The resulting string will then need to be stored in a location where the application can retrieve it if instances of the control will be created. For example, you could save the keys in a database table, a flat file, or even in the Windows Registry.

## Events

The method for handling events of referenced ActiveX controls is the same as intrinsic controls. First, declare an object variable of the type of the control using the **WithEvents** keyword and then set the variable to the result of the **Controls.Add** method.

However, more is required to handle events for unreferenced controls. VB exposes a special object type called **VBControlExtender** that can be used as a catch-all object to refer to controls referenced and created at runtime. By declaring on object variable of type **VBControlExtender** using the **WithEvents** keyword, you can handle the events through the object's **ObjectEvent** event.

For example, to code for the events of an unreferenced Slider control, first declare an object variable to refer to the control:

```
Private WithEvents objSlider As VBControlExtender
```

Then add the license key and create the control, using the newly dimensioned **objSlider** variable to refer to the control:

```
Licenses.Add "MSComctlLib.Slider", strSliderKey
Set objSlider = Form1.Controls.Add("MSComctlLib.Slider", "Slider1")
```

You can now use the **objEvent** event of the objSlider control to handle all the specific events raised by the slider control class. The **objEvent** event passes in an object of type **EventInfo** that contains the properties **EventParameters** and **Name** to identify the event and pass in its arguments. **EventParameters** is actually a collection of **EventParameter** objects that specify the name-value pairs for each parameter.

The code in Listing 4.6 uses **objEvent** to trap for the **Change** and **MouseMove** events of objSlider and prints the arguments and their values to the immediate window.

## Listing 4.6 Handling events for dynamically created unreferenced controls.

```
Private Sub objSlider_ObjectEvent(Info As EventInfo)
Dim objParm As EventParameter

Select Case Info.Name
    Case "Change"
        'Here is the new value of the slider
        Debug.Print "Value = " & objSlider.Value
    Case "MouseMove"
        For Each objParm In Info.EventParameters
            Debug.Print objParm.Name & " = " & objParm.Value
        Next
    Case Else
        'Unhandled event
End Select

End Sub
```

# Using COM Components

Much of the code in the user services of a distributed application—and indeed almost everything we've dealt with thus far—involves the creation and manipulation of objects that adhere to the *Component Object Model (COM)*.

These objects can be ActiveX controls residing on the client machine or ActiveX components implementing business services running in MTS. For this reason, it is essential to have a basic understanding of the foundations of COM and how to use it efficiently.

## Essential COM

At its core, COM defines a binary standard through which programs can communicate using an agreed-upon set of rules; each does not have to know how the other is internally implemented. In fact, the programs can be written in different languages, as long as each adheres to the rules of COM.

### Interfaces

In COM the shared set of rules that allow two programs to communicate takes the form of *interfaces*. These interfaces define the functionality one program exposes to others. For example, a COM object that deals with customers may implement a Customer interface. The interface itself is made up of methods and properties that define the functions of the interface and store its data. Methods for the Customer interface may include **CheckCredit** to check the customer's credit and **GetBalance** to calculate and retrieve the customer's current balance. Properties of the Customer interface might include name, address, and phone number.

These interfaces are each assigned a *globally unique identifier (GUID)* at compile time that allows them to be differentiated from all other interfaces. In this way, a calling program can be certain that the interface it is communicating with is the correct one. This relationship between the calling program and the interface is often explained in the language of a legal contract—and indeed it is similar. Once the interface has been defined and published, any program that uses the interface is relying on its constancy. If the interface is changed, the contract is broken and a new GUID must be generated. For this reason, COM interfaces are also often referred to as *self-versioning*. A developer who makes changes to the interface is in effect creating a new version that cannot be used by calling programs that used the previous version.

### IUnknown

All COM interfaces inherit from a standard interface known as *IUnknown*. This interface can be used by calling programs to retrieve pointers to other interfaces in the component through a method called **QueryInterface**. It is also used to keep track of how many clients are currently accessing an object through **AddRef** and **Release** methods. Other interfaces can then be added to support specific functionality. In fact, Microsoft and other vendors have created standard interfaces that may be implemented by components to perform functions such as data access, document storage, data exchange, control implementation, and many others.

## Role Of The Registry

The COM specification defines these rules and then leaves it to the operating system to carry them out. In a Windows operating system, information about the COM components and their interfaces is stored in the system Registry. The Registry contains a reference to a GUID and a programmatic identifier (ProgID) that can also be used to refer to the class of the object. Other key information that is stored includes the DLL or EXE component that houses the object. This information is important, because the calling program does not need to know where the component actually resides. In fact, COM is referred to as *location transparent*, because you can use it to interact with components that are both local and that reside on the network. When a calling program attempts to reference a component, the Registry can then be consulted to provide the actual location of the component so that it can be loaded into memory. In Windows, the OLE system DLLs known as the *COM Library* serve the function of searching the Registry and creating instances of the components. This process and its steps is depicted in Figure 4.2:

1. A client program references an object by its ProgID.

2. The COM Library locates the GUID (also known as a *CLSID*) in the Registry to discover the name and location of the component.

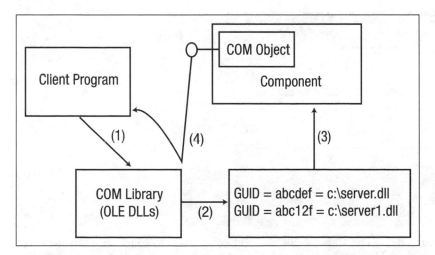

**Figure 4.2**  The Registry is used to store references to interfaces and components.

3. The component is loaded into memory.

4. A pointer to the interface is returned via the COM Library. From this point on, all communication happens directly between the client and the COM object.

## Type Libraries

In order for development tools to provide type checking and make the calls to the interfaces more efficient, COM also provides a mechanism called a *type library*. Simply put, type libraries provide calling programs with the specifications of each interface. They are themselves COM objects that are registered in the system Registry and can be queried by the development tools. VB provides the Project|References (see Figure 4.3) and Project|Components menu items to allow your application to read the type libraries of ActiveX components and ActiveX controls, respectively.

## Automation

Because COM specifies adherence to a strict binary standard that is based on pointers, some development tools cannot call COM interfaces without assistance. To accommodate these tools, Microsoft created a special dispatch interface, IDispatch, through which applications created by these tools can communicate with COM objects that implement this interface. This method is termed *automation* and can be used by languages such as VBScript and JavaScript. The idea behind IDispatch is that it exposes methods such as **GetIDsOfNames** and **Invoke** that allow a calling program to discover the assigned identification

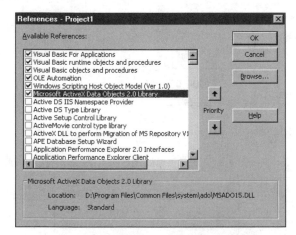

**Figure 4.3**   The References dialog box is used to load type libraries. By loading a type library, VB can use early binding to make interface calls more efficient.

number, called a *dispatch identifier (DISPID)*, of each method (**GetIDsOfNames**) or property in the interface and call them using this number (**Invoke**). In this way the dispatch interface acts as a kind of proxy through which calls are made.

Components may provide the traditional pointer-based method of invocation, called a *virtual table* or *vtable*, the dispatch interface, or a combination of both (termed a *dual interface*).

Although the details of COM are much more complex than depicted here, this provides the foundation to discuss the mechanisms VB uses to call COM components.

# Understanding Binding

*Binding* is the term used to refer to how VB sets up a call to a COM method or property. The mechanism used affects the overhead of the call and—as a result—the performance. The mechanism that is used is determined by several factors, including the way the component was compiled, whether it has a type library, and the syntax used in the calling program to make the call.

There are three ways VB can bind to a component: late binding, DispID binding, and vtable binding.

## *Late Binding*

*Late binding* is used when the VB code declares a variable as **Object** or **Variant**. In these cases the compiler cannot tell ahead of time which interface will be instantiated, so the determination must be made at runtime. An example declaration, creation, and use of a Customer interface using late binding follows:

```
Dim objCustomer as Object
Set objCustomer = CreateObject("ACME.Customer")
objCustomer.Name = "Sammy Sosa"
```

At runtime VB uses the dispatch interface and calls **GetIDsOfNames**, passing it the name of the property; it then uses the returned DISPID to call the **Invoke** method to set the property. Essentially this means that two calls to the component must be made for each method or property access, decreasing performance. For components that reside in a separate process from the caller or perhaps even on a separate server, this greatly affects the responsiveness of the call.

Therefore, you should use late binding only when the function of the program dictates that the class of the object is truly not known at compile time or when the component containing the class does not provide a type library.

## DispID Binding

*DispID binding* is a form of early binding that is used when the component provides a type library, but does not provide a dual interface. In this case, VB uses the **IDispatch::GetIDsOfNames** method to return the DISPID of each method or property call at compile time, rather than runtime. This allows the compiler to essentially replace the name of the method or property with the DISPID in the compiled code so that the **Invoke** method may be called directly at runtime.

To use *early binding*, the ACME.Customer interface first must be added to the References dialog box through the Project|References menu so that its type library may be loaded and used. Second, the declaration of the object must be changed to use the explicit ProgID:

```
Dim objCustomer as ACME.Customer
```

> *Note: Using early binding also enables the Intellisense feature of the VB editor so that you can view the available methods and properties. In addition, the Object Browser provides a look at all the COM components whose type libraries have been referenced.*

## Vtable Binding

Using this form of early binding, the VB compiler uses an offset into a virtual function table, or *vtable*, to set up the calls into the component. This method is the fastest way to call COM interfaces (500 to 1,000 times faster than late binding) and actually takes no more overhead than calling a function in a DLL if the component is loaded in the same process as the caller. If the component is being called out of process or across the network, vtable binding is still the fastest, but the performance gain is not as significant.

VB will always use vtable binding if the component supports it and the interface is explicitly dimensioned with its ProgID. Consequently, the form of early binding (DispID or vtable) the VB compiler uses is not up to the caller, because the syntax is identical, but is dependent on the component.

All components created with VB automatically support dual interfaces and provide a type library so they will be early bound using vtable binding when called from VB using an explicit ProgID.

# CreateObject Vs. New

When using early binding, you can create an instance of a COM object in three ways. All three of the following code snippets for the ACME.Customer component are functionally equivalent:

```
Dim objCustomer as New ACME.Customer

Dim objCustomer as ACME.Customer
Set objCustomer = CreateObject("ACME.Customer")

Dim objCustomer as ACME.Customer
Set objCustomer = New ACME.Customer
```

In all three cases the component is created using the COM creation services in the OLE DLLs discussed previously. However, the first method is not recommended because the object will not actually be created until the first time it is referenced. This requires the compiler to essentially wrap all subsequent calls to the object in if-then logic to determine when the object is actually created. The second two methods perform identically for objects that are provided by a component outside the calling program. This is not the case, however, if the object resides in a class module inside the calling program. In this case, the third technique is recommended because the compiler will bypass the standard COM creation services and use a private and more efficient method to create the object.

### GetObject

You can also use the **GetObject** function to return a reference to an already instantiated COM object or create a new instance initializing it with a file. The function takes two optional arguments, **pathname** and **class**. By setting the pathname to an empty string ("") a new instance will be created. To create a new instance of ACME.Customer you would execute the following code:

```
Dim objCustomer as ACME.Customer
Set objCustomer = GertObject("","ACME.Customer")
```

If the pathname is omitted, an existing instance of the object will be returned if possible or a trappable error will occur. If the pathname contains a file, the object will be instructed to load the file upon initialization. For example, to create an instance of Word and load it with a document you would code:

```
Dim objDoc as Word.Document
Set objDoc = GetObject("c:\My Documents\report.doc","Word.Document")
```

# Binding To Data

The ability to display and manipulate data are the most important functions of most VB applications. With VB6 the capabilities for data manipulation and display have been enhanced. VB6 now sports a new *ActiveX Data Objects (ADO)* Data Control and several OLE DB data-bound controls that can use the ADO Data Control as a data source. For the exam it is important to know how to use the ADO Data Control to execute a statement against an OLE DB provider and bind the result set to one of the new bound controls.

The full explanation of OLE DB and ADO will have to wait for Chapter 9, but suffice it to say that OLE DB is Microsoft's strategic direction for data access and ADO provides a way for VB to take advantage of OLE DB. Among ADOs strengths are the ability to connect to relational as well as nonrelational data sources (called providers) and its flexible object model.

# Using The ADO Data Control

For those familiar with the DAO and RDO data controls that have been a part of VB for several years, the new ADO version will not be difficult to comprehend. The key properties and methods of the control are in Table 4.3.

| Table 4.3 ADO Data Control key methods and properties. | |
| --- | --- |
| **Member** | **Description** |
| CommandTimeout | Specifies how long the control will wait for a single command to execute before returning an error. |
| CommandType | Specifies the format of the command that will be sent to the data provider. Options include the name of a table, stored procedure, or SQL statement. |
| ConnectionString | Specifies the connection information used to connect to the data provider. |
| ConnectionTimeout | Specifies how long the control will wait for the connection to the data provider before returning an error. |
| Mode | Specifies the permissions in use for modifying data returned by the control. |
| Password | Specifies the password to be sent to the data provider upon initiating a connection. |
| Recordset | Property that returns or sets a reference to the underlying recordset returned by the control. |
| RecordSource | Specifies the text of the command to be sent to the data provider. This may include a table name, stored procedure, or SQL statement. |
| Refresh | Method that instructs the data control to refresh its recordset. This can be used after the **RecordSource** property is changed programmatically to repopulate the control. |
| UpdateControls | Method that restores the contents of all bound controls to their original values and is used when a user decides to cancel changes to the current record. |
| UserName | Specifies the user name to be sent to the data provider upon initiating a connection. |

After placing an instance of the ADO Data Control on a form, the important properties to set for the control are as follows:

```
Adodc1.CommandType = adCmdText
Adodc1.ConnectionString = "DRIVER=SQL Server;SERVER=ssosa;" & _
    "DATABASE=Northwind"
Adodc1.Mode = adModeRead
Adodc1.RecordSource = "SELECT * FROM Products"
Adodc1.UserName = "sa"
Adodc1.Password = ""
Adodc1.Refresh
```

Each of these properties can also be set at design time. Once the **Refresh** method has executed, the data control is synchronously populated with data. Like other data controls, the ADO Data Control also exposes a series of events that can be used to determine when data in the control is manipulated or updated. The key events of the control are listed in Table 4.4.

| Table 4.4 ADO Data Control events. | |
|---|---|
| **Event** | **Description** |
| **EndOfRecordset** | Fired when an attempt is made to move to a record that is past the end of the recordset. |
| **Error** | Fired when a data access error occurs and passes in arguments to determine the error number, description, and source, as well an argument that can used to suppress display of the error. |
| **WillChangeField** and **FieldChangeComplete** | Fired before and after the value of one or more fields in the recordset changes. The event passes in information about the fields and their status, as well as a reference to the underlying recordset. |
| **WillChangeRecord** and **RecordChangeComplete** | Fired before and after one or more records in the recordset changes in response to an **Update**, **Delete**, or **AddNew** operation. This event also passes in information about the status and reason for the change, as well as a reference to the recordset. |
| **WillChangeRecordset** and **RecordsetChangeComplete** | Fired before and after the underlying recordset changes in response to the **Requery**, **Resync**, **Close**, **Open**, or **Filter** methods. This event also passes in information about the status and reason for the change, as well as a reference to the recordset. |

*Note: The events exposed by the ADO Data Control are the same as those exposed by the ADO Recordset object discussed in Chapter 9, with the exception of the **FetchComplete** and **FetchProgress** events, which are used for asynchronous processing.*

## Using Data-Bound Controls

In order to display data from an ADO Data Control, VB6 now ships with six ActiveX controls designed specifically for use with the control, in addition to the intrinsic controls that support data binding. You can see the new controls and their functions in Table 4.5.

All of the controls listed in Table 4.5 and any bound controls support the **DataSource** property that is used to tie the bound control to an instance of an ADO Data Control. Once bound, the control can expose properties such as **DataField** to determine which field from the data control's recordset will be displayed. Additionally, controls like **DataCombo** and **DataList** provide properties such as **RowSource**, **ListField**, and **BoundColumn** to allow the control to display data from one data control and update the contents of a second.

## Using The Data Environment

VB6 now sports another method for putting bound controls on a form. The *Data Environment Designer* is a graphical tool that makes it easier to create ADO connections to data sources and commands to query those connections.

**Table 4.5    New data-bound controls that can be used with the ADO Data Control.**

| Control Name | Description |
| --- | --- |
| Microsoft Chart | Displays a retrieved recordset as a two-dimensional or three-dimensional graph. |
| Microsoft DataCombo | Provides a drop-down combo box that can be used to ensure proper data entry. |
| Microsoft DataGrid | Displays the recordset in a standard tabular format. Also allows the data to updated. |
| Microsoft DataList | Provides a drop-down listbox that can be used ensure proper data entry. |
| Microsoft DataRepeater | Allows other controls that are bound to a data source to be repeated for each record returned from the data source. This allows the creation of custom tabular type data controls. |
| Microsoft Hierarchical FlexGrid | A read-only grid control that allows images, formatting, and both summary and detail data to be displayed. |

Both the connections and commands are available at design time or programmatically at runtime and can be reused throughout the project.

To add a Data Environment, right-click on the project in the Project Explorer window and select Add|Data Environment. By default, a connection called Connection1 is created. To set its properties, right-click on it and select Properties. The resulting dialog box can be used to specify the OLE DB Provider to use, the login credentials, and specifics of the connection including server name and database. As you'll see in Chapter 9, this is the graphical representation of an ADO **Connection** object.

Once the connection has been created you can encapsulate ADO **Command** objects by right-clicking on the connection and selecting Add Command or Insert Stored Procedure. In either case, a command is added to the Data Environment that can be manipulated by right-clicking on it. Each command can encapsulate a user-defined SQL string, a table name, or a stored procedure. There is also a SQL Builder included to make it simple to create the query graphically.

After the graphical design is finished you can drag the command from the Data Environment Designer to a form to automatically create bound controls on the form. You'll notice the **DataSource, DataMember,** and **DataField** properties of the bound controls are set to the Data Environment, command, and column name, respectively.

To provide more control you can access the Data Environment commands programmatically. For example, to programmatically save changes that have been made to a recordset created using a Data Environment with a command called **rsAuthors**, the syntax would be as follows:

```
DataEnvironment1.rsAuthors.Update
```

# Implementing Callbacks

In certain cases the user services of a distributed application will require access to services that employ asynchronous processing. Obviously, events are one type of asynchronous processing, but another type exists and is referred to as a *callback*. Depending on the origin of the callback, VB uses different techniques to handle them. The two types of callbacks that you will encounter are those in standard DLLs, such as the Win32 DLLs, and those in ActiveX components.

## Callbacks In The Win32 API

In DLLs, callbacks occur when a DLL function is passed the address of a function in the calling program. The DLL function then uses this address to call back into your VB program to report status information or when its work is complete.

To implement callbacks of this type, VB5 introduced the **AddressOf** operator. This operator, when passed the name of a VB procedure, returns its address, which can then be passed to a DLL function.

Several Win32 API functions employ callbacks. One of the most commonly used is the **SetTimer** function. This function sets a timer for a specific window and is passed the address of a function to call back in your program when the timer goes off. Many of the other functions that employ callbacks are called *enumeration functions*. These functions enumerate multiple items, such as the fonts installed on the computer (**EnumFontFamilies**) or the windows that are currently open (**EnumWindows**).

To use the **SetTimer** function, first declare the function using the **Declare** statement that can be found using the API Text Viewer that installs with Visual Studio:

```
Public Declare Function SetTimer Lib "user32" _
(ByVal hwnd As Long, ByVal nIDEvent As Long, _
ByVal uElapse As Long, ByVal lpTimerFunc As Long) As Long
```

Next, create a public procedure in a code module that will be used as the callback procedure. This procedure must have a specific set of arguments for the function you are calling. You can consult the MSDN documentation on the Win32 API to find the proper declaration for the procedure. For **SetTimer**, the procedure will take on the declaration as follows:

```
Public Sub TimerProc(ByVal hwnd As Long, _
ByVal uint As Long, ByVal idevent As Long, _
ByVal dwtime As Long)
```

 Remember that the callback function must be a public procedure in a code module.

To initiate the callback, call the **SetTimer** function, passing it the handle of the window to set the timer for, the ID of the timer, the length of the interval in milliseconds, and the address of **TimerProc**:

```
SetTimer Me.hwnd, 1, 1000, AddressOf TimerProc
```

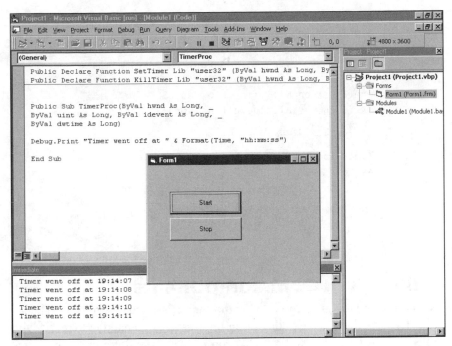

**Figure 4.4**    Using the Win32 **SetTimer** function to provide a callback.
Notice that the Immediate window is printing the notifica-
tions of each call to **TimerProc**.

The callback procedure **TimerProc** will now be called each time the timer goes
off. The complete code in Listing 4.7 also implements the Win32 **KillTimer**
function to stop the timer when the user clicks on the button. Figure 4.4 shows
the application running in the development environment.

## Listing 4.7    A simple application that uses the Win32 **SetTimer** callback.

```
'Form1 Code*******************************************
Private Sub cmdStart_Click()

SetTimer Me.hwnd, 1, 1000, AddressOf TimerProc

End Sub

Private Sub cmdStop_Click()

KillTimer Me.hwnd, 1

End Sub
```

```
'Module1 Code*****************************************
Public Declare Function SetTimer Lib "user32" _
(ByVal hwnd As Long, ByVal nIDEvent As Long, _
ByVal uElapse As Long, ByVal lpTimerFunc As Long) As Long

Public Declare Function KillTimer Lib "user32" _
(ByVal hwnd As Long, ByVal nIDEvent As Long) As Long


Public Sub TimerProc(ByVal hwnd As Long, _
ByVal uint As Long, ByVal idevent As Long, _
ByVal dwtime As Long)

Debug.Print "Timer went off at " & Format(Time, "hh:mm:ss")

End Sub
```

# Callbacks In COM Components

Asynchronous processing in COM components is analogous to the callbacks in DLLs. In both cases the calling program must create a handler to receive the callback. However, when using COM components, the communication is accomplished through interfaces rather than a public procedure. Because we're only dealing here with the user services of a distributed application, we'll discuss what a client program must do to use a COM component that implements a callback.

For this example, assume that a COM component exists that processes customer orders, ACME.Customer. This component contains a method, **ValidateCard**, that validates a customer's credit card and returns a status as to whether the purchase is allowable. Rather than implement this as a synchronous operation, the component implements the operation asynchronously using a callback to allow the user services to continue processing.

COM components like ACME.Customer will provide an interface through which the component will make the callback. The client program must then create an object using the interface and pass it into a method of the component. When the component completes its processing, it calls a method of the object that was passed in to perform the notification.

In this example, an interface called ACMEUtil.Notify has been created to handle the notification. This interface includes one method, **ValidateReturned**, that passes in an argument that returns the status of the processing. In VB, this interface is created as a separate ActiveX DLL project and includes only definitions of the methods, but no implementation. This creates a type library that other programs can use to create objects of the same class:

```
Option Explicit

Public Sub ValidateReturned(validated As Boolean)

End Sub
```

The ACME.Customer component includes a method called **ValidateCard** that takes as arguments the purchase amount and a reference to an object that will be used to call back into the client. It also includes a private procedure, **DoValidation**, to perform the validation and then calls the **ValidateReturned** method of the notification object when the processing is complete. You can find the code for the ACME.Customer component in Listing 4.8.

## Listing 4.8    The ACME.Customer component.

```
Option Explicit

Public objNotify As ACMEUtil.Notify

Public Sub ValidateCard(PurchaseAmount As Currency, _
                        objClient As ACMEUtil.Notify)

    Set objNotify = objClient

    Call DoValidation

End Sub

Private Sub DoValidation()

    'Do some work here to validate it

    'Finished, call the client
    objNotify.ValidateReturned True

End Sub
```

In order to implement the callback, the client program must create a class module to implement the notification interface. This is accomplished through the **Implements** keyword. Essentially, this keyword allows COM objects to be *polymorphic*, allowing multiple objects to share the same definition. This enables you to write code that is more flexible and reusable. The code for this internal class, called **Class1**, follows:

```
Option Explicit
Implements ACMEUtil.Notify
```

```
Private Sub Notify_ValidateReturned(validated As Boolean)

'The process is complete
MsgBox validated

End Sub
```

The only task that remains is for the form to create instances of both the customer component and the internal class that implements the notification interface. The client then calls the **ValidateCard** method of the customer component, passing it the purchase amount and a reference to the notification object:

```
Option Explicit
Private objCustomer As New ACME.Customer
Private objNotify As New Class1

Private Sub Form_Load()

    objCustomer.ValidateCard 5000, objNotify

End Sub
```

Once the process is complete the **ValidateReturned** method of **objNotify** will be called, in this case producing a message box displaying the result of the validation.

# Error Handling

All user interfaces should employ sound error-handling techniques, and those created in VB are no exception. For the exam you'll need to be familiar with the basics of handling errors and some typical techniques that are used. Space prohibits a complete discussion of all the variations of this topic, but we'll cover the basics and you can look for more information in the "Need To Know More?" section at the end of the chapter.

## Setting Traps

VB uses error traps to handle runtime errors. Basically, *error traps* are sections of code within a procedure that can be executed in the event of an error. This is the same concept as raising exceptions in C++ and Java. By default, no error traps are enabled in an application and any runtime error produces an obtuse dialog box that ends the application after it is dismissed. To set a trap you use the **On Error Goto** statement followed by a line label. For example, to set an error trap in a click event in a command button you would code the following handler:

```
Private Sub Command1_Click()
On Error Goto MyErr

'Other code goes here

Exit Sub
MyErr:
    'Handle the error here
End Sub
```

In this case, any runtime errors that occur between the **On Error** statement and the **Exit Sub** will immediately redirect the flow of control to the **MyErr** statement.

To disable a trap you use the **On Error Goto 0** statement, which disables any error trap that was set. You can only have one error trap enabled in a procedure at any point in time. You may also skip all errors that occur in a procedure by using the **On Error Resume Next** statement, although this is not normally recommended for obvious reasons.

Inside the error trap you can use the **Err** object to view the source, description, and number of the error using its properties.

## Exiting A Trap

Once inside an error trap, you can take five courses of action. They are enumerated in Table 4.6.

| Table 4.6 | Ways to exit an error trap. |
| --- | --- |
| **Statement** | **Description** |
| **Resume** | Forces program execution to continue at the statement that caused the error. This is the preferred method for certain kinds of errors that the user can correct. For instance, a runtime error occurs when a floppy disk or CD-ROM is not ready for reading. By inserting the proper media, the statement can be re-executed successfully. |
| **Resume *line*** | Forces program execution to continue at a specific line label. |
| **Resume Next** | Forces program execution to continue with the statement following the one that caused the error. |
| **Err.Raise number** | Raises an error from within the error handler so that it can be handled by another procedure. |
| ***Nothing*** | By doing nothing in the error trap, the procedure will simply end once the error handler has finished executing. In many cases, this is the desired action. |

## Error Sequences

In the event that a runtime error is generated in a procedure that does not have an error trap set, VB will search the call stack to determine if a procedure that is lower in the stack contains an error handler. In other words, if procedure A calls procedure B and procedure B generates a runtime error without an error trap set, the error trap in procedure A is called if it exists. This process continues until every active procedure has been checked. This functionality means that not every one of your procedures must contain error traps, only those that are called directly from the interface. However, in many instances you'll still want to trap for specific errors in individual procedures.

The key point to remember about the sequence of an error handler is that the **Resume** and **Resume Next** statements only execute code with the procedure in which the error handler is actually found. In the previous example, for instance, this means that if the error handler in procedure A issues a **Resume** statement, the statement that gets re-executed is actually the call to procedure B and not the actual statement in procedure B that first caused the error. Likewise, if procedure A issues a **Resume Next**, the statement after the call to procedure B is executed.

 Be sure you understand the concept in the previous paragraph. Test writers love questions about procedures calling procedures and often ask you to figure out which line of code will execute after the error handler.

## Inline Error Handling

In some situations you may want to bypass the trapping mechanisms of VB and check for specific errors after each line of code. To do this you'll need to turn off all error traps using the **On Error Resume Next** statement and then check the **Number** property of the **Err** object.

For example, a procedure that deletes a file using the **Kill** statement may use inline error handling to make sure the file exists, as shown in Listing 4.9.

### Listing 4.9 Implementing inline error handling.

```
Public Function DelFile(strFile As String) As Boolean

On Error Resume Next

Kill strFile
If Err.Number = 53 Then
    'file not found
    DelFile = False
    Err.Clear
```

```
Else
    'success
    DelFile = True
End If

End Function
```

# Centralized Error Handling

Rather than rewrite the same error handlers in multiple applications, you can centralize much of this error-handling code by writing procedures to handle specific types of errors. These procedures can even prompt the user and return the appropriate action to the procedure that generated the error.

The case of disk errors is a good example of where you can use a centralized error handler. The set of possible errors when dealing with disks and files can be checked within a centralized procedure. The procedure can then create a message to prompt the user and pass back the result. You can see the code for the **DiskErrors** procedure in Listing 4.10.

## Listing 4.10   A centralized DiskErrors procedure adapted from the MSDN online help.

```
Function DiskErrors() As Integer
Dim intMsgType As Integer
Dim strMsg As String
Dim intResponse As Integer

    Select Case Err.Number
        Case 68
            strMsg = "That device appears unavailable."
        Case 71
            strMsg = "Insert a disk in the drive "
        Case 57
            strMsg = "Internal disk error."
        Case 61
            strMsg = "Disk is full. Continue?"
        Case 76
            strMsg = "That path doesn't exist."
        Case 54
            strMsg = "Can't open your file."
        Case 55
            strMsg = "This file is already open."
        Case 53
            strMsg = "This file is not found."
        Case 62
            strMsg = "There was a problem with this file."
        Case Else
```

```
         DiskErrors = 1
         Exit Function
      End Select

   intResponse = MsgBox(strMsg, _
      vbExclamation + vbAbortRetryIgnore, "Disk Error")

   Select Case intResponse
    Case vbAbort
         DiskErrors = 1
    Case vbRetry
         DiskErrors = 2
    Case vbIgnore
         DiskErrors = 3
    End Select

End Function
```

This procedure can then be called in the error handler for the **DelFile** procedure seen previously, rather than using inline error handling. Listing 4.11 shows this code.

## Listing 4.11    Calling the centralized error handler.

```
Public Function DelFile(strFile As String) As Boolean

On Error GoTo DelFileErr

Kill strFile

Exit Function
DelFileErr:
    Select Case DiskErrors
    Case 1  'Abort
        Exit Function
    Case 2  'Retry
        Resume
    Case 3  'Ignore
        Resume Next
    End Select

End Function
```

# Implementing Help

Because the user interacts directly with the user services in a distributed application, this is the place where you need to provide assistance to that user. In a VB interface you can provide help using the traditional Windows Help System (WinHelp) or the newer HTML Help. Although the exam does not cover how to compile help files for use in either of these two engines, you do need to know how to integrate these help files with your application.

## Assigning A Help File

To associate a help file with your application you need to set the **HelpFile** property of the built-in **App** object. You can access this property through the Project Properties dialog box by selecting Project|Project Properties.

Keep in mind that if you specify a help file with a hard-coded path in the dialog box, the path will be compiled into the EXE and must exist on each client machine that runs your executable. For this reason, you should specify a help file without the path and place it in the same directory as the executable or in a directory that is always searched, like Windows\System32, or a directory referenced in the **PATH** environment variable.

To avoid this situation you can also set the property programmatically using the **App** object. The following code uses the **App.Path** property to set the **HelpFile** property to point to the directory in which the application is running:

```
App.HelpFile - App.Path & "\myapphelp.hlp"
```

Once the property is set, VB will automatically view the help file whenever the user presses F1. If the help file is not set, the VB help file will be displayed.

The **Err** object also exposes a **HelpFile** property that can be set so that when runtime errors occur the **Err** object will be able to return the help file that can be consulted. In this way you can specify separate help files for error messages that may be shared by multiple applications and application-specific help files. By storing the reference to the help file in the **Err** object, you can allow the user to get more information on the error that was trapped. The code in Listing 4.12 shows how you can use this to pop up a message box with a help button that takes the user to a specific help topic in a help file that elucidates common errors.

## Listing 4.12   Setting the **HelpFile** property of the Err object.

```
Const DISKERRORS As Long = 1000

Private Sub Form_Load()
  Err.HelpFile = App.Path & "\commonerrors.hlp"
  App.HelpFile = App.Path & "\myapp.hlp"
End Sub
```

```
Private Sub OpenDiskFile()

On Error GoTo DiskErr

'Code goes here to open the disk file

Exit Sub
DiskErr:
    'Display an error message to the user
    'Using the common errors help file
    MsgBox err.Description, _
        vbExclamation + vbMsgBoxHelpButton, _
        App.Title, Err.HelpFile, DISKERRORS
End Sub
```

# Providing Help Context

When a user presses the F1 key to activate the help file, the topic in the file that is displayed is determined by the **HelpContextID** property of the control that currently has focus. For example, if you set the **HelpContextID** of a textbox to 1050, place your cursor in the textbox, and then press the F1 key, the help file specified in the **HelpFile** property will be displayed and opened to the topic specified in the **HelpContextID** property. As with the **HelpFile** property, you can set **HelpContextID** at design time or runtime. To set the property at runtime, refer to the name of the control:

```
txtName.HelpContextID = 1050
```

Menu items also contain a **HelpContextID** property that you can set programmatically or at design time.

If the **HelpContextID** is set to zero or not specified, VB will look in the container of the control to see if a **HelpContextID** exists at the higher level. It does this until all containers are exhausted and finally displays the default topic in the help file if no context can be found.

# Practice Questions

## Question 1

Assume you have two controls on a form, txtName and txtAddress. You set the **CausesValidation** property of txtName to **True** and write code in the **Validate** event for txtAddress to check if the user has entered data. If not, you set the **Cancel** argument to **True**.

If the initial focus is on the txtName control, what sequence of events occurs when the user presses the Tab key without entering data in txtName?

○ a.  The **Validate** event fires for the txtAddress control, causing the validation code to run and the focus to remain on txtName.

○ b.  The **Validate** event fires for the txtName control, causing the validation code to run and the focus to remain on txtName.

○ c.  Focus moves to the txtAddress control.

○ d.  Focus remains on the txtName control and its **CausesValidation** property is reset to **False**.

The correct answer is c. In this case, the **Validate** event for txtName was not coded, so even though the **CausesValidation** property is set to **True** (the default), focus will be allowed to move. Answer b is incorrect because only by setting the **Cancel** argument to **True** in the **Validate** event of txtName would focus remain on txtName. Answer a would be correct if the focus was initially set to txtAddress. Answer d is incorrect because VB never resets the **CausesValidation** property.

Remember that the key concept here is that the **Validate** event will fire as a control is losing focus if and only if the **CausesValidation** property of the control about to receive focus is set to **True**.

## Question 2

You've coded the following events for textboxes called **txtName** and **txtAddress**:

```
Private Sub txtName_LostFocus()
    If Len(txtName) = 0 Then
        txtName.SetFocus
    End If
End Sub

Private Sub txtAddress_LostFocus()
    If Len(txtAddress) = 0 Then
        txtAddress.SetFocus
    End If
End Sub
```

What will happen when the user tabs from **txtName** to **txtAddress** without entering any data in **txtName**?

○ a.  The focus will remain on **txtName**.

○ b.  The focus will move to **txtAddress**, but a trappable error will occur.

○ c.  A stack overflow message will appear and the program will halt.

○ d.  An trappable error will occur.

The correct answer is c. Remember that without using a form-level variable to control when the validation code should run, these two controls will fight for focus until VB runs out of stack space, causing the program to halt. The key concept here is that the **LostFocus** event does not fire until after the control receiving focus has already done so.

Obviously, answers a and b are incorrect because the infinite loop that is created will not allow focus to ever settle on either control. Answer c is incorrect because an error handler is not allowed to be called while the controls are vying for focus.

## Question 3

You want to retrieve data from a SQL Server database using the ADO Data Control. How must you set the properties of the control?

○ a.  Set **ConnectionString** to a valid table name in the database. Set **CommandText** to a valid SQL statement. Set **CommandType** to a constant specifying the type of command to run.

○ b.  Set **ConnectionString** to a string specifying the data provider and database. Set **RecordSource** to a valid SQL statement. Set **CommandType** to a constant specifying the type of command to run.

○ c.  Set **CommandString** to a valid SQL statement. Set **Connect** to a string specifying the data provider and database. Set **CommandType** to a Boolean indicating that you are processing a command.

○ d.  Set **ConnectionString** to a string specifying the data provider and database. Set **DataSource** to a bound data control. Set **CommandType** to a Boolean indicating that you are processing a command.

The correct answer is b. The **ConnectionString** property specifies all the connection information, including the data provider, server name, database name, and even the login ID and password. The **RecordSource** property is used to hold the valid SQL statement; the **CommandType** property must be set to an enumerated type that specifies the type of command contained in the **RecordSource** property.

Answer a is incorrect because the name of the table is specified in the **RecordSource**. Answer c is incorrect because the ADO Data Control does not support a **Connect** property. Answer d is incorrect because bound controls use the **DataSource** property to bind to an ADO Data Control, not the other way around.

## Question 4

> You want to dynamically add a label control to the form Form1 and name it txtLabel. Which syntax is valid?
>
> ○ a. Form1.AddControl "VB.Label", "txtLabel"
>
> ○ b. Load "txtLabel", "VB.Label"
>
> ○ c. Form1.Controls.Add "VB.Label", "txtLabel"
>
> ○ d. Form1.Controls.Add "txtLabel","VB.Label"

The correct answer is c. To add a control dynamically you must use the **Add** method of the **Controls** collection of the **Form** object. This adds the control to the collection and allows it to be referenced. The two arguments are the ProgID or programmatic identifier and the name of the control. Answer a is incorrect because no **AddControl** method of the **Form** object exists. Answer b is incorrect because the **Load** statement can only be used to add controls to a control array dynamically, although the syntax shown in the answer is also incorrect. Answer d is incorrect as the arguments are reversed.

## Question 5

> You want to call a Win32 callback function such as **Enum-ChildWindows**. How should you declare the procedure that will receive the callback in VB?
>
> ○ a. As a public procedure in the form that is to receive the callback
>
> ○ b. As a public method in a class module
>
> ○ c. As a private procedure in a code module
>
> ○ d. As a public procedure in a code module

The correct answer is d. When calling Win32 API functions that produce callbacks, the procedure that is to be notified must be declared as a public procedure in a code module. The address of this procedure is then passed into the API function using the **AddressOf** keyword.

Obviously the other answers are incorrect and represent other ways of declaring procedures.

## Question 6

You want to declare an ActiveX component, ACME.Customer, in a local procedure in your VB application. You want VB to use early binding. Which of the following declarations can you use? [Check all that apply]

☐ a.  Dim objCustomer as New ACME.Customer

☐ b.  Dim objCustomer as New Object

☐ c.  Dim objCustomer as ACME.Customer

☐ d.  Dim objCustomer as Variant

Answers a and c are correct. To use early binding you need to use the explicit class name of the component in the declaration. By doing so, VB will read the type library information of the component, providing Intellisense help and making the calls to the component more efficient. Answers b and d are incorrect because declaring an object as **Object** or **Variant** instructs VB to use late binding, which does not resolve the references to the object until runtime.

Using the **New** keyword, as in answers a and b, simply instructs VB to create the object upon first use, rather than using an explicit **CreateObject** statement. Whether the **New** keyword is used or not does not affect the binding method VB uses.

## Question 7

You want to add help to your application so that when the user presses the F1 key while the focus is on a control called lstProducts, the help file is opened and the appropriate topic for the control is displayed. What do you need to do? [Check all that apply]

☐ a.  Set the **App.HelpFile** property to the name of the help file to use. Set the **Tag** property of lstProducts to the help topic number associated with the control.

☐ b.  Set the Help file field in the Project Properties dialog to the help file to use. Set the **HelpContextID** property of lstProducts to the appropriate help topic.

☐ c.  Set the **App.Helpfile** property to the name of the help file to use. Set the **HelpContextID** property of lstProducts to the appropriate help topic.

☐ d.  Set the **Helpfile** property of the **Form** object to the name of the help file to use. Set the **HelpContextID** property of lstProducts to the appropriate help topic.

The correct answers are b and c. To set the help file for the application you can use either of the methods in these two answers. However, by programmatically setting the **HelpFile** property, you have more control over the path to the help file. The **HelpContextID** must be set to the help topic that should be displayed when the user presses F1.

Answer a is incorrect because the **Tag** property is used to store any miscellaneous information about the control that you wish. However, because the control provides a specific property for the help topic, you would not use it for this purpose. Answer d is incorrect because the help file is set at the application level and not at the form level.

## Question 8

Assume you've coded the following two procedures:

```
Public Sub ProcA()
On Error Goto ErrA
        Call ProcB
        'More statements
Exit Sub
ErrA:
        Resume Next
End Sub

Public Sub ProcB()
Dim x as Integer
        x = 1/0
End Sub
```

What happens when the variable x is set to the value 1/0?

○ a. VB displays a default error message and the program terminates.

○ b. The error handler in **ProcA** is called and statement following the call to **ProcB** is then executed.

○ c. The error handler in **ProcA** is called and **ProcB** is then re-executed.

○ d. Nothing.

The correct answer is b. Remember that if no active error handler exists in a procedure, the error handler in the calling procedure is run in the event of a runtime error. If ProcA did not have an error handler, VB would move down the call stack to see if the procedure that called ProcA had one, and so forth. Because the error handler issues a **Resume Next** statement, the statement following the one that caused the error is executed. In this case that is the statement following the call to ProcB, because error handlers only reference statements in their own procedures.

Answer a is incorrect because ProcB is called by ProcA. If ProcB was called directly by the user interface, VB would display a message and terminate. Answer c is incorrect because the **Resume Next** statement, rather than **Resume**, was issued in the error handler. If **Resume** were executed, the call to ProcB would be re-executed and an infinite loop would result. Answer d is incorrect because the **On Error Resume Next** statement was not invoked in ProcB. Invoking it would not activate any trappable errors.

# Question 9

To allow a stored procedure, **GetAuthors**, that returns a recordset to be executed at runtime using the Data Environment Designer, what actions below are not required?

- O a.  Add a Data Environment object to the project.
- O b.  Insert a command and set its Object Name to
  **GetAuthors.procedure**.
- O c.  Execute the code:
  **DataEnvironment1.rsGetAuthors.Open**.
- O d.  Set the **Connection** object's properties by right-clicking on it.
- O e.  Set the **ActiveConnection** property of the **Command** object programmatically.

The correct answer is e. To set up the Data Environment to reference and execute a stored procedure you do need to add the Data Environment object (answer a), set the **Connection** object's properties (answer d) or create a **Command** object to reference the stored procedure (answer b). To execute it you can either open the recordset programmatically using the code in answer c or drag and drop the **Command** object to a form at design time and then simply run the project. The **ActiveConnection** property does not need to be set at runtime and is normally set at design time when the command is being defined.

# Need To Know More?

 Appleman, Daniel: *Dan Appleman's Visual Basic 5.0 Programmer's Guide to the Win32 API*. Ziff-Davis Press, 1997. ISBN:1-56276-446-2. This is the bible for the intersection of VB and Win32 programming. It includes references to all the relevant API calls that you'd want to make from VB, not just the callback functions explored in this chapter.

 Chappell, David: *Understanding ActiveX and OLE for Developers and Managers*. Microsoft Press, 1996. ISBN: 1-57231-216-5. This is an excellent introduction to the concepts of COM and provides a solid foundation for topics such as automation, type libraries, and late versus early binding.

 For the basics on validation see the MSDN online help that ships with Visual Studio 6 and search for "Validating Control Data by Restricting Forms" in the Visual Basic Programmer's Guide. This section walks through the **Validate** event and **CausesValidation** property.

 Also in the online help see "Asynchronous Notifications Using Call-Back Methods." This topic discusses the COM notification procedure and points you to the sample application that ships with the Enterprise edition of Visual Studio.

 For an overview of creating COM interfaces and the **Implements** keyword, see the "Creating Standard Interfaces with Visual Basic" and "Providing Polymorphism by Implementing Interfaces" topics in the MSDN online help.

# Creating Web-Based Clients

**5**

## Terms you'll need to understand:

√ **Application** object

√ **ObjectContext** object

√ **OnTransactionCommit**

√ **OnTransactionAbort**

√ **Session** object

√ **Server** object

√ **Request** object

√ **Response** object

√ IIS application

√ **WebClass** object

√ **StateManagement** property

√ HTML template file

√ **WriteTemplate** method

√ **ProcessTag** event

√ Indicator tags

√ **TagPrefix** property

√ **BeginRequest** event

√ Start event

√ **NextItem** property

√ DHTML Page Designer

## Techniques you'll need to master:

√ Creating **Application** and **Session** object variables

√ Accessing form element values and query string variables using the **Request** object

√ Initiating client browser redirects using the **Response** object

√ Adding code to HTML output using the **Response** object

√ Transacting ASP scripts

√ Sending HTML template Webitem to client

√ Adding indicator tags

√ Setting initial HTML template used by **WebClass**

√ Modifying page content and styles by using the DHTML Page Designer

# Basic Active Server Page Concepts

No discussion concerning Web-based clients can exist, or even begin, without discussing Active Server Page extensions for Internet Information Server (IIS), or the Personal Web Server variations of IIS. Formerly code-named "Denali," *Active Server Pages (ASP)* are a server-side scripting execution platform or environment for providing server-side script execution. Active Server Pages provide a layer of executable script that is evaluated prior to packetizing HTTP-requested data that is sent to the client; they allow requested pages to be dynamically produced, based on information provided to IIS through a number of different mechanisms. Active Server Pages are not inherently tied to any one scripting language; they allow for any language for which a scripting engine or interpreter is properly installed in the system. ASP provides built-in support for the Visual Basic-based VBScript scripting language and for JScript, which is Microsoft's implementation of JavaScript and is ECMAScript 262 compliant.

 Moving a Perl-based script requires a Perl interpreter to be installed on the destination Web server.

## Built-In Objects

The Active Server Pages framework provides six built-in objects for accessing common properties or information for the server, HTTP requests and responses, MTS ObjectContexts, and assorted information commonly used in an ASP-based application. These six objects are the **Application, Session, Request, Response, Server,** and **ObjectContext** objects. The objects are "built in" to the Active Server Page extension to IIS, which makes them automatically available to any server-side ASP code without first requiring that the developer create them in the page.

Several of the built-in objects work off of the concept of an application. An *ASP-based application* is generally defined as the sum total of all ASP files that are placed within a virtual directory, including all of its subdirectories. When a user accesses any one of the ASP files within an application, a user session is initiated if it is the first attempt at accessing an ASP file by that user. The concepts of an *application* and *user session* are important in understanding the functionality and uses of the built-in ASP objects.

## ASP Delimiters

You can use either of two ways to separate ASP scripting from client-side script. Server-side ASP script can be delimited, or separated, from client-side script and

HTML code by using the <% and %> tag elements. Any script found within these tags will be processed on the server. Optionally, you can use the <SCRIPT> tag, traditionally used to identify client-side script, to signify that script be run at the server. This is accomplished by setting the optional **RUNAT** attribute to the value of **SERVER**.

# Active Server Page Built-In Objects

The Active Server Page ISAPI extension to IIS 4 provides six built-in objects for use by the ASP developer to access server information and HTTP packet and header information. It also persists state information across individual instances of an ASP page, within a given user session, or across all instances of ASP currently in memory. As mentioned earlier, the six objects are the **Application, Session, Request, Response, Server,** and **ObjectContext** objects.

## Application Object

The **Application** object is used to share information among all current users of an application; it can be used to create application-level variables that are available to all users of an application at any given time. Because application-level variables are accessible simultaneously by an unknown—and potentially unlimited—number of users, the **Application** object has two methods, **Lock** and **Unlock,** for ensuring that only one instance of an ASP file can access any given **Application** object variable at a time, as seen here:

```
<%
Application.Lock
Application.("CurrentUserCount") = Application.("CurrentUserCount")+ 1
Application.Unlock
%>
```

If the code was executed without the **Lock** method being performed, then two different users accessing the ASP file at the same time would result in the exact value being read from the **Application.(CurrentUserCount)** variable. When the variable is incremented in the next line of code, the exact same result will simply be written to the **Application** object variable, resulting in the loss of result from one or more instances of the code being executed. If the **Unlock** method was removed from the previous example, IIS would unlock the variable automatically when either the script concludes or times out. Although the **Unlock** method will be fired implicitly when the ASP script concludes execution or times out, it is important to explicitly call the **Unlock** method to allow other clients to access the **Application** object variables, rather than wait for the ASP script to conclude. This increases ASP-based application scalability and ASP script execution performance.

Because the **Application** object is implemented as a collection of elements (see the **Contents** collection mentioned shortly), elements within an array stored within an **Application** object variable cannot be accessed directly. Arrays should be stored locally in a page-level variable. After the necessary array member modification has been completed, the array can be restored in the **Application** object variable.

## *Application* Object Events

The **Application** object has two events that are available to the application for initializing **Application** object variables for use by any ASP file in the application: **Application_OnStart** and **Application_OnEnd**. These files are found in the GLOBAL.ASA file that serves as the root of the ASP-based application.

The **Application_OnStart** event fires the first time anyone accesses a page in the application, but prior to the session for that first client actually being established. For this reason, only the **Application** object and the **Server** object, seen later, are available for reference within the **Application_OnStart** event. Any attempt to access any of the other built-in objects at this time results in an ASP script execution error.

The **Application_OnEnd** event is fired after the application ends. This occurs most commonly when the GLOBAL.ASA file is modified and saved. This forces IIS to queue any additional requests for user sessions and then fire the **Application_OnEnd** event after the last client session has been ended. After the GLOBAL.ASA file is saved, normal processing continues, beginning with the **Application_OnStart** event firing.

## *Application* Object Collections

The **Application** object provides two collections for enumerating all of the items that have been added to the application through script: **Contents** and **StaticObjects**. The **Contents** collection contains all items or objects that have been established or declared as an application-level variable through script commands, except through use of the **<OBJECT>** tag. The **Contents** collection is considered the default collection for the **Application** object, therefore the following commands result in the same variable assignments:

```
<%
    Dim intClientNum
    Dim intClientNum2
    intClientNum = Application.("CurrentUserCount")
    intClientNum2 = Application.Contents("CurrentUserCount")
%>
```

You can see the two most common script commands used to add elements to an application at the application level in the following code. It is not necessary to declare the name of an **Application** object variable prior to setting a value to it in script. Note that the second line uses the **CreateObject** method of the **Server** object, which will be detailed later in the chapter:

```
<SCRIPT LANGUAGE=VBSCRIPT RUNAT=SERVER>
    Application.("UserCount") = Application.("UserCount") + 1
    Set Application("CustomerValidator") = _
                        Server.CreateObject("MLT.Customer")
</SCRIPT>
```

The **StaticObjects** collection includes all application-level instantiated objects except ASP built-in objects. Objects instantiated within an ASP file by use of the <**OBJECT**> tag are included as a part of the **StaticObjects** collection when the **Scope** attribute is set to **Application**. Create objects at the application level carefully, as resources can be significantly affected by the threading model of the objects. Additionally, apartment-threaded objects declared at the application level must be instantiated with the <**OBJECT**> tag.

# Session Object

The **Session** object is used to store information for a given user session; it performs almost identically to the **Application** object. A **Session** object is created the first time a client requests an ASP file from an application, assuming the client is not already engaged in an existing session. As the client moves from page to page, the values assigned to **Session** object variables continue to be accessible in script. The values stored with **Session** variables are unique to the particular user session and are not available between sessions. When either the established session timeout value is exceeded without an additional ASP page request, the user closes the browser engaged in the session, or the user navigates away from the application, the user session is abandoned and the **Session** object is destroyed. When the **Session** object is removed from memory, all **Session** variables are cleared.

## *Session Object Methods*

The **Session** object exposes only one method for use in script. The **Abandon** method is used to force the **Session** object to be destroyed, which effectively releases all object resources, including those used to maintain **Session** object variables. This method mimics a user quitting an application or an application timing out. Use of the **Abandon** method performs a queued delete request, allowing any scripts on the same page to continue to process and access any **Session** object variables.

## *Session* Object Events

The **Session** object provides two events, identical in nature to the two events provided by the **Application** object. The **Session_OnStart** event is fired the first time any given client requests a page from an application and is executed prior to the initial page request being fulfilled. All of the ASP built-in objects are available for reference within the **Session_OnStart** event. If the user session being established is the first after the application starts, the **Session_OnStart** event fires after the **Application_OnStart**. **Session_OnStart** is often used to set application-wide variables, similar to global variables, at the session level, as shown here:

```
<SCRIPT RUNAT=Server Language=VBSCRIPT>
Sub Session_OnStart
     Session("MagicWord") = "Goofy"
     Session("TheKing") = "Elvis"
End Sub
</SCRIPT>
```

The **Session_OnEnd** event fires whenever a user session either times out or is abandoned. During this event, only the **Application, Server,** and **Session** built-in objects are available for referencing.

## *Session* Object Collections

The **Session** object provides two collections for accessing, iterating through, or enumerating available **Session**-level items. These collections, the **Contents** and **StaticObjects** collections, perform identical functions as the collections of the same names exposed by the **Application** object. Similar to the **StaticObjects** collection exposed by the **Application** object, the **Session.StaticObjects** collection contains all objects instantiated at the session level by use of the <OBJECT> tag, with the **Scope** attribute set to **Session**.

## *Session* Object Properties

The **Session** object, although similar in functionality to the **Application** object, differs in a few ways. One primary difference lies in properties that the **Application** object does not expose. The **Session** object exposes four properties: **CodePage, LCID, SessionID,** and **Timeout**. The **CodePage** property is used to change the codepage, or character set, that is used to display dynamic data. The **LCID** property is used to set the location identifier used to display dynamic data. The **SessionID** property returns the unique session identifier generated by the server when the user session is established. Easily the most useful property is the **Timeout** property. As seen in the following code, you can set the **Timeout** property anywhere within ASP script to reset the maximum amount of time, in minutes, that a session will remain active without a subsequent page request. When this time has elapsed since the last ASP file request, the user session will be abandoned and the **Session** object is destroyed automatically. The default value for this property is 20 minutes:

```
<SCRIPT LANGUAGE=VBSCRIPT RUNAT=Server>
    Session.Timeout = 10 'Setting Session Timeout to 10 minutes
</SCRIPT>
```

# Server Object

The **Server** object provides server-specific information and access to methods that provide utility functions. The **Server** object reveals only one property and four methods. Although the **Server** object provides a very limited set of functionalities, the exposed methods provide some very powerful features that could be considered indispensable in creating Web-based applications.

## Server Object Properties

The only property exposed by the **Server** object is **ScriptTimeout**. It is used to set the maximum amount of time, in seconds, that an ASP script is allowed to run without concluding, before an error is returned to the client. For this property value, a script is considered to be all ASP code within a given requested ASP file. When setting this property, any currently running server component will be unaffected by the new setting. The default value for this behavior is 90 seconds.

## Server Object Methods

The **Server** object provides four highly functional methods for either obtaining server information, instantiating server components, or converting character information based on valid HTML or URL encoding rules. These methods are **HTMLEncode**, **URLEncode**, **MapPath**, and **CreateObject**.

The **HTMLEncode** method is used to apply HTML encoding rules to a given string to ensure that the character string does not contain ASCII characters that might be mistaken for portions of HTML tags or code. Any character that might be mistaken for portions of HTML tag code are converted to the equivalent character code syntax to ensure that the client browser rendering engine does not mistake the character string for HTML code. For example, the greater than and less than operators are used to begin and end HTML tags, so in HTML code these characters would normally be mistaken for HTML tag declarations. The **HTMLEncode** method can be used, as seen in Listing 5.1, to convert a character string involving these characters into acceptable character code syntax equivalents.

## Listing 5.1 The **HTMLEncode** method averts confusion.

```
<%
  If blnShowHTML Then %>
     <%=Server.HTMLEncode("This is going to be <I>big!</I>")%>
<%
  Else%>
     <%="This is going to be <I>big!</I>")%>
<%
  End If%>
```

According to the code in Listing 5.1, if the variable **blnShowHTML** evaluates to **TRUE**, then the HTML output looks like

```
This is going to be &lt;I&gt;big!&lt;/I&gt;
```

which will be rendered by the client browser as:

```
This is going to be <I>big!</I>
```

If the variable **blnShowHTML** evaluates to **FALSE**, then the HTML output will look like

```
This is going to be <I>big!</I>
```

which will be rendered by the client browser as:

```
This is going to be big!
```

The **URLEncode** method is used to apply URL encoding rules to a given string. This method helps ensure that the provided string does not contain ASCII characters that would be invalid when used as a portion of a URL string. Any characters that might invalidate a URL when appended to it are converted to acceptable control codes. For example, valid URLs are often passed between pages by appending them as variables to the URL. This would cause the URL to be syntactically incorrect without any intervention. By using the **URLEncode** method of the **Server** object, the appended URL can be converted as necessary, as shown here:

```
<%
  Response.Redirect ("http://www.thefastlane.com?OrigUrl=" + _
                     Server.URLEncode("http://www.krell.com"))
%>
```

The resulting client-side output from the script looks like the following:

```
http://www.thefastlane.com?OrigUrl=http%3A%2F%2Fwww%2Ekrell%2Ecom
```

The **MapPath** method is used to provide the physical path on the Web server local drive that corresponds to the relative or full virtual path provided. The physical path does not necessarily exist on the server, but is primarily a concatenated result of combining a partial physical path with the provided virtual path. The **MapPath** follows slightly different rules in returning physical paths, depending on whether the path provided begins with a slash. If the path begins with a forward (/) or a backward (\) slash, the **MapPath** returns a physical path that includes the physical installation path of Internet Information Server concatenated with the virtual path. In other words, the provided path is treated as if it represents the entire or full virtual path from the server installation directory. If the exact same path is provided, sans slash, then the path is treated as a relative virtual path from the actual location of the script file calling the **MapPath** method. One exception to the general behavior of the **MapPath** method is when the provided path consists of only a slash. Instead of returning the installation directory, the actual home directory for the Web server is returned:

```
<%=Server.MapPath("/images/hello.gif")%>
<%=Server.MapPath("images/hello.gif")%>
<%=Server.MapPath("/")%>
```

If this code is executed from a script file in the local physical path c:\inetpub\ wwwroot\demo, then the output of the code will look like the following:

```
C:\inetpub\images\hello.gif
C:\inetpub\wwwroot\demo\images\hello.gif
C:\inetpub\wwwroot
```

The **CreateObject** method of the **Server** object is probably the most powerful of all of the available object methods. With this method, instances of server components can be created, opening the door of Web server programming to an unlimited variety of tasks. When combined with ActiveX or COM DLL Visual Basic projects that make COM objects available as server components, you can achieve significant functionality enhancements. You can instantiate objects that are installed onto the Web server by passing the **CreateObject** method the ProgID of the object as registered in the system Registry. Objects created by the **CreateObject** method have page scope. To create objects that have either session or application scope, the objects must first be created, and then assigned to either a **Session** or **Application** object variable. If a COM component with the ProgID of **WebApp.Customer** is installed on the server, an instance of the component can be instantiated on the server and given session with the following code:

```
<%
    Set Session("Customer") = Server.CreateObject("WebApp.Customer")
%>
```

# Request Object

The **Request** object is used allow the retrieval of information passed by the client to the Web server by way of the HTTP request headers. It is the primary built-in object used to retrieve and pass information from the client to the server. You use the **Request** object primarily by referencing one of its five different collections: **Cookies, ServerVariables, ClientCertificate, Form,** and **QueryString**. Accessing a member of one of the collections requires using a variable name that identifies the collection member. You can access collection members without actually specifying the collection. The Web server will attempt to locate the member in each collection in the following order:

1. **Cookies**

2. **ServerVariables**

3. **ClientCertificate**

4. **Form**

5. **QueryString**

If multiple members exist in different collections but have the same name, the first member found will be returned.

## *Request* Object Collections

The **Cookies** collection allows the values of cookies passed in an HTTP request to be accessed or set. Members of the **Cookies** collection can either be single values or arrays whose members are identified by a key value. Members of the **Cookies** collection that exist as an array are known as *cookie dictionaries*. To determine whether or not a cookie is actually a cookie dictionary, the **Cookies** collection has one property, **HasKeys**, which is used to determine the existence of key values. The syntax used for accessing the **Cookies** collection of the **Request** object is as follows:

```
Request.Cookies(cookie)[(key)]
```

Therefore, you can access a series of cookies that store user information by using code similar to this:

```
<%
    strUserName = Request.Cookies("UserName")
    strAccessLevel = Request.Cookies("UserAccessLevel")
    strTitle = Request.Cookies("UserTitle")
%>
```

The **ServerVariables** collection includes a number of established members whose values represent different pieces of server information or environment variables. You can use these variables to retrieve a wide range of values that represent server, HTTP, and client information. The syntax for using the **ServerVariables** collection is **Request.ServerVariables**(*server environment variable*). Some of the more useful variables are listed in Table 5.1.

**ServerVariables** collection members can be extremely useful. For example, as shown in the following code, you can use **SERVER_NAME** to dynamically create an anchor tag **HREF** attribute that inserts the correct server name into an anchor tag. This is extremely useful for creating ASP scripts that use non-relative URLs without requiring recoding when moved into production on an intranet.

```
The following is a <B><A HREF =
    "http://<%=Request.ServerVariables("SERVER_NAME")%>/notes.asp>
    link to My Notes</A></B>
```

| Table 5.1 | Environment variables available through the ServerVariables collection. |
|-----------|------------------------------------------------------------------------|
| **Variable** | **Description** |
| ALL_HTTP | All the HTTP headers sent by the client to the server |
| AUTH_TYPE | The user authentication method used by the server to authenticate clients when accessing a protected ASP file |
| HTTPS | Returns **ON** if the HTTP request came through a secure channel (SSL) |
| LOGON_USER | The NT user account the user is logged in to |
| QUERY_STRING | URL query string information appearing after the "?" in the HTTP request |
| REMOTE_ADDR | IP address of the remote system making the HTTP request |
| REMOTE_HOST | Host name, if available, of the remote system making the HTTP request |
| SERVER_NAME | Host name, DNS alias, or IP address of the Web server |
| URL | Base portion of the URL requested |

The **ClientCertificate** collection is used in connection with a server that is configured to request client digital certificates. When IIS is configured as a secure server using SSL, the Web server pages are accessed by using HTTPS as the listed protocol, instead of the typical HTTP. This format for an HTTP request informs the server that the client is requesting a secure session. If IIS also requests that the client sends certification of its identity, then the client replies with a client certificate consisting of standard fields, as specified in the X.509 digital certificate standard. When the client sends the requested certification information, the information is made available to ASP script by way of the members of the **ClientCertificate** collection. For Web servers that are not configured to request client certificates, this collection returns **EMPTY**. Key values for some of the more common collection members are:

➤ **Issuer**

➤ **SerialNumber**

➤ **ValidFrom**

➤ **ValidUntil**

➤ **Subject**

The **Form** collection is used to retrieve form element values posted to the HTTP request body. The form element values represent members of a standard HTML form that have been posted to the HTTP request body by using the **POST** method. This is accomplished by setting the **METHOD** attribute of the <FORM> tag to **POST**. For example, consider the code in Listing 5.2.

## Listing 5.2    A typical HTML form.

```
<FORM action=Process.asp method=POST>
    <P>Please provide the following information:
    <P>Name: <INPUT type=TEXT name=txtName>
    <P>Favorite football team:
    <SELECT name=selTeam>
        <OPTION>Denver Broncos
        <OPTION>K-State Wildcats
        <OPTION>Temple City Over-40 Men's football league
        <OPTION>Any NFL team besides the Oakland Raiders
    </SELECT>
    <P><INPUT type=Submit>
</FORM>
```

In order to retrieve the values for the **txtName** and **selTeam** elements in Listing 5.2 from ASP script, you could use the **Forms** collection. The values of the two input elements would be assigned to members of the **Forms** collection with the same names, namely **txtName** and **selTeam**:

```
Welcome <%=Request.Form("txtName")%>,
you are wise in picking (the)
<%=Request.Form("selTeam")%>
as your favorite team!!!
```

The **QueryString** collection is used to retrieve values of variables from the HTTP query string. The same information that is available when using **Request.ServerVariables** (**QUERY_STRING**) is also available when using the **QueryString** collection without specifying a specific member or variable. The **QueryString** collection membership is obtained by parsing the query string list into specific variables. The HTTP query string is formed by appending the URL information to the HTTP request after the question mark (?). This can be accomplished by either hard-coding the values into an anchor **HREF** attribute value, by using the **GET** method of form submittal, or by a user hand-typing a URL with the proper syntax into the address bar of the browser. Variables in an HTTP query string are separated by using the ampersand (&), and the values are assigned by using the equal sign (=) after the variable name. Repeating variables in a query string results in the assignment of multiple values to the variable. By using **Request.QueryString(*variable*).Count**, the number of values assigned to a given query string variable can be determined, and the individual members of a query string variable can be accessed by using the index value when requesting the **QueryString** collection member.

### *Request* Object Properties And Methods

The **Request** object exposes only one property, **TotalBytes**, which indicates the total number of bytes the client is transmitting through the HTTP request body. The **Request** object exposes one method, **BinaryRead**, which is used to read the raw data sent by the client when submitting a **POST** request.

## Response Object

The **Response** object is used to send information back to the client. This HTTP response information can control the resulting behavior of the browser by sending either HTML information or control information, which instructs the client browser to exhibit certain standard behavior.

### *Response* Object Collections

The **Response** object provides only one collection: The **Cookies** collection is identical to that exposed by the **Request** object. The **Cookies** collection exposed by the **Response** object provides a write-enabled access method for the collection of user cookies stored by the server on the client system, just as the **Request** object **Cookies** collection provides a read-only access to this same collection. The **Cookies** collection of the **Response** object is the mechanism provided by the Web server for adding cookies to the client system.

Individual members of the **Cookies** collection have a number of properties or attributes that can be set to alter the behavior of the cookie implementation. The available attributes are:

➤ **Domain** If set, only requests originating from this domain will utilize the cookie.

➤ **Expires** Indicates the date the cookie will expire. If not set, the cookie will last only for the duration of the current user session.

➤ **HasKeys** Indicates whether the cookie has keys, thus indicating if it is a cookie dictionary.

➤ **Path** If set, only requests to the provided path will utilize the cookie.

➤ **Secure** Indicates whether the cookie is secure or not.

## *Response Object Properties*

The **Response** object provides nine properties for use in tailoring the behavior or characteristics of the HTTP headers or client browser behavior concerning the current ASP file: **Buffer, CacheControl, Charset, ContentType, Expires, ExpiresAbsolute, IsClientConnected, PICS,** and **Status.**

The **Buffer** property is used to signify whether the current page output being generated by ASP script is buffered in memory. When page output is buffered, all server scripts on the current page are allowed to finish processing before any HTTP responses are sent to the client. Also, the **Flush** or **End** methods (detailed shortly) will cause an HTTP response to occur prior to the server scripts finishing processing. If output has already been sent to the client, attempts to alter the **Response** object's **Buffer** property will fail. When set to **TRUE,** the server will honor HTTP Keep-Alive requests.

 Take care in setting this property to **TRUE,** as long scripts may cause a noticeable delay.

The **CacheControl** property is used to configure whether proxy servers will be allowed to cache the server script output. The default value is **Private,** with the opposing valid value for this property being **Public.**

The **Charset** property is used to specify whether the name of the page's character set is appended to the end of the content-type header. A default content-type header would appear as "content-type:text/html." Then the **Response.Charset** property is set to a text string equal to the applicable character set for the current page; this string is appended to the end of the content-type header. All strings are accepted for the character set parameter, despite validity. Multiple instances of setting the **Charset** property will result in the last instance taking precedence.

The **ContentType** property is used to set the content-type header for the current page. The default setting is "text/html." Additional typical content-type values include "image/GIF," "image/JPEG," and "application/x-cdf." You can find the full, up-to-date list of content-type string identifiers by referring to the current HTTP specifications.

The **Expires** property is used to identify the length of time a page will be allowed to be reviewed from the client's local cache; in other words, it determines how long a given page can live in the cache on a client browser. This allows a user to return to a page within a given time frame and benefit from the performance boost of loading the page locally instead of reissuing a new HTTP request. This property is assigned a numerical value that represents the time in minutes before the page expires. If this property is set twice within a script, the shortest value will be used for the page.

 In order to force a cached page to expire immediately after downloading by the client, set the **Expires** property to a value of **zero**.

The **ExpiresAbsolute** property is used in a similar fashion to **Expires**, except that an absolute date and/or time is provided. The value used must conform to the standard RFC-1123 date format, including surrounding the date/time value with the pound sign (#). If the **ExpiresAbsolute** property is provided with a date only, but no specific time, then the page will expire at midnight on the date provided. If a time, but no date, is provided, then the page will expire at the specified time on the date the page is accessed. When the **ExpiresAbsolute** property is set more than once in a page, the earliest time will be used. For example, to ensure that a page will expire at exactly one second before the turn of the millennium, you can use the following code:

```
<%
    Response.ExpiresAbsolute=#December 31,1999 23:59:59#
%>
```

The **IsClientConnected** property indicates whether the client requesting the page is still connected to the server. It is possible that an extended amount of time may have elapsed between the client request and the server response. Checking the value of the **IsClientConnected** property can help in scripting for this scenario.

The **PICS** property is used to add a value, valid or not, to the pics-label field of the HTTP response header. If used multiple times, the last assignment is used.

The **Status** property can be used to set the server status line message returned by the server in response to a client HTTP request. The acceptable values are defined as a part of the HTTP specification. Examples of valid status lines include "401 Unauthorized" and "200 OK."

## *Response* Object Methods

The **Response** object provides eight methods for use within script: **AddHeader**, **AppendToLog**, **BinaryWrite**, **Clear**, **End**, **Flush**, **Redirect**, and **Write**. These methods can be used to adjust, impact, or configure various aspects of the HTML output or HTTP response header information.

The **AddHeader** method is used to create and add a brand-new custom HTTP header to the response. This method accepts two parameters: *name* and *value*. The *name* signifies the name of the new header to send. The *value* parameter provides the value to assign to the new header. This method cannot be used to replace existing headers, nor can the custom headers be removed once added.

The **AppendToLog** method allows additional information to be appended to the end of the Web server log entry for this specific HTTP request. The method can be used multiple times in a script, with the specified strings being appended to the existing entry.

 Using **AppendToLog** is restricted because information is stored in the IIS fields in comma-delimited format. Therefore, commas cannot be used in the designated append string.

The **BinaryWrite** method allows an array of bytes to be written to the current HTTP output without incurring any character conversions. This method can be used to send binary or non-string information to custom applications through the HTTP response headers.

The **Clear**, **End**, **Flush**, and **Write** methods often are used together in some capacity to affect the HTML output being directed to the client. The **Clear** method causes any currently buffered HTML output to be cleared from the memory buffer. The **Clear** method only applies to the response body, not the response headers, and requires that the **Response.Buffer** property be previously set to **TRUE**.

The **Flush** method sends the buffered HTML output immediately to the client. It requires that **Response.Buffer** be set to **TRUE**.

The **End** method instructs the server script to immediately cease processing. The current result is sent to the client, whereas the remaining script is not processed. When calling the **End** method, setting **Response.Buffer** to **TRUE** will result in the **Flush** method being implicitly called. To avoid this, the **Clear** method should be called prior to calling the **End** method.

The **Write** method is used to add a given string to the HTTP output. Any character string, excluding the character combination "%>", can be used as the parameter for the **Write** method.

The **Redirect** method is used to send a server status message of "302 Object moved" to the client, causing the client to redirect and reconnect to the URL attached to the message header. Response body content set within the page is ignored when the **Redirect** method is called. The **Redirect** takes one parameter, *URL*, which represents the URL the client should attempt to connect to.

# ObjectContext Object

The **ObjectContext** object is used to allow server-side ASP scripts to participate in transactions, as administered and managed by Microsoft Transaction Server. When working with Visual Basic projects that reference the Microsoft Transaction Server Type Library, the **ObjectContext** object normally exposes eight methods. However, when made available through the ASP built-in **ObjectContext** object, only two methods, **SetAbort** and **SetComplete**, are exposed. By exposing these two methods, as a minimum requirement, ASP scripts participating in an MTS managed transaction can provide the necessary informational feedback. This notification mechanism allows the script to inform other transaction components called within the script as to whether the script code has initiated a transaction abort scenario. The **ObjectContext** object also exposes two event handlers, **OnTransactionCommit** and **OnTransactionAbort**, to handle the two possible transactional outcomes.

For an ASP script to participate in an MTS managed transaction, the script directive **@TRANSACTION** must appear as the first element of server script at the top of the ASP file. When an ASP file begins with **@TRANSACTION=** *value*, depending on the value assigned, MTS creates a transaction within the MTS environment to coordinate the events processing by the ASP script. The possible values for the **@TRANSACTION** directive are **Required, Requires_New, Supported,** and **Not_Supported.** Only the first two values listed will result in a script-initiated MTS transaction. Once a new transaction has been established, a reference to the specific MTS **ObjectContext** instance is then made available to the ASP script through the built-in **ObjectContext** object.

## *ObjectContext Object Methods*

The **SetAbort** method is used to indicate that based on current environment settings or script results, the transaction initiated by the ASP script should not be completed and any resources updated by the script should be reversed. This is used primarily to ensure that additional COM components created and used within the ASP script will be properly notified of the transaction abort declaration. This guarantees that if these components are designed to participate in transactions, any currently executing method will be terminated and previous resource modifications performed by component methods will be reversed.

The **SetComplete** method is used to declare that the ASP script, acting in the context of transactional component, has determined the initiated transaction is safe to commit. The transaction is not completely committed by MTS until all components agree to the commit event. If the ASP script creates and calls methods of additional MTS-aware components, the transaction will only commit after any currently executing methods of the components have finished executing and have run the **SetComplete** method. Calling the **SetComplete** method explicitly is not required by the ASP script, as the script will invoke **SetComplete** implicitly upon script completion, given that **SetAbort** was not explicitly called. Calling **SetComplete** also revokes any previously issued **SetAbort** method invocation.

## *ObjectContext Object Events*

The **ObjectContext** object exposes two event handlers, **OnTransactionCommit** and **OnTransactionAbort**, to provide ASP script processing of any transaction termination or completion processing within the transaction-originating ASP script. When an ASP script initiates an MTS transaction (referred to as *being transacted*) the exposure of the MTS transaction's **ObjectContext** instance by the built-in **ObjectContext** informs MTS to provide notification of transaction status events for both abort and commit declarations to the **OnTransactionAbort** and **OnTransactionCommit** events of the ASP built-in **ObjectContext** object. Neither event requires that a subroutine be coded by the ASP script to handle the event, but will run if present.

# Using WebClass With IIS Applications

With Visual Basic 6, a brand-new form of Visual Basic project called an *IIS application* is now available. This is essentially an ActiveX DLL project with the standard class module removed and replaced with an instance of the WebClass ActiveX Designer. The **WebClass** object is a special type of server-side COM component that is used to intercept HTTP requests and respond accordingly. In essence, **WebClass** is used to provide custom HTTP request processing. The **WebClass** object acts as the base for a Web server-based application; it also is physically implemented as a special type of object compiled into an ActiveX DLL that runs on the Web server. The **WebClass** object, as seen in Figure 5.1, provides six default events, five of which comprise the standard life cycle of the **WebClass** object.

Each **WebClass** object contained within an IIS application has a corresponding ASP file that is used to load an instance of the corresponding **WebClass**. The ASP file acts as the starting gateway for accessing the **WebClass** and is automatically generated when the IIS application is compiled; it serves two purposes. First, the ASP file checks for an existing instance of the **WebClass-Runtime.WebClassManager** object stored within an **Application** object variable. If the object does not exist, the ASP file creates an instance of the object and assigns it to an **Application** object variable. This object, provided by the MSWCRUN.DLL runtime file, is used to provide management services

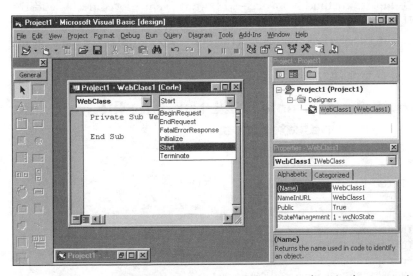

**Figure 5.1**  The **WebClass** ActiveX Designer code window provides six default events.

for the custom **WebClass** objects contained within the IIS application project ActiveX DLL. Once the **WebClassManager** object creation is confirmed, then either the **ProcessRetainInstanceWebClass** or the **ProcessNoStateWebClass** method is invoked, based on the value assigned to the **StateManagement** property of the **WebClass** object. The ProgId of the **WebClass** object is passed as a parameter of the method used, therefore identifying the specific **WebClass** object to instantiate.

**WebClass** still uses HTML as its user interface, but with a different implementation mechanism than ASP-based applications. ASP-based applications are inherently designed for script developers who combine HTML and script in the same ASCII text files. A **WebClass**, as exposed through Visual Basic IIS applications, separates the application logic entirely from the HTML. Therefore, the use of **WebClass** is tailored for Visual Basic developers who may also create the HTML template files that are contained within the **WebClass** as Webitems. This frees the Visual Basic application developer to focus on the important programming tasks at hand without having to become an expert at HTML. The development of the HTML templates can be left to the Web developer who specializes in the HTML coding aspect of creating Web-based applications.

The HTML template files, representing the primary form of Webitem that can be contained within a **WebClass**, serve as the user interface by containing special indicator tags that represent areas of information within an HTML template file that are marked for text replacement processing. The **WriteTemplate** method is invoked within an event procedure to send the HTML template file to the client browser. If the template file contains indicator tags, the **ProcessTag** event is also fired for each indicator tag found as the HTML template is parsed. You can see a sample HTML template file, including indicator tags, in Listing 5.3.

## Listing 5.3    A sample HTML template file, including indicator tags.

```
<HTML>
<HEAD>
     <TITLE>This is a test Template</TITLE>
</HEAD>
<BODY>
<P>  Thank you, <WC@Fname>ACME Member<WC@Fname>,
     for choosing to buy from ACME Online!
<P>  Your purchase will be shipped on
     <WC@ShipDate>unknown</WC@ShipDate>.
</BODY>
<HTML>
```

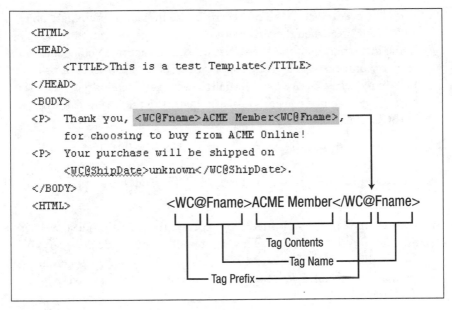

**Figure 5.2**  Indicator tag components.

As seen in Figure 5.2, the indicator tags enclose tag content. The areas within an HTML template that are to be processed for content replacement consist of three parts. The tag prefix is determined by the value assigned to the **TagPrefix** property of the HTML template Webitem. The default is **WC@**, and any modification to this property should maintain a letter as the first character. The inclusion of a unique character, such as "@," is recommended to improve or optimize the parsing algorithm used within the **WriteTemplate** method to determine when the **ProcessTag** event should be fired.

As the HTML template is parsed, the **ProcessTag** event will fire when an instance or an indicator tag prefix is located. The **ProcessTag** event is passed the indicator tag name and the tag contents as string parameters. A Visual Basic **Select** statement can be used on the **TagName** parameter to determine which indicator tag name fired that instance of the **ProcessTag** event. Within the **Select** statement, the value of the **TagContents** parameter can be modified to take on the desired value. This will initiate a text replacement of the tag contents of the HTML template file with the desired new contents. Once all the indicator tags are replaced, the final rendition of the HTML file is sent to the client.

# Events Of The WebClass Life Cycle

The **WebClass** object has a series of events that define its lifetime, much in the same way as the **Form** object in a standard Visual Basic EXE application. The key events within the life of a **WebClass** object are listed here:

➤ **Initialize event** This is the first event in the life of the **WebClass** object. This event fires when the **WebClass** ASP file is requested, thus resulting in the instantiation of the **WebClass** object. If the **StateManagement** property of the **WebClass** object is set to **wcNoState**, then each time an HTTP request is received, the **Initialize** event is refired for the **WebClass** object. This event is considered the first event in the life cycle of the **WebClass** object.

➤ **BeginRequest event** This event begins the processing of an HTTP request. It is fired each time a request is received from the browser. Any processing required by each and every HTTP request should be placed within this event.

➤ **Start event** This event is fired the first time the **BeginRequest** event is fired for a **WebClass** object. This event contains the code necessary to initiate the user interface of the IIS application. This event generally contains the necessary code to identify the first Webitem to be sent to the browser.

➤ **WebClass_Start event** This event is used to identify which Webitem should be the first to be returned to the client browser. Setting the **NextItem** property of the **WebClass** object to a desired Webitem within the **Start** event causes that Webitem to be the first element sent to the client when requesting that **WebClass**.

➤ **EndRequest event** This event is fired when the HTTP request processing has been concluded and a response has been generated and sent to the client. This event will not fire until all events and templates are completely processed and concluded.

➤ **Terminate event** This event is used to notify the Microsoft **WebClass** runtime DLL (MSWCRUN.DLL) to destroy the instance of the **WebClass** in memory. If the **StateManagement** property is set to **wcNoState**, then the **Terminate** event is fired after each response is sent to the client. If the **StateManagement** property is set to **wcRetainInstance**, the **Terminate** event is not fired and the **ReleaseInstance** method must be called to fire the **Terminate** event.

➤ **Start event** This event is normally used to identify which Webitem is to be the first element sent back to the client, in response to requesting the **WebClass** object for the first time, typically when starting the application. This can be established by setting the **NextItem** property of the **WebClass** object, as seen here:

```
Private Sub WebClass_Start()
    Set NextItem = DemoWebItem
End Sub
```

## Storing State And Passing Information With WebClass

Storing information while working with the **WebClass** object is a relatively simple process. Because the ASP object model is available to the **WebClass** object, both the **Session** and **Application** objects can be used to store information. Also, depending on the value set for the **StateManagement** property, information can be stored in variables. The primary methods of storing state or passing information can be summarized as:

➤ If the **StateManagement** property is set to **wcRetainInstance**, then the **Terminate** event is not fired. This allows the **WebClass** instance to remain in memory; therefore any global variables created for the **WebClass** object will continue to be accessible between method invocations (HTTP requests).

➤ Because each **WebClass** object is loaded by navigation to a corresponding ASP file, a user session is established for the client. While this user session exists, any **Session** object or **Application** object variables generated from within the **WebClass** event code will continue to be available to future instantiations of the **WebClass** object.

➤ If the type of information being stored is complex in nature, or would benefit from persistent storage, then Visual Basic objects can be created for storing the data. If the data needs to be stored in a database, then setting the properties of server COM components that save the data to a database can be used. The object must be assigned to a **Session** object or an **Application** object variable, in order to be accessible from multiple instantiations of the **WebClass** object.

## Creating Pages Using The DHTML Page Designer

Along with the IIS application projects, Visual Basic 6 now provides us with another project type dedicated to creating Web-based applications. The *DHTML application project* provides the ability to offload the application logic to a client-side DLL file while still utilizing HTML pages as the user interface. Unlike IIS applications that offload the processing logic for HTTP requests and ASP-like dynamic page generation to a server-side COM DLL, DHTML applications offload the client-side dynamic processing of DHTML scripting logic to a DLL loaded by the HTML pages involved in the application user interface. By shifting the client-side application or user-interface logic to a client-side DLL, performance improvements, as well as proprietary code protection, can be easily established.

When creating a DHTML application within Visual Basic, an ActiveX Designer is utilized to allow dynamic design, modification, and visually enhanced page creation procedures. This DHTML Page Designer, unlike the Webclass ActiveX Designer used by IIS applications, provides a visual design palette for laying out a DHTML page for an application. We refer to the page as a *DHTML page*, because without the extensive use of scripting supported by the Document Object Model, the concept of a client-side DLL housing application logic would be a moot point. In Figure 5.3, an example of a default DHTML Page Designer is shown.

Although it is possible to make extensive changes to a DHTML page from within the DHTML Page Designer, many times the developer will need to load an existing page as a link for the designer. For simpler interfaces, the pages should be designed within Visual Basic, but for more complex pages, or for times when greater control is desired, linking a DHTML Page Designer to an existing page is desirable. Let's assume a page exists with the code shown in Listing 5.4.

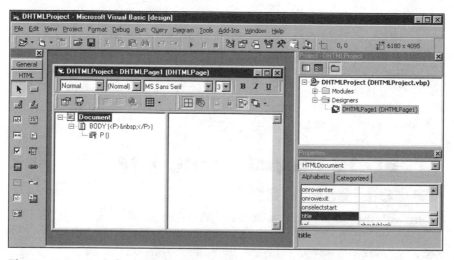

**Figure 5.3** A default DHTML Page Designer in the VB6 IDE.

## Listing 5.4    A sample HTML page.

```
<HTML>
<HEAD>
     <TITLE>Test Title</TITLE>
</HEAD>

<BODY>
This is a test page.
<INPUT TITLE="Click to earn a million dollars"
     TYPE=button VALUE="Hello world"><BR>
<IMG SRC="C:\WINDOWS\Desktop\VB6demo\kaleid.gif">
</BODY>
</HTML>
```

After starting Visual Basic with a new or existing DHTML application, your project should look a little like Figure 5.3. To import an existing HTML page for use as a template, add another instance of the DHTML Page Designer by right-clicking on the Visual Basic Project Explorer, choosing Add, and then DHTML Page. The screen shown in Figure 5.4 should appear.

After choosing Open and then browsing to the desired HTML page, your page might look like Figure 5.5, which uses the code provided in Listing 5.4.

Once the existing page created by your Web developer has been loaded into the DHTML Page Designer, you can now make changes to the elements within the page using the designer. You can dynamically change attributes, content, styles, and element positioning.

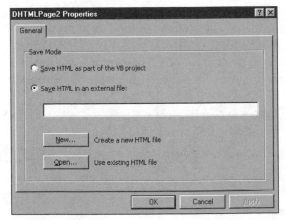

**Figure 5.4**    Assign the source of the DHTML Page Designer.

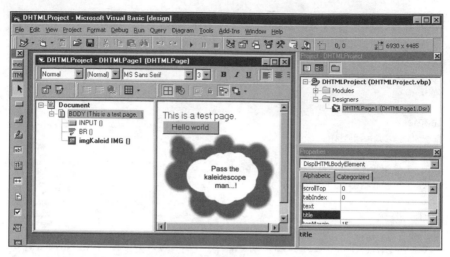

**Figure 5.5** A DHTML Page Designer loaded with an existing HTML page.

## Changing Element Attributes

After linking an HTML page to a DHTML Page Designer, the Page Designer will consist of two panes and assorted toolbars. The left-hand pane shows a hierarchical view of the elements within the HTML page. The right-hand pane provides a visual look at what the layout of the page will be when rendered within a Web browser. Notice in Figure 5.6 that choosing a tag element listed in the left-hand pane results in changes to the right-hand pane and to the elements listed in the Visual Basic Properties window. For example, when choosing the **INPUT** element shown in Figure 5.6, the right-hand pane emphasizes the same element visually just as if it were a constituent control selected from a **Form** object in a standard EXE application project. Also, the available elemental attributes are now listed in the standard Visual Basic IDE Properties window shown in the bottom right corner of Figure 5.6. We can see that for the **INPUT** element selected, some of the configurable attributes shown include **Id, accessKey, className,** and the **disabled** condition. Assigning values to elements within the HTML page via the DHTML Page Designer is as simple as any other type of Visual Basic project.

Changing attributes visually within the DHTML Page Designer is helpful, but it is limited to runtime. Remember that a DHTML application merely shifts the processing of page element events off to a client-side DLL, but the same HTML pages are still requested, rendered, and viewed just like a regular static set of HTML pages. If we assigned a value to the **Id** property of the **INPUT** element selected in Figure 5.6, we can now access the same element programmatically within the code window. By right-clicking on the Designer

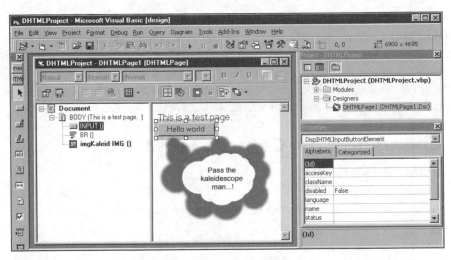

**Figure 5.6** Choosing a page element in the left-hand pane reveals configurable properties in the Properties window.

from within the Visual Basic Project Explorer, we can choose View Code. This loads a code editor just like any other standard **Form, UserControl,** or **UserDocument** object. All of the page elements that have been previously assigned a value to the **Id** property/attribute will show up in the object drop-down menu, as seen in Figure 5.7.

In Figure 5.7, notice that the default **BaseWindow, DHTMLPage,** and **Document** objects are listed. We also see the **Id** we assigned to the **INPUT** tag element,

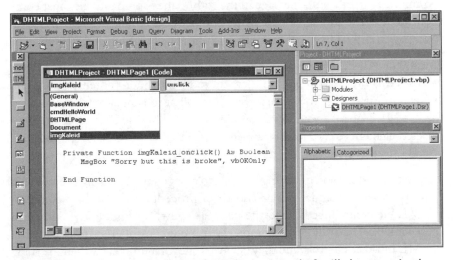

**Figure 5.7** All page elements with an assigned **Id** will show up in the object drop-down menu.

**cmdHelloWorld,** and a previously assigned **Id** of **imgKaleid** was assigned to the **IMG** element prior to linking to the DHTML Page Designer. If we choose, we can then proceed to assign Visual Basic code to the available events of the page elements, such as firing a standard Msgbox in response to the **onclick** event of the **imgKaleid** element. This is the Visual Basic code that will automatically fire, acting as event handlers for the elements as they receive user actions.

## Changing Page Content From The Page Designer

Changing content on a DHTML page is performed in one of four main ways in the DHTML Page Designer interface. These four methods include:

➤ Pasting elements from the Windows clipboard

➤ Typing text-based content directly

➤ Using the File or Element toolbar bands

➤ Dragging and dropping elements available on the HTML toolbox

When pasting elements into the page, the right-hand pane is used. Right-clicking on the visual layout pane (right-hand pane) reveals an enabled Paste option when the object within the Windows clipboard is suitable for pasting directly into the DHTML Page Designer. Adding content to the page in this manner is limited to text and images that have been previously copied directly from the page.

Typing text directly onto the page in the right pane is probably the most common method for adding content. Text comprises the bulk of the content on Web pages, and adding such content is as simple as clicking and typing.

The DHTML Page Designer provides four toolbars for designing pages. You can use two of these, the File and Element toolbars, to add content to the page. As seen in Figure 5.8, you can use the File toolbar to launch the default editor for HTML pages on your development system. The Element toolbar allows selected elements to be either wrapped in <DIV> or <SPAN> tags, or be converted into a hyperlink in the form of an HTML <A> tag.

The last major method of adding content to a page involves using the HTML toolbox to allow standard drag-and-drop procedures for adding common HTML elements directly onto the page, as shown in Figure 5.9. Although these look like the Windows common constituent controls, they're actually the HTML intrinsic controls, and they behave somewhat differently than the standard Windows control counterparts.

**Figure 5.8**    The DHTML Page Designer provides toolbars for common tasks.

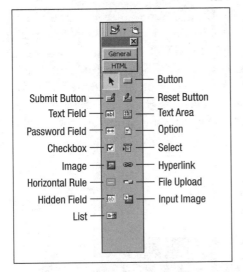

**Figure 5.9**    The Page Designer toolbox provides access to common HTML elements.

## Changing Element Styles

The DHTML Page Designer provides the Format toolbar for altering or setting various characteristics of an element's style. Shown in Figure 5.10, this toolbar provides several buttons for assigning format and style aspects, including HTML Block Element attributes such as Address, Heading 1-6, and Numbered List, to select elements. The second drop-down menu, CSS Styles, allows the assignment of existing custom styles to selected elements. The styles must have been previously defined within the page. The remainder of the drop-down menus or buttons allow for standard assignment of font properties, such as family, bold, italics, and generally positioning of appropriately selected elements.

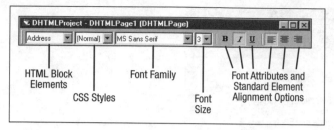

**Figure 5.10**   The Format toolbar provides quick assignment of style and formatting.

# Position Page Elements

Positioning elements within an HTML page is one of the benefits that DHTML has over standard HTML. Positioning elements exactly where the developer desires on a page requires using the **STYLE** attribute. Positioning elements isn't limited to the x and y planes. By using the **zindex** attribute available with styles, you can layer elements on top of each other when the DHTML page is rendered by the client browser. You can assign both of these forms of positioning from within the DHTML Page Designer by using the Design toolbar, as shown in Figure 5.11.

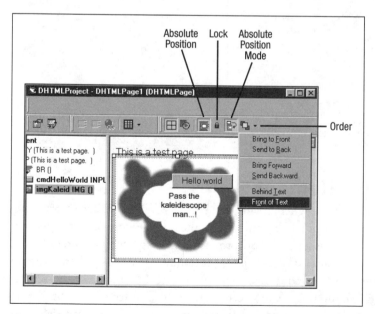

**Figure 5.11**   The Design toolbar provides element positioning functions.

As seen in the right-hand pane of the DHTML Page Designer, from within the visual layout of the DHTML page you can set elements to load and render whenever desired. Each element can be selected individually and the **position** property of the **STYLE** attribute can be toggled between relative and absolute by using the Absolute Position button on the Design toolbar. Buttons also exist for toggling the default positioning status of a new element as it is created or added to the page by using the Absolute Position Mode button. The Lock button is a design-time-only setting for ensuring that precisely positioned elements will stay where placed. Use of this button does not affect programmatic ability to position elements by changing their attributes. Finally, the Order button alters the **zindex** property of the **STYLE** attribute by changing this value relative to the other elements around it on the page. All of these buttons add the necessary standard DHTML attributes, properties, and values to implement the desired positioning modifications.

# Practice Questions

## Question 1

The Active Server Page built-in objects consist of six different COM objects. Which of the following are part of those six objects? [Check all that apply]

❑ a. **Request**

❑ b. **Response**

❑ c. **ContextObject**

❑ d. **Client**

❑ e. **Application**

The correct answers are a, b, and e. The **Request**, **Response**, and **Application** objects comprise three of the six ASP built-in objects. These objects are made available by the ASP.DLL file.

Answer c is not correct, although it is very close. One of the remaining objects is the **ObjectContext** object, not the **ContextObject** object. The **Server** object is one of the built-in objects, however the **Client** object does not exist, therefore answer d would be incorrect.

# Question 2

The **Application** object contains user-defined variables that can be assigned values to be accessible to all users of the application at a given time. Because of this, several methods of the **Application** object, such as **Lock** and **Unlock**, are also available to ensure consistency in the values. What would be the result of accessing an **Application** object variable without using the **Lock** method?

- ○ a.  Nothing. Application variables cannot be accessed without first using the **Lock** method. Attempting to do so would result in a **NULL** or **EMPTY** value being returned for the variable.

- ○ b.  An error would occur, because the **Application** variable must first be locked before attempting to access.

- ○ c.  The **Lock** method would perform implicitly. Explicit use of the **Lock** method Is like varlable declaratlon: It's not needed, but is recommended for better documentation.

- ○ d.  The access attempt would succeed, but any attempt to use a corresponding **Unlock** would result in an error.

- ○ e.  Nothing would happen initially, but simultaneous attempts to access the same **Application** variable by different clients might result in variable value modifications being lost.

The correct answer is e. Although no explicit error will be generated by the Web server of the ASP script, the possibility that at least one modification to an **Application** variable will be lost due to simultaneous reads is very real. Also, transacted ASP scripts that are aborted might result in incorrect values being read by other clients.

Because **Application** variables can indeed be accessed without using the **Lock** method, answer a would be incorrect. The variable will not return an inaccurate value. Similarly, an error would not initially occur, as in answer b, therefore answer b is also incorrect. The **Lock** method is never performed implicitly. Only explicit invocation of the **Lock** method will result in the desired safeguards, therefore answer c would be incorrect. Although the **Lock** method is not inherently required, merely suggested, a corresponding **Unlock** method would not generate an error if it failed to be preceded by explicit use of the **Lock** method. For this reason, answer d is incorrect.

## Question 3

> Which events are made available in the GLOBAL.ASA file for use in conjunction with the **Application** object? [Check all that apply]
>
> ❑ a. **Application_OnClose**
>
> ❑ b. **Application_OnStart**
>
> ❑ c. **Application_OnBegin**
>
> ❑ d. **Application_OnLoad**
>
> ❑ e. **Application_OnUnload**

The correct answer is b. The **Application** object provides two events for initializing variables and coding necessary settings each time the application is restarted. These events, the **Application_OnStart** and **Application_OnEnd** events, are found in the GLOBAL.ASA file. Any changes to this file result in the application restarting and the **OnStart** event firing.

The **Application** object does not have **OnClose** or **OnUnload** events. The event that fires when the application is shutting down is known as the **OnEnd** event, therefore answers a and e are incorrect. Because **Application_OnStart** represents the beginning of the application, answers c and d, **OnBegin** and **OnLoad**, are also incorrect.

## Question 4

> Which of the following pieces of code will result in a proper declaration of server-side ASP script? [Check all that apply]
>
> ❑ a. `<SCRIPT LANGUAGE=VBSCRIPT PROCESS=SERVER> </SCRIPT>`
>
> ❑ b. `<SCRIPT LANGUAGE=VBSCRIPT RUNAT=SERVER> </SCRIPT>`
>
> ❑ c. `<SCRIPT LANGUAGE=VBSCRIPT RUN=SERVER> </SCRIPT>`
>
> ❑ d. `<% LANGUAGE=VBSCRIPT RUNAT=SERVER></%>`
>
> ❑ e. `<%></%>`

The correct answer is b. The valid answers would include enclosing the code with `<%` and `%>` tags, or using `<SCRIPT LANGUAGE=`*script_type* `RUNAT=SERVER></SCRIPT>`.

Answer a is incorrect because the **RUNAT** attribute is missing. It should be present and set to **SERVER**. Answer c is also incorrect because the **RUNAT** attribute has been replaced with an invalid **RUN** attribute. Answer d is incorrect because it is a combination of valid ASP script delimiters that do not match the chosen value. Answer e is almost correct, except it uses normal tag syntax. When using the % sign, the correct syntax is <% *enter code here* %>.

## Question 5

The **Session** object is used to store information for a user session. User sessions have a limited life. Which of the following events will cause the **Session** variable values to be removed from memory and lost? [Check all that apply]

- ❏ a. The total time since the first ASP page requested has exceeded the **Session** timeout value.

- ❏ b. The client closes the browser engaged in the session.

- ❏ c. The **Abandon** method for the **Session** object is invoked.

- ❏ d. The **Session_OnEnd** event has been initiated.

- ❏ e. The GLOBAL.ASA file has been changed.

The correct answers are b, c, and e. When a client closes a browser that initiated the user session, that particular user session is terminated, resulting in the removal of the session variables from memory. Alternatively, the **Session** object exposes one method, the **Abandon** method, which can be used to force the **Session** to be terminated. Whenever the GLOBAL.ASA file is modified and saved, the application is restarted. This causes all sessions to terminate and all **Session** object instances are destroyed.

The **Session** timeout value, which defaults to 20 minutes, represents the total amount of maximum allowed time between HTTP requests. If another ASP page is requested, the time elapsed counter is reset. Answer a is incorrect because it refers to the total time elapsed since the first HTTP request, instead of the most recent page request. Within the **Session_OnEnd** event, the **Session** object is still accessible, therefore the fact that the event has been fired does not alone removed the session variables from memory. Therefore, answer d is incorrect.

## Question 6

---

Which of the following physical path locations would be returned by the Active Server Page script listed below?

```
<%=Server.MapPath("/images/hello.gif")%>
```

○ a.  c:\inetpub\wwwroot\images\hello.gif

○ b.  c:\inetpub\images\hello.gif

○ c.  file://c:\inetpub\images\hello.gif

○ d.  \inetpub\images\hello.gif

○ e.  wwwroot\mages\hello.gif

---

The correct answer is b. When using the **MapPath** method of the **Server** object, string values passed that begin with a slash, forward or backward, cause the string to be interpreted as a full virtual path. The output of the **MapPath** method will represent the installation directory of the Web server plus the partial path passed to the method. Hence, answer b would be the result of the **MapPath** method listed.

Answer a is incorrect because it is the result of appending the given string to the physical path of the installation directory for the Web root, not for the entire Web server, hence the addition of the wwwroot subdirectory. Answers c, d, and e are incorrect because they do not represent valid physical paths, so they would not be returned by the **MapPath** method. Answer c includes a protocol indicator that might be necessary for navigating, but is not part of a normal physical path. Answers d and e are missing the physical drive indicators.

## Question 7

---

Which of the following code segments represent proper syntax for indicator tags for use in an HTML template file and IIS applications? [Check all that apply]

❑ a.  <WC@ShipDate><WC@ShipDate>

❑ b.  <WC@ShipDate></WC@ShipDate>

❑ c.  <WC@>ShipDate</WC@>

❑ d.  <@WCShipDate></@WCShipDate>

❑ e.  <W@CShipDate></W@CShipDate>

The correct answers are b and e. Indicator tags consist of a prefix, name, and optional default content between the tags. Tag prefixes must begin with a letter, and are recommended to have a unique character. Answers b and e both satisfy the criteria, with answer b using the default tag prefix.

Answer a is missing the standard forward slash on the closing tag, therefore it is incorrect. Answer c is missing a tag name after the tag prefix, hence it does not represent a valid indicator tag; therefore answer c is incorrect. Answer d is incorrect because the tag prefix starts with a non-alphabetical character, which is not allowed.

## Question 8

> When running an IIS application, which event of the **WebClass** object is normally used to set the first Webitem to be returned to the user accessing the application?
>
> ○ a.  **Initialize**
>
> ○ b.  **BeginRequest**
>
> ○ c.  **Start**
>
> ○ d.  **EndRequest**
>
> ○ e.  **Terminate**

The correct answer is c. Assigning the first Webitem to return to the user is normally performed within the **Start** event of the **WebClass** object by assigning the **NextItem** property equal to the Webitem to be returned. This causes the Webitem, usually an HTML template file, to be sent to the client.

The **Initialize** event does not always fire each time the application is accessed, therefore it is a poor choice for setting the first Webitem and answer a is incorrect. The **BeginRequest** event is fired every time an HTTP request is received, so setting the **NextItem** property to the same Webitem would cause the same Webitem to be returned for every request, hence answer b is incorrect. Answers d and e are incorrect because both the **EndRequest** and **Terminate** events are fired after HTTP responses are sent, thus they cannot be used to set the first Webitem sent to the client.

# Need To Know More?

 Isaacs, Bruce: *Inside Dynamic HTML*. Microsoft Press, 1997. ISBN: 1572316861. This book provides an excellent framework for exploring the integral parts of DHTML, from cascading style sheets to the Document Object Model. This book comes with a CD-ROM full of sample code.

 Pardi, William and Eric Schurman: *Dynamic HTML in Action*. Microsoft Press, 1998. ISBN: 1572318201. This book, about to show up in a new edition, goes deeper into using CSS, Active Channels, and scripting. It also briefly talks about XML and filters.

 For more information regarding the topics covered in this chapter, search the MSDN Visual Studio 6.0 Library with the following phrases:

➤ DHTML Page Designer Main Screen

➤ Building Web Applications with Visual Basic

➤ The Object Model for IIS Applications

➤ An Introduction to Web Classes

➤ Built-in ASP Objects Reference

# Creating ActiveX Controls

6

## Terms you'll need to understand:

√ **UserControl** object

√ Constituent controls

√ Container

√ **PropertyBag** object

√ **SelectedControls** collection

√ Ambient properties

√ **ReadProperties** event

√ **WriteProperties** event

√ **InitProperties** event

√ **ApplyChanges** event

√ **SelectionChanged** event

√ **PropertyChanged** method

√ **CanPropertyChange** method

√ **GetDataMember** event

√ **DataMembers** collection

## Techniques you'll need to master:

√ Creating properties and methods

√ Saving and loading persistent properties

√ Testing an ActiveX control

√ Debugging an ActiveX control

√ Creating property pages

√ Enabling simple data binding

√ Creating an ActiveX control that is a data source

# Defining ActiveX Controls

As you're certainly aware by now, Visual Basic (VB) can act as a container for ActiveX controls to enhance the user interface of your applications. In fact, this ability to reuse components developed by others is what makes VB such a popular rapid application development environment. These controls, such as the tree view or list view controls that are distributed with the 32-bit releases of Windows, take advantage of the *Component Object Model* (COM) to provide user-interface services to distributed applications. As with other COM-related services, the primary benefits of controls are reusability and encapsulation.

You may also be aware that starting with version 5, VB has also had the ability to create ActiveX controls. By creating your own controls you can add functionality to the user services of a distributed application and encapsulate that functionality to be reusable. In this chapter we'll go through the basics of creating, testing, and debugging a simple control used to select multiple values from a listbox and place those values into a selected list. We'll also look at adding property pages and enabling controls for data binding and acting as a data source. By creating the controls yourself and touching all areas of their development, you should be able to handle any exam questions that come your way.

# UserControl Template

To create a control, open a new project with the File menu and choose the ActiveX control template. The resulting project will contain one **UserControl** template object, also called a *control class*, named **UserControl1**. This template acts as the canvas that will contain the user interface for the control and is analogous to the **Form** object used when creating a standard VB EXE. The **UserControl** object also exposes some specific events that the control container will call upon initialization and when properties are modified. You can see a list of these key events and the conditions under which they are fired in Table 6.1.

The *control container* is the form in the application that will house an instance of the control after it is compiled. The most common containers are VB itself and Internet Explorer.

It's important to note that your ActiveX control project may contain more than one **UserControl** object. Upon compilation, the resulting OCX file or ActiveX control component will contain one control for each **UserControl** template in the project. In this way, you can package related controls together in the same distributable file just as the Windows common controls are distributed in the comctl32.ocx file.

| Table 6.1   Important UserControl events. | |
|---|---|
| **Event Name** | **Use** |
| Initialize | Fired when the control is placed on a container in design mode and when the control is created at runtime. |
| InitProperties | Fired when the control is placed on a container in design mode. It is used to set default properties in the control. |
| Resize | Fired when the control is placed on a container and when the control is created at runtime. It is used to adjust the size of the constituent controls if needed. |
| ReadProperties | Fired when the control is created at runtime by the container and again when the runtime instance is destroyed. It is used to read properties from persistent storage and to set their values. |
| Terminate | Fired when the control instance is destroyed by the container. |
| WriteProperties | Fired when the control instance is destroyed by the container. It is used to save properties to persistent storage |

# Creating The User Interface

To create the user interface for a control you can simply select one or more controls from the toolbox and place them on the **UserControl** object. These controls are then referred to as *constituent controls*; you can manipulate them normally. For this example, add two listboxes, two label controls, and two command buttons as constituent controls, as shown in Figure 6.1.

> *Note: Using any of the standard controls that ship with VB (except the DBGrid control) is permissible. However, using a third-party control or the previous exempted control as a constituent control requires that all the licensing requirements for the third party be met before distribution. Microsoft also states that if you use constituent controls, you must add "significant and primary" functionality. In other words, you cannot simply repackage the TreeView control and sell it as your own.*

Next, to implement the functionality of this simple control, write the trivial code required to move items from one listbox to the other in the clicked events of the command buttons, as shown in Listing 6.1.

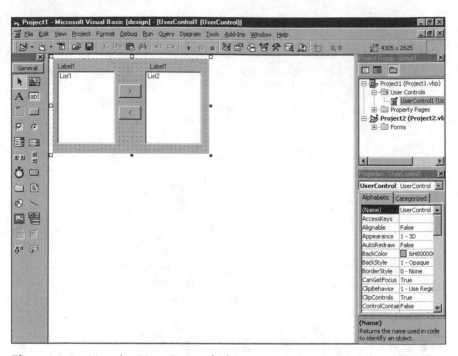

**Figure 6.1**  Use the **UserControl** object to create the user interface for your control.

## Listing 6.1  Moving items from one listbox to another.

```
Private Sub Command1_Click()

On Error Resume Next
List2.AddItem List1.List(List1.ListIndex)
List1.RemoveItem List1.ListIndex

End Sub

Private Sub Command2_Click()

On Error Resume Next
List1.AddItem List2.List(List2.ListIndex)
List2.RemoveItem List2.ListIndex

End Sub
```

# Exposing Properties, Methods, And Events

Once the user interface is established, you can determine what properties, methods, and events your control class should expose. These will comprise the public members or interface that the developer using your control will be able to call from code or through the container in which your control is placed at design time. Keep in mind that the methods, properties, and events of the constituent controls we've placed on the **UserControl** object will not be visible to the user of this control. For example, if we want to allow the developer to view and change the **Caption** property of the Label1 constituent control, we'll need to provide a property through which we'll interact with the constituent control.

## Coding Properties, Methods, And Events

One simple method for creating user-defined members is to use the Tools|Add Procedure menu option that is available once you view the code for the **UserControl** object. The resulting dialog box allows you to specify whether the member will be a property, method (sub or function), or event. Keep in mind that all public procedures, both sub and function, that you create in the **UserControl** automatically become methods. If you wish to create a procedure for use only within the control, declare it as **Private**.

For this example, create two public properties called **FromLabel** and **ToLabel**. The object now contains four new procedures. Each property contains a **Get** procedure that is called when the user of the control requests the value of the property and a **Let** procedure that is called when the user changes the value of the property.

Note that these properties employ **Variant** data types by default. To make the code more efficient, you should change these to the data type that is required, in this case a string.

The code you'll place in these procedures should interact with the Label1 and Label2 constituent controls. The **Get** procedures simply return the values in the label controls; the **Let** procedures modify the constituent controls and change their captions to the value passed in, as seen in Listing 6.2.

## Listing 6.2    **Get** and **Let** property procedures.

```
Public Property Get FromLabel() As String
FromLabel = Label1.Caption
End Property
```

```
Public Property Let FromLabel(ByVal vNewValue As String)
Label1.Caption = vNewValue
End Property

Public Property Get ToLabel() As String
ToLabel = Label2.Caption
End Property

Public Property Let ToLabel(ByVal vNewValue As String)
Label2.Caption = vNewValue
End Property
```

Public methods and events can be exposed in a similar fashion by creating public sub, function, or event procedures.

In some cases you should consider creating an enumerated type for the data type of your property. *Enumerated types* allow the user of your control to choose from a drop-down list of available choices, rather than having to assign a value. The syntax for creating an enumerated type is:

```
Public Enum FieldingPosition
    posFirstBase
    posSecondBase
    posThirdBase
End Enum
```

To use the type, set the return value of the property **Get** and **Let** procedures to the name of the enumerated type.

# ActiveX Control Interface Wizard

Rather than coding all the members of the control by hand, an easier method is to use the *ActiveX Control Interface Wizard*. This wizard allows you to create and map members to your constituent controls and writes all the necessary code. The other nice feature of the wizard is that by running it multiple times you can make changes as necessary; the wizard will modify the underlying code.

To invoke the wizard, you'll first need to load it as an add-in from the Add-Ins menu. Next, choose ActiveX Control Interface Wizard from the menu. After a short explanation, the wizard allows you to choose from a list of common members that you might want to use in your control. For our example choose the **AddItem** method and add it to the list of Selected Names. The wizard then shows the custom interface members—the two properties we created earlier—and allows you to edit or delete them. The Set Mapping dialog box then lets you map the **AddItem** method to one of the constituent controls. In this case, map the **AddItem** method to the **AddItem** method of the listbox List1 as shown in Figure 6.2.

In the final dialog box you are allowed to add a description and modify the return values and data types of all the members of the control. After closing the wizard, the code is inserted into the **UserControl's** code module. You'll notice that the wizard added the code for the public sub **AddItem**:

```
Public Sub AddItem(ByVal Item As String, _
    Optional ByVal Index As Variant)
    List1.AddItem Item, Index
End Sub
```

By mapping our **AddItem** method to the constituent control List1, we're actually wrapping the call to **List1.AddItem** in our method. Notice also that the arguments the wizard creates for the method are identical to those defined by the constituent control.

Make sure you know how to reference user-defined properties from within the code of your control. You can either simply type the name of the property or use the **Me** object, which refers to the **UserControl** object. For example, to reference the **FromLabel** property from procedures within the **UserControl** use the code:

```
Me.FromLabel
```

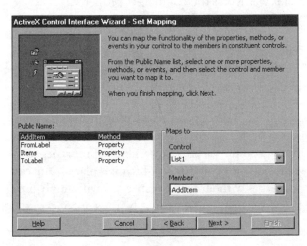

**Figure 6.2**    The ActiveX Control Interface Wizard allows you to map the members of your control to the members of constituent controls.

## Ambient And Extended Properties

Some properties are, in fact, not exposed by the control but are provided by the container. These can be classified as *extender* properties and *ambient* properties. Extender properties are provided by the container to give the developer the ability to name and work with your control in his or her development environment. The standard Extender object properties include **Name**, **Visible**, **Default**, **Cancel**, and **Parent**, although a container like VB also adds the additional properties **Top**, **Width**, **Left**, **Tag**, **Index**, **HelpContextID**, **TabStop**, **TabIndex**, and **ToolTipText**. To access these properties simply use the **Extender** object and refer to the property by name:

```
strName = Extender.Name
```

Keep in mind, however, that if you reference properties that are not implemented by the container the developer is using with your control, errors will result. Make sure to use copious error handling to avoid this problem.

For the exam, make sure you know what happens when your control defines a property that may also be defined by the container. For example, if your control and the container both define a **Visible** property, the user of your control can only access your property by using the syntax:

```
yourcontrol.Object.Visible
```

The normal syntax will access the container's property.

The other type of container-supplied properties are referred to as ambient properties. Generally these properties have to do with how the control will be displayed in the container. You can use the **AmbientChanged** event of the **UserControl** object to respond to changes in ambient properties. The event is simply passed the name of the property as a string. Some of the ambient properties for all containers include **Font**, **BackColor**, **ForeColor**, and **UserMode**. To see all the standard ambient properties use the Object Browser and select the **AmbientProperties** object. The primary use of ambient properties is to ensure that your control blends into the container in which it is placed. You can use the standard ambient properties without fear, because VB will simply provide a default value if the property is not implemented by the container.

## Saving And Loading Persistent Properties

Because your control will be loaded and unloaded multiple times when it is used by a container, make sure that the appropriate properties are saved to disk (*persistent storage*) by the container. For example, if we did not tell the container to save the **FromLabel** and **ToLabel** properties of our control, each time a developer closed and re-opened a project that uses the control, the two label captions would be reset to their default values of Label1 and Label2.

The **UserControl** object contains the **ReadProperties** and **WriteProperties** events that are called whenever the container attempts to read in property values from persistent storage or when it tries to write those values out. The events are passed in a **PropertyBag** object that contains just two methods: **ReadProperty** and **WriteProperty**. You can think of the **PropertyBag** as a "black box" object that you simply pass values into and then let the container take care of them. Call those methods once for each property you want to read and save, as in Listing 6.3.

### Listing 6.3   Reading and writing persistent properties.

```
Private Sub UserControl_ReadProperties(PropBag As PropertyBag)
On Error Resume Next
    Label1.Caption = PropBag.ReadProperty("FromLabel")
    Label2.Caption = PropBag.ReadProperty("ToLabel")
End Sub


'Write property values to storage
Private Sub UserControl_WriteProperties(PropBag As PropertyBag)
    Call PropBag.WriteProperty("FromLabel", Label1.Caption)
    Call PropBag.WriteProperty("ToLabel", Label2.Caption)
End Sub
```

> *Note: You can use the **InitProperties** event of the **UserControl** to override the default values for properties provided by VB.*

# Testing And Debugging

Luckily, testing and debugging an ActiveX control created in Visual Basic is a straightforward process. VB's ability to load multiple projects into the Project Explorer allows you to test your control from within VB itself without having to first compile and register the control as you would in Visual C++.

*Note: Although VB doesn't use the term workspace as the rest of the Visual Studio tools do, the projects that are loaded into the Project Explorer can be saved together in what is termed a group. This group of projects can then be reloaded by opening the VBG file that maps to the group.*

To test the control we've been working on, add a new project to the Explorer using File|Add Project and select Standard EXE for the project template. We're going to use this new project as the client project that will create and use an instance of your control. You'll notice that in the toolbox an icon has been added that represents the control in your control project.

 If the Toolbox icon for your control is grayed out, you'll need to close the UserControl designer. Likewise, a control placed on a form will be hatched if you open the UserControl designer.

Place the control on Form1 and note the properties that are available in the Properties window. To make sure the property procedures work correctly, set the **FromLabel** and **ToLabel** properties from the window. Then open the code window for the form and write some code in the **Form_Load** event to call the **AddItem** method:

```
UserControl1.AddItem "Sammy Sosa"
```

Finally, to test the complete functionality, be sure to make the standard EXE project the current project by right-clicking on the project name and selecting Set As Startup; then click on Start or press F5 to run the project. At this point you should be able to fully test the control within the client project. In this case, that means being able to move the item from the "from" box (Players) to the "to" box (Pitchers) and back again, as shown in Figure 6.3.

To debug the control, place breakpoints anywhere within either the code in the client project or the code within the control project. Likewise, if a runtime error occurs when running the control in the development environment, the debugger will automatically take you to the line that caused the error within the control project. By stepping through the code, you can move from the client to the control project seamlessly. This certainly simplifies debugging.

*Note: Keep in mind that even when your control is in the development environment, its events may be firing and its code running if it is placed on a form in another project. This is what allows you to debug the control without actually compiling it.*

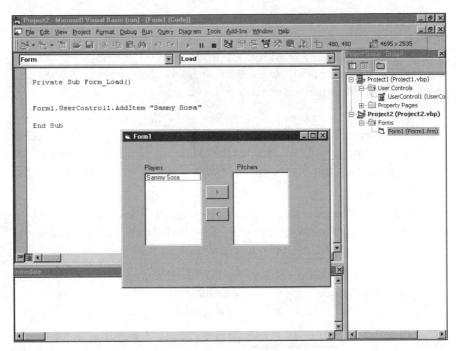

**Figure 6.3** Testing the control is accomplished through a second project added to the Project Explorer.

To handle errors within ActiveX controls, your procedures within the control should raise an error back to the container. In this way the container can handle the error as it deems appropriate. The proper method for this is to use the **Raise** method of the **Err** object to raise an error number that is offset from the constant **vbObjectError** like so:

```
Err.Raise vbObjectError + 1024, Err.Description
```

This method is preferred, rather than creating message boxes that cause the user to have to respond to each error.

# Creating Property Pages

Property pages are not required when creating ActiveX controls, but they are a convenient way to organize properties exposed by your control so that developers will have an easier time setting those properties at design time. For example, you can provide a property page that uses a custom interface to set the background color or font properties of your control, rather than forcing the developer using your control to type in these values. This also allows you to group related properties together in different pages.

In addition, all the property pages you create are available from a single tabbed dialog box that the developer can access by simply right-clicking on your control in the development environment. Also keep in mind that property pages are desirable because not all containers that house your control will allow developers to set the properties as easily as VB does.

The way in which you create these pages is similar to the concept of the **UserControl** class. You need to add a **PropertyPage** object to your project using the Add menu when right-clicking on the project in the Project Explorer. The resulting borderless form represents one of the tabs in the Tabbed Properties dialog box.

Continuing with our example control from earlier in the chapter, you should create the user interface for setting the **FromLabel** and **ToLabel** properties using standard controls, as shown in Figure 6.4.

Much like the **UserControl** object, the **PropertyPage** object contains special events that are called when the object is manipulated. In this case, the two primary events that you must write code for are **SelectionChanged** and **ApplyChanges**.

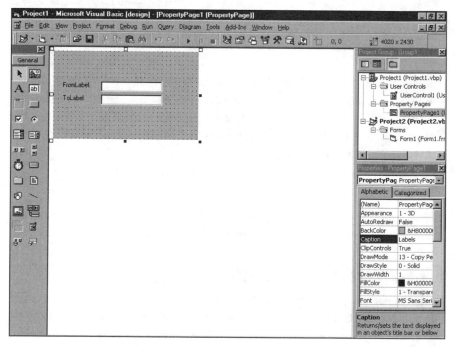

**Figure 6.4** Use the **PropertyPage** object to create the user interface for the property page.

The **SelectionChanged** event is fired when the property page is opened and should contain code that populates the user interface of the page with the current values of the properties from the control. In our case, the code in **SelectionChanged** would populate the two textboxes in the property page with the values of the label controls on the **UserControl** object:

```
Private Sub PropertyPage_SelectionChanged()
    Text1.Text = SelectedControls(0).FromLabel
    Text2.Text = SelectedControls(0).ToLabel
End Sub
```

The **SelectedControls** collection is a special object that contains all the instances of your control that are currently selected by the developer. In other words, a developer could put several instances of your control on a form and then select all of them before invoking the properties dialog. By referencing item 0 in the collection, as we've done in the previous example, the properties for only the first selected control will be made visible. To determine whether or not multiple instances of your control have been selected, you can check the **Count** property of the **SelectedControls** collection.

The second event that must be coded is the **ApplyChanges** event. This event is fired when the properties dialog box is closed, when the developer clicks on OK or Apply, or when he or she selects another property page. This event is where you place the code to write any changed values back to the properties of your control. In this case, we'll write code that is the inverse of that in the **SelectionChanged** event:

```
Private Sub PropertyPage_ApplyChanges()
    SelectedControls(0).FromLabel = Text1.Text
    SelectedControls(0).ToLabel = Text2.Text
End Sub
```

However, as with **SelectionChanged**, the preceding code handles only the first instance of your control selected on a form. To handle multiple selected instances, you can simply loop through each item in the **SelectedControls** collection and set the properties:

```
For Each objControl in SelectedControls
    objControl.FromLabel = Text1.Text
    objControl.ToLabel = Text2.Text
Next
```

The final bit of code to add to the property page is to make sure that the page itself is notified when the developer modifies one of the properties. You need to notify the page so that the Apply button will be enabled and the **ApplyChanges** event will fire. To make the notification, set the property page's **Changed** event to True in the change event of the controls that are used to change the properties; in our case, these are the Text1 and Text2 controls:

```
Private Sub Text1_Change()
    Changed = True
End Sub

Private Sub Text2_Change()
    Changed = True
End Sub
```

Now that the coding is complete, the final step is to connect the property page to the control. Double-click on the **UserControl** object to display the properties window. The ellipses next to the **PropertyPages** property will invoke the Connect Property Pages dialog box. You'll notice that in addition to the property page you just created, standard property pages are available for setting a font, color, picture, and data format. Any property that you define with these standard types automatically invokes the corresponding standard property page from the VB properties window. By checking them in this dialog box, a property page is added to the properties dialog box, which contains a list of all the properties that correspond to the checked data type.

One last thing you'll want to do is change the **Caption** property of your property page to the name you wish to see as the name of the tab in the properties dialog box. In this case, name it "Labels". To test the property page, close the **PropertyPage** object and switch to the client project. Activate Form1 and then right-click on the instance of your control that you placed on the form. You should now see a Properties menu at the bottom of the context menu. When you select this menu, the properties dialog box should appear with the user interface for the **FromLabel** and **ToLabel** properties (see Figure 6.5).

Be sure to test changing the properties and re-invoking the property page to see the changed values.

# Enabling Data Binding

As you probably know, VB ships with intrinsic controls such as the textbox and checkbox that can bind to fields in recordsets created by the data controls that also ship with the product. What you may not have realized is that the controls you create can also act as *bound controls*.

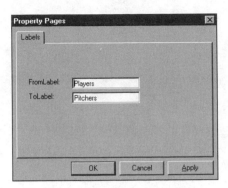

**Figure 6.5**   The completed Property Pages dialog box.

> *Note: This is especially interesting in the latest release of VB, because now VB sports three different data controls that you can use: one for Data Access Objects (DAO), one for Remote Data Objects (RDO), and one for ActiveX Data Objects (ADO).*

In order to make a control bound, you'll first need to create a property or properties that contain the data from the bound recordset. In the case of the control we've been building, we can use the **FromLabel** and **ToLabel** properties. Of course, our control may not be an ideal candidate for data binding, but you'll understand how to apply the concept to other controls that are more suitable for data binding. You'll also need to set the **DataBindingBehavior** property of the **UserControl** to **vbSimpleBound**. This allows your control to expose individual properties to be bound to fields in the data control.

> *Note: Although space prohibits an example, you can also set the DataBindingBehavior property to vbComplexBound. This setting allows your control to bind to the entire recordset returned by a data control. This might be useful for controls that wish to display the entire recordset at one time, such as a grid or tabular control.*

Once the properties are created, invoke the Procedure Attributes dialog box from the Tools menu. After selecting the **FromLabel** property, click on the Advanced button to view the data-binding options. To make the property data bound, check the Property Is Data Bound checkbox. This should enable the other checkboxes, which you should also check, as shown in Figure 6.6.

In a similar manner, check all the options for **ToLabel** except the This Property Binds To DataField. Each control can support only one property that binds to the **DataField** property. You can think of this as the primary property

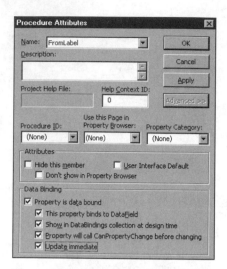

**Figure 6.6** The Procedure Attributes dialog box allows you to choose which properties are data bound.

through which a field from a recordset is bound to your control. Other properties that wish to bind to fields will be associated through the **DataBindings** collection at design time, as specified in the second checkbox.

After dismissing the dialog box, you'll need to write a little code in the property procedures for **FromLabel** and **ToLabel**. This ensures that the data control is notified when the bound property is changed and checks to make sure the data control will allow changes to the property. Normally, to notify the data control you would call the **PropertyChanged** method of the **UserControl**, passing it the name of the property, in the event that it is fired when the developer modifies the property. In the case of our **FromLabel** and **ToLabel** properties, the developer using the control cannot modify the properties, except through the properties window or the properties dialog box; in both cases the control already recognizes that the property has changed. However, before we modify the properties in the property **Let** procedures, we should call the **CanPropertyChange** method of the **UserControl**, passing it the name of the property, which will return a True or False to let us know if the property can be changed:

```
Public Property Let FromLabel(ByVal vNewValue As String)
    If CanPropertyChange("FromLabel") Then
        Label1.Caption = vNewValue
    End If
End Property
```

```
Public Property Let ToLabel(ByVal vNewValue As String)
    If CanPropertyChange("ToLabel") Then
        Label2.Caption = vNewValue
    End If
End Property
```

Finally, to test the data binding, you'll need to add one of the data controls to the client project and populate the properties required to create a recordset. In the case of the ADO data control, you need to populate the **CommandType**, **ConnectionString**, and **Recordsource** properties. Next, set the **DataSource** and **DataField** properties of the instance of your control to map to the ADO data control and one of the fields returned from the **Recordsource**, respectively. You should now be able to run the client project and watch the **FromLabel** property change as you traverse the recordset.

# Controls As Data Sources

The final concept you'll need to master is to make your control act as a data source for other controls. In other words, you can roll your own custom data controls and encapsulate specific behavior that you want to provide. One possible use of this technique is to create and distribute ActiveX controls that encapsulate recordsets that developers in your company need access to. This alleviates the developers from having to code SQL or remember where the data is stored.

To demonstrate the technique, you'll need to create a new ActiveX control project. For this control we'll create a simple ADO data control with a user interface that contains two command buttons to traverse the **authors** table found in the SQL Server **pubs** database. The key property we need to set in the **UserControl** is **DataSourceBehavior**. By setting this property to **vbDataSource**, we allow other bound controls to use their **DataSource** property to select our control.

In VB6, each data source control can expose multiple recordsets, each of which is referred to as a *DataMember*. The recordsets that your control will include should be created in the **Initialize** event of the **UserControl**. Within this event you should first add a **DataMember** to the **DataMembers** collection of the **UserControl**, giving it an appropriate name. In this case we'll add a **DataMember** called "Authors" using the following code:

```
DataMembers.Add "Authors"
```

Now the remainder of the code in the **Initialize** event will create the ADO recordset:

```
Set rs = New ADODB.Recordset
Set cn = New ADODB.Connection

cn.ConnectionString = _
  "DRIVER={SQL SERVER};SERVER=SSOSA;DATABASE=pubs;UID=sa"
cn.Open

rs.Open "SELECT * FROM authors", cn, adOpenStatic, adLockReadOnly
```

In this case be sure that you declare the **rs** (recordset) and **cn** (connection) variables as module-level variables, because we'll need to manipulate the recordset in other events within the control. Note that the preceding code also connects to a SQL Server database using a DSN-less connection. In other words, all the information needed to connect to the server is passed directly to the ADO **Connection** object, rather than simply passing a reference to an ODBC data source. This allows the code to be more portable; you don't have to set up an ODBC data source at each client workstation that instantiates your control.

> *Note: You may want to expose some of the connection information as properties and allow the developer to set them at runtime or design time. Good candidates would be the server name and login id and password.*

The other important point to note in the preceding code is that the recordset is opened with the attributes **adOpenStatic** and **adLockReadOnly**. These specify that no updates are allowed in the recordset, and it can be traversed both forward and backward.

Now that the **DataMembers** have been initialized, you'll need to write the code to provide the underlying recordsets to the bound control when it is requested. Luckily, the **UserControl** exposes an event, **GetDataMember**, for just such a purpose. This event will be called whenever the bound control requests information about the recordset, for instance when the bound control uses its **DataField** property to select the field within the recordset it will bind to.

The **GetDataMember** event itself is passed two arguments: **DataMember**, a string that identifies which data member was requested, and **Data**, an object that is passed by reference and which you'll populate with the desired recordset. For our control the code will look as follows:

```
Private Sub UserControl_GetDataMember(DataMember As String, _
    Data As Object)

If DataMember = "Authors" Then
    Set Data = rs
End If

End Sub
```

*Note: If you have more than one **DataMember**, a **Select Case** statement would be a better choice.*

To give our data source control more functionality, we'll also write a little code behind the **Command1** and **Command2** click events. These events will simply issue a **MoveNext** or **MovePrevious** on the module-level recordset variable **rs**:

```
Private Sub Command1_Click()
    If rs.BOF Then
        rs.MoveLast
    Else
        rs.MovePrevious
    End If
End Sub

Private Sub Command2_Click()
    If rs.EOF Then
        rs.MoveFirst
    Else
        rs.MoveNext
    End If
End Sub
```

*Note: These events also take into account that as you traverse the recordset, you'll encounter the beginning (BOF) and end (EOF) of the recordset. Runtime errors will be generated if you move beyond these markers. Therefore, the prevous code performs a wrapping operation by moving to the last or first record, depending on whether you've reached the BOF or EOF condition.*

Once again, to test our data source control you'll need to add a new Standard EXE project to the "workspace" or project group. Place an instance of your control on the form and set the **DataSource** property. To test the binding, place a textbox on the form and set its **DataSource** property to **UserControl1** (or whatever you've named your instance). The act of instantiating your control on the form will call the **Initialize** event, creating the **authors** data member and the underlying recordset. By selecting the **DataField** property, the **GetDataMember** event is fired and a list of columns from the **authors** table should be visible. After selecting a column such as **au_lname,** run the client project. You should now be able to traverse the **authors** table using the two command buttons you created (see Figure 6.7).

**Figure 6.7**  The completed application that uses a data-bound ActiveX control.

# Practice Questions

## Question 1

> A constituent control is:
>
> ○ a. An ActiveX control created using Visual Basic.
>
> ○ b. An ActiveX control that is shipped with Windows.
>
> ○ c. A control that is placed on the **UserControl** object.
>
> ○ d. A control that performs multiple functions.

The correct answer is c. Constituent controls are those controls that you use to create the user interface for an ActiveX control. By placing these controls on the **UserControl** object, you can integrate their functionality through code and package them together within the control. Constituent controls can include those that ship with VB and Windows or third-party controls. Keep in mind that the licensing restrictions for third-party controls still apply.

Answers a and b are incorrect because constituent controls can be standard controls that ship with VB, third-party ActiveX controls, or controls that you create in VB. In other words, the term *constituent* refers to how the control is used and not how it is created. Answer d is incorrect because although a constituent control may perform multiple functions, it certainly is not required.

## Question 2

> The **PropertyBag** object is used to:
>
> ○ a. Pass data from a client program into the ActiveX control.
>
> ○ b. Read the values of ambient properties.
>
> ○ c. Store and read properties saved to persistent storage by the container.
>
> ○ d. Asynchronously read properties from a Web server.

The correct answer is c, because the **PropertyBag** object is exposed as an argument in the **ReadProperties** and **WriteProperties** events of the **UserControl**. Within these events you can call the **ReadProperty** and **WriteProperty** methods of the **PropertyBag** to tell the container to retrieve or save them, respectively.

The **PropertyBag** acts as a conduit through which communication to the container occurs. Remember that the container determines how the properties are actually stored and retrieved.

Answer a is incorrect because the **PropertyBag** is used by the container in which the control is placed and not by the final client program that may be created by the container. Answer b is incorrect because ambient properties are those supplied by the container itself and so do not have to be passed into the control. Answer d is incorrect because the **PropertyBag** is used to communicate with a container, such as a development environment, not a Web server. Your ActiveX control can be used in a Web page and can read data from a Web server using the **AsyncRead** method of the **UserControl** object, but the **PropertyBag** is unrelated.

## Question 3

Properties that are exposed by the container of a control, but may not be implemented by the control, are called [Check all correct answers]:

❑ a. Constituent properties

❑ b. Ambient properties

❑ c. Extender properties

❑ d. Public member properties

The correct answers are b and c, because containers may implement properties for your control that allow the container to more easily manipulate the control and modify its appearance. Examples of common ambient and extender properties include **Name, BackColor, Top, Left, Width,** and **Height.** Your control is notified as ambient properties are changed through the **AmbientChanged** event of the **UserControl** object. You can use this event to resize constituent controls or otherwise change the appearance of your control based on the ambient property. Extender properties can be accessed using the **Extender** object and simply referenced with their name. Generally, ambient properties are used to give your control hints as to how it should display itself, whereas extender properties are simply used by the container to place and name your control.

The term "constituent properties" is nonsensical, rendering answer a incorrect. Answer d is incorrect because public member properties are by definition user-defined and not defined by the container.

# Question 4

> In order to populate controls on a **PropertyPage** when the page is loaded you would need to:
>
> ○ a. Write code in the **SelectionChanged** event to read the values of the **SelectedControls** collection.
>
> ○ b. Write code in the **ApplyChanges** event to read the values of the **SelectedControls** container.
>
> ○ c. Write code in the **InitProperties** event to read the values of the **PropertyBag** object.
>
> ○ d. Write code in the **SelectedControls** event to read the values of the **SelectionChanged** collection.

The correct answer is a, because the **SelectionChanged** event is fired when the **PropertyPage** object is initialized. The **SelectedControls** collection is available as a property of the **PropertyPage** and contains references to all the instances of your control that have been selected in the container. As a result, each item in the **SelectedControls** collection contains the same properties as your control. The code within the event should then read these properties and populate any user interface controls on the property page.

Answer b is incorrect because the **ApplyChanges** event is fired when the property page is closed. Answer c is incorrect because the **InitProperties** event occurs on the **UserControl** object and not the **PropertyBag** object. Answer d is incorrect because it confuses the name of the collection with the name of the event.

# Question 5

> The purpose of the **GetDataMember** event of the **UserControl** object is to:
>
> ○ a. Initialize recordsets to use in controls that bind to data sources.
>
> ○ b. Indicate which properties of the control are data bound.
>
> ○ c. Return a recordset to bound controls from a control acting as a data source based on a given **DataMember**.
>
> ○ d. Pass recordsets to controls that act as data sources based on a given **DataMember**.

The correct answer is c. On controls that act as data sources (**DataSourceBehavior** set to **vbDataSource**), the **GetDataMember** event of the **UserControl** object is fired when a bound control binds to the data source and attempts to retrieve the recordset. The event is passed in the name of the requested **DataMember** and your code should return a reference to the recordset that is implemented for the **DataMember**. Remember that you initialize the recordsets in the **Initialize** event of the **UserControl** object, which is why answer a is incorrect.

Answer b is incorrect because selecting properties that are data bound is done through the dialog box that pops up after selecting Tools|Procedure Attributes. Answer d is incorrect because it is your control that is acting as the data source, not the control that is receiving the recordset.

## Question 6

The function of the following code

```
Public Property Get FromLabel() As String
FromLabel = Label1.Caption
End Property
```

is to:

○ a.  Allow developers to set the value of the **FromLabel** property.

○ b.  Allow developers to change the value of **Label1.Caption**.

○ c.  Set the value of a label control on a property page.

○ d.  Allow developers to retrieve the value of the **FromLabel** property.

The correct answer is d. This is an example of a **Get** property procedure. You can remember that this is used by developers using your control to *get* the value of the property. Property **Let** or **Set** procedures are used to change the value of a property, hence answer a is incorrect.

Answer b is incorrect because the code reads the value of **Label1.Caption** and does not allow the user of your control to change it. Answer c is incorrect for the same reason.

## Question 7

You plan to create an ActiveX control that is used by different containers. How can you ensure that properties of your control can be set correctly at design time?

- ○ a. Create your control as a data source so that containers can bind to your properties.

- ○ b. Use the ActiveX Control Interface Wizard to map constituent control properties to your control's properties.

- ○ c. Create a property page that provides an interface to set the properties.

- ○ d. Create property procedures for each of your properties.

The correct answer is c. Because all containers do not expose their own property windows like VB, you'll want to create property pages. These pages can then be accessed by the developer using your control by right-clicking on the control and choosing Properties on the context menu. Property pages ensure that you control the way in which the property is presented to the developer.

Answer a is incorrect because data binding is used to provide recordsets from a database to other controls and is not a mechanism to expose standard properties. Answer b is incorrect because using the ActiveX Control Interface Wizard simply creates properties and does not specify how they are presented to the user of your control. Likewise, answer d is incorrect because creating property procedures exposes them, but does not provide an interface to them.

## Question 8

Which is the best approach for testing an ActiveX control you've developed in Visual Basic?

- ○ a. Compile the control and use the **<OBJECT>** tag to embed it in a Web page.

- ○ b. Add a new Standard EXE project to the project group and put an instance of the control on Form1.

- ○ c. Create a new ActiveX EXE project to act as a client for your control.

- ○ d. Use the ActiveX control test container installed as a part of Visual Studio 6.

The correct answer is b, because you can test your control and even step through its code line by line if you use it in a project that is in the same project group. You do this by adding a new Standard EXE or ActiveX EXE project to the group and placing an instance of your control on a form in the new project. Immediately upon creating the instance, the code in your control will start running. You can set breakpoints in events such as **InitProperties** and **ReadProperties** to see your code work.

Once you are confident in your code, compile it and create a new EXE project to test the compiled version. You'll have to add your control to the toolbox through the Project|Components menu.

Answer a is incorrect because using your control in a Web page will use the compiled control rather than the control in the development environment. Testing in the development environment allows you to place breakpoints within the control code and debug it line by line. Answer c is incorrect because creating a new project will automatically close the control project. However, you may use the ActiveX EXE template to test since the important factor is that both projects are in the project group, not which template is used. Answer d is incorrect because the ActiveX control test container can host only compiled controls and as such is not the best way to test a control written in VB.

# Need To Know More?

 Appleman, Dan: *Dan Appleman's Developing ActiveX Components with Visual Basic 5.0: A Guide to the Perplexed*. Ziff Davis Press, 1997. ISBN: 1-56276-510-8. Because little has changed in this topic from VB 5, this should still be a good reference. However, the scope of this book (over 700 pages) also includes ActiveX DLLs and EXEs and a more in-depth discussion on COM.

 Williams, Al: *Creating ActiveX Controls with Visual Basic 5.* The Coriolis Group, 1997. ISBN: 1-57610-128-2. This book provides step-by-step instructions for creating and customizing ActiveX controls with VB. As with the previous book, this book should still be useful with VB 6.

 For a fairly complete reference on creating controls, see the MSDN online help that ships with Visual Studio 6 and search for "Building ActiveX Controls." You can also look in the *Microsoft Visual Basic 6.0 Programmer's Guide* by Microsoft Press (ISBN: 1572318635). This section of the guide steps you through the process and contains almost everything you need to create professional ActiveX controls in Visual Basic. This guide is more formally written and does a good job of defining the terms used, then sticking to them.

 For a more basic approach, see the article, "Creating Your First ActiveX Control" on the MSDN Web site at **msdn.microsoft.com/vbasic/technical/tutorial/activex.asp**.

# Creating An ActiveX Document

## Terms you'll need to understand:

√ **UserDocument** object

√ ActiveX document container

√ ActiveX document object

√ OLE document object

√ **PropertyBag** object

√ **ReadProperties** event

√ **WriteProperties** event

√ **InitProperties** event

√ **PropertyChanged** method

## Techniques you'll need to master:

√ Creating properties

√ Saving and loading persistent properties

√ Testing an ActiveX document

√ Debugging an ActiveX document

√ Navigating using the **HyperLink** object

# Defining An ActiveX Document

Lurking in the shadows of ActiveX controls is another form of ActiveX component known as *ActiveX documents*. ActiveX documents are a somewhat unusual hybrid between a Visual Basic (VB) application, an OLE embedded object, and an OLE automation server. Originally created as a Microsoft Binder-based technology, ActiveX documents require the use of a host application to provide a container frame. ActiveX documents, unlike ActiveX controls, utilize the entire container or client frame window serving as the host to the ActiveX document and have the ability to merge menus with those of the container. ActiveX documents, like ActiveX controls, expose properties, methods, and events, and adhere to the standards and rules of the Component Object Model (COM).

Although ActiveX controls provide user-interface and encapsulated application logic services, ActiveX documents tend to provide full-blown application functionality, appearing to take over the entire application functionality of the host container. This behavior allows the developer to create full-blown Visual Basic applications that can be called from Internet Explorer (IE) just like any other traditional HTML page request.

In this chapter, we'll take a look at the process of creating, testing, and debugging an ActiveX document designed to provide Windows application-like functionality. We will also compare ActiveX documents to ActiveX controls, discuss the parts of an ActiveX document, and explain how to use the **HyperLink** object to provide navigation capabilities. By stepping through the creation of an ActiveX document and exploring the core concerns, you should be able to address ActiveX document-related questions that appear on the exam.

# The Origins Of ActiveX Documents

The concept of ActiveX technology-based documents, borrowing liberally from the definition of documents we most often compare to the commonplace Word document, has its origins back with the Office 95 suite of applications. These humble beginnings are owed to the introduction of the Microsoft Binder technology. Originally known as *OLE document objects*, ActiveX document technology was designed to provide a document-centric methodology for designing and working with related documents (produced in Office suite applications, of course).

The Office Binder was designed to be a basic host container, or *ActiveX document container*, to allow the siting of multiple ActiveX documents produced in various Office products. This provided a user with the ability to rapidly move between document functionalities, with all OLE automation server functionality fully available. Technically, the Office applications themselves are referred to as the ActiveX document, saving the document data as a single *Office Binder Document (OBD)* file. This file, an OLE-structured storage file, stored the actual file data, making it available to the ActiveX documents when loading.

The OLE Document Object technology was expanded with VB5, allowing Visual Basic developers to create ActiveX documents of a customized class, outside those generated in conjunction with Office applications. The OLE structured data is now stored in a VBD file, with a customized compiled application file produced during compiling that provides the OLE automation functionality previously provided by executables such as Winword.exe or Excel.exe. The resulting documents can also now exist as either in-process and out-of-process varieties.

# Comparison With ActiveX Controls

ActiveX documents have a number of characteristics that are similar to ActiveX controls, but differ in implementation and usage. A comparison between the two should highlight the characteristics that separate these different implementations of ActiveX technology.

ActiveX documents are similar to ActiveX controls in many ways:

➤ An ActiveX document cannot be instantiated on its own. A host container, quite often an ActiveX-based object, is required to act as a host for the document. This process, therefore, is referred to as *siting*. Siting an ActiveX document by hooking into the container services of the host exposes the available properties of the document.

*Note: Until an ActiveX document is sited, the **Parent** property and the **HyperLink** object are both unavailable. The process of siting an ActiveX document is very similiar to the act of instantiating an ActiveX control within a host container.*

➤ ActiveX documents expose properties, methods, and events through a public interface.

➤ They adhere to the communication specifications of the Component Object Model.

➤ Lifetime issues are experienced similar to ActiveX controls, involving similar events.

ActiveX documents differ from ActiveX controls in several ways:

➤ They fill the entire client window of the hosting container. ActiveX documents take over the entire visual interface, including menu bar integration, whereas ActiveX controls are basically limited to the physical·boundaries of the controls interface.

➤ ActiveX documents are designed to store document information directly in the VBD file.

➤ ActiveX documents can utilize menu items, which become part of the container's menu bar upon loading.

# Preview Of Building An ActiveX Document

Creating an ActiveX document is a simple process, no different than building a Visual Basic application using any one of the available Visual Basic project types:

1. Open Visual Basic and open a new project using either the ActiveX Document DLL or the ActiveX Document EXE project.

   *Note: Both ActiveX Document DLL and EXE projects provide a single UserDocument as the base template object. This object provides the visual interface for a single ActiveX document.*

2. Add constituent controls onto the document interface.

3. Add code to respond to the appropriate user-initiated actions by using the code window.

4. Add additional **UserDocument** template objects to act as additional pages in your ActiveX document application.

5. Debug the ActiveX document project by starting an instance of the intended host container and view the document.

6. After successful debugging, compile the project into the appropriate in-process or out-of-process component.

7. Deploy the component and accompanying Visual Basic document file (VBD) to the destination server location.

ActiveX documents can be hosted in many different containers, including being used to create add-in tools for the Visual Basic design environment itself.

Therefore, the previous steps are by no means the ultimate listing of steps you can take.

# The Anatomy Of An ActiveX Document

When creating an ActiveX document project, either of the EXE (out-of-process) or DLL (in-process) varieties, the core object class, **UserDocument**, will be stored in DOB and DOX files. These files are similar to the FRM and FRX files used by standard **Form** objects. The DOB files are standard text files that contain source code and property values of the **UserDocument** object and constituent controls on the document interface. If any binary elements, such as graphic files, are used on a **UserDocument,** they are stored in a binary DOX file. The combination of code, properties, and binary elements stored collectively within the DOB and DOX files completely define the visual appearance and exposed interface of the ActiveX document.

> *Note: Examples of common ActiveX document containers include Internet Explorer, Microsoft Office Binder, and even the Visual Basic IDE itself. Corresponding to the traditional concept of the client, an ActiveX document container is capable of hosting, or siting, ActiveX documents by reading the OLE structured data file (VBD file), loading the services of the ActiveX document server, and integrating that functionality within its own application and menu framework.*

Upon compiling an ActiveX document project, the DOX and DOB files, plus any additional required files, are compiled into two main files. Visual Basic creates an ActiveX EXE or ActiveX DLL file, based on the type of project started, to provide the same OLE Server functionality as Winword.exe or Excel.exe provides for Microsoft Binder OBD files. Visual Basic also creates a Visual Basic document (VBD) file. This file provides the initial OLE structured data read by the ActiveX document EXE or DLL. If the ActiveX document provides for data storage through use of the **PropertyBag,** the VBD file is also used to persist this data between requests for the ActiveX document.

To be viewable, an ActiveX document requires three elements. The previously mentioned ActiveX DLL or EXE files (also referred to as the *ActiveX Document Server*) plus the document (VBD) file represent the first two elements; the OLE document container, or host container, finishes out the list of required components in an ActiveX document solution. All three elements are inherently required to allow successful viewing of the ActiveX document.

ActiveX documents, to the casual observer, may provide only minor advantages over full-blown Win32 applications, while instituting additional implementation complexities. But the benefit of providing almost complete window application functionality and maintaining the rapid updatability of ActiveX documents provides numerous benefits:

➤ Separation of the data defining presentation tier visual elements from the actual distributed client application container

➤ Use of a generic client application ActiveX document container (Internet Explorer)

➤ Use of a familiar design environment (Visual Basic IDE)

➤ Greater flexibility in application distribution and updatability by simply recompiling and deploying augmented ActiveX document solutions

➤ Integration of ActiveX document technology with additional Internet-based application technologies

# Creating An ActiveX Document

You must take several steps in order to create and view an ActiveX document. Start by making sure that both Visual Basic and a suitable ActiveX document container, such as Internet Explorer, are available. Once this is done, take the following steps:

1. Open Visual Basic and start an ActiveX Document Dll or ActiveX Document Exe project, as shown in Figure 7.1.

2. The project includes one **UserDocument** object by default. This provides the visual interface for the ActiveX document. Add any constituent controls to the **UserDocument**. For example, adding a FileListBox, Textbox, and CommandButton would look something like Figure 7.2.

3. After adding all desired controls and user interface elements, compile the project into the appropriately named EXE or DLL file. Leaving the default project alone, initiate compiling by clicking on File|Make Project1.exe, as shown in Figure 7.3.

4. After successfully compiling the project, use Internet Explorer to load the resulting VBD file, as shown in Figure 7.4. Notice that the ActiveX document has the same full-blown application functionality a similar Standard EXE project would have, when using Internet Explorer as the container application. Loading the VBD file into Microsoft Office

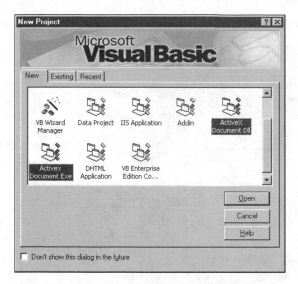

**Figure 7.1**    Starting Visual Basic with either an ActiveX DLL or EXE project is the first step.

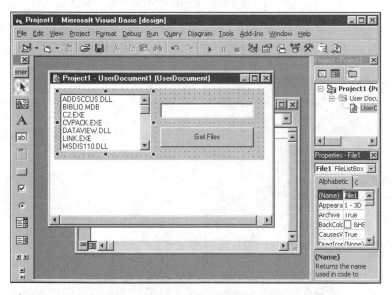

**Figure 7.2**    Adding constituent controls onto **UserDocument** provides functionality to the ActiveX document.

Binder, as seen in Figure 7.5, results in a similar view as if the VBD file was loaded into Internet Explorer, except the functionality of the Binder adds a little extra file representation in a display pane on the left side of the screen.

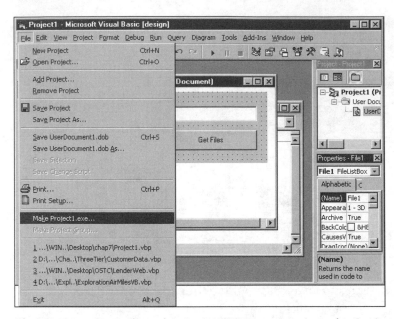

**Figure 7.3** Compiling the ActiveX EXE project into the Project1.exe
out-of-process ActiveX document server allows the
corresponding VBD data file to be loaded into the intended host container.

**Figure 7.4** Internet Explorer is the most commonly used ActiveX
document container, allowing access to application
functionality directly over the Web.

You load an ActiveX document into Internet Explorer by navigating to the location of the VBD file generated when the ActiveX
document project is compiled. Starting with Visual Basic 6, VBD
files now contain the **CODEBASE=** and **VERSION=** values that
were previously loaded via **<OBJECT>** tags embedded in a
starting HTML file.

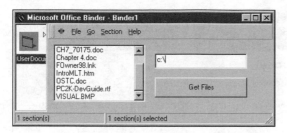

**Figure 7.5**    Loading an ActiveX document into Microsoft Office Binder also adds a reference to the VBD file name in a special document pane.

# Using The UserDocument Template

The **UserDocument** is the base object used in an ActiveX document project. Similar to the **UserControl** class control used to make an ActiveX control, the **UserDocument** is analogous to the basic **Form** object used in standard Visual Basic projects. The events exposed by the **UserDocument** object differ somewhat from the events exposed by the standard **Form** object. Some standard **Form** object events not used by **UserDocument** objects are:

➤ Activate

➤ Deactivate

➤ LinkClose

➤ LinkError

➤ LinkExecute

➤ LinkOpen

➤ Load

➤ QueryUnload

➤ Unload

You can see these similarities and differences in Table 7.1.

Whereas the **UserDocument** object is the source of the user interface that an ActiveX document exposes to the user, an ActiveX document can actually contain more than one **UserDocument** object. In this scenario, multiple VBD files will be generated, although only one ActiveX document EXE or DLL will actually be generated. Similar to ActiveX controls, this allows multiple objects to be contained or grouped into one ActiveX project.

| Table 7.1 | UserDocument object events not used by the standard Form object. |
|---|---|
| **Event Name** | **Purpose** |
| AsyncReadComplete | Fired when an asynchronous read request is completed. |
| EnterFocus | Fired when either the **UserDocument** or one of its constituent controls receives focus. |
| ExitFocus | Fired when either the **UserDocument** or one of its constituent controls loses focus. |
| Hide | Fired when **UserDocument**'s **Visible** property changes to False. |
| InitProperties | Fired when a new instance of the **UserDocument** object is created until the document has been saved. |
| ReadProperties | Fired in place of the **InitProperties** event when an instance of the **UserDocument** object has been loaded. |
| Scroll | Fired when the scroll box is repositioned, scrolled horizontally, or scrolled vertically on an instance of an ActiveX document sited within a container. |
| Show | Fired when the **UserDocument**'s **Visible** property changes to True. |
| WriteProperties | Fired when an instance of an ActiveX document object is saved. This event notifies the **UserDocument** object that the state of the object needs to be saved. This information is saved in the VBD file. |

# Primary UserDocument Events

The **UserDocument** is subject to several events that define its lifetime, much in the same way as ActiveX controls or standard **Form** objects. You can see the sequential ordering of the primary events in the life of a **UserDocument** object in Figure 7.6.

Understanding the use and meaning of the object events that help define the lifetime of the **UserDocument** object is fundamental in properly designing ActiveX document-based applications:

➤ **EnterFocus** This event fires whenever either the document or a constituent control receives focus.

➤ **ExitFocus** This event fires whenever neither the constituent controls nor the document itself have focus.

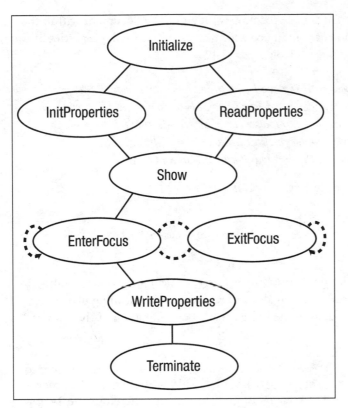

**Figure 7.6**   The key events in the lifetime of the **UserDocument** object help define the sequential behavior of the **UserDocument** object.

➤ **Initialize**  This event occurs each time a document (VBD) file is created by navigating to the appropriate VBD file. This is the first event that transpires in the lifetime of the document.

*Note: The **Initialize** event is a good location for code that should be run each time a document is created or re-created by loading the VBD file.*

➤ **InitProperties**  This event occurs after **Initialize**. The occurrence of this event is conditional on no properties having been saved by using the **PropertyBag** object. If state information has been saved by way of **PropertyBag**, this event is replaced by the **ReadProperties** event, listed next.

➤ **ReadProperties**  If the **PropertyBag** object has been used to save and persist document property values, the **ReadProperties** event will replace the **InitProperties** event in the life of the ActiveX document.

➤ **Show** This event signals the process of siting the document within the ActiveX document container. Once this event has fired, properties of the document become available.

*Note: The **Show** event is a good way to check for global variable object references, such as a globally defined variable set to reference a previously visited document. For example, a global object reference can be made to the previously visited document from within the **Click** event of a command button on the previous document, as seen here:*

```
Private Sub cmdGoNext_Click()
    Set gPrevious = Me
    HyperLink.NavigateTo _
        "http://www.go-chiefs.com/UserDocument2.vbd"
End Sub
```

➤ **Terminate** This event fires just before the document is completely destroyed. **Terminate** provides a good location for cleaning up object references no longer needed because of the termination of the current document.

Internet Explorer versions 3.x and 4.x behave differently. Due to the caching behavior of Internet Explorer 3.x, ActiveX documents are subject to a cache of four documents. Therefore, the **Terminate** event does not fire until a fifth document, page, or unique URL is loaded. Internet Explorer 4.x does not cache documents in the same manner, therefore the **Terminate** event is fired immediately upon navigating away from an ActiveX document. Beware of this behavior when deciding the nature of the code to implement within the **Terminate** event.

➤ **WriteProperties** If a property has been changed during the life of the document, this event will fire. This event firing is usually the result of the **PropertyChanged** statement having been performed. This notifies the container that one or more properties have changed, resulting in the **WriteProperties** event being fired.

The **WriteProperties** event is the appropriate event in which to use the **ProjectBag** object to save state information, as shown here:

```
Private Sub UserDocument_WriteProperties (PropBag As _
    VB.PropertyBag)
    UserDocument.WriteProperty "DocCaption", Text1.Text, _
        "Page One"
End Sub
```

> Using a globally defined variable that is declared as public within a code module added to an ActiveX document project can provide an excellent mechanism for sharing information between **UserDocument** objects. Setting the variable prior to using the **NavigateTo** method of the **HyperLink** object will make the information available to additional **UserDocument** objects provided by the project.

# Using The HyperLink Object

ActiveX document solutions rarely contain only one **UserDocument** object. With this being the case, the resulting VBD files require a convenient method to move back and forth between documents. ActiveX controls and documents have a built-in object known as the **HyperLink** object that provides basic hyperlink functionality. **HyperLink** functionality requires that the ActiveX document be sited within a hyperlink-aware document container, such as Microsoft Internet Explorer.

The **HyperLink** object contains no properties or events, and provides only three methods, as shown in Table 7.2. Despite having such limited programmability features, the **HyperLink** object provides a very important navigational capability to ActiveX documents. Without such functionality, almost all ActiveX document solutions would be single document projects.

Use of any of the provided **HyperLink** methods requires that the container support OLE hyperlinking. If the document container in use does not support OLE hyperlinking, an error will occur.

The **GoBack** and **GoForward** methods are useful for dictating user movement through a distinct series of documents that represent a multistep user process. The **NavigateTo** method is the primary method used to freely navigate between desired ActiveX documents. The syntax for the **NavigateTo** method is as follows:

```
object.NavigateTo Target [, Location [, FrameName]]
```

| Table 7.2    Methods available for the HyperLink object. | |
| --- | --- |
| **Method Name** | **Description** |
| GoBack | Executes a hyperlink jump to a location back in the history list. |
| GoForward | Executes a hyperlink jump to a location forward in the history list. |
| NavigateTo | Executes a hyperlink jump to a provided location. |

Assigning a value to the *Target* parameter requires that either the intended target document or URL be in the same location as the current document initiating the **HyperLink** object method invocation, or that the target parameter include the full URL path, including the appropriate protocol identification:

```
Private Sub cmdGoToMS_Click()
    Hyperlink.NavigateTo "http://www.microsoft.com"
End Sub
```

# Creating The User Interface

You create the user interface for an ActiveX document using the same steps identified in Chapter 6. By simply adding constituent controls from the toolbox and placing them on the face of the **UserDocument** object, you can perform precise placement of the user interface element just with **Form** and **UserControl** objects. You add code to the controls placed on the **UserDocument** in the same way as for **Form** and **UserControl** objects. Add the code to the appropriate events for the constituent controls via the standard code editor window.

One primary difference between creating the user interface for an ActiveX document and creating the user interface for other ActiveX components, such as controls, lies in the availability of menu items. ActiveX documents can utilize the Menu Editor to assign menus to the **UserDocument**, as seen in Figure 7.7.

When adding menus to a **UserDocument** object, the visual behavior of the menus differs within the design environment from menus added to a standard

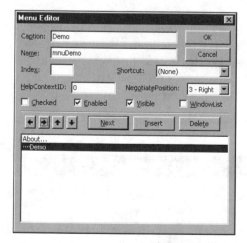

**Figure 7.7**   You can use the Menu Editor to create **UserDocument** menu items that will merge with document container menus.

**Form** object. A standard **Form** object has a full window border as a portion of the object's visual interface, but **UserDocument** objects do not, so after using the Menu Editor, no immediate visual element is generated within the design environment, as seen in Figure 7.8.

Although the menus added to a **UserDocument** object are not visually represented within the appropriate **UserDocument** designer, a look at the Code Editor will reveal that the appropriate menu objects and events are available for coding, as seen in Figure 7.9.

Adding code to menu items provided by the ActiveX document can provide some additional functionality to that provided by the host container, as seen in Figure 7.10.

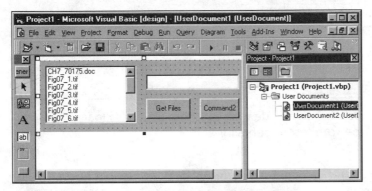

**Figure 7.8**    Menus added to a **UserDocument** object by the Menu Editor are not visually revealed within the design environment.

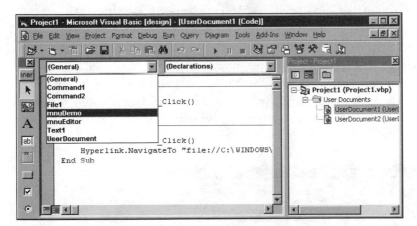

**Figure 7.9**    Although menus are not visually identifiable when added to **UserDocument** objects, you can add code for them in the Code Editor.

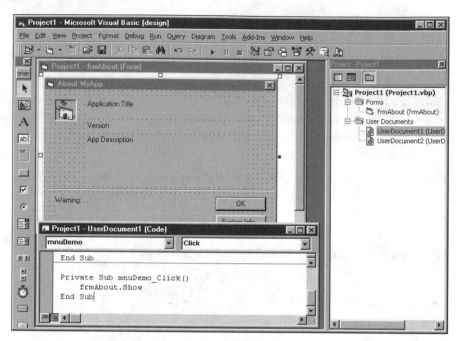

**Figure 7.10** You can add code to menu item events to load forms and perform other behaviors.

 Adding at least one menu item that can load a simple "About" form can provide a way for users of your ActiveX document to read basic information about your document or application. The position of this menu, as well as the document container menus, will be negotiated and placed based on the **NegotiatePosition** value chosen when creating the menu.

Part of the process of creating a menu for a **UserDocument** requires setting the **NegotiatePosition** value. If the **NegotiatePosition** setting is left to the default value of **None**, the menu will not be aligned with the existing menus of the document container. Any other value chosen will cause the menu to be integrated with the existing menus, as seen in Figure 7.11.

**Figure 7.11** **UserDocument** menus integrate with existing document container menus.

# Exposing Document Properties

After completing the user interface design, the **UserDocument** should have the necessary properties, methods, or events added to the **UserDocument** object. The procedures to create this public code interface are identical to that of the **UserControl** object, as described in Chapter 6. The following issues, true of **UserControl** objects, are also true concerning creating the public members or interface of the **UserDocument**:

➤ Methods, properties, and events of constituent controls are not automatically exposed to users or containers of the **UserDocument** object.

➤ Use of the Tools|Add Procedure menu option is available while using the Code Editor.

➤ All subs or functions declared as public become methods.

➤ Creating a public property requires adding a **Get** or **Let** procedure, either manually or through the Add Procedure dialog.

Adding a **Get** procedure without a corresponding **Let** or **Set** procedure will add a public property for the **UserDocument** object that is read-only.

# Persisting Document Properties

Quite often, the user of your document will come back to your document at a later time, possibly wanting to return the document to a previous state. Also, because Internet Explorer is the most common form of ActiveX document container, it is quite possible that a document might be added to the Favorites list. Returning to a document that is part of a series of steps in a process, each represented by a different document, may also require that the state of the document be preserved. You can provide persistent storage of this nature by using the **PropertyBag** object, in the same way you use it to preserve persistent state for ActiveX controls.

Use of the **PropertyBag** object is normally confined to the **ReadProperties** and **WriteProperties** events. In order for the **ReadProperties** event to fire in place of **InitProperties**, you must invoke the **PropertyChanged** method, as seen in Listing 7.1, passing it the name of a properly defined property that has changed. This method notifies the document container to fire the **WriteProperties** event, in which the **WriteProperty** method of the **PropertyBag** object should be used. In the case of ActiveX documents, this data is stored in the VBD file.

### Listing 7.1    Saving persistent property values.

```
Private Sub Text1_Change()
    PropertyChanged "Location"
End Sub

Private Sub UserDocument_ReadProperties(PropBag As PropertyBag)
    Text1.Text = PropBag.ReadProperty("Location")
End Sub

Private Sub UserDocument_WriteProperties(PropBag As PropertyBag)
    Call PropBag.WriteProperty("Location", Text1.Text)
End Sub

Public Property Get Location() As Variant
    Location = Text1.Text
End Property

Public Property Let Location(ByVal vNewValue As Variant)
    Text1.Text = vNewValue
End Property
```

# Testing And Debugging

Testing an ActiveX document requires a slightly different approach than testing an ActiveX control. The document container for the ActiveX document acts as the client application, as opposed to the use of a Standard EXE project to test an ActiveX control. This requires that you load the VBD file into the document container in order to initiate debugging.

When running an ActiveX document project from Visual Basic, a VBD file is automatically generated for each **UserDocument** object that exists in the project. This VBD file is placed in the same location as where the project is saved. The steps for testing can be performed in a number of ways, with the primary steps shown here:

1. Start the project from within Visual Basic.

2. Start the appropriate ActiveX document container, usually Internet Explorer.

3. Load the temporary VBD file into the document container.

4. Use the document as designed, switching back to Visual Basic as necessary to manually invoke Break mode and so forth.

The recommended way to invoke Internet Explorer for purposes of debugging an ActiveX document is as follows:

1. Start the project by using the F5 key. This generates a VBD file in the project directory, if one does not already exist.

2. If this is the first time debugging the project, the Project Properties dialog box will appear. Choose Start Browser With URL and enter the file location of the VBD file.

3. Internet Explorer will automatically start, loading the VBD file.

4. Use any of the standard debugging tools, such as Ctrl+Break, to enter Break mode; or, use the **STOP** command to debug the project while it is being hosted within Internet Explorer.

Although the standard method of debugging the project involves invoking the document container (Internet Explorer) from Visual Basic, including the automatic loading of the target document into the container, any procedure that involves running the project, starting the container, and loading the file will suffice.

An alternative to the preceding steps might involve starting the project and then dragging the VBD file into an existing instance of Internet Explorer that is already running. This will provide the same result and also allows for the use of multiple test document containers at the same time.

Debugging an ActiveX document project can utilize all the same tools that a Standard EXE project has at its disposal, including watch variables, setting breakpoints, using the **Debug** object, and so on. In the event that a runtime error occurs, Visual Basic will stop on the offending line. The difficult issue in debugging ActiveX documents is that a separate, compiled binary executable is used as the client, as opposed to an added Standard EXE project, which runs within the same Visual Basic design environment. This induces some additional logistical issues, plus the occasional need to press Alt+Tab to move between the client and Visual Basic applications. Fortunately, though, the vast array of debugging tools provided by Visual Basic helps avoid significant difficulties.

# Practice Questions

## Question 1

> The **HyperLink** object is provided automatically as a part of the **UserDocument** base class object. The **HyperLink** object, although available, does not become accessible until what activity or process occurs?
>
> ○ a.  The ActiveX document container is loaded into memory.
>
> ○ b.  The ActiveX document container fires the **Show** event of the **UserDocument** class object.
>
> ○ c.  The **HyperLink** object's **Initialize** event is fired.
>
> ○ d.  The **UserDocument**'s **GetFocus** event is fired.
>
> ○ e.  The ActiveX document is sited in the ActiveX document container.

The correct answer is e. The **HyperLink** object is part of the **UserDocument** class object, although it does not actually become accessible until the object is sited by loading into the ActiveX document container. Specifically, siting by a hyperlink-aware ActiveX document container is required.

Simply loading the intended ActiveX document container into the memory of the client is insufficient to make the **HyperLink** object accessible, because the **HyperLink** object requires an ActiveX component to provide a framework or source from which the **HyperLink** object will navigate. Therefore, answer a is incorrect. The **HyperLink** object is already available by the time the **Show** or **GetFocus** events are fired. Therefore answers b and d would not be correct. The **Initialize** event of the **HyperLink** object is available after the **HyperLink** is technically first available, due to the fact that an event handler for an object is not fired until the parent object for which the event is fired exists. For this reason, answer c is also incorrect.

## Question 2

> ActiveX document projects, upon successful compilation, will by default include several different files that are needed for successful siting in an ActiveX document container. These files will include which of the following? [Check all that apply]
>
> ❑ a. An EXE or DLL file matching the name of each **UserDocument** object that has been added to the ActiveX document project
>
> ❑ b. An EXE or DLL file matching the name of the ActiveX document project
>
> ❑ c. A VBD file matching the name of each **UserDocument** object that has been added to the ActiveX document project
>
> ❑ d. A DOB file matching the name of each **UserDocument** object that has been added to the ActiveX document project
>
> ❑ e. A DOX file matching the name of each **UserDocument** object that has been added to the ActiveX document project

The correct answers are b and c. After successfully compiling an ActiveX document project, Visual Basic will create either an EXE or a DLL file. An EXE is created when the type of Visual Basic project chosen is of the type ActiveX Document Exe project. This produces an out-of-process ActiveX document server application. When the project compiled is of the type ActiveX Document Dll, Visual Basic will compile an in-process ActiveX document server. Either the EXE or DLL files will be given the same name as the project name, by default, although you can alter this. In addition to the base document server, Visual Basic will create a file with a .VBD extension to match each of the **UserDocument** objects that exist within the project. Because b is correct, a is obviously incorrect.

Answers d and e are incorrect because DOB and DOX files are part of the ActiveX document project, but are not compiled files. They store the source code and binary elements of a **UserDocument** object until the project is ready to be compiled. These files provide the same function as the FRM and FRX files provide for the **Form** object in a standard application project.

## Question 3

> The data contained within a DOB file represents what type of information for an ActiveX document project? [Check all that apply]
>
> ❑ a. Persisted state information for the **PropertyBag** object
>
> ❑ b. OLE structured data for the document server
>
> ❑ c. Source and event code for the **UserDocument** object
>
> ❑ d. Binary information, such as graphic files, contained within the **UserDocument** object
>
> ❑ e. Property values for the **UserDocument** object

The correct answers are c and e. Visual Basic creates a DOB file for each **UserDocument** object added to a Visual Basic ActiveX document project. The DOB files function identically to the FRM files for the **Form** object by providing storage for the source code and properties configured and written for the **UserDocument** object.

State information persisted by the **PropertyBag** object is written to the compiled VBD file when while viewing the document from within an ActiveX document host container. Therefore, answer a is incorrect. Answer b is incorrect because the OLE structured data is contained with the compiled VBD file that the client loads into Internet Explorer. Finally, the binary information for a **UserDocument** object is stored in a DOX file, so answer d is incorrect.

## Question 4

> You decide to create a multidocument solution using ActiveX documents that will be loaded into Internet Explorer. You want to allow the user to navigate to the second document directly if so desired. What file should the URL request to provide this capability?
>
> ○ a. UserDocument2.dob
>
> ○ b. UserDocument2.vbd
>
> ○ c. UserDocument2.dox
>
> ○ d. UserDocument2.exe
>
> ○ e. UserDocument2.dll

The correct answer is b. Starting with Visual Basic 6, navigating directly to the compiled VBD file will properly invoke the appropriate ActiveX document server EXE or DLL. The necessary codebase and version attributes are now stored within the VBD file.

The DOB and DOX files are precompiled files that store **UserDocument** object code, properties, and binary elements, but are not part of the compiled, finished document, so answers a and e are therefore incorrect. Any EXE or DLL compiled files produced as a part of the compiled ActiveX document project provide the function of the document server, but are not directly loaded into the browser. Therefore answers d and e are incorrect.

# Question 5

You are in the middle of designing an ActiveX document solution that requires sharing information between documents. In order to provide a reference to methods and properties of one of the **UserDocument** objects after navigation to one of the remaining **UserDocument** objects, what steps must you take?

○ a. Use the **PropertyBag** object to store references to the desired properties and methods.

○ b. Define a global variable and set a reference to the current **UserDocument** prior to navigating to the next **UserDocument**.

○ c. Store the property values in public variables.

○ d. Save the current state of the **UserDocument** by saving the document in the **WriteProperties** event.

○ e. You cannot make an object reference for this purpose.

The correct answer is b. By creating and defining a global variable in the Declarations section of a code module added to an ActiveX document project, you can store information and make it available to subsequently navigated document files (by loading the appropriate VBD file). By setting an object reference to the current **UserDocument** object prior to navigating to other ActiveX documents, the properties and methods of the referenced object will be made available to any other document.

The **PropertyBag** object stores information for persistent storage purposes locally within the cached VBD file, thus this information would not be accessible directly from the next **UserDocument** object. So answer a is incorrect. Answer c is incorrect because storing information within public variables would not provide access to methods of the first **UserDocument** as desired. Saving the current state of the **UserDocument** object from within the **WriteProperties** event would entail use of the **PropertyBag** object, and would be used for persistent storage of state information. Therefore, answer d is incorrect. And if answer b is correct, then answer e is obviously incorrect.

# Question 6

ActiveX documents and ActiveX controls are similar in several ways. Being applications of ActiveX technology, these elements are similar for what reasons? [Check all that apply]

❑ a. A host container is required to instantiate the element.

❑ b. A public interface is provide to expose properties, events, and methods.

❑ c. To adhere to the Component Object Model industry open specification for component communication.

❑ d. To allow for menu item integration and negotiation with the hosting container.

❑ e. To fill the entire client viewing area provided by the hosting container.

The correct answers are a, b, and c. Both ActiveX documents and ActiveX controls require a hosting container for instantiation. By adhering to the Component Object Model (COM), ActiveX documents and ActiveX controls expose properties, methods, and events through a public interface, as stipulated by the COM specification.

Answer d is incorrect because ActiveX controls are not able to use or provide for menu bars. They are limited to the visual interface area defined by the **UserControl** object's default width and height properties or by the explicitly configured width and height property values altered at instantiation.

ActiveX documents are capable of expanding to fill the available Viewport, or client area, provided by the host container. This allows ActiveX documents to integrate and include menu item objects compiled into the document with those menu items provided by the host container. ActiveX controls do not fill the entire viewing area presented by the host container, hence answer e is incorrect.

# Question 7

> Examples of valid ActiveX document host containers include which
> of the following applications? [Check all that apply]
>
> ❑ a.  Visual Basic 5 IDE
>
> ❑ b.  Microsoft Office Binder
>
> ❑ c.  Internet Explorer 4.x
>
> ❑ d.  Internet Explorer 3.x
>
> ❑ e.  Visual Basic 6 IDE

The correct answers are a, b, c, d, and e. Internet Explorer 3.x and 4.x are capable of
hosting or siting ActiveX documents, although caching behavior can create some
functionality differences. Microsoft Office Binder is the original ActiveX document host container designed for siting one or more ActiveX documents. Visual
Basic versions 5 and 6 are both capable of acting as host containers for ActiveX
documents, as a means for expanding the design environment. Additional functionality is provided by ActiveX documents in the form of Visual Basic Add-Ins.

# Question 8

> Starting with Visual Basic 6, ActiveX documents are now capable
> of self-registration within Internet Explorer, when used as the host
> container for the ActiveX document. This ability is accomplished
> by what process?
>
> ○ a.  The **Initialize** event of the **UserDocument** object now
>       provides a call-back routine to provide the necessary
>       registration information.
>
> ○ b.  The **Initialize** event now includes a reference to the
>       parent object of the **UserDocument** object, allowing for
>       self-registration of the **UserDocument** object within the
>       host container.
>
> ○ c.  Starting with Visual Basic 6, ActiveX documents no
>       longer require registration with the hosting container.
>
> ○ d.  Visual Basic 6 compiled ActiveX documents are now
>       capable of including within the VBD file the same
>       **CODEBASE** and **VERSION** values previously provided
>       by an initializing HTML file through use of the
>       **<OBJECT>** tags.
>
> ○ e.  VBD files now provide the necessary registration
>       Information as a part of the HTTP request headers.

The correct answer is d. Starting with Visual Basic 6, compiled ActiveX documents now provide the same codebase and version information previously provided by an <**OBJECT**> tag embedded within an initialization or hosting HTML page. This provides the necessary registration information to register the ActiveX document server EXE or DLL file directly from the VBD file. This allows direct navigation to the VBD file.

The **Initialize** event doesn't initiate any call-back routines, nor is it passed any information regarding the host container or parent object that would allow for registration of the ActiveX document server for the VBD file on the client system. Therefore, answers a and b are incorrect. ActiveX documents do continue to require registration on the client system as ActiveX document servers (making answer c incorrect), yet this information is not provided in any way within the information passed through HTTP headers between the client and the server (making answer e incorrect).

# Need To Know More?

 For the most complete reference on creating controls, see the MSDN online help and search for the following: "What Is an ActiveX Document?," "Creating an ActiveX Document," and "Parts of an ActiveX Document."

 For a demo Mastering Series chapter entitled "Creating and Using ActiveX Documents," point your Web browser to **premium. microsoft.com/msdn/mastering/mvb510/**.

 To navigate to the online version of the MSDN Library section entitled "ActiveX Document Creation Basics," go to **premium. microsoft.com/msdn/library/** and search for "ActiveX Document Creation Basics."

# Creating Business Services

**8**

## Terms you'll need to understand:

- ✓ COM DLL and COM EXE
- ✓ **Property Get**, **Set**, and **Let**
- ✓ **Instancing** property
- ✓ **ObjectContext** object
- ✓ **GetObjectContext** method
- ✓ **IsCallerInRole** method
- ✓ **IsSecurityEnabled** method
- ✓ Declarative security
- ✓ Programmatic security
- ✓ **MTSTransaction** property
- ✓ **SetAbort** and **SetComplete** methods
- ✓ **EnableCommit** and **DisableCommit** methods
- ✓ Version, Binary, and Project compatibility

## Techniques you'll need to master:

- ✓ Creating component properties and methods
- ✓ Creating a read-only property
- ✓ Designing an object model
- ✓ Setting the **Instancing** property
- ✓ Registering and unregistering a component
- ✓ Using the **GetObjectContext** function
- ✓ Configuring transactional behavior of a component
- ✓ Creating MTS packages
- ✓ Importing and exporting packages
- ✓ Installing components into a package
- ✓ Creating and applying roles to packages
- ✓ Assigning accounts and groups to roles

The middle layer of the Microsoft Solutions Framework Application Model is generally referred to as the *business services layer*. Within this layer, the business rules and logic that provide the competitive advantages of the business are encapsulated within COM components, generally running within the MTS environment. Just like in an Oreo cookie, the good stuff—in this case the COM components—is sandwiched in the middle tier, providing the precious business rules that govern how raw market data is processed and made available to the user interface.

Within this chapter, we will be taking a look at creating COM components, using Microsoft Transaction Server, and numerous settings, configurations, and programming concerns relating to the use of business COM objects within the MTS environment.

# Compiling Projects With Class Modules Into COM Components

When we start to talk about encapsulating business services into components, we are naturally talking about COM components. To create a COM component, you must start with a Visual Basic ActiveX DLL or EXE project, as seen in Figure 8.1. Because the bulk of this chapter relates to COM components running within MTS, which inherently require the components to be contained

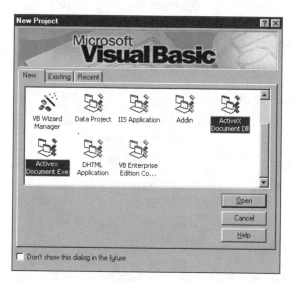

**Figure 8.1**   Also known as COM DLLs or EXEs, ActiveX DLL and EXE projects in Visual Basic 6 are used to create COM components for use in client applications.

within in-process servers or ActiveX DLLs, I will refer entirely to the use of the Visual Basic ActiveX DLL project.

Starting up an ActiveX DLL project will provide one initial class module. Class modules are used as the foundation or starting point for creating COM components. Class modules can be used in many other types of Visual Basic projects, but when used in ActiveX DLL or EXE projects, they provide templates for creating new objects. These objects can have customized properties and methods that are publicly available for any instance of the object. Within an ActiveX DLL project, each class module equates to a single object that is subsequently available for instantiation. For example, as seen in Figure 8.2, an ActiveX DLL project can contain as many class modules as desired. Five separate modules, such as INews, IDocLibrary, and IFaq, will provide—after successful compilation into a DLL—five completely separate objects for use in your code.

Code written within the class modules is used to implement the custom properties, events, and methods of the custom objects. Once all the desired properties and methods are created, use of the **New** keyword within client code allows instances of the object to be created. If the ActiveX DLL project is compiled, then the resulting DLL contains the COM components that are subsequently available upon successful installation of the DLL onto a target system. After successfully compiling an ActiveX DLL project into a COM DLL, referencing this DLL from within another Visual Basic project allows the use of the **New** keyword to instantiate any of the included objects, as seen in the Visual Basic auto-complete feature shown in Figure 8.3.

Because class modules allow the creation of custom objects or COM components, including properties and methods, any desired attributes must be properly provided for within code by creating the supporting **Property** and **Sub** functions.

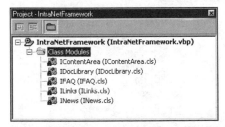

**Figure 8.2**    Visual Basic ActiveX DLL projects can contain numerous class modules, each representing an individual object that can be instantiated.

**Figure 8.3** The Visual Basic auto-complete feature reveals the available properties and methods within the class module.

# Creating A Public Object Property

Establishing a public property for a class module can provide numerous benefits. Every instance of the object that is instantiated will include this property. Setting this property can provide a method of information storage for details about the object that are pertinent to the life of that particular instance of the object. Creating a public property starts with declaring a module-level public variable in the Declarations section of the class module, as seen in Figure 8.4.

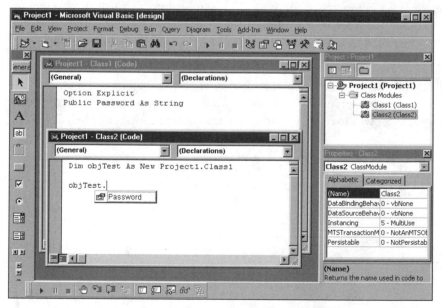

**Figure 8.4** Adding a property to an object begins with declaring a module-level variable of the desired property name.

Notice that in the second class module added to the project in Figure 8.4, dimensioning a variable, **objTest,** as a new instance of the **Class1** object allows the Visual Basic auto-complete feature to immediately recognize the available public property named **Password.** If the Object Browser is immediately opened from within the same project, viewing the details of Project1 reveals the two available objects, **Class1** and **Class2,** and the defined properties and methods of the selected object **Class1,** as seen in Figure 8.5. Notice that the detailed information at the bottom of the Object Browser shows the exact same variable declaration command that was added to the Declarations section of the **Class1** class module.

One particular difficulty arises in defining custom properties by simply declaring module-level public variables: Property value validation cannot be performed. For this reason, a different approach is typically taken. The variable declared to hold the property value is declared as private, thereby preserving its value from access by direct object instantiation. In order to allow retrieval and modification of the property value stored within this private variable, Visual Basic provides several special **Property** functions, as seen in Listing 8.1.

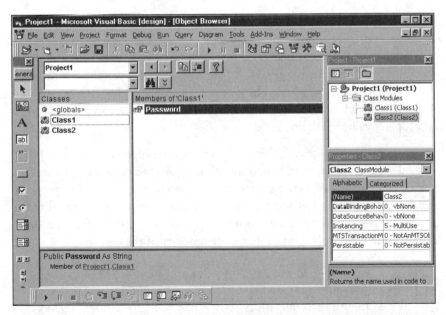

**Figure 8.5**    Using the Object Browser can reveal the available properties and methods of the selected object.

## Listing 8.1 Property procedures are used to retrieve and modify public properties.

```
' Internal private variable storage for property value.
Private mstrPassword As String

Public Property Get Password() As String
    Password  = mstrPassword
End Property

Public Property Let Password (ByVal NewValue As String)
  ' Insert code to validate property value here!
    mstrPassword = NewValue
End Property
```

Property procedures are public by default within Visual Basic, therefore the declaration of **Public** may be omitted without negative consequences. It is highly recommended to retain the explicit **Public** declaration to avoid confusion. Declaring property procedures **Private** is also acceptable, although doing so will render the variable inaccessible for read/write procedures.

Property procedures are a cross between functions and events. For example, whenever an attempt is made to retrieve a property value, the appropriate **Property Get** procedure is automatically fired, like an event would fire, with the procedure being assigned the value of the local private variable storing the actual property value, as selected in Listing 8.1. Whenever a variable is being set, the **Property Let** procedure is fired. This would be the correct location to add property value validation code.

Special property types that reference objects as the property value type being returned use the **Set** keyword to accomplish the object reference assignment. In these situations, the **Property Set** procedure is used in place of the **Let** property procedure. Because the **Let** and **Set** property procedures are used to modify the values of properties, not providing either, as appropriate for the defined property data type, will effectively create a read-only property of the object.

Providing a combination of a **Get** and a **Let** or **Set** property procedure will create a read/write public property. In order to create a read-only property, it is necessary to remove any **Let** or **Set** property procedures that may exist.

## Setting The Instancing Of A Class Module

In order to restrict the instancing abilities and behavior of class modules, Visual Basic provides an **Instancing** property for controlling the availability of the class module for use by other applications. The **Instancing** property dictates whether instances of the class can be created by other applications. This property is used to determine whether a class module is available for public instantiation or for use solely by internal, private code modules. The **Instancing** property is also used to determine what part objects play within a given component's object model. The **Instancing** property provides six possible settings:

➤ Private

➤ PublicNotCreatable

➤ MultiUse

➤ GlobalMultiUse

➤ SingleUse

➤ GlobalSingleUse

## Private

If marked as **Private**, client applications are unable to create instances of the class and type library information for the class is inaccessible to them. **Private** class modules are used only internally within the component and cannot be seen by outside applications. This setting defines an internally creatable object only.

## PublicNotCreatable

Outside applications can use instances of this class, but can't create new instances on their own. Instances of this class can only be created internally by the component and can't be created externally by using either the **CreateObject** method or the **New** keyword. Objects of this class are commonly referred to as *dependent objects* and are typically parts of more complex objects. This setting defines an internally creatable object only.

## MultiUse

**MultiUse** allows any number of objects or instances of this class to be created by other applications from one instance of the component. If the objects are provided by an out-of-process component, then multiple objects can be provided by multiple clients. If an in-process component is the source, then multiple instances can be generated to the client and any components within the same process. Properties and methods of instances of the classes can only be invoked if an instance of the class is explicitly created.

Classes provided by ActiveX EXE components marked for unattended execution should have their **Instancing** property set to **MultiUse** to allow separate threads (multithreading) to be used by each instance.

### GlobalMultiUse

Instancing behavior of the **GlobalMultiUse** class behaves exactly as if set to **MultiUse**, except that explicit creation of instances is not required to invoke class methods and properties. In other words, class methods and properties are treated as if they were global in scope. Invoking a class method will automatically instantiate an instance of the class.

### SingleUse

**SingleUse** can only be used with out-of-process COM components. This setting allows other applications to create instances of this class, but each object instance will create a new instance of the component in memory.

### GlobalSingleUse

Also allowed only with out-of-process COM components, **GlobalSingleUse** results in the creation of a new component instance for each object instance being created by other applications. Explicit creation of class instances is not required for invoking class methods and properties.

## Implementing An Object Model Within A COM Component

Programming with objects instantiated from class modules would be somewhat limiting to the programmer if relationships, collections, or object hierarchies could not also be developed with our components. The concept of an *object model* provides for containment of objects within other objects. This expands the capabilities of the programmer in some valuable directions; it also provides a mechanism for dealing with the development of extremely complex objects, allowing for the creation of a simpler and more easily manageable object structure and layout.

Object models help define hierarchies of objects that represent the relationships between related objects within a complex object-based application or component. Object models consist of parent and dependent objects, object collections, and internal private objects, and they are used to define containment between objects.

Establishing an object model focuses on the creation of object properties that link objects together by returning references to objects. When objects contain other objects, properties of the parent object are used to reference the dependent objects or object collections. You can see an example of an object model in Figure 8.6. Consider a component that consists of a publicly creatable **House**

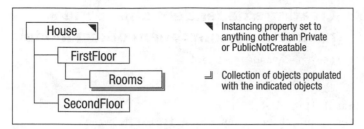

**Figure 8.6**    An object model typically consists of one or more dependent objects or collections of objects.

object. This object contains two dependent objects, **FirstFloor** and **SecondFloor**. The **FirstFloor** object, in turn, contains a dependent collection of **Room** objects known as **Rooms**.

 To ensure that a private property referencing a dependent object used internally by a component does not appear in the objects type library, follow these two steps:

➤ Set the dependent object **Instancing** property to **Private**.

➤ Declare the **Referencing** property as **Friend**.

Creating a dependent object within a desired object model involves a number of steps that ensure undesired actions can't be performed on the dependent object and that the proper relationship is supported. These steps include:

1. Create the dependent class module, using an **Instancing** property setting of **PublicNotCreatable**.

2. Declare a private module-level variable to serve as internal object reference to the dependent object.

3. Provide a single **Get** property procedure to allow referencing ability to the dependent object by the client.

4. Instantiate the dependent object within the **Initialize** event of the parent object class.

You can see the latter three steps implemented in Listing 8.2. A private module-level variable, **mFirstFloor**, is created and set as an object reference to an instance of the **FirstFloor PublicNotCreatable** class module. This reference is set within the **Class_Initialize** event within the **House** class module. Finally, a **Get** procedure allows read-only access to this dependent object.

## Listing 8.2 Creating a dependent object and rudimentary component object model.

```
'Allows for referencing dependent object
Private mFirstFloor As FirstFloor

Private Sub Class_Initialize()
' Instantiate dependent object when House is initialized.
    Set mFirstFloor = New FirstFloor
End Sub

Public Property Get FirstFloor () As FirstFloor
    Set FirstFloor = mFirstFloor
End Property
```

Sometimes the relationships desired within the object model under construction include an indefinite number of dependent objects of an identical class. In order to implement this one-to-many relationship, you must use a collection object. Implementing a collection class requires the use of three different class modules; these three classes can be generally categorized as:

➤ **Collection element class** Implemented as the **Rooms** class module.

➤ **Collection class** Implemented as the **Rooms** class module.

➤ **Collection parent class** Implemented as the **FirstFloor** class module.

The collection element class, implemented as the **Rooms** class module in Figure 8.6, is the simplest in terms of designing and coding the class module. This module can be coded with whatever properties or methods you wish. In order to behave properly as a part of the object module, the **Instancing** property must be set to **PublicNotCreatable**. This prevents applications from explicitly creating new or accessing existing instances of this class. In order to allow instances of this class module to be added as members of the parent collection, an **Add** method must be added to the collection class module. This allows new collection members to be added, but within the confines of the application rules defined within the **Add** function.

Creating a collection class module involves four minimal steps, in order to provide the necessary ability to add new objects to the collection. After setting the **Instancing** property to **PublicNotCreatable**, you must perform the following code activities:

1. Declare a private, module-level variable as a **Collection** object type.

2. Instantiate the private, module-level variable as a new **Collection** object in the **Class_Initialize** event of the collection class module.

3. Cascade the standard properties and methods of the **Collection** object as properties and methods of the collection class module being created.

4. Create a public **Add** function to allow applications to instantiate new collection element objects, invoke the standard **Add** method of the **Collection** object with the new object instance, and return the newly instantiated object to the calling application for use in setting an object reference to the new collection member.

Additionally, it is suggested that you add the necessary methods to the collection class module to allow access to this internal collection object. The steps we just outlined are implemented in Listing 8.3 for the object module shown in Figure 8.6.

## Listing 8.3    Using a read-only property and instance of a PublicNotCreatable class module.

```
' Place this declaration in the General Declarations section
Private mcolRooms As Collection

' This event is found in the Rooms class module
Private Sub Class_Initialize()
     Set mcolRooms = New Collection
End Sub

Public Function Add(ByVal Color As String, _
                    ByVal SquareFeet As Integer)

    Dim rmAddition As New Room

    ' Assigned the pass parameters to the Room object properties
    rmAddition.Color = Color
    rmAddition.SquareFeet = SquareFeet

    ' Use the standard collection object Add method to implement the
    ' actual adding of the new collection member
    mcolRooms.Add rmAddition

    ' Return the new Room object for future object reference
    Set Add = rmAddition

End Function
```

After creating the collection element and collection class modules, the final class module to create is the class that will act as the parent of the collection. In our example, this is fulfilled by the **FirstFloor** class module. The **Instancing** property of the **FirstFloor** class should be set to **MultiUse**. This allows any application to create explicit instances of the **FirstFloor** object. If the **FirstFloor** object is to remain a fully dependent object within the object model being constructed, it is possible that setting the **Instancing** property to **PublicNotCreatable** would be preferred. The primary distinction is that when linking objects where the number of dependent objects of a particular class is unknown, the linkage must be supported by creating a collection class module. This collection class serves as the dynamic object linkage between the externally creatable collection parent class and the collection element class instances. The final act of making the dependent collection class available to the application or external clients involves creating a private module-level variable and a **Property Get** procedure, as seen in Listing 8.4.

## Listing 8.4   A private variable and Property Get link the collection parent class to the dependent collection class.

```
' Create a private variable to store the Rooms collection object
' Found in the Declarations section
Private mRooms As New Rooms

' This event is found in the FirstFloor class module
Public Property Get Rooms() As Rooms
     Set Rooms = mRooms
End Property
```

By providing a reference to the **Rooms** dependent object only through a **Property Get** procedure, the object is protected. An object reference to new members of the collection can be made by setting a variable reference to the results of the collection's exposed **Add** method, as seen in Listing 8.5.

## Listing 8.5   The Add method is used to create new collection members.

```
Dim fFlr as FirstFloor
Dim Bedroom as Room

' FirstFloor can be created if it is set to MultiUse
Set fFlr = New FirstFloor

Set Bedroom = fFlr.Rooms.Add Color:="Blue", SquareFeet:=420
```

In Listing 8.5, the only way to instantiate a new **Room** object as a member of the **Rooms** collection is to invoke the exposed **Add** method of the **Rooms** collection. The **Rooms** collection is generated on demand within the **FirstFloor** object by implicitly invoking the **Property Get** procedure when accessing the **Rooms** property.

Concerning the naming of the collection parent object, if several instances of the collection parent class are to be created, then a generic class module name may be chosen, such as **Floor**. The **FirstFloor** and **SecondFloor** objects can then be created as read-only properties of the root object **House**. The resulting **Property Get** procedures would then expose, as read-only, two instances of the **Floor** class as the property object type. This would allow multiple instances of the same dependent object type.

 The key issues to remember in creating an object model are summarized in the following list:

➤ The value of the **Instancing** property controls the object linking limitations.

➤ All dependent objects should be set to **PublicNotCreatable**.

➤ Parent dependent objects should be set up as read-only (**Property Get**).

# Registering And Unregistering A COM Component

Once a component has been compiled, you need to ensure that the component is properly registered on a client system before it can be utilized. Registration of a COM component refers to ensuring that the information needed for locating the component DLL or EXE when an object is created can be found in the system Registry. Visual Basic provides several methods for registering components:

➤ Auto-registration by executing a setup program generated through the Package and Deployment Wizard

➤ Registration by the Visual Basic IDE on the system used to create the component

➤ Use of the command-line utility RegSvr32

Sometimes it is necessary to use the command-line registration utility RegSvr32 to manually register a component on a system. This adds the necessary entries into the system Registry to map ProgIds—used to reference or create objects in code—to class IDs, which are mapped in turn to the physical location of the component file. RegSrv32 can also be used to unregister a component from a system to assist in testing solutions by creating a clean system relative to the component. Passing the name of a DLL to RegSvr32 will register any

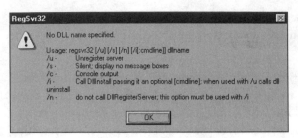

**Figure 8.7** Providing no parameters generates a standard dialog box listing possible parameters.

components contained within the DLL onto the system. You can use the /u parameter to unregister a component from a system; however, using no parameters generates a list of possible parameters, as shown in Figure 8.7.

 For development systems, where registering DLLs and ActiveX controls is a common occurrence, placing a shortcut to regsvr32.exe in your SendTo folder can provide a convenient tool. This allows fast registration by right-clicking and choosing to register from the SendTo option.

# Choosing Threading Models

Choosing the threading model for a COM component can have drastic results on the capabilities, behavior, and performance of the component. Starting with Visual Basic Service Pack 2, and now continuing with Visual Basic 6, applications and components can be set to use the apartment model for thread allocations to component code execution. The apartment model for thread allocation provides a form of thread safety, allowing individual threads of execution to work entirely within the apartment and maintain separation from any other threads or objects created inside a separate apartment.

Setting the threading model within a Visual Basic 6 ActiveX DLL or Control project is performed by opening the Project Properties dialog box, which provides Threading Model options, as shown in Figure 8.8. The general options are Apartment Threaded and Single Threaded. Within Visual Basic 6, even single-threaded projects or components are actually configured as apartment-threaded, with the number of apartments used limited to one.

When an ActiveX DLL or in-process COM component is created and configured as apartment-threaded, the threads that are created to define the apartment belong to or are defined by the client application calling or using the in-process component. Out-of-process components, or ActiveX EXEs,

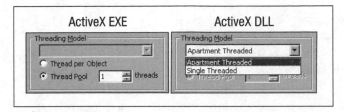

**Figure 8.8**    Threading Model options for ActiveX projects.

initiate their own threads, thus the Threading Model settings differ somewhat. As seen in Figure 8.8, COM EXEs provide the ability to decide if one thread is created for each and every externally created object (Thread Per Object) or whether a pool of threads is used to service the component (Thread Pool). Choosing Thread Per Object and leaving the number of threads set to one creates a single-threaded component; setting the value higher than one results in an apartment-threaded project. When Thread Per Object or Thread Pool is set to greater than one thread for an ActiveX EXE project, only externally created objects are created on new threads.

Implementation of apartment-model threading within Visual Basic provides numerous and distinct thread execution behaviors, such as:

➤ Each thread defines a separate apartment.

➤ Object instances can only be accessed on the threads where they were originally created.

➤ Dependent objects share the same apartment as the object that created them.

➤ A copy of all global data is maintained for each of the apartments.

 Starting with Visual Basic 6, applications no longer need to be marked for unattended execution or to suppress visual elements in order to leverage apartment threading.

Although apartment threading can provide numerous benefits for certain types of applications, a project configured as apartment-threaded does endure certain limitations:

➤ MDI forms are not allowed in apartment-threaded projects due to the nature of the data sharing that must occur between MDI parent and child forms.

➤ Visual Basic does not allow single-threaded ActiveX controls to be added to projects where the Threading Model is set to Apartment Threaded.

Apartment-threaded applications can be made to allow single-threaded controls by manually editing the VBP file. Take great care before attempting to perform this step to avoid unpredictable execution results.

➤ Component properties and methods defined as **Friend** can only be called by objects on the same thread.

➤ Forms shown with **vbModal** are only modal to code and forms on the same threads. Any forms shown by code from other threads will still be active and code running within other threads will not be blocked.

➤ Standard drag and drop between forms and controls will only work if they are running within the same thread. OLE drag and drop is unaffected.

# Designing MTS-Enabled COM Components

The ability to create COM components that run in the middle or business services tier has existed prior to Visual Basic 6. In Visual Basic 5, COM components, including ActiveX DLL (in-process) or EXE (out-of-process) projects, could be compiled. The ability to create these components and encapsulate business rules and logic for reuse within a middle tier of the basic three-tier architecture has been extended to include designing components that can run within the runtime component infrastructure provided by Microsoft Transaction Server (MTS). MTS-enabled components require certain programming considerations to provide the necessary hooks to communicate with the MTS services. These programming hooks allow a business component to notify the MTS runtime of the status of the component's code execution. The business components participate in the programming model provided by MTS by utilizing public objects made available to the component project through referencing the MTS object type library found in MTXAS.DLL, and by using the new **MTSTransactionMode** property of VB6 class modules.

Because MTS is a transaction-processing, component-based runtime environment, understanding the basic transactional concepts is important in understanding the coding considerations required to design an MTS-enabled COM component. In order to support execution within the MTS runtime environment, certain considerations must be implemented:

➤ COM components must be in-process components (ActiveX DLLs).

➤ A project reference to the MTS object type library must be made.

➤ Components should be designed as stateless. No public properties should be coded for the component.

 Designing components for execution within the MTS runtime environment inherently requires that the component run as in-process. In order to participate within the runtime environment of MTS, the component must be written as an ActiveX DLL. Thread creation for an in-process component is handled by the client application; therefore, only in-process ActiveX DLL components will allow the MTS service, acting as the client, to provide the thread management services of MTS.

## Using The ObjectContext Object To Participate In Transactions

MTS provides an API, **GetObjectContext**, and an interface, IObjectContext, for use in designing MTS-enabled components. Because MTS maintains a transactional context reference point for managing communication between objects participating in a given transaction, a component must have a reference point to this transactional context. This reference point is provided by the **GetObjectContext** method and the **ObjectContext** object, as seen in Listing 8.6.

### Listing 8.6 Using ObjectContext and GetObjectContext to enlist a component in an MTS transaction.

```
Public Function Validate (ByVal LenderID As String, _
    ByVal UserName As String, ByVal Password As String) As Boolean

On Error GoTo ValidateError:

Dim adoConn As New ADODB.Connection
Dim adoRS As New ADODB.Recordset
Dim adoCmd As New ADODB.Command
Dim adoSQL As String

    'Obtain the MTX Context Object
Dim objContext As ObjectContext
Set objContext = GetObjectContext()

If Trim$(LenderID) = "" Then
    If Not objContext Is Nothing Then
        objContext.SetAbort
    End If
```

```
    Err.Raise Number:=Err.Number, _
            Source:="LenderWeb.User(Validate)", _
            Description:="This was a test abort. Not a real error!"
    Exit Function
End If


adoConn.Open "DSN=OSTCWeb;UID=LenderWeb;PWD=concept"
adoCmd.ActiveConnection = adoConn

adoSQL = "Select UserName from Login Where LenderDB = '" & _
        LenderID & "' AND UserName = '"& UserName & _
        "' AND Password = '" & Password & "'"

adoCmd.CommandType = adCmdText
adoCmd.CommandText = adoSQL
Set adoRS = adoCmd.Execute

If adoRS.EOF And adoRS.BOF Then
    Validate = False
Else
    Validate = True
End If

   'Indicate to the MTX Context Object that method succeeded
If Not objContext Is Nothing Then
   objContext.SetComplete
End If

Exit Function

ValidateError:
'Indicate to the MTX Context Object that it should abort
If Not objContext Is Nothing Then
   objContext.SetAbort
End If
Err.Raise Number:=Err.Number, Source:="LenderWeb.User(Validate)", _
          Description:=Err.Description

End Function
```

When a component runs within the MTS environment, the **GetObjectContext** method can be used to get an object reference to the specific transactional context within which the object is participating. If the object is the first instantiated within the transaction, invoking the **GetObjectContext** method causes MTS to establish a new transaction, as long as the object supports transaction through the appropriate **MTSTransactionMode** setting. The **GetObjectContext** method returns an object reference of the type **ObjectContext**. As shown in the first code selection in Listing 8.6, a COM component must declare a variable of the **ObjectContext** object type, and then set it to reference the results of the **GetObjectContext** method. If the component has been called by another component participating in an existing transaction, the component will be able to enlist in the existing transaction by obtaining a reference to the transaction context through the return value of the **GetObjectContext** method.

Once the object has enlisted in an MTS transaction, the component can use any of four methods provided by the **ObjectContext** object. These four methods allow the object to help determine the outcome of the transaction. The primary methods, **SetComplete** and **SetAbort**, are implemented in Listing 8.6. The **SetComplete** method indicates that the object has given its permission to commit the transaction. The **SetAbort** method indicates that the transaction cannot be committed, based on the results of the object's code execution. Either **SetComplete** or **SetAbort** will result in the object being deactivated within the MTS runtime environment.

Two other methods are provided to offer additional options. The **EnableCommit** method instructs the MTS runtime that the state of the object code execution is sufficiently successful to allow committal of the transaction at the time of invocation, but that processing is not yet complete, thus this condition may yet change. The **DisableCommit** method instructs the MTS runtime that the current status of the object code execution is such that the transaction can't be currently committed, although this condition may change.

# Using **IsSecurityEnabled** To Determine Security Status

The **IsSecurityEnabled** method of the **ObjectContext** object allows the object to check the existence of security on the object. If the object is running within a server process, such as the MTS runtime environment, and security is enabled either on the component providing the object or the package the component resides within, then the **IsSecurityEnabled** method can be used to confirm this fact. You can see implementation of the **IsSecurityEnabled** method in Listing 8.7.

### Listing 8.7    The **IsSecurityEnabled** method determines whether component security is enabled.

```
Dim objContext As ObjectContext
Set objContext = GetObjectContext()
```

```
If Not objContext Is Nothing Then
    ' Check to see if security is enabled on the component
    If objContext.IsSecurityEnabled Then
        ' Check for role membership
        If objContext.IsCallerInRole("Developer") Then
            ' If the caller of the object is in the specified
            ' role, then perform the desired code
        Else
            ' If the caller fails in the role membership test,
            ' then a limited set of code is executed.
        End If
    End If
End If
```

# Using IsCallerInRole To Determine Caller Role Membership

Occasionally, the code within a COM component needs to check whether the direct caller of the object is a member of the specified MTS role. *Direct caller* refers to the client application or COM component that has caused the instance of the object to be created. Occasionally, programmatic security checking, through use of **IsCallerInRole**, is desired to alter the code execution of the object based on the roles that the direct caller is a member of. Use of **IsCallerInRole** is often combined with the **IsSecurityEnabled** method, as shown in Listing 8.8.

### Listing 8.8 The IsCallerInRole method provides a direct link to the membership roster of a role defined within MTS.

```
Dim objContext As ObjectContext
Set objContext = GetObjectContext()

If Not objContext Is Nothing Then
    ' Check to see if security is enabled on the component
    If objContext.IsSecurityEnabled Then
        ' Check for role membership
        If objContext.IsCallerInRole("Developer") Then
            ' If the caller of the object is in the specified
            ' role, then perform the desired code
        Else
            ' If the caller fails in the role membership test,
            ' then a limited set of code is executed.
        End If
    End If
End If
```

Remembering the **IsCallerInRole** and **IsSecurityEnabled** method syntax may help with two or three questions on the exam.

# Setting Transactional Properties Of Components

When using Visual Basic 6 to create MTS-enabled COM components, an additional property of class modules is available to provide additional control in configuring the transactional behavior of the resulting objects. Prior to Visual Basic 6, the transactional behavior of the class was determined by component runtime configuration settings modified from within the MTS Explorer. The property in question, **MTSTransactionMode**, dictates at the code level the degree of support and cooperation the class provides for transaction participation within the MTS runtime environment.

The **MTSTransactionMode** property has five possible values that class modules can choose from to vary the component transactional behavior. The value of this property is applicable only to components that are running within MTS. MTS-enabled COM components not currently running within the MTS runtime environment, or components not designed for MTS at all, simply ignore this property. The five possible settings for this property, in order of transactional autonomy, are:

➤ NotAnMTSObject

➤ NoTransactions

➤ UsesTransaction

➤ RequiresTransaction

➤ RequiresNewTransaction

## NotAnMTSObject

When creating a component within Visual Basic, setting the **MTSTransactionMode** property to **NotAnMTSObject** causes the component to ignore any checks normally made to determine whether the component is running within the MTS environment. An object created from a class module configured with **NotAnMTSObject** will not attempt to determine the existence of MTS, and thus will not provide any MTS-related communication or information. This results in MTS failing to create an object context for the object. This is the default setting for class modules within Visual Basic 6 and programmatically this setting assumes a value of zero.

## NoTransactions

When you set **MTSTransactionMode** to **NoTransactions**, the component objects created or requested by a client do not participate in transactions. If a client application, such as a Web-based ASP application, creates an instance of an MTS-enabled component, a transaction will not be created for that object. If the client creating the object is another object currently running within the context of an MTS transaction, the object created from a class configured with **NoTransactions** will not participate in the transaction. When the object is created, an MTS object context is still created for the object, unlike the **NotAnMTSObject** property setting, only without a transaction. Programmatically, this setting uses an integer value of 1.

## UsesTransaction

This value for the **MTSTransactionMode** property results in the component object behaving with "transactional inertia." In other words, when the client, be it a full application or another component, creates an object configured as **UsesTransaction**, the newly created object will assume the same transaction participation of the client. If the client is participating in a transaction, MTS will create an object context for the new object that will be configured to participate within the scope of the client's transaction. If the client is not currently operating within a transaction, the new object will also execute outside the scope of any established transactions. Programmatically, this setting assumes an integer value of 3.

## RequiresTransaction

If a class module's **MTSTransactionMode** property is set to **RequiresTransaction**, then any resulting objects generated from this template will include a transaction with the object context created by MTS. In other words, the object must run within a transaction scope if it is to execute within the MTS runtime environment at all. When a new object is created, the object context for this object inherits, or assumes, the transaction of the client. If the client is not running within an MTS transaction, the object context for the new object will be created with a new MTS transaction. Programmatically, this setting assumes an integer value of 2.

## RequiresNewTransaction

The **RequiresNewTransaction** setting for the **MTSTransactionMode** property of class modules is the most aggressive and independent setting, in terms of transactional autonomy. Component objects created with this setting are created with a new MTS transaction, no matter the transactional participation of the client creating the object. This setting ensures that components can perform their activities, such as recording the initiation of activities of the client object, without being rolled back or aborted by the failure of the client object activities. Programmatically, this setting uses an integer value of 4.

# Creating Packages In The MTS Explorer

Once the process of designing and coding a business COM component is completed, the final step in preparing to install an MTS-enabled component involves the creation of an *MTS package*. This is a containment concept that groups objects and components together for purposes of security, increased performance, and to facilitate the management of resources and object requests. Much like a folder on a file system, an MTS package allows objects to be grouped together in a container. The overall organization of packages is designed to improve the relative performance of objects when using system resources, thread pooling, database connections, and security requirements. Packages help define the boundaries of MTS server processes, which contribute to process isolation of individual component threads, increasing application reliability.

Creating an MTS package starts by opening the Microsoft Management Console and expanding the Microsoft Transaction Server node until the Packages Installed node is available. Then, as shown in Figure 8.9, right-clicking on the Packages Installed node reveals the ability to choose New|Package on the pop-up menu.

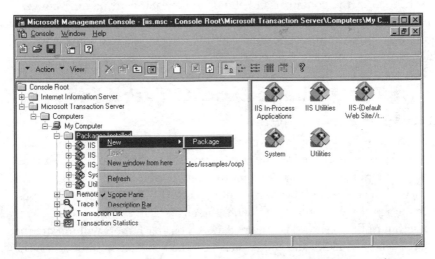

**Figure 8.9**    Create a new MTS package by right-clicking on the Packages Installed node.

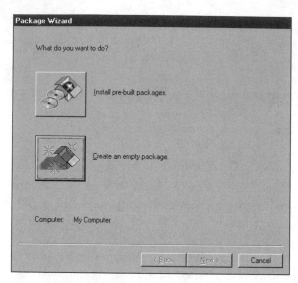

**Figure 8.10**    The Package Wizard is used to import existing packages or to create a new, empty package.

Figure 8.10 shows the Package Wizard screen that subsequently loads when you attempt to either create a new package or import an existing package (discussed later in this chapter).

Clicking on Create An Empty Package continues the Package Wizard, asking next for the name to give the package. The name chosen is merely for unique identification of the container and should follow standard naming conventions. After providing a name, the next screen of the Package Wizard, seen in Figure 8.11, provides the opportunity to identify the security context within which elements in the package will run.

## Using The Package Export Wizard To Create A Package

Once a package has been created and the desired components have been added to the component package (see the next section for details), the package might become a candidate for moving to another MTS server. The package might also need to be re-created due to corruption issues or for rebuilding purposes. To create a package installation folder, right-click on an existing package created within MTS, as shown in Figure 8.12. Choosing Export will initiate the Export Package Wizard, allowing a package to be installed on remote servers.

The Export Package Wizard begins with a screen that asks for the destination location for the exported package. An exported MTS package creates two forms of package exports. All the necessary files for installing the components and

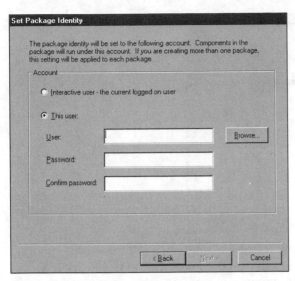

**Figure 8.11**   Creating a new package includes choosing the
security context.

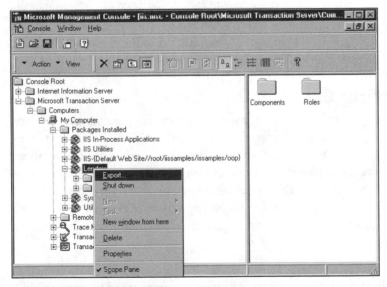

**Figure 8.12**   Access the Export Package Wizard by right-clicking on an
existing package.

package onto another MTS server are copied into the chosen destination directory. This generally includes the necessary ActiveX DLLs and a PAK file that
houses all the necessary registration and file information. One single folder, called
"clients," is included in the destination directory, as shown in Figure 8.13. The
clients folder contains an executable that includes all the same required files,

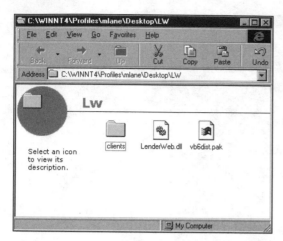

**Figure 8.13** The destination export directory contains the files needed to install the components and package on a remote MTS server.

including information necessary to properly install and register the components on the client system on which the executable is subsequently run. Given that the destination PAK file is given the name of vb6dist.pak, the contents of the export directory would look as in Figure 8.13. The contents of the clients subdirectory, not shown, include a single file named vb6dist.exe.

## Importing Existing Packages

Once a package has been created, populated with components (see the next section), and exported to a folder, the natural process would be to—at some point—use the Package Wizard, shown earlier in Figure 8.10, to import an existing package. Clicking on the option to import an existing package brings up a dialog box requesting the names and locations of the PAK files to use in importing MTS packages. Once these package files are chosen, the resulting MTS packages are created, including registering the components, if necessary, on the server.

The client application executable generated by the Package Wizard is used to configure client machines to access application components on the remote MTS server.

Do not run the client package executable found in the clients subdirectory on the MTS server. This will result in corrupting Registry settings pertaining to the components within the package and will require that the package be completely removed and then reinstalled.

# Adding Components To An MTS Package

Of course, creating, exporting, and importing MTS packages provides no benefit unless components are actually added to the packages. Adding components, contained within ActiveX DLLs, is a relatively simple matter, as all the aspects of MTS explored so far have been. You can add a component through one of three main methods:

➤ Use the Component Wizard by right-clicking on the desired components folder.

➤ Drag and drop an existing object from another package.

➤ Drag and drop an existing COM DLL into the desired components folder.

Invoking the Component Wizard starts off the client by displaying a dialog box, as shown in Figure 8.14. The Component Wizard allows the identification of files, in the form of DLLs, that contain components to be added to the MTS package.

Besides using the Component Wizard to identify ActiveX DLLs containing components for inclusion in an MTS package, you can simply drag the same DLLs into the right-hand panel of the Microsoft Management Console when the desired package's Component node is selected in the MMC hierarchy. Finally, components can also be added to a package by merely dragging or

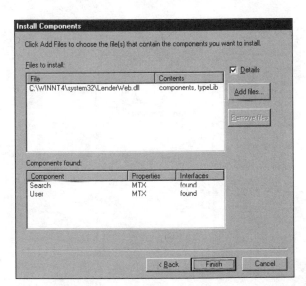

**Figure 8.14**    You can add components to an MTS package by way of the Component Wizard.

moving an existing component from within an existing package into the desired package. Whatever method is used, once the files have been fully chosen, the wizard is finished, and the addition concludes. If the Package node is expanded within the Microsoft Management Console, it might look a little like Figure 8.15.

# Limiting Component Use Through Roles

Microsoft Transaction Server provides several methodologies for restricting the exposure of component functionality to the clients calling and creating MTS-enabled objects. Use of the **IsCallerInRole** and **IsSecurityEnabled** methods of the **ObjectContext** object were discussed earlier. These methods provide a mechanism, known as *programmatic security*, for restricting the exposure of functionality. The primary method provided for securing access to component functionality within MTS is through roles. As discussed in Chapter 3, a *role* is an abstract concept used to organize NT users and/or groups for establishing access to packages or individual components through a process known as *declarative security*. Declarative security requires that authorization checking be enabled on the Security tab of the package's property sheet, as shown in Figure 8.16.

Assuming authorization checking is properly enabled, declarative security involves three primary steps: creating roles within the MTS Explorer, assigning roles to components or component interfaces, and assigning NT accounts or

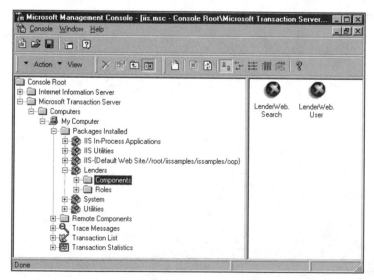

**Figure 8.15**   Installed components are revealed in the right-hand panel of the MMC.

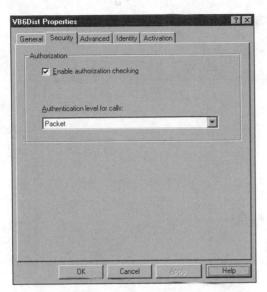

**Figure 8.16**  Authorization checking is enabled on the property sheet of the package involved.

groups to the defined roles. Once these three steps have been accomplished, any client attempting to create and/or access a component will be first checked for membership within the list of assigned roles.

## Creating Roles

Before declarative, or role-based, security can be initiated, roles must be pre-pared for use. The roles are merely abstract concepts involving containment or grouping capabilities. Roles are package-specific, therefore roles must be added one package at a time. To define a new role for a package, start by expanding the desired package and selecting the Roles folder. Follow this by either click-ing on the toolbar Action button and choosing New or by right-clicking on the Roles folder and choosing New|Role, as shown in Figure 8.17. This brings up a simple one-page dialog box, asking for the name of the role to create.

## Assigning Roles To Components Or Component Interfaces

Simply defining a role within a package is not enough to actually restrict or enforce any manner of security. Once one or more roles have been defined for a specific MTS package, assignment of the roles to components, or com-ponent interfaces, must be performed. Applying a role can be initiated by right-clicking on the Role Membership folder and choosing New|Role, as shown in Figure 8.18.

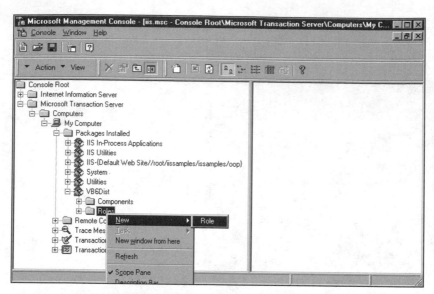

**Figure 8.17** Roles are package-specific and can be added by right-clicking on a package's Roles folder.

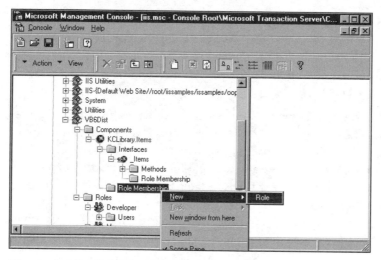

**Figure 8.18** Adding a role to the Role Membership folder is required to apply role-based security.

The only roles that are available to be applied to a chosen component or component interface are those having been not only previously defined, but specifically defined for the same package within which the component itself has been installed. Defining a role for use within a different package will result in the role not showing up in the dialog box shown in Figure 8.19.

**Figure 8.19**    Applying a role to a component is limited to the previously defined roles for the package affected.

MTS provides the flexibility to assign roles either for a component or for a component's interface. COM components written in Visual Basic 6 are created with a single interface that encompasses all the public functions coded for the class module. The definition and generation of interfaces, as specified by the Component Object Model, is handled "behind the scenes" for components written in Visual Basic. Therefore, the only additional interfaces exposed by components written in Visual Basic are typically those added using the **Implements** keyword. For this reason, application of roles to specific component interfaces is rarely a necessity, or desire, for Visual Basic written components, as shown in Figure 8.20.

# Adding Users To Roles

Once the roles have been both defined for a package and assigned to components or component interfaces, the last step in setting up declarative security entails adding valid NT user accounts or groups to the roles. Once accounts are added and assuming authorization checking was enabled as previously described, then only the users who have membership in the roles assigned to the individual components or component interfaces will have the ability to access these objects.

Adding a user to a role starts by expanding, one by one, the folder for the desired package, the Roles folder, the role to be modified, and finally the Users folder, as shown in Figure 8.21. Right-clicking on the Users folder and choosing New|User provides a dialog for choosing users or NT groups, as shown in Figure 8.22.

After a user or group is added to a role for a chosen package, note that the icons used for both are identical, as shown in Figure 8.21.

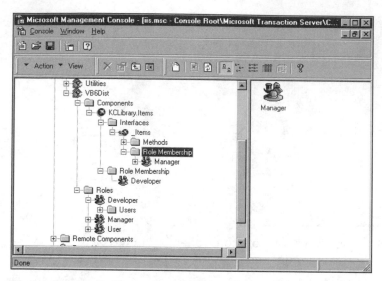

**Figure 8.20** Roles can either be applied to a component or to a particular interface defined for a component.

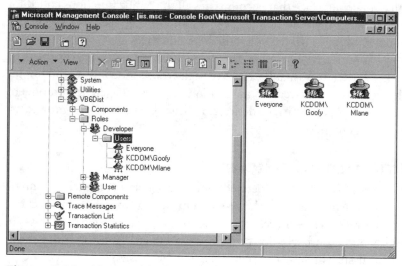

**Figure 8.21** Users added to roles show both in the hierarchy on the left-hand tree and in the right-hand display panel.

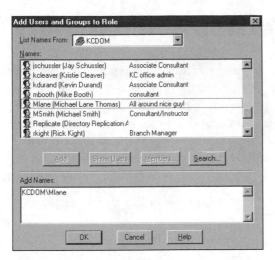

**Figure 8.22**  Adding users to roles is accomplished by a dialog box nearly identical to that used to add NT accounts to NT groups within User Manager for Domains.

MTS provides a special, built-in package called the *System package*. Enabling authorization checking on this package is necessary for completely securing access to packages and components. Included in this package are Administrator and Reader roles. The System package restricts the ability to modify configuration settings on other packages and components within the MTS Explorer. A suggested security practice is to enable authorization checking on the System package. This process should include the following steps:

➤ Map the current account in use to the Administrator role. Failure to do so will result in the inability to modify (add users to) packages.

➤ Remove any undesired NT accounts or groups from the Administrator roles.

➤ Check the Enable Authorization Checking checkbox on the property sheet for the System package.

Fortunately, MTS will warn the user prior to removing either the last account or group assigned to the Administrator role, or before enabling security on the System package when no accounts or groups are actively mapped to the Administrator role.

# Component Version Compatibility

Invariably, the widespread use of business COM components will result in the necessity to enhance, improve, or otherwise modify the components. This gives rise to the concern for compatibility among the original and modified or updated versions of the components. Failure to ensure that component projects maintain compatibility can easily result in updated components breaking older applications relying on the explicit interface contracts provided by the previous component versions. Visual Basic provides two methods for dealing with version compatibility:

➤ Version Compatibility on the Component tab of Project Properties

➤ The **Implements** keyword

## Version Compatibility

The primary method for ensuring compatibility among newer versions of a component is to leverage the project version compatibility settings for the Project Properties. Visual Basic provides three possible settings for dictating the underlying decisions made by Visual Basic when saving component projects, as shown in Figure 8.23. The decisions affected involve the maintenance or modification of existing type library information, class IDs, and interface IDs:

➤ No Compatibility

➤ Project Compatibility

➤ Binary Compatibility

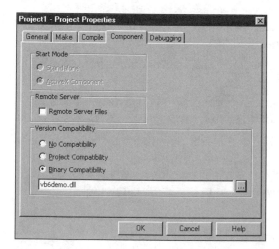

**Figure 8.23**    Version Compatibility has three possible choices for component projects.

## No Compatibility

Subsequent project compiling operations will result in new type library information, new class IDs, and new interface IDs. No relationships exist between the class IDs and interface IDs for subsequent versions of components. Use this option when you want to completely break or separate from a previous version of the component. Using this setting will force all identifiers to be completely regenerated. With this change, existing applications will not be able to access the new version of the component. After compiling for the first time with the No Compatibility setting, switch to one of the following settings for future compiling. In conjunction with this setting, you should take additional steps to ensure a complete separation from the previous compiled version of the component:

➤ Rename the component file name so the new version won't overwrite the older version and break applications relying on the older version.

➤ Change the project name so the programmatic ID (ProgID) generated as a part of the object type library is different from the previous ProgID. This will avoid confusion with previous applications.

## Project Compatibility

Compiling a component project maintains type library identifiers and all class IDs from previous project versions. Interface IDs are regenerated when classes are determined to be binary incompatible with the previous versions. Use this option when starting the first version of a component or when breaking from a previous version of the component, after having compiled once with the No Compatibility setting.

## Binary Compatibility

Binary Compatibility is the setting generally associated with the concept of version compatibility. This setting requires that the binary file (such as VB6DEMO.DLL) be identified for which the component project is to maintain binary compatibility. When compiling a project with this setting, changes in binary compatibility will generate a warning dialog box. Accepting the warning results in project compatibility behavior, with object type library identifiers and class IDs remaining consistent. Interface IDs are changed only for classes that endured binary incompatibilities. Ignoring the warning causes the interface IDs to also remain consistent with previous versions.

Use the Binary Compatibility setting when modifying a component to produce a subsequent version of the component. This setting allows applications designed to use the previous version of the component to continue to work with the new version of the component.

# Practice Questions

## Question 1

Not all COM components created within Visual Basic can be used within the Microsoft Transaction Server environment. Which type of Visual Basic projects can be used to create MTS-enabled components?

○ a. ActiveX DLL project

○ b. ActiveX EXE project

○ c. ActiveX Control project

○ d. ActiveX Document DLL project

○ e. ActiveX Document EXE project

The correct answer is a. Because thread creation and management is controlled by MTS for MTS-enabled components, only an in-process component will allow this to perform correctly. This means that only an ActiveX DLL project can be used. Any other projects, such as ActiveX EXE (answer b), ActiveX Control (answer c), ActiveX Document DLL (answer d), or ActiveX Document EXE projects (answer e) would be incorrect.

## Question 2

Which of the following procedure declarations might be used in creating a write-only property of a component? [Check all that apply]

❏ a. **Public Property Get**

❏ b. **Private Property Set**

❏ c. **Public Property Let**

❏ d. **Property Let**

❏ e. **Public Property Set**

The correct answers are c, d, and e. The property procedures to be used for creating a write-only property are the **Let** and **Set** procedures. These procedures must be declared as **Public**. Answer d is also okay because the default scope declaration for property procedures is **Public**.

Because answer b shows a property declaration of **Private,** the **Set** procedure cannot be used for public writing. Declaring a **Public Get** property will certainly further the creation of a read-only property, but not a write-only property, therefore answer a is incorrect.

## Question 3

> With the addition of the **Instancing** property of class modules, developers of components can now set or control how the component will behave in regard to transactions. Which of the following are acceptable settings for this property when creating externally creatable objects? [Check all that apply]
>
> ❑ a. **Private**
>
> ❑ b. **MultiUse**
>
> ❑ c. **PublicNotCreatable**
>
> ❑ d. **PublicCreatable**
>
> ❑ e. **SingleUse**

The correct answers are b and e. In order for an object to be externally creatable by a client, the class module should have its **Instancing** property set to either **SingleUse, MultiUse, GlobalMultiUse,** or **GlobalSingleUse.**

Answer d is incorrect simply because **PublicCreatable** is not a valid setting for this property. **Private** and **PublicNotCreatable** are used for dependent objects and do not allow objects to be created externally, therefore answers a and c are incorrect.

## Question 4

> When attempting to create an object model within a component, what settings must be chosen for the **Instancing** property of a dependent object? [Check all that apply]
>
> ❑ a. **MultiUse**
>
> ❑ b. **PublicNotCreatable**
>
> ❑ c. **Private**
>
> ❑ d. **GlobalMultiUse**
>
> ❑ e. **PublicCreatable**

The correct answers are b and c. Creating an object as **PublicNotCreatable** protects it from accidental deletion of creation. Creating an object as **Private** also protects the object by making it completely inaccessible to the client for instantiation.

Setting an object to either **MultiUse** or **GlobalMultiUse** will allow outside clients to create instances of the object independent of its parent, violating the dependent status of the object. Therefore, answers a and d are incorrect. Answer e, **PublicCreatable**, does not actually exist, therefore it is incorrect also.

# Question 5

Creating a read-only property of an object is performed by which combination of property procedures?

○ a. **No Set, Let, No Get**

○ b. **Set, No Let, Get**

○ c. **Set, Let, Get**

○ d. **No Set, No Let, Get**

○ e. **No Set, Let, Get**

The correct answer is d. In order to create a read-only property for a component, only the **Property Get** procedure should be provided. This procedure is fired when the property is read.

If any combination of **Let**, **Set**, and/or **Get** procedures is generated, then the property is not read-only. Answer a is incorrect because it would create essentially a write-only property. Answer b is incorrect because it would create a normal property used to return object types. Answer c provides two write-based property procedures, thus it is definitely incorrect. Answer e is incorrect because it represents the normal property procedures used to create a basic read/write property.

# Question 6

> Which of the following is true of a Visual Basic project set to apart-
> ment threading?
>
> ○ a.  MDI forms are not allowed.
>
> ○ b.  Single-threaded ActiveX controls cannot be used.
>
> ○ c.  Forms shown with **vbModal** are universally modal to all
>       threads.
>
> ○ d.  OLE drag and drop is not allowed.
>
> ○ e.  Standard drag and drop is unaffected.

The correct answer is a. When a project is set to apartment-threaded, MDI
forms are not allowed due to the nature of the data sharing requirements between MDI parent and child forms. For this reason, Visual Basic does not
allow MDI elements to be added to an apartment-threaded project.

Although Visual Basic does not normally allow ActiveX controls to be configured as apartment-threaded projects, for very good reasons, the VBP file can
be manually edited to allow such behavior, thus answer b is technically incorrect. Answer c is incorrect because in apartment-threaded projects, forms shown
with **vbModal** are only modal to code and forms on the same threads. In apartment-threaded projects, standard drag and drop operations are not allowed
because the controls might not exist on the same thread, therefore generic or
standard drag and drop functionality may fail. This is not true of OLE drag
and drop, therefore answers d and e are incorrect.

# Question 7

> Which of the following values are valid settings for the
> **MTSTransactionMode** property for class modules inserted into
> ActiveX DLLs within Visual Basic 6? [Check all that apply]
>
> ❏ a.  **NotAnMTSObject**
>
> ❏ b.  **UsesNoTransactions**
>
> ❏ c.  **RequiresMTSTransaction**
>
> ❏ d.  **RequiresNewTransaction**
>
> ❏ e.  **NoTransactions**

The correct answers are a, d, and e. The **Instancing** property has five possible values: **NotAnMTSObject**, **NoTransactions**, **UsesTransaction**, **Requires-Transaction**, and **RequiresNewTransaction**. Therefore, answers b and c are incorrect.

## Question 8

> Visual Basic provides a Version Compatibility feature that assists the process of ensuring that class IDs and interface IDs do not induce a violation of the Component Object Model's requirement that published interfaces are immutable. Which combination of Version Compatibility settings will properly ensure that a new version of a component is completely separated, or broken free, from a previous version of the component, but that all future work on that new version of the component remains compatible with itself as the version is slowly developed?
>
> ○ a.  Project Compatibility, followed by Binary Compatibility
>
> ○ b.  No Compatibility, followed by Project Compatibility
>
> ○ c.  No Compatibility, followed by No Compatibility
>
> ○ d.  Project Compatibility, followed by Project Compatibility
>
> ○ e.  Binary Compatibility, followed by Project Compatibility

The correct answer is b. In order to make a clean break in a component project from a previous version, No Compatibility must be chosen for the initial recompile. This ensures that the class IDs, object type library identifiers, and interface IDs are regenerated. Additionally, the recompiled file should be given a different physical name and project name. After compiling once with No Compatibility, the project should be switched to either Project Compatibility or Binary Compatibility.

Because the first compiling of the new version should be performed under No Compatibility, answers a, d, and e are all incorrect. Continuing on with No Compatibility will cause the IDs for the component to continually change, generating locally what would appear as multiple versions of the identically named component, just under different class IDs in the Registry. Answer c is incorrect for this reason.

# Need To Know More?

For more information on creating COM components within Visual Basic 6, we highly recommend either one of the following books for additional reading:

 Lhotka, Rocky: *Visual Basic 6 Business Objects*. Wrox Press, November 1998. ISBN: 186100107X. This book provides an excellent focus on business services objects.

 Pattison, Ted: *Programming Distributive Applications With COM and Microsoft Visual Basic 6.0*. Microsoft Press, October 1998. ISBN: 1572319615. This book covers MTS and COM very well.

 For more information regarding the topics covered in this chapter, search the MSDN Library Visual Studio 6.0 with the following phrases:

➤ Creating ActiveX components (excellent collection of links)

➤ Apartment-Model threading in Visual Basic (good detail)

➤ Instancing for classes provided by ActiveX components (good comparisons)

# Implementing Data Services

**9**

. . . . . . . . . . . . . . . . . . . . . . . . . . . . . . . . . . . . .

## Terms you'll need to understand:

√ OLE DB

√ ActiveX Data Objects (ADO)

√ OLE DB provider

√ Cursors

√ ADO **Command** object

√ ADO **Connection** object

√ ADO **Recordset** object

√ Disconnected recordsets

√ **UpdateBatch** method

√ Inner join

√ Optimistic locking

√ Pessimistic locking

√ Stored procedures

√ Transactional commit and rollback

## Techniques you'll need to master:

√ Writing SQL statements that retrieve and modify data

√ Using SQL statements that use joins to combine data from multiple tables

√ Using the ADO Execute Direct technique

√ Using the ADO Prepare/ Execute technique

√ Calling stored procedures with parameters

√ Selecting cursor types and locations for different data access scenarios

√ Creating and manipulating disconnected recordsets

√ Using the ADO **Errors** collection to handle database errors

√ Managing database transactions to ensure data consistency and recoverability

√ Using locking strategies including Read-Only, Pessimistic, Optimistic, and Batch Optimistic

# Introduction To Data Services

Data services are the third tier in distributed three-tier applications covered in the exam. The topics that will be covered on the exam relate strictly to the various options for getting data from data sources and how to interact with backend servers such as Microsoft SQL Server. Keep in mind that distributed applications serve data from COM components that are managed by Microsoft Transaction Server, as seen in Chapter 8. As such, these components are not concerned with the visual appearance of the data, but only the interaction with the data source to insert, update, delete, and retrieve data. Accordingly, this section of the exam will not cover any user interface-related issues such as how to display data in a grid control.

When you look at accessing distributed data in an enterprise application, you can consider basically two approaches. One approach is to identify and extract data from its current locations and import it into a relational database management system (RDBMS) such as SQL Server or Oracle. This approach is often called *Universal Data Storage* and has been championed by database vendors Sybase and Informix. Although this approach centralizes data, it does so at the expense of being able to easily manipulate the data in its native format. Microsoft's approach, and consequently the emphasis in this chapter, has been one of Universal Data Access (UDA), rather than centralized data storage. *UDA* at its core simply means accessing data from where it already is stored.

At the center of this strategy lies OLE DB. OLE DB is a set of COM interfaces that provides a standard way for data consumers such as C++, VB, or Active Server Pages (ASP) applications to access a data provider. These interfaces are analogous to the standard ODBC APIs in use today. However, COM's ability to run in multiple tiers—known as *location transparency*—through DCOM, and its extensibility through the addition of interfaces make OLE DB a perfect vehicle for accessing data from the data services tier of a distributed application. Consequently, OLE DB, through data providers created by application vendors, can access data from such diverse sources as the upcoming Windows 2000 Active Directory Services, SQL Server, Oracle, and DB2. This chapter will focus on how VB developers use OLE DB to access data from the data services tier.

# Introduction To SQL

Before we can get into OLE DB, you need to have a basic grounding in Structured Query Language (SQL). The exam will assume you have a basic understanding of SQL and may even throw a couple of questions your way to be sure you do.

SQL is the standard language that relational databases use to communicate with client applications and middle-tier components. Although all vendors customize SQL by adding extensions (Microsoft's dialect is called *Transact-SQL* and Oracle's is *PL/SQL*), the basics of the language are universal. In fact, a standard SQL implementation exists that is known as *ANSI SQL-92*. Microsoft SQL Server 6.5 and higher implement much of the ANSI standard and will be used for the examples in this chapter.

 The SQL questions on the exam will all be able to be answered using Microsoft's Transact-SQL. In other words, assume that the SQL will execute on Microsoft SQL Server.

SQL can be broken down into three subsets of commands: *Data Manipulation Language* (*DML*), *Data Control Language* (*DCL*), and *Data Definition Language* (*DDL*). For the purposes of the exam you'll need to understand DML or how to manipulate data rather than how to implement security (DCL) or define database objects (DDL). The basics of DML can be broken down into four SQL statements:

➤ SELECT

➤ INSERT

➤ UPDATE

➤ DELETE

## SELECT Statement

The **SELECT** statement is used to retrieve data from a database. The basic format of the statement is:

```
SELECT [column list]
FROM [tables]
WHERE [search conditions]
ORDER BY [column list]
```

The **column list** is a comma-delimited list of any columns within the **tables** referenced in the **FROM** clause. If you want to return all the columns, you can simply use an asterisk. For example, to select the author's first and last names from the **authors** table the statement would be:

```
SELECT au_fname, au_lname
FROM authors
```

Note that the columns can be displayed in any order, regardless of how the table was defined.

> *Note: Keep in mind that you should always include only those columns in the column list that your component or client program actually needs. Specifying columns that are not used or simply using an asterisk wastes precious server processing cycles and network bandwidth.*

The other key aspect of the columns list is that you can assign your own column names to the result set, rather than use the names of the columns from the table. In Transact-SQL you can achieve this by using the **AS** keyword or the alternate syntax using the equal sign. Note that the following two statements are functionally equivalent:

```
SELECT au_fname AS 'First Name', au_lname AS 'Last Name'
FROM authors

SELECT 'First Name' = au_fname, 'Last Name' = au_lname
FROM authors
```

The **FROM** clause of the **SELECT** statement is used to specify from which tables you wish to retrieve data. In the previous examples the statements were selected from only one table. In this case, you simply place the name of the single table after the **FROM**. However, in many instances you'll want to retrieve data from multiple tables by joining those tables together and displaying data from both tables in a single result set.

## Using Joins

*Joins* are specified in either the **FROM** or **WHERE** clauses, although using the **FROM** clause is recommended, because this adheres to the ANSI standard. There are three types of joins that can be implemented:

➤ **Inner joins** This is the most common join operation and uses a comparison operator like = or <>.

➤ **Outer joins** Outer joins can be a left, right, or full outer join.

➤ **Cross joins** Also called *cross products*, these are used infrequently.

*Inner joins* are specified using the **INNER JOIN** keywords and use a comparison operator to match rows from two tables based on the values in common columns from each table. The following example retrieves all rows where the author identification number is the same in both the **authors** and **royalty** tables:

```
SELECT au_lname, au_fname, royaltyper
FROM authors INNER JOIN royalty ON authors.au_id = royalty.au_id
```

The resulting set of records will only contain data from rows in both tables where the **au_id** column is the same.

*Outer joins* are specified with one of the following sets of keywords in the **FROM** clause:

➤ LEFT JOIN or LEFT OUTER JOIN

➤ RIGHT JOIN or RIGHT OUTER JOIN

➤ FULL JOIN or FULL OUTER JOIN

The result set of a *left outer join* includes not only the rows that match from the **ON** clause but all rows in the table on the left side of the statement. When a row in the left table has no matching rows in the right table, the result set contains null values for all the columns selected from the table on the right.

A *right outer join* is the reverse of a left outer join and returns all rows from the right table and only those from the left table that intersect using the **ON** clause. As you just read, null values are returned for the left table any time a right table row has no matching row in the left table. An example of a left outer join would be to try and retrieve all the authors, even those that do not have associated records in the **royalty** table:

```
SELECT au_fname, au_lname, royaltyper
FROM authors LEFT OUTER JOIN royalty ON authors.au_id = royalty.au_id
```

A *full outer join* can be thought of as the sum of the left and right outer joins. This type of join returns all rows in both the left and right tables. Any time a row has no match in the other table, the columns in the select list from the other table contain null values. When there is a match between the tables, the row in the result set contains the columns from both tables.

The final type of join, the *cross join* using the **CROSS JOIN** keywords, is used infrequently. This type of join matches each row in the left table with each row in the right table, generating a result set that is the product of the row counts of the individual tables. For example the cross join

```
SELECT au_lname
FROM authors CROSS JOIN royalty
```

returns 500 rows if there are 50 rows in **authors** and 10 in **royalty**. Obviously, using a cross join is not recommended, because it returns such a large set of records.

## Specifying Criteria

As previously noted, you should always specify only the columns that are needed by the component or client program. This same rule applies to the rows that you return as well. By using the **WHERE** clause, you instruct the server to return only those rows that meet the criteria specified.

The **WHERE** clause consists of search conditions that evaluate as Boolean (True or False) expressions that may be connected by the logical operators **AND** and **OR** or preceded by the negation operator **NOT**. For example, to return only those rows in which the author is from Overland Park, Kansas, you would write the following SQL:

```
SELECT au_lname
FROM authors
WHERE au_state = 'KS' AND au_city = 'Overland Park'
```

If you use more than two criteria separated by **AND** or **OR**, it's recommended that you specify the order of evaluation using parentheses, because different databases may specify different orders of precedence, resulting in differing result sets.

In addition to using equality comparison you can also use the following operators:

➤ **Other comparison operators** <, >, <=, >=, and <>.

➤ **BETWEEN and NOT BETWEEN** Use these to return rows within a range that covers both end points or excludes the range using **NOT**. If you wanted to return all the rows from the **sales** table in which the sale price was between $5 and $10, the syntax would look like this:

```
SELECT sale_price
FROM sales
WHERE sale_price BETWEEN 5 AND 10
```

➤ **LIKE and NOT LIKE** Use these to do pattern matches within a column that contains text. For example, to return only those authors who live in states that start with K, you would issue the following SQL:

```
SELECT au_lname
FROM authors
WHERE au_state LIKE 'K%'
```

Note that the % acts as the wildcard. You can use the wildcard at the beginning of the pattern as well. Transact-SQL also contains syntax for matching on ranges of values within a string (starts with A through C for example) and even matching a pattern that specifies characters in specific locations.

*Note: Generally you'll want to restrict using the **LIKE** clause to columns that you know are indexed by the database server and avoid using the wildcard as the first character in the pattern. If you violate these rules, you'll incur extra overhead on the server as it scans through each row in the table.*

➤ **IN and NOT IN**  These allow you to check for the existence of column values within a parenthesized list. The syntax for returning all authors who are in the states of Kansas, Iowa, and Illinois would be:

```
SELECT au_lname
FROM authors
WHERE au_state IN ('KS', 'IA ', 'IL')
```

 The **BETWEEN** and **IN** operators are essentially shorthand operators, because both can be written using the standard operators.

➤ **NULL and NOT NULL**  These are used to check for the existence of data within a column. Relational databases allow you to leave a column empty when a row is inserted. These columns do not contain blank spaces or a zero-length string for character columns or zero for numeric columns. No data is actually in the column, so the way to test for that condition is to use the **NULL** keyword. To return the authors that do not have a title you would use the syntax:

```
SELECT au_lname
FROM authors
WHERE au_title IS NULL
```

## Sorting Results

You can sort results by using the **ORDER BY** clause after the **WHERE** clause. The clause contains the column names and the sort method that you should use. For example, to sort the authors by last name in ascending order you would use:

```
ORDER BY au_lname ASC
```

SQL also supports the ability to do multilevel sorts by specifying a comma-delimited list of columns. In this way, you could sort by last name and within each last name sort the first names alphabetically as well.

# INSERT Statement

The **INSERT** statement is the second of the SQL DML statements you'll need to understand and is used to add new rows to a single table in the database. Basically, the **INSERT** statement comes in two forms and can be used to either add a single row or multiple rows to a table.

To add a single row to a table, you use the **INSERT INTO VALUES** form of the statement. Using this form to insert a row into the **authors** table might look like the following:

```
INSERT INTO authors (au_fname, au_lname, au_city)
VALUES ('George', 'Will', 'Chevy Chase')
```

In this form you'll notice that the parenthesized list after the table name corresponds to the parenthesized list after the **VALUES** clause. By specifying the column list, you are allowed to provide values for only those columns you wish to specify. In addition, by specifying the column list, the columns can be in any order. However, if you do not specify the column list, the **VALUES** clause must contain values for all the columns in the table in the order in which they were defined when the table was created.

In both cases you can use the keyword **NULL** if you wish to leave the column without a value in the new row. Of course, this is only allowed when the column has been defined in the table as allowing null values. You also do not have to specify the column if it has been defined with a default value. The default values of all columns will automatically be populated by the database when the row is inserted.

> *Note: By default, in Microsoft SQL Server you do not explicitly refer to identity columns (those that are self-incrementing) in the INSERT statement. SQL Server will automatically populate these columns as the row is inserted.*

The other form of the **INSERT** statement is referred to as **INSERT INTO SELECT**. This statement allows you to insert multiple rows into a table based on the rows returned from a **SELECT** statement. For example, to populate the **authors_temp** table with data from the **authors** table you would use:

```
INSERT INTO authors_temp (au_fname, au_lname, au_city)
SELECT au_fname, au_lname, au_city
FROM authors
```

The caveat to performing this sort of operation is that the number and data types of the columns in the column list of the **SELECT** statement must match those in the table in which you are attempting to insert data. Note that the columns do not have to have the same names and that you can provide a column list after the table name to specify a subset of columns to insert.

 A form of the **SELECT** statement called **SELECT INTO** allows you to create a table on the fly from data in a **SELECT** statement. Don't confuse this statement with **INSERT INTO SELECT**.

With both forms of the statement you must always provide enough columns so that all columns defined as **NOT NULL** or that do not have default values provided are accounted for.

## UPDATE Statement

The **UPDATE** statement is used to modify the columns of a row or rows within a single table. The general syntax of the statement is:

```
UPDATE [table]
SET [column name] = [expression], [column name] = [expression]
WHERE [criteria]
```

The **SET** clause is used to specify which columns are being updated and what their new values should be. You can provide multiple columns to be updated by simply creating a comma-delimited list:

```
UPDATE authors
SET au_lname = 'Gould', au_fname = 'Stephen'
WHERE au_id = 1
```

The **WHERE** clause is simply used to determine which rows should be updated using the rules discussed in the preceding "Specifying Criteria" section. Note that in most cases the **WHERE** clause will contain the primary key of the table so that only one row will be updated. By leaving off the **WHERE** clause, all the rows in the table will be affected.

## DELETE Statement

The **DELETE** statement is similar to the **UPDATE** statement in that it also uses a **WHERE** clause to determine which rows to delete, but it is simpler because no column list needs to be defined. In order to delete the author whose last name is "Gould," you would issue the statement:

```
DELETE FROM authors
WHERE au_lname = 'Gould'
```

*Note: Although the syntax is beyond the scope of this book, depending on the implementation, both the UPDATE and DELETE statements can be performed based on join values from other tables. For example, you can write a DELETE statement that will only delete the authors who do not have a corresponding author ID in the royalty table.*

# ActiveX Data Objects

As we discussed at the start of this chapter, Microsoft has put significant technical and marketing effort into the concept of Universal Data Access through its OLE DB COM interfaces. These interfaces allow C++ programmers to use an OLE DB provider to interact with databases like SQL Server or Oracle. Unfortunately, VB does not have the ability to use these interfaces directly. To alleviate this difficulty Microsoft created ActiveX Data Objects (ADO) to expose the underlying OLE DB interfaces to programming tools that do not support pointers. Figure 9.1 shows the architecture of UDA and highlights the fact that ADO can be used to access a number of data providers.

The remainder of this chapter will focus on how VB developers use ADO to interact with databases in a variety of ways. The questions you'll encounter on the exam will be related to the proper use of ADO and syntax when using ADO objects.

 Although ADO is Microsoft's strategic direction and the vast majority of the data services questions will pertain to ADO, you should familiarize yourself with how to create a connection and return a recordset using Remote Data Objects.

ADO is a very simple and flexible object model composed of seven objects: **Connection, Command, Recordset, Parameters, Fields, Property**, and **Errors**. You can see the relationship of these objects in Figure 9.2 and their definitions in Table 9.1.

An interesting feature of the diagram shown in Figure 9.2 is that it is not strictly hierarchical in nature, as are the previous object models released by Microsoft—Remote Data Objects (RDO) and Data Access Objects (DAO). In ADO, the **Connection, Command, Parameter**, and **Recordset** objects can be created independently using either the **New** keyword or the **CreateObject** statement. These objects can then be freely associated with each other at runtime. As we'll see, this flexible model makes ADO great for applications that access multiple data sources or work with disconnected recordsets.

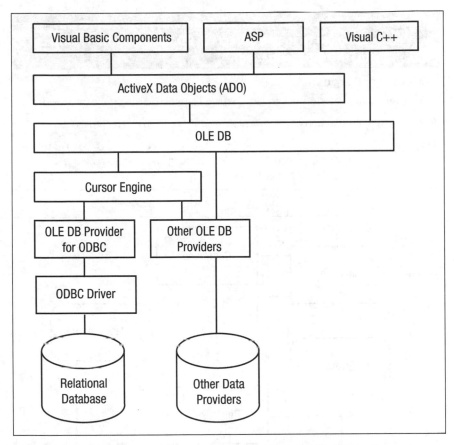

**Figure 9.1**  The data access architecture defined by UDA allows multiple types of clients access to data from a variety of sources.

| Table 9.1 | The ADO 2.0 object model contains just 7 objects, as opposed to the 10 objects in RDO 2.0 and the 17 objects in DAO 3.5. |
|---|---|
| **Object** | **Purpose** |
| **Connection** | Represents a single connection with a data provider. |
| **Errors** | A collection that exposes the errors that occur during the session with a data provider. |
| **Command** | Specifies a data definition or data manipulation to be executed. This could refer to a SQL statement or stored procedure. |
| **Parameters** | A collection that specifies the arguments to be passed to a **Command** object. |

*(continued)*

| Table 9.1 | The ADO 2.0 object model contains just 7 objects, as opposed to the 10 objects in RDO 2.0 and the 17 objects in DAO 3.5 *(continued)*. |
|---|---|
| **Object** | **Purpose** |
| Recordset | Represents the interface to the data retrieved from the data provider. |
| Fields | A collection of column information contained in a recordset. |
| Property | A collection of provider-specific properties contained by each of the other ADO objects. This allows ADO to dynamically expose the capabilities of a specific provider. |

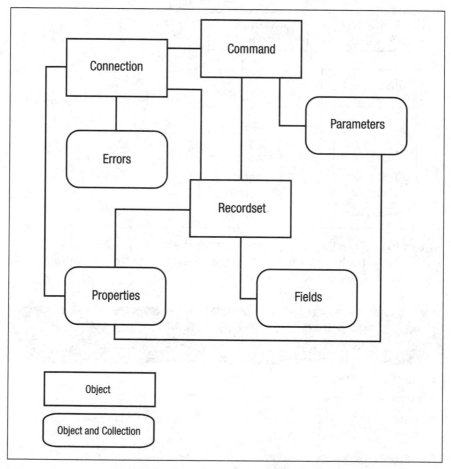

**Figure 9.2** The ADO object model is simpler and more flexible than previous Microsoft data access interfaces.

# Connecting To A Data Provider

To begin accessing data using ADO, you must first create a connection to the data provider using the **Connection** object. This requires that you first set a reference to the Microsoft ActiveX Data Objects 2.0 Library in the Project|References menu in VB. After setting a reference, declare a **Connection** object, instantiate it, set its properties, and, finally, open the connection. This process is shown in Listing 9.1.

## Listing 9.1    Opening an ADO connection.

```
Dim cnSQL as ADODB.Connection
Set cnSQL = New ADODB.Connection

With cnSQL
    .Provider = "MSDASQL"
    .ConnectionString = "DRIVER={SQL SERVER};DATABASE=pubs;" & _
        "SERVER=myserver;uid=sa;pwd=admin"
End With

cnSQL.Open
```

In the listing you can see that the **Provider** property of the **Connection** object specifies which data provider to access. By default ADO always uses the OLE DB provider for ODBC, MSDASQL, to allow ADO to use any ODBC driver available. However, this should be a temporary situation, as ADO 2.0 already ships with native OLE DB providers for SQL Server 7, Oracle, and Access. As they become available, you'll want to specify the native providers to both increase performance and enable the enhanced features of the provider.

Two other important properties you should be aware of are the **CommandTimeout** and **ConnectionTimeout** that specify how long each command may execute before ADO will cancel it and how long ADO will wait for a connection to be established, respectively.

> *Note: You can also dimension the **Connection** object using the **WithEvents** keyword if the object will be module level or global in scope. This creates nine event procedures that you can use to handle events fired by the **Connection** object, such as **ConnectComplete** and **ExecuteComplete**.*

When you have finished working with the data provider you can close the connection and deallocate the **Connection** object:

```
cnSQL.Close
Set cnSQL = Nothing
```

*Note: Even if you do not explicitly close and deallocate the **Connection** object, it will automatically be destroyed when the object goes out of scope.*

# Retrieving Data And Navigating A Recordset

In order to retrieve data from a data provider you must specify the SQL that is to be executed and create a **Recordset** object. In ADO there are actually three techniques that will accomplish this:

➤ Creating a new **Recordset** object and using its **Open** method

➤ Calling the **Execute** method of the **Connection** object

➤ Calling the **Execute** method of the **Command** object

In all cases ADO will return a **Recordset** object that represents the set of records returned by the data provider. As with the **Recordset** and **Resultset** objects exposed by DAO and RDO, the ADO **Recordset** exposes a cursor that contains a pointer to the current record, and methods and properties that are used to manipulate the pointer and the underlying records. You can find the key properties and methods of the **Recordset** and their descriptions in Table 9.2.

| Table 9.2 | Properties and methods of the Recordset object. |
|---|---|
| **Member** | **Use** |
| **AbsolutePosition** | Property that returns the position of the current pointer in the recordset |
| **ActiveCommand** | Property that returns a reference to the **Command** object used to create the recordset |
| **ActiveConnection** | Property that returns a reference to the **Connection** object used to create the recordset |
| **AddNew** | Method that moves the pointer to a new record at the end of the recordset |
| **BOF** | Property that returns True if the pointer is at the beginning of the recordset |
| **Bookmark** | Property that can be used to uniquely identify a record in the recordset |
| **CacheSize** | Property that determines how many rows a provider puts in its buffer initially and how many it subsequently retrieves when the buffer is exhausted. |
| **Close** | Method used to close the recordset |

*(continued)*

| Table 9.2   Properties and methods of the Recordset object *(continued)*. | |
| --- | --- |
| **Member** | **Use** |
| **CursorLocation** | Property that determines where the recordset is created, normally on the client or on the server |
| **CursorType** | Property that determines what functionality is available to the recordset |
| **Delete** | Method that deletes the current record in the recordset |
| **EOF** | Property that returns True if the pointer is at the end of the recordset |
| **Fields** | Property that returns a reference to a collection of **Field** objects |
| **Find** | Method that searches the recordset for a search condition and moves the pointer to the first record that satisfies the condition |
| **GetRows** | Method that returns rows from the recordset into a multidimensional array |
| **MoveFirst** | Method that moves the pointer to the first record in the recordset |
| **MoveLast** | Method that moves the pointer to the last record in the recordset |
| **MoveNext** | Method that moves the pointer to the next record in the recordset |
| **MovePrevious** | Method that moves the pointer to the previous record in the recordset |
| **Move** | Method that moves the pointer to an offset based on the current record |
| **Open** | Method that is used to pass a SQL statement to a **Connection** object to create the recordset |
| **Requery** | Method that re-executes the query against the data provider |
| **Save** | Method that allows the recordset to be saved to persistent storage as a file |
| **Update** | Method that instructs the data provider to update changed records |

Keep in mind that not all the properties and methods will be available at all times. For example, the **CursorType** and **CursorLocation** properties affect whether the **MovePrevious, Bookmark,** and **Update** methods are available. You can see a typical scenario for creating and traversing a **Recordset** in Listing 9.2. Like the **Connection** object, the ADO **Recordset** object can also be dimensioned as a module-level or global variable using the **WithEvents** keyword. This allows you to write code in response to events for the recordset.

## Listing 9.2 Dimensioning and using the **Recordset** object's properties.

```
Dim rsAuthors as ADODB.Recordset

'Code to create the recordset goes here

'Traverse the records
Do While Not rsAuthors.EOF
    strName = rsAuthors.Fields("au_fname") & " " & _
        rsAuthors.Fields("au_lname")
    rsAuthors.MoveNext
Loop

'Close the recordset
rsAuthors.Close
```

## *Recordset Open*

As previously mentioned, three methods exist for creating the **Recordset** object, the first being the **Open** method of the **Recordset**. To use this method you simply dimension and create a recordset and call the **Open** method. This method takes the SQL statement and a reference to a **Connection** object as parameters to connect to the data provider and return the **Recordset** object:

```
Dim rsAuthors As ADODB.Recordset
Set rsAuthors = New ADODB.Recordset
rsAuthors.Open "SELECT * FROM authors", cnSQL
```

The advantage to this method is that the **Connection** object can be passed as a parameter and specified in a variable. This is useful in applications that may not decide until runtime which **Connection** object to execute the SQL against.

## *Execute Direct*

The second method for creating a recordset is to execute a **SELECT** statement directly using the **Execute** method of the **Connection** object:

```
Dim rsAuthors As ADODB.Recordset
Set rsAuthors = cnSQL.Execute("SELECT * FROM authors")
```

As we'll see shortly, if the SQL statement you specify does not return a recordset, such as an **INSERT** or **UPDATE** statement, you do not have to capture the return value in a **Recordset** object. Using this method has the advantage of decreasing memory usage, because no information about the statement is saved; however, it always creates a server-side forward-only cursor, which—as we'll soon see—may not always be desirable.

## *Command* Objects

The third technique to create a recordset is to use the **Command** object. Basically, the **Command** object allows you to encapsulate all the characteristics of a command you wish to execute against a data provider. For most providers this includes a SQL statement and properties that tell ADO what type of command is being executed, the **Connection** object to use, and the parameters that should be packaged with the command, if any.

> *Note: Although it is not required, you will usually want to create a Connection object and associate it with multiple Command objects. Each Command object can create its own implicit Connection object by specifying a connect string in the ActiveConnection property, but this creates more objects and is less efficient.*

The code to use the **Command** object to retrieve the **authors** table can be seen in Listing 9.3.

## Listing 9.3    Creating and using a **Command** object.

```
Dim cmSQL As ADODB.Command
Set cmSQL = New ADODB.Command

With cmSQL
    .ActiveConnection = cnSQL
    .CommandText = "SELECT * FROM authors"
    .CommandType = adCmdText
    .CommandTimeout = 10
End With

Set rsAuthors = cmSQL.Execute
```

You'll notice that the **Command** object also exposes a **CommandTimeout** property that can override what is set by the **Connection** object.

## *Persisting A Recordset*

After opening a recordset with one of the methods shown earlier you can then use the provided methods and properties shown in Table 9.2 to traverse and manipulate the data. One of the new methods in ADO 2.0 that you may not be familiar with is the **Save** method. The **Save** method allows your application to persist the data in the recordset to a disk file and then open it back up at a later time for processing. This is especially useful for disconnected applications that run on a laptop or browser-based applications using Remote Data Services (RDS).

For example, to save the recordset **rsAuthors** to disk, simply call the method on the open recordset passing it the disk file to use and the format:

```
rsAuthors.Save "authors.rs", adPersistADTG
```

Note that in ADO 2.0 the second argument denoting the format can only be set to the ADTG format. In addition, if you have first applied a filter to the recordset, only the filtered records will be saved. If you subsequently call the **Save** method for this recordset, you must omit the filename.

To re-open this recordset you would then call the **Open** method, passing it the name to retrieve from in the *source* argument.

```
rsAuthors.Open "authors.rs"
```

# Executing A Prepared Statement

One of the advantages of a **Command** object is that it allows you to define all the properties of a SQL statement, encapsulate them, and then reuse the **Command** throughout your application, perhaps even against different **Connection** objects. This type of reuse certainly can boost developer productivity and make your code easier to write and maintain. However, **Command** objects can also boost performance by allowing you to take advantage of a data provider's ability to compile and reuse commands that you wish to execute repeatedly against the same connection.

The **Command** object exposes a **Prepared** property that instructs the data provider to save a prepared or compiled version of the command specified in the **CommandText** property before it is first executed. In this way the data provider can reuse this compiled version on subsequent calls and not incur the overhead of reparsing and compiling the statement. The default value for the **Prepared** property is False, indicating that the provider will not compile and save the statement.

> *Note: Some data providers may not support this property and may even throw a trappable error if your code attempts to set the property. Other providers may simply ignore the property when set.*

In many instances this technique can give your code a big performance boost, especially when the SQL in the **CommandText** property is complex and you want to execute it multiple times. You can see an example of creating and executing a prepared statement in Listing 9.4.

## Listing 9.4    Creating and executing a prepared statement using a **Command** object.

```
Dim cmSQL As ADODB.Command
Set cmSQL = New ADODB.Command

With cmSQL
    .ActiveConnection = cnSQL
    .CommandText = "SELECT * FROM authors _
        WHERE au_id = '123-45-6789'"
    .CommandType = adCmdText
    .CommandTimeout = 10
    .Prepared = True
End With

Set rsAuthors = cmSQL.Execute
'Do other logic
rsAuthors.Close
'Do even more logic

'Execute the command again
Set rsAuthors = cmSQL.Execute
```

# Calling Stored Procedures

Just as prepared commands allow the data provider to execute compiled statements and thus increase performance, you can think of *stored procedures* as permanently compiled statements that reside on the data provider. However, stored procedures not only contain basic SQL statements but can also include control-of-flow syntax that allows them to process if-then style conditional logic. Because of this advantage, stored procedures are ideal for encapsulating logic that is provider-specific. As was mentioned in Chapter 8, business logic that is not particular to the provider should be located in your ActiveX components so they are isolated from the data services tier.

Not only do stored procedures provide a performance advantage, they also allow your code to be isolated from the underlying database schema. This may not seem important when developing simple two-tier applications, but in a more complicated environment, isolating your code from table changes will save you a lot of development time in the long run.

As with prepared statements, you use the **Command** object to identify the stored procedure you wish to execute, setting its **CommandText** and **CommandType** properties to the name of the stored procedure and a constant indicating that a stored procedure is being called:

```
Dim cmSQL As ADODB.Command
Set cmSQL = New ADODB.Command

With cmSQL
    .ActiveConnection = cnSQL
    .CommandText = "GetAuthors"
    .CommandType = adCmdStoredProc
    .CommandTimeout = 10
End With

Set rsAuthors = cmSQL.Execute
```

## Using Parameters

Many times stored procedures require that parameters be passed to them so that the result set or statement can be customized. ADO contains **Parameter** objects that can be appended to a **Command** object, each of which represents a parameter or return value of a stored procedure.

There are basically two ways to create the parameter objects for a stored procedure. The easiest method—although less efficient—is to simply call the **Refresh** method of the **Parameters** collection of the **Command** object.

> *Note: The **Refresh** method is less efficient because ADO needs to query the data provider to discover the number and types of parameters for the stored procedure. This incurs an extra network round trip to the server.*

Once the parameters are defined, you can populate them using the **Parameters** collection before executing the command. For example, to execute the stored procedure **GetAuthors** that takes the author ID as a parameter, you would use the following ADO code:

```
Dim cmSQL As ADODB.Command
Set cmSQL = New ADODB.Command

With cmSQL
    .ActiveConnection = cnSQL
    .CommandType = adCmdStoredProc
    .CommandText = "GetAuthors"
    .Parameters.Refresh
    .Parameters(1) = "123-45-6789"
End With

Set rs = cmSQL.Execute
```

Notice that to populate the first parameter you reference index 1 of the **Parameters** collection, although the collection is zero-based. In Microsoft SQL Server, index 0 is reserved for the return value from the stored procedure. If a return value is not specified, the stored procedure automatically assigns one based on the status of the stored procedure. You can see the possible return values from Microsoft SQL Server in Table 9.3.

Listing 9.5 shows the **GetAuthors** stored procedure written in Microsoft Transact-SQL.

## Listing 9.5    The **GetAuthors** stored procedure takes one argument.

```
CREATE PROCEDURE GetAuthors
@au_id char(11)
AS

SELECT *
FROM authors
WHERE au_id = @au_id

return 0
```

| Table 9.3 | Microsoft SQL Server stored procedure return values. |
|---|---|
| **Value** | **Meaning** |
| 0 | Procedure executed successfully |
| -1 | Object missing |
| -2 | Datatype error occurred |
| -3 | Process was chosen as deadlock victim |
| -4 | Permission error occurred |
| -5 | Syntax error occurred |
| -6 | Miscellaneous user error occurred |
| -7 | Resource error, such as out of space, occurred |
| -8 | Non-fatal internal problem encountered |
| -9 | System limit was reached |
| -10 | Fatal internal inconsistency occurred |
| -11 | Fatal internal inconsistency occurred |
| -12 | Table or index is corrupt |
| -13 | Database is corrupt |
| -14 | Hardware error occurred |

The second method for populating the **Parameters** collection is to create a **Parameter** object and append it to the collection yourself. As noted previously, this method ensures that extra network round trips are not incurred and can be done even before the **Command** object is associated with a **Connection** object. You can see this method in Listing 9.6.

## Listing 9.6   Creating a parameter and appending it to the Command object.

```
Dim cmSQL As ADODB.Command
Dim prmSSN As ADODB.Parameter
Dim strSSN As String

Set cmSQL = New ADODB.Command

With cmSQL
    .ActiveConnection = cnSQL
    .CommandType = adCmdStoredProc
    .CommandText = "GetAuthors"
End With

strSSN = "123-45-6789"

Set prmSSN = cmSQL.CreateParameter("@au_id", adChar, _
    adParamInput, Len(strSSN), strSSN)
cmSQL.Parameters.Append prmSSN

Set rsAuthors = cmSQL.Execute
```

Note that the parameter is created using the **CreateParameter** method of the **Command** object. This method takes five parameters that include the name, data type, direction, length, and value of the parameter to be passed. The direction parameter is particularly interesting, because it determines whether the parameter is an input, output, or return parameter. *Input parameters* are those you pass into the stored procedure, whereas *output parameters* can additionally return values as well. As noted earlier, *return values* might be returned by the stored procedure and always appear first in the **Parameters** collection. When creating the parameters, you should always create them in the same order in which they are defined in the stored procedure, with the return value first if you wish to read it. You can find an example of calling a stored procedure that returns the total number of books sold by an author as the return value in Listing 9.7.

## Listing 9.7    Using the **Parameters** collection to read a return value from a stored procedure.

```
Dim cmSQL As ADODB.Command
Dim prmSSN As ADODB.Parameter
Dim strSSN As String
Dim intSales as Integer

Set cmSQL = New ADODB.Command

With cmSQL
    .ActiveConnection = cnSQL
    .CommandType = adCmdStoredProc
    .CommandText = "GetAuthorSales"
End With

strSSN = "123-45-6789"

Set prmSSN = cmSQL.CreateParameter("Return", adInteger, _
    adParamReturnValue, 4, 0)
Set prmSSN = cmSQL.CreateParameter("@au_id", adChar, _
    adParamInput, Len(strSSN), strSSN)
cmSQL.Parameters.Append prmSSN

cmSQL.Execute
intSales = cmSQL.Parameters("Return")
```

> *Note: If you execute a stored procedure that returns a recordset as well as a return value, you must close the recordset before attempting to read any output or return values. This is documented in the Microsoft Knowledge Base article Q167908.*

# Modifying Data

When your business objects need to modify data, you can use two techniques. The first is to use the **Recordset** object's **AddNew, Update,** and **Delete** methods, and the second is to execute SQL that instructs the data provider to modify the data directly.

## Adding Records

Using the methods of the recordset has the limitation of allowing only one row in the recordset to be modified at a time. In order to insert a new record you can call the **AddNew** method of the **Recordset** and then use the **Fields**

collection to fill in the values. Once populated, you instruct the data provider
to actually perform the insert by calling the **Update** method. An example of
inserting a record with ADO follows:

```
With rsAuthors
    .AddNew
    .Fields("au_lname") = "Will"
    .Fields("au_fname") = "George"
    .Fields("city") = "Chevy Chase"
    .Fiel ds("state") = "MD"
    .Fields("phone") = "555-1212"
    .Fields("au_id") = "123-45-6789"
    .Fields("zip") = "55555"
    .Fields("contract") = 0
    .Update
End With
```

When accessing the **Fields** collection, you'll often see different
forms of the syntax used—actually five different sets—which can
be a little confusing. The following lines of code are all functionally equivalent:

```
rsAuthors.Fields("state") = "MD"
rsAuthors("state") = "MD"
rsAuthors.Fields(6) = "MD"
rsAuthors(6) = "MD"
rsAuthors!state = "MD"
```

Which one you use is largely a matter of choice. Using the ordinal
number to refer to the field is obviously more cryptic; using a literal string to contain the field gives the advantage of being able
to substitute the literal with a variable. Traditionally, the last syntax has been rumored to yield the best performance, but I have
not done any tests to that effect.

Rather than use a separate line of code for each field you wish to modify, the
**Update** method optionally takes two variant arrays as parameters. You can fill
the first with the names or positions of the fields you wish to modify; the
second contains the values to place in those fields. This can make the code
more compact, but perhaps more difficult to read.

Keep in mind that just as with the SQL **INSERT** statement, you must fill in
all the fields that are either marked as **NOT NULL** in the database or that do
not have default values associated with them.

## Updating Records

To update records already in the recordset, ADO only requires that you modify the field or fields using the **Fields** collection (as seen previously) and call the **Update** method. Unlike the older RDO and DAO data access models, there is no **Edit** method on the recordset that must be called before a field is modified.

As with inserting a record, you can also use the optional parameters of the **Update** method to pass in variant arrays that contain the fields to be modified and their new values.

## Deleting Records

Deleting a record with ADO is as simple as positioning the recordset to the row you wish to delete and calling the **Delete** method. When using connected recordsets, which is the default, the **Delete** method has the effect of immediately executing the delete against the data provider:

```
rsAuthors.MoveNext
rsAuthors.Delete
```

Although the default is to delete a single record at a time, the **Delete** method optionally takes one parameter defined as a constant that determines how many records are deleted. The default for this parameter is **adAffectCurrent**, which deletes the row at the current pointer, as shown earlier. The other possible value is **adAffectGroup**, which deletes all the records that satisfy the current **Filter** property setting.

The **Filter** property of the recordset allows you temporarily view a subset of the records in the recordset. By setting the filter to a criteria string, you shield your code from working with any records that are not a part of the filter. For example, to see only those authors who live in California you would specify the filter as:

```
ssAuthors.Filter = "state = 'CA'"
```

Activating a filter has the effect of immediately repositioning the recordset to the first row satisfied by the filter and will also affect the values of other properties, such as **RecordCount** and **AbsolutePosition**. To turn off the filter and return all rows to the recordset, set the **Filter** property to the constant **adFilterNone**.

## Performing Direct Modifications

Although it is possible to use the methods described previously to perform modifications against the data provider, they are not usually the best option. For ActiveX components that are running in Microsoft Transaction Server

(MTS), a more efficient method is to execute the updates directly against the data provider using the **Connection** or **Command** objects. This is because the methods described earlier require that a **Recordset** object be created and available to perform the modifications. Remember that to take full advantage of MTS, your ActiveX components should be stateless and not provide recordsets to the client and then simply wait around to process updates or deletes. This would be an inefficient use of MTS and require that a component instance be dedicated for each client accessing your application the entire time the client is running.

Instead, use the **Execute** method of either the **Connection** or **Command** object to perform the direct update using the SQL **INSERT**, **UPDATE**, and **DELETE** statements. For example, to perform the equivalent insert into the **authors** table we saw previously, you could use the following statement:

```
cnSQL.Execute "INSERT INTO authors (au_id,au_lname, " & _
    "au_fname,city,state,zip,contract) VALUES " & _
    "('123-45-6789','Will','George','Chevy Chase','MD','55555',0)", _
    ,adExecuteNoRecords
```

 The **adExecuteNoRecords** constant specified as the third parameter to the **Execute** method instructs ADO 2.0 to bypass creating and verifying any recordset properties since no recordset will be returned. This will enhance performance.

However, even this code is not ideal. A better method is to create a stored procedure that takes the necessary parameters to perform the insert and then calls the procedure using the **Command** object. This procedure call is then wrapped in a method exposed by your component that takes all the arguments required by the procedure. For example, if I created a component called Authors that contained methods to manipulate the **authors** table, I would create an **Add** method in the component to allow the client to insert a new record in the **authors** table. This method would contain ADO code to call an **AddAuthor** stored procedure, passing in its arguments. You can see the code for the stored procedure in Listing 9.8 and the code for the method in Listing 9.9.

## Listing 9.8 A stored procedure used to insert a new author.

```
CREATE PROCEDURE AddAuthor
@au_id char(11),
@au_lname varchar(40),
@au_fname varchar(20),
@city varchar(20),
@state char(2),
```

```
@zip char(5),
@contract tinyint

AS
INSERT INTO authors
    (au_id,au_lname,au_fname,city,state,zip,contract)
VALUES (@au_id,
    @au_lname,
    @au_fname,
    @city,
    @state,
    @zip,
    @contract)
```

## Listing 9.9    An **Add** method of an authors component that uses a stored procedure to execute the insert into the database.

```
Public Function Add(ByVal strId As String, _
    ByVal strLName As String, ByVal strFName As String, _
    ByVal strCity As String, ByVal strState As String, _
    ByVal strZip As String, ByVal intContract As Integer) As Boolean

Dim cnSQL As ADODB.Connection
Dim cmSQL As ADODB.Command
Dim prmParm As ADODB.Parameter

On Error GoTo AddErr

Set cnSQL = New ADODB.Connection
cnSQL.ConnectionString = "driver={Sql server};" & _
    "database=pubs;server=ssosa;uid=sa"
cnSQL.Open

Set cmSQL = New ADODB.Command

With cmSQL
    .ActiveConnection = cnSQL
    .CommandType = adCmdStoredProc
    .CommandText = "AddAuthor"
End With

Set prmParm = cmSQL.CreateParameter("@au_id", adChar, adParamInput, _
                                    Len(strId), strId)
cmSQL.Parameters.Append prmParm
```

```
Set prmParm = cmSQL.CreateParameter("@au_lname", adVarChar, _
                               adParamInput, Len(strLName), _
                               strLName)
cmSQL.Parameters.Append prmParm
Set prmParm = cmSQL.CreateParameter("@au_fname", adVarChar, _
                               adParamInput, Len(strFName), _
                               strFName)
cmSQL.Parameters.Append prmParm
Set prmParm = cmSQL.CreateParameter("@city", adVarChar, _
                               adParamInput, Len(strCity), _
                               strCity)
cmSQL.Parameters.Append prmParm
Set prmParm = cmSQL.CreateParameter("@state", adChar, adParamInput, _
                               Len(strState), strState)
cmSQL.Parameters.Append prmParm
Set prmParm = cmSQL.CreateParameter("@zip", adChar, adParamInput, _
                               Len(strZip), strZip)
cmSQL.Parameters.Append prmParm
Set prmParm = cmSQL.CreateParameter("@contract", adTinyInt, _
                               adParamInput, 2, intContract)
cmSQL.Parameters.Append prmParm

cmSQL.Execute

Add = True
Exit Function
AddErr:
    Err.Raise Err.Number, "Author:Add", Err.Description
    Add = False

End Function
```

I prefer this technique because it takes advantage of the performance gain realized in SQL Server when using stored procedures and at the same time isolates your code from the underlying database schema.

# Advanced Retrieval Topics

Now that we've covered all the basics relating to using ADO to retrieve and modify data, we can discuss four additional concepts that you'll need to master for the exam. These have to do with cursors, disconnected recordsets, locking, and using transactions.

## Using Cursors

Whether you realized it or not, all the code you've previously seen that uses ADO recordsets employs cursors. Simply defined, *cursors* are what provide your code the ability to scroll through the recordset, maintain the pointer to the current record, and determine whether or not the recordset is updateable. Each cursor is defined by two properties exposed by the **Connection** and **Recordset** objects: **CursorType** and **CursorLocation**. All the recordsets we've created thus far have employed the default cursor type and location, so now we need to look at these properties more closely to determine how they should be set.

In ADO there are four types of cursors that you can employ. Each one is useful in different situations and consumes differing amounts of client, server, and network resources. Table 9.3 summarizes the four types, the constant used when setting the property, and what functionality each provides.

You can find a summary of the functionality provided by the cursor types in Table 9.4. As mentioned previously, to set the cursor type you can either change the **CursorType** property of the **Connection** object or the **Recordset** object be-

| Table 9.3 | ADO cursor locations. | |
|---|---|---|
| **Cursor Type** | **Constant** | **Summary** |
| Forward Only | **adOpenForwardOnly** | This type of cursor is the default, requires the least amount of overhead, and is thus generally the fastest. As the name implies, this cursor allows only **MoveNext** operations on the recordset. The records may also be updateable, but you cannot see data that is changed by other users. |
| Static | **adOpenStatic** | This type of cursor copies all the data in the recordset and allows you to scroll backward and forward through the recordset. It consumes more memory than a forward-only cursor because it has to copy all the data. As the name implies, other users' changes will not be able to be seen and it is updateable. |
| Keyset | **adOpenKeyset** | This type of cursor constructs and stores only a key value for each row in the recordset, and each row is retrieved only as it is accessed. Because less data is stored in the cursor, it consumes less memory than Static cursors. This type of cursor is scrollable and updateable, and deletes and updates by other users are visible. |
| Dynamic | **adOpenDynamic** | This cursor type allows the maximum functionality, but also consumes the most resources. It is fully scrollable and updateable, and all changes made by other users are visible. |

| Table 9.4 | Cursor functionality. | | | |
|---|---|---|---|---|
| Type | Scrollable | Updateable | Changes Visible | Resource Usage |
| Forward Only | No | Yes | No | Low |
| Static | Yes | Yes | Yes | Medium |
| Keyset | Yes | Yes | Delete/Update | Medium |
| Dynamic | Yes | Yes | Yes | High |

fore opening a recordset. The property of the **Connection** object controls the default type used for all recordsets, although you can override it on each recordset.

The second cursor-related property that influences how the cursor is created in ADO is **CursorLocation**. This property specifies where the cursor resides and can be set to the constants **adUseClient** or **adUseServer**.

By changing the cursor location to **adUseClient**, you instruct ADO to use a cursor engine located on the client machine. Remember that in a distributed application the client machine is the machine running the MTS components. By using client cursors, you decrease the load on the data provider while perhaps sacrificing increased functionality, such as seeing changes other users have made to the data. However, the client-side cursor library that Microsoft provides supports disconnected recordsets that allow offline modifications, as we'll discuss shortly.

Server-side cursors are the default setting and ensure that the data provider keeps the cursor on the server. Although this option is efficient for large recordsets where only a few records are accessed or updated, and provides the most flexibility when selecting a cursor type, it can quickly lead to server resource problems as more clients create cursors. For that reason, and because most applications should be designed to work with small recordsets (several hundred records at most), I recommend the use of client-side cursors almost exclusively.

For the exam you'll need to be prepared to select a cursor type and location based on a specific set of requirements given in the question.

The cursor location also has an impact on what cursor types are supported by the data provider. For example, when using Microsoft SQL Server, dynamic cursors cannot be created when the cursor engine is located on the client, because the client is not aware of changes made on the server. If you attempt to set the cursor type to **adOpenDynamic** in this situation, ADO will automatically reset it to

| Table 9.5 | The cursor types that are supported by SQL Server and their locations. | | | |
|---|---|---|---|---|
| **Cursor Location** | **Static** | **Dynamic** | **Keyset** | **Forward Only** |
| Server | Yes | Yes | Yes | Yes |
| Client | Yes | No | No | Yes |

**adOpenStatic** when the recordset is opened. Table 9.5 shows which cursor types can be created for the cursor locations when using Microsoft SQL Server.

## Locking

Recordsets also support different lock types through the **LockType** property, which determines how the data is locked by the data provider while it is being edited. By default, all recordsets are created with the lock type **adLockReadOnly**. To allow the recordset to be edited you'll need to use one of the other types. The available lock types are shown in Table 9.6.

The primary considerations when choosing a lock type are concurrency and data consistency. By using optimistic locking, you are ensuring greater concurrency, because more users will be able to modify the data. However, this comes with the cost of reducing the data consistency, because there is a greater potential for a second user to update the record while others are viewing it. On the other hand, pessimistic locking ensures that the data will remain consistent, because it is locked earlier. However, it allows less concurrency, because subsequent users may encounter row or page locks while the modification is being performed.

## Using Disconnected Recordsets

One of the advanced features of ADO is the ability to create *disconnected recordsets*. These recordsets can be created on the client and then, as the name suggests, be disconnected from the **Connection** object. The records can then

| Table 9.6 | Recordset lock types. |
|---|---|
| **Lock Type** | **Description** |
| **adLockReadOnly** | The data cannot be altered. This is the default and consumes the least amount of overhead by the recordset. |
| **adLockPessimistic** | The data is locked when it is edited. |
| **adLockOptimistic** | The data is only locked when the **Update** method is called. |
| **adLockBatchOptimistic** | The data can be updated on the client and later synchronized with the data provider. This is known as a *disconnected recordset*. |

be scrolled and modified without a persistent connection to the database. When the client is ready, a new connection can be associated with the recordset and the changes submitted to the data provider. ADO then provides a mechanism for determining whether or not the updates were successful and for handling conflicts with existing data.

To create a disconnected recordset, you must use a client-side cursor opened as **adOpenStatic** or **adOpenKeyset** and use the lock type **adLockBatchOptimistic**. After creating the recordset, you can set its **ActiveConnection** property to **Nothing** to disconnect it:

```
Dim rsAuthors As ADODB.Recordset
Set rsAuthors = New ADODB.Recordset

rsAuthors.CursorType = adOpenStatic
rsAuthors.CursorLocation = adUseClient
rsAuthors.Open "SELECT * FROM authors", cnSQL, , adLockBatchOptimistic
Set rsAuthors.ActiveConnection = Nothing
```

With the recordset disconnected, you can now modify, add, or delete records with the same techniques we discussed earlier. The difference is that to save the changes you must now reset the **ActiveConnection** property to a valid **Connection** object and call the **UpdateBatch** method rather than the **Update** method.

The **UpdateBatch** method creates SQL statements for each row modified and sends them to the data provider. The statements that are sent use SQL that determines whether the row has been modified since it was first downloaded. If the row has changed on the server, ADO marks the record as a conflict and changes the **Status** property for that record to indicate why the record could not be changed. If any of the records are in conflict, then the entire recordset is not updated. In addition, a trappable error is generated in Visual Basic and the **Errors** collection of the **Connection** object is populated with the errors. Once the method returns, you can filter the recordset by setting the **Filter** property to the constant **adFilterConflictingRecords**. Only those records that had conflicts will now be visible and you can scroll through them, interrogating each record's **Status** property to determine why the update failed. You can see an example of the code required in Listing 9.10.

## Listing 9.10   Updating a disconnected recordset and checking for conflicts.

```
On Error Goto UpdateErr

'Reset the ActiveConnection
Set rsAuthors.ActiveConnection = cnSQL
rsAuthors.UpdateBatch
```

```
'Other code goes here

UpdateErr:
'Set the filter
rsAuthors.Filter = adFilterConflictingRecords
Do While Not rsAuthors.EOF
   'Check the status
    Debug.Print rsAuthors.Status
   'Fix the error
    rsAuthors.MoveNext
Loop
Resume 'Resubmit the recordset
```

The **Status** property can be one of 18 different values that determine the cause of the update failure. The most common values to check for include **adRecModified**, **adReIntegrityViolation**, and **adRecCantRelease**.

After looking at the reason why the updates failed, you may want to see what the new values are in the database. To tell ADO to retrieve these values you must use the **Resync** method of the recordset and pass it the constants **adAffectGroup** and **adResyncUnderlyingValues**:

```
rsAuthors.Resync adAffectGroup, adResyncUnderlyingValues
```

This method populates the **UnderlyingValue** property of each **Field**, which you can then query. Once you are satisfied with your changes, you can resubmit them by simply calling **UpdateBatch** again, as shown in Listing 9.10. Any modified records will then be overwritten in the database by ADO.

> *Note: The **Field** object also exposes the **OriginalValue** and **Value** properties that allow you to view the value that was originally retrieved from the data provider, as well the current value in the recordset.*

In a distributed application you can take advantage of disconnected recordsets to pass the recordset to the base client application, which frees up your component to be recycled by MTS. Once the updates are complete, you can then pass the recordset to a method in your component that calls the **UpdateBatch** method and checks for conflicts. With this technique, ADO must be installed on the base client, but it frees up resources on the machine running MTS.

## Using Transactions

The ADO **Connection** object supports methods that allow you to control when modifications to the data provider are committed or rolled back. The **BeginTrans**, **CommitTrans**, and **RollbackTrans** methods are used to control when a transaction is started, committed, and cancelled, respectively. Normally you would use transactions with the ADO methods just described to ensure that multiple data modifications to a single data provider either all succeed or are all rolled back. This ensures data consistency between tables in a relational database.

However, in distributed applications the situation is a little more complex. In these applications, multiple components may be interacting with multiple databases and the modifications made by all of these may need to be included in the scope of a single distributed transaction. In other words, the work of several components must be coordinated. When your components run in MTS, it uses the *Distributed Transaction Coordinator* (DTC) service to coordinate the modifications with the data providers (called *Resource Managers* in DTC) and your components. When you call the **SetComplete** or **SetAbort** methods of the context object in your component, MTS instructs the DTC to send a commit or rollback command to the Resource Manager if all the components participating in the transaction agree. This ensures that all the Resource Managers either commit their transactions or roll them back together. This process used by the DTC is what is commonly called a *two-phase commit*.

# Handling Errors

Errors in ADO are handled through a collection of **Error** objects that are accessed through the **Connection** object. Each time an error is returned by the data provider, an **Error** object is created and appended to the collection for the appropriate **Connection** object and a trappable error is thrown. Similar to VB's own **Err** object, the **Error** object exposes properties for viewing the **Description, Source, Number, HelpFile,** and **HelpContext** of the error. In addition, it also provides raw information from the data provider in the properties **SQLState** and **NativeError**.

Because a single statement can generate multiple errors, you should always check the entire **Errors** collection to view all the errors that were returned. The first error in the collection will also be mirrored in the **Err** object.

Because components do not have a user interface, you must avoid using message boxes or other UI elements in your error handlers. Instead, one strategy for error handling is to log the error to the Windows NT event log using VB's **App** object and then simply notify the client program that the error occurred. Listing 9.11 shows the code of a method that uses the **Errors** collection to construct a string that will be logged to the NT event log and then will raise a custom error back to the calling program.

## Listing 9.11    Using the Errors collection.

```
Dim cnSQL As ADODB.Connection
Dim rsAuthors As ADODB.Recordset
Dim objErr As ADODB.Error
Dim strEvent As String

On Error GoTo ADOErr

'Create and open a connection...

Set rsAuthors = New ADODB.Recordset
rsAuthors.Open "SELECT * FROM sdfauthors", cnSQL

Exit Sub
ADOErr:
    For Each objErr In cnSQL.Errors
        strEvent = objErr.Number & ":" & _
            objErr.SQLState & ":" & _
            objErr.Description & ":" & _
            objErr.NativeError
    Next

    'Log to the NT event log
    App.LogEvent strEvent, 1

    Set rsAuthors = Nothing
    Set cnSQL = Nothing

'Raise a custom error to the client
Err.Raise vbObjectError + 1024, "MyComponent:MyMethod", Err.Description
```

The **Errors** collection will be automatically cleared when the next error is returned. Otherwise, you may use the **Clear** method of the collection to clear the errors. Keep in mind that only errors returned by the data provider are stored in the **Errors** collection. Errors returned by ADO itself are simply returned, as are all other errors in VB, through the **Err** object.

# ADO Techniques In Distributed Applications

Distributed applications have a few techniques that you may want to take advantage of to make your applications more scalable and perform better:

➤ Always perform modifications using the **Execute** method of the **Connection** object or a **Command** object. This is especially true when you want to update multiple rows in a table. You can accomplish this with a single SQL statement rather than a cursor and looping.

➤ Always use the least expensive cursor for the job. Generally this a forward-only, read-only, client-side cursor. If the data is going to be traversed immediately and the recordset closed, then using a server-side cursor with SQL Server is actually more efficient. Using server-side cursors with recordsets that remain active can quickly bog down a database server.

➤ Always create ADO objects as late as possible and release them as early as possible. This minimizes the number of open connections on the database server and the amount of resources your components consume.

➤ Use stored procedures whenever possible for data access. This has both a performance and maintenance advantage.

➤ You can use the **CacheSize** property of the **Recordset** object to optimize the number of records the OLE DB provider retrieves from the data provider. For some types of cursors, adjusting this properly can significantly reduce the number of network round trips that must be made when retrieving rows.

# Practice Questions

## Question 1

You want to write a SQL statement to retrieve only those books in the **titles** table who have authors, along with the author's name. The **SELECT** clause you construct is:

```
SELECT a.title, b.au_fname, b.au_lname
```

Assume the **au_fname** and **au_lname** columns are found in the **authors** table and the **title** column is found in the **titles** table. Which **FROM** clause will join the tables together correctly?

❍ a.  FROM titles b INNER JOIN authors a ON a.au_id = b.au_id

❍ b.  FROM titles a INNER JOIN authors b ON a.au_id = b.au_id

❍ c.  FROM titles a LEFT OUTER JOIN authors b ON a.au_id = b.au_id

❍ d.  FROM titles AND authors WHERE a.au_id = b.au_id

The correct answer is b. There are two keys to this question. The first is to discern whether an inner or outer join is required. Because the question asks specifically for those rows in the **titles** table "who have authors," you can deduce that an inner join is needed. Remember that an outer join returns all the rows that intersect between two tables and those that do not in one of the tables. Therefore, answer c is incorrect.

The second key is to know the syntax for an inner join. The reason a is incorrect is that the tables' aliases are mismatched. The alias "b" should belong to the **authors** table and not the **titles** table, because the question states that the **au_fname** and **au_lname** columns belong to the **authors** table and are specified with alias b in the **SELECT** clause.

Answer d is incorrect because the syntax is fictitious.

# Question 2

You want to write a SQL statement to insert all the rows from the **authors_temp** table into an existing **authors** table. Both tables have identical structures. Which statement is correct?

- a. INSERT INTO authors SELECT * FROM authors_temp
- b. INSERT INTO authors VALUES FROM authors_temp
- c. SELECT * FROM authors_temp INTO authors
- d. INSERT INTO authors WHERE authors.au_id = authors_temp.au_id

The correct answer is a. Remember that to insert a row from one table into another you use the **INSERT INTO SELECT** syntax. As long as the columns are of the same number and data type (as this question states), you can simply use the **SELECT** * to retrieve all the columns. To insert a single row into a table you use the **VALUES** clause of the **INSERT** statement. Therefore, b is incorrect, and in fact uses invalid syntax. Answer c is incorrect because it uses the **SELECT INTO** syntax rather than **INSERT INTO SELECT**. The **SELECT INTO** has the effect of creating a table as well as populating it. In this case, the statement would create the **authors** table and the question specifically states that the **authors** table already exists. Answer d is incorrect because the syntax is invalid, although in Transact-SQL you may use joins inside of **INSERT** statement in some circumstances.

# Question 3

You want to write a distributed application using components that will be used by different client front ends. The components must access a relational database. What is the best approach for developing this solution?

- a. Create COM objects in VB that use the database vendor's native API to access the data using stored procedures.
- b. Create COM objects in VB that use the ODBC API to access the relational database using SQL statements.
- c. Create COM objects in VB that use OLE DB directly to access the relational database using SQL statements.
- d. Create COM objects in VB that use ADO to call stored procedures in the relational database.

The correct answer is d; the COM objects you develop in VB should use ADO to communicate with the database. Using ADO allows your code to be more flexible and does not tie you to one vendor's API (as answer a would). Using the ODBC API, as in answer b, would work, but because ADO ships with an OLE DB Provider for ODBC (MSDASQL), which will use an ODBC driver to access the database, it is not the best approach. Answer c is incorrect because VB cannot use the OLE DB interfaces directly since it cannot reference the necessary pointers.

The latter part of each answer refers to the technique used to get at the data. For databases that support them, stored procedures are usually the best method for data access. Using stored procedures, your code is shielded from changes to the database schema, reducing maintenance; also, stored procedures often provide a performance advantage.

## Question 4

Which of the following are valid ways to populate an ADO **Recordset** object? [Check all that apply]

❑ a. Use the **Execute** method of the **Connection** object, passing it a SQL statement that returns a result set.

❑ b. Use the **Open** method of the **Recordset** object, passing it a SQL statement that returns a result set and a reference to a valid **Connection** object.

❑ c. Use the **Execute** method of the **Command** object to execute the SQL stored in the **CommandText** property of the **Command** object.

❑ d. Use the **CreateRecordset** method of the **Command** object, passing it a SQL statement that returns a result set.

The correct answers are a, b, and c. All three of the methods are valid for populating a **Recordset** object; which one you use depends on what type of recordset will be created and the SQL needed to generate it. For example, the method in answer a is the most efficient when you want a forward-only, read-only recordset that you read and quickly dispose of. The method in answer b is useful when you want to create the recordset object independently of the **Connection** and **Command** and associate with a **Connection** object at a later point. The method described in answer c is most useful when calling a stored procedure that uses parameters.

Answer d is incorrect because the **Command** object does not support a **CreateRecordset** method.

## Question 5

In what situation would you open up the recordset **rs** with the following properties:

```
rs.CursorType = adOpenStatic
rs.CursorLocation = adUseServer
rs.LockType = adLockOptimistic
```

○ a. When you are going to access and possibly update most or all of the records in the recordset and must scroll forward and backward

○ b. When you want to use a disconnected recordset to make changes on the client and marshal those changes back across the network

○ c. When you are going to access proportionally few records in a large recordset and must scroll and update the recordset

○ d. When you want to read the records sequentially, loading them into an array for display only

The correct answer is c. The question specifies that the recordset will use a static, server-side, updateable cursor. Static cursors allow the recordset to be fully scrollable, therefore it would be overkill for answer d where a forward-only, read-only cursor would be more appropriate. Creating the cursor on the server consumes shared resources on the server although, as in this question, you may want to do it since the alternative is to possibly download a large recordset to the client and only access a few records. Using optimistic locking with server-side cursors is especially important since using pessimistic locking may create contention on the server for the same records.

Remember that to use disconnected recordsets you must set the **CursorLocation** to **adUseClient** and the **LockType** to **adLockBatchOptimistic**. Therefore, answer b is incorrect.

The scenario in answer a would be better suited to a cursor type of **adOpenKeyset** or **adOpenStatic** and a location of **adUseClient** since you are going to access most or all of the records. Using a server-side cursor would generate excessive network traffic. Therefore, answer a is incorrect.

# Question 6

Which method(s) can you use to populate and pass parameters to an ADO **Command** object? [Check all that apply]

❑ a. Call the **Parameters.Refresh** method of the **Command** object. Use the **Parameters** collection to assign the values.

❑ b. Create the **Parameter** objects using the **CreateParameter** method of the **Command** object specifying the values. Append the **Parameter** object to the **Parameters** collection of the **Command** object.

❑ c. Create a **Parameter** object using the **Parameters.Add-Parameter** method of the **Command** object. Use the **Parameters** collection to assign the values.

❑ d. Call the **Parameters.Populate** method of the **Command** object. Use the **Parameters** collection to assign the values.

The correct answers are a and b. Both of these methods are valid for creating and setting parameters, although they are not the same. The method described in answer a is the easiest in terms of lines of code, but is less efficient because the **Refresh** method instructs ADO to query the data provider for the names, directions, and data types of the parameters. Therefore an extra network round trip is required.

The method described in answer b requires more code, because you must fully specify the name, data type, and direction of each parameter using the **CreateParameter** method. You then must append the **Parameter** object to the **Parameters** collection for the **Command** object.

Answers c and d are incorrect because there is no **AddParameter** or **Populate** method of the **Parameters** collection.

## Question 7

When using a disconnected recordset, **rs**, which series of actions can you take to update the server and check for conflicts in the event that an error or errors is discovered?

○ a. Associate the recordset with a connection using the **rs.ActiveConnection** property. Call the **UpdateBatch** method of the **Connection** object. Set the **rs.Filter** property to **adFilterConflictingRecords**. Check the **rs.Status** property of each record.

○ b. Associate the recordset with a connection using the **rs.ActiveConnection** property. Call the **rs.UpdateBatch** method. Set the **rs.Filter** property to **adFilter-ConflictingRecords**. Check the **rs.Status** property of each record.

○ c. Associate the recordset with a connection using the **rs.ActiveConnection** property. Call the **rs.Update** method. Set the **rs.Filter** property to **adFilter-ConflictingRecords**. Check the **rs.Status** property of each record.

○ d. Associate the recordset with a connection using the **rs.Connection** property. Call the **rs.UpdateBatch** method. Set the **rs.Filter** property to **adCheckConflictingRecords**. Check the **rs.Status** property of each record.

The correct answer is b. To update the recordset you must first use the **ActiveConnection** property of the recordset to reassociate the recordset with a valid connection to the data provider. By calling **UpdateBatch** on the recordset, the SQL statements are then sent to the data provider. If any errors occur, a trappable error will be thrown, and the **Errors** collection of the **Connection** object will be populated. You can then set the recordset's **Filter** property to **adFilterConflictingRecords** to view only those records that had conflicts. After checking each record's **Status** property and perhaps using the recordset's **Resync** method to view the changed values in the database, you can then correct your changes and resubmit them again using the **UpdateBatch** method.

Answer a is incorrect because the **UpdateBatch** method does not belong to the **Connection** object. Answer c is incorrect because the **Update** method is used to update connected recordsets. Answer d is incorrect because the proper method for reconnecting the recordset is **ActiveConnection** and the constant you use with the **Filter** property is not **adCheckConflictingRecords**.

# Question 8

What are the primary differences between the **LockType adLockOptimistic** and **adLockPessimistic**? [Check all that apply]

❑ a. **adLockOptimistic** locks records from the time they are modified through the call to the **Update** method of the recordset. This ensures greater concurrency, but less data consistency.

❑ b. **adLockOptimistic** locks records only during the call to the **Update** method of the recordset. This ensures greater concurrency, but less data consistency.

❑ c. **adLockPessimistic** locks records from the time they are modified through the call to the **Update** method of the recordset. This ensures greater data consistency, but less concurrency.

❑ d. **adLockPessimistic** locks records from the time they are modified through the call to the **Update** method of the recordset. This ensures greater concurrency, but less data consistency.

The correct answers are b and c. remember that the issues to be concerned with related to locking are data consistency and concurrency. Optimistic locking provides greater concurrency because the locks are held for a shorter time. However, it provides less consistency because other users may be updating the record while it is being viewed and before the **Update** method is called.

The reverse is true of pessimistic locking. Locks are held longer and thus serve to reduce simultaneous access to the data (concurrency). On the other hand, the data is more consistently updated, because only one user may lock the record at one time.

## Question 9

You are designing an application that uses ADO for salesmen who work in field. One of the requirements is that they be able to download sets of records to their laptop and manipulate them while not connected to the network. Which methods of the ADO **Recordset** object can assist you in this design? [Check all that apply]

❑ a. **Filter**

❑ b. **Save**

❑ c. **Open**

❑ d. **GetRows**

The correct answers are b and c. The **Save** method has been added in ADO 2.0 to persist recordsets to files when passed a filename and format. The **Open** method can then be used to re-open the recordset during a later session of the application. Answer a is incorrect because the **Filter** method simply specifies which records are visible to be saved, but does not actually save them. Answer d is incorrect because it is not the easiest method, although it is possible to use the **GetRows** method to return a variant array of the records and then write your own code to save the array to disk.

# Need To Know More?

 Bowman, Judith S. and Emerson, Sandra L.: *The Practical SQL Handbook: Using Structured Query Language*. Addison Wesley, 1996. ISBN: 0201447878. Although not as long on theory as Date, this book covers all aspects of SQL. One nice aspect of this book is the table that describes the differences between Microsoft, Sybase, and Oracle.

 Date, Chris J.: *An Introduction to Database Systems*. Addison Wesley, 1994 (sixth edition). ISBN: 020154329X. This is a classic book for understanding relational theory and providing a foundation for using SQL. This edition also is expanded to cover some object oriented database concepts.

 Fox, Dan: "ADO 2.0 Adds Performance, Flexibility." July 1998 issue of the *Visual Basic Programmer's Journal*. I wrote this article to discuss the differences between ADO and the legacy RDO and DAO data access models from Microsoft. This should be particularly helpful for those developers who have used RDO and DAO in the past.

 Homer, Alex and Sussman, David: *ADO 2.0 Programmer's Reference*. Wrox Press, 1998. ISBN: 1861001835. This book is a handy one to have around when programming with ADO. It explains each property and method in depth and provides some examples.

 Vaughn, William R.: *Hitchhiker's Guide to Visual Basic and SQL Server*. Microsoft Press, 1998 (sixth edition). ISBN: 1572318481. If previous editions of this book are any indication, it will be one you'll want to include in your library. This new edition covers ADO and always contains fascinating nuggets about performance and optimization.

 Although it is not emphasized in this book, you could run across several questions on RDO on the exam. To prepare for these you should read the topics "Running ADO Asynchronously" and "Performing an Action Query" in the MSDN Online help.

 Microsoft's Universal Data Access Web site at **www.microsoft.com/data** is a good place to start reviewing the concepts behind OLE DB and ADO. You'll find links to white papers that describe the architecture as well as downloads to the most current releases of the technology.

# Testing Strategies For Distributed Applications

**10**

## Terms you'll need to understand:

- √ Compiler options/switches
- √ Conditional compiler constants
- √ Conditional compiler directives
- √ Locals window
- √ Immediate window
- √ Watch window
- √ Call stack
- √ Breakpoint
- √ **Assert** method
- √ **Print** method

## Techniques you'll need to master:

- √ Setting breakpoints
- √ Defining watch expressions
- √ Adding conditional compiling directives to code
- √ Printing to the Immediate window using **?**, **Print**, and **Debug.Print**
- √ Evaluating variable values during break mode by using debug windows
- √ Choosing the correct compiler options in a given scenario
- √ Stepping through code by using the Debug toolbar
- √ Entering break mode by using **Debug.Assert**
- √ Resolving scope issues with watch expressions

# Testing The Solution

Once you have developed a solution, testing that solution is a vital part of the development process. Testing and debugging applications is a necessary hurdle that you must successfully traverse before delivering a working solution to the client. Unfortunately, testing the solution is not a one-time event. In fact, numerous loops through the compiling process are generally required to test for multiple scenarios and to ensure that the complex changes made to the application will continue to produce a stable solution. To aid in the compiling process, Visual Basic provides a large number of compiler options that you can use to optimize the resulting compiled binary executable or to tailor the nature of the resulting binary for different systems. These compiling options can be separated into *basic optimization* and *advanced optimization* choices.

Prior to compiling, testing a solution generally involves a large degree of repetitive debugging activities. While developing a solution within the Visual Basic IDE, numerous tools are provided to aid in the debugging process. In fact, most debugging typically occurs within the design environment. Many types of Visual Basic applications are far too complex to traverse the compiling procedures every time a minor change is made to the application. Therefore, Visual Basic provides numerous tools to assist in the process of eliminating the numerous instances of unpredictability that crop up at the least opportune times. Familiarity with the use of these tools is essential for both efficient solution development and success in the exam.

# Compiling Choices

The choices supported by Visual Basic for configuring, optimizing, or controlling the compiling process can be separated into two main camps. The first camp, collectively referred to as *compiler options*, provides an avenue for optimizing and configuring the characteristics of the resulting compiled binary executable. These options instruct Visual Basic as to how to proceed in compiling the high-level instructions of your Visual Basic application into lower-level code. The second camp of compiling instructions is collectively referred to as *conditional compiling*. These conditional compiling constants or directives are programmatic instructions used to instruct Visual Basic during the compile process as to what portions of code to include or ignore. These code elements allow for variations in the resulting compile binary executable at a far more complex level than otherwise would be possible through simple configuration settings.

## Selecting The Appropriate Compiler Options

Accessing compiler options is performed by adjusting the project properties. Within Visual Basic, click on Project|Properties. The Project Properties page contains five tabs: General, Make, Compile, Component, and Debugging. For selecting compiling options, we are primarily concerned with the Compile tab. Basic compiling options are listed directly on the tab face; you'll find the advanced optimization choices on a separate dialog box by clicking on the Advanced Optimizations button.

## Basic Optimization Choices

On the Compile tab, shown in Figure 10.1, numerous options are available for configuring how the application is compiled. They are separated rather lopsidedly into two segments. The main decision to be made is whether to Compile To P-Code or Compile To Native Code. What is the difference between the two choices? *P-code*, or *pseudocode*, was the standard type of VB compiled executable produced in Visual Basic 4 or earlier. The binary compiled into p-code requires translation of the instructions into native code instruction. This interpretation is handled by the VB runtime DLL. Starting with version 5, and carried into version 6, the Professional and Enterprise Editions of VB allow projects to be compiled directly into native code. This eliminates the need for numerous translation functions within the Visual Basic runtime DLL and provides visible performance improvements for certain types of applications.

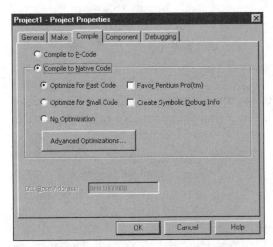

**Figure 10.1**    The Compile tab of Project Properties provides numerous compile switches.

The following list shows application characteristics that might benefit from compiling directly to native code:

➤ Numerous, repetitive, or complex nonstring calculations, such as financial calculations

➤ Computationally rich applications, especially if involving the movement or modification of large amounts of data in local memory

Other types of application characteristics tend to receive very little benefit from directly compiling to native code, including:

➤ Heavy use of subroutine calls compared to basic inline procedures. The process of setting up call stacks, variable initialization, and cleanup maintain a negligible benefit from the compiled native code versus the p-code engine routines.

➤ VBA runtime function-intensive applications.

➤ Extensive use of COM method calls or Windows API calls.

➤ Extensive string manipulation.

If the choice is made to compile directly to native code, then the bulk of the VB-supported compiling switches become available for use, as seen in Figure 10.1. The switches are centered around optimizing the native code to run more efficiently if certain decisions or assumptions can be made.

The first decision to be made concerns general optimization preferences, including whether to optimize for speed, size, or not to attempt general optimization routines. After the general optimization decision is made, two additional choices are provided concerning specific forms of optimization.

## Optimize For Fast Code

This compiler option instructs the compiler to favor any instruction routines that produce faster executing code over those that produce tighter or smaller code. Because numerous machine code variations often exist that can accurately represent any given Visual Basic statement, variations in the resulting size will occur. Choose this option to produce faster, but potentially larger code sequences, and hence executable sizes.

## Optimize For Small Code

This option is the opposite of the Optimize For Fast Code switch. This instructs the compiler to produce the machine code sequence variation that will produce the smallest or most compact series of commands for a given Visual Basic statement. Notice in Figure 10.1 that Optimize For Small Code and Optimize For Fast Code are both radio buttons. This indicates their status as mutually exclusive options.

### No Optimization

This option effectively turns off all forms of native code compilation optimization decisions. Native code is still produced, which is faster—in some cases—than p-code. This is the last mutually exclusive option for generic optimization, hence it is also a radio button.

### Favor Pentium Pro

This choice provides an additional level of basic, but specific, compiling optimizations that are used to favor the Pentium Pro or P6 line of processors. The Pentium Pro line provided an architecture that favors (and therefore improves) performance for certain types of machine code sequences. Code produced to leverage this favoritism would yield significant performance improvements on Pentium Pro systems, but tend to run sluggishly on earlier processor architectures. Choose this option only if your solution will be run primarily on Pentium Pro systems.

### Create Symbolic Debug Info

This is the slightly oddball option in the pack of basic optimization switches. Choosing this switch results in symbolic debug information being added to the executable, increasing the size slightly, but allowing for enhanced debugging options. The inclusion of the symbolic debug information, along with the accompanying PDB file generated by the compiler, will allow the executable to take advantage of debugging procedures made available through Visual C++ or compatible debuggers. Obviously, this switch is not a form of runtime binary executable optimization, but rather a form of solution testing optimization.

## Advanced Optimization Choices

In addition to the basic compiling choices listed, Visual Basic provides six advanced optimization choices, as seen in Figure 10.2, for further tailoring the choices made by the compiler when compiling directly to native code. Using these choices can carry some heavy negative ramifications, as numerous assumptions must be made in order to ensure the proper conditions for obtaining the optimization results. Use these options with care.

Be sure you really understand the meaning of the optimization options, primarily focusing on the advanced optimization options. This will help you understand the consequences of using the options, and you will be able to recognize when certain options are beneficial. For this reason, study the meaning of the six advanced optimization options listed in this chapter. Be prepared to pick the proper choice when given a scenario.

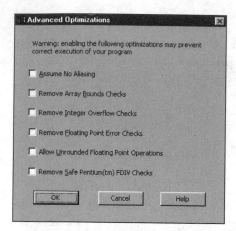

**Figure 10.2** Advanced optimization choices provide enhanced compiler configuration settings. Use of these settings requires certain assumptions to be made.

## Assume No Aliasing

The process of *aliasing* involves assigning a name (variable) to refer to a memory location that holds the value of a variable, when that memory location is already referred to by another name. This issue occurs when variables are passed into methods by reference (**ByRef**). Passing variables by reference is the default behavior of Visual Basic; it involves Visual Basic passing a reference to the actual memory location where the variable's value is held. This allows the variable to be directly accessed and its value to be directly modified, as opposed to accessing a copy. You can see an example of aliasing in Listing 10.1.

## Listing 10.1  Aliasing occurs when variables are passed by reference.

```
Sub BeginExample
    Dim x As String
    SecondSub x,x
End Sub

Sub SecondSub (y As String, z As String)
    y = "FirstValue"
    z = "SecondValue"
End Sub
```

In Listing 10.1, the **BeginExample** subroutine calls the **SecondSub** subroutine, passing the value of x for both parameters. Because **ByRef** is the default method for passing values, the **BeginExample** routine passes the memory location of the variable x to the **SecondSub** routine. Within the **SecondSub** routine, the variable y is used to refer to that memory location passed for the variable x. The variable z is then used as an alias to the same memory location. Checking the Assume No Aliasing option instructs the compiler to perform code compiling optimization techniques that are only possible if no aliasing occurs within the application. Checking the option when aliasing is present within the application will result in incorrect program execution and incorrect variable memory location references.

## Remove Array Bounds Checks

Whenever Visual Basic statements access an array, checks are made to determine if the array element being accessed is a valid or existing array member. If not, a runtime error is generated. The overhead for these checks can be significant for some applications. If an application can be reasonably confirmed to stay within all defined array boundaries, then choosing this option will instruct the compiler to not include the necessary machine code sequences to implement these standard boundary checks. Significant speed improvements can be obtained for array accesses by skipping these checks in a compiled application, but attempts to access an invalid array memory will result in invalid memory location accesses. This will result in unpredictable application behavior.

## Remove Integer Overflow Checks

The use of assorted data types provides for more efficient storage of variable data, but limits are imposed on the type or range of data that different data types can store. Integer-style data types (**Integer, Currency, Long**, and the like) are checked by Visual Basic for each access to ensure that any modification to the variable value remains within the valid range for that data type. If this option is selected, these checks will not be performed, which can provide significant improvements in variable value assignments. If an overflow occurs, incorrect values will result, causing incorrect calculations.

## Remove Floating Point Error Checks

Modifications to floating point data types are checked by Visual Basic to ensure that the result remains within the valid range for the data type. This check is similar to the integer overflow checks performed by Visual Basic for the integer-style data types. The floating point error checks performed by Visual Basic include checks for invalid floating point operations, such as division by zero. Using this option will turn off the checks in the compiled binary produced by the compiler, yielding execution performance improvements, but possibly resulting in incorrect values.

### Allow Unrounded Floating Point Operations

Floating point data types (**Single** and **Double**) are declared with a precision value that is implemented whenever a floating point calculation occurs. This ensures that subsequent comparisons to the same calculation or values yield the expected equalities. Using the option instructs the compiler to skip the machine code sequences in the compiled binary that produces these checks. This yields performance boosts, but may result in calculations being held to a higher than desired precision. Also, comparisons may fail when the results of floating point calculations are later compared to the same variable assigned the results.

 Pay extra-careful attention to the advanced optimization options that deal with floating point operations.

### Remove Safe Pentium FDIV Checks

The Visual Basic native code compiler adds special code to ensure that floating point division operations are accurate when the application is run on a Pentium system that has the *floating point division (FDIV)* bug. Because this code is only beneficial to the Pentium FDIV systems, combined with the relative rarity of these systems and the minor degree of error induced, using this option can provide benefits with relatively few downsides.

## Using Conditional Compilation

*Conditional compilation* provides the application developer with the ability to enforce selective code compiling. You can selectively compile portions of code to create variations of your solution designed to run on different platforms, including language-specific code segments, or to use different currency and date display filters. You can also use conditional compiling directives to conditionally compile debugging code into your application. However, starting with version 5, the **Debug.Assert** method is provided. This method of the **Debug** object is automatically stripped from the application during the compiling process.

Four conditional compiling directives exist for use within your Visual Basic code. These directives, **#If...Then**, **#Else**, **#ElseIf**, and **#EndIf**, provide the same conditional logic functionality as their standard counterparts, except certain usage rules apply:

➤ **#If...Then** can't stand by itself; it must be followed by **#EndIf**.

➤ **#Else, #ElseIf,** and **#EndIf** must be preceded by **#If...Then**.

➤ No other code can appear on the same line as **#If, #ElseIf, #Else,** or **#EndIf**.

➤ Only one **#Else** can follow **#If...Then**.

To induce conditional compiling directives into your code requires the use of conditional constants. These are similar to their standard counterparts because they are used to represent values throughout the application. The difference is that conditional constants are only recognized by the conditional compiling directives, effectively using only two values and a limited choice of scopes. Conditional constants effectively use only the values of **-1**, which evaluates to **True,** and something other than **-1**. Any other value besides **-1** will always evaluate to **False**.

Be conscious of the fact that **-1** evaluates to **True**. This is not intuitive and questions on the exam may ask which code will be included in an application during compile.

Setting conditional constants can be performed in three ways. As seen in Figure 10.3, the Make tab of the Project Properties dialog box provides a Conditional Compilation Arguments textbox. You can use this textbox to set conditional constants, such as **cndDebug** or **cndWin32**. The constants themselves can be named anything that adheres to standard naming limitations for variables, but following a naming convention of some type is recommended.

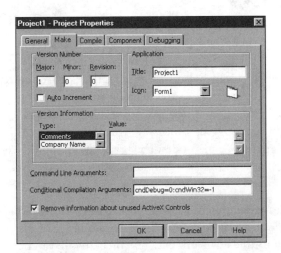

**Figure 10.3**    You can use the Make tab of Project Properties to set conditional constants.

The second method of setting conditional compilation constants is by using the **/d** command-line parameter for the VB6 executable in conjunction with the **/make** command-line parameter, as shown here:

```
Vb6.exe /make DemoApp.vbp /dcndWin32=-1:cndDebug=0
```

Notice that no space is placed after the **/d** switch, and multiple conditional compilation constants are added by using the colon (:) as the separator. Use of command-line conditional compilation constant value declarations overrides those values set on the Make tab of the Project Properties dialog box, but does not replace them.

The final method for setting the value of conditional compilation constants is programmatically through the use of the **#Const** statement, as seen here:

```
#Const cndDebug = -1
```

The scope of conditional compilation constants set either from within the Make tab or by use of the **/d** command-line parameter is effectively public to all modules within the project. Constants set programmatically are private to the module in which they are declared. Public conditional compiler constants can't be created in code, and although private, they are at the module level, no matter at what point they are declared in code. Attempting to use a standard constant defined with **Const**, instead of the conditional directive **#Const**, will result in an error, as will using an undefined conditional compiler constant.

# Debugging Tools

Testing a solution is, as we've already mentioned, an iterative process. To a large extent, this is true simply for the fact that applications rarely stop at Version 1.0. Although application versioning induces repetitive rides through the solution testing blueprints, debugging—concurrent with the application development process itself—is the real source of reliance on solution testing strategies. Constant checking and rechecking of application functionality requires good tools for facilitating the debugging process. Fortunately, Microsoft provides built-in tools for design-time, run-mode debugging of an application, eliminating the need for runtime-only, compiled binary executable debugging.

The Visual Basic IDE provides three modes: design mode, run mode, and break mode. It is the latter mode that is used to test the inner workings of the application in the context of a runtime environment. The break mode can be aptly described as a freeze-frame analysis of the application execution. Debugging is essentially supported by two classes of elements: those that invoke break mode, and those tools that are used when in break mode. Visual Basic supports numerous elements for enhancing debugging procedures. The following capabilities are not all those provided, but simply some of the most common:

➤ Breakpoints

➤ Break expressions

➤ Watch expressions

➤ Three variations of step-by-step code execution

➤ Runtime variable value display

➤ Break mode code modifications

➤ Code execution sequence modification

The debugging process aims to eliminate the three types of errors that can occur within an application's code: compile errors, runtime errors, and logic errors.

*Compile errors* are the product of incorrect code, in syntax or structure. This type of error includes missing punctuation, missing parameters, or omission of corresponding code elements. These errors are mostly noted when the application is compiled, hence its name. Many of these errors will provide the developer with some sort of early warning due to the advanced features of VB, such as Auto-Complete and Intellisense.

*Runtime errors* occur during the execution of the application, either during Visual Basic run mode or during actual compiled application execution. This type of error centers around the attempt to perform operations that are impossible, such as division by zero.

The final type of error is called *logic errors*; these refer to those results of code execution that do not live up to the expected outcome. Though the code is syntactically correct and no operations requested were impossible to carry out, the result of the code execution differed from what was intended.

The source of the errors, or bugs, is the ultimate target of any debugging efforts. Finding that source allows the code generating the issue to be removed or modified. To assist in finding those sources, numerous tools are provided by Visual Basic. The Debug toolbar, shown in Figure 10.4, provides quick access to several of these tools.

The following is a brief explanation of the different items on the Debug toolbar. A more detailed explanation of the Locals, Immediate, and Watch windows will appear in the remainder of this chapter:

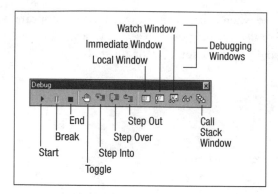

**Figure 10.4** The Debug toolbar provides access to many different debugging actions and tools.

➤ **Start** Initiates the run mode of Visual Basic, beginning the object or subroutine chosen as the Startup Object in the General tab of the Project Properties dialog box.

➤ **Break** Forces the running application to enter into break mode. From break mode, the three main debugging windows can be used extensively.

➤ **End** Terminates run mode, returning the application back to design mode.

➤ **Toggle Breakpoint** Toggles the line of code the current cursor is on to switch between being a breakpoint or not. Visual Basic will halt execution of application code when a breakpoint is reached.

➤ **Step Into** Used in break mode to step through code, line by line, including entering procedural code.

➤ **Step Over** Used in break mode to step through code, line by line, without entering procedural code.

➤ **Step Out** Used in break mode to conclude execution of the remainder of code in the current procedure, re-entering break mode after the procedure is completed.

➤ **Locals Window** Displays the value of current local variables.

➤ **Immediate Window** Used in break mode to execute code and query variable values.

➤ **Watch Window** Displays the value of selected or predefined expressions.

The last three items in the preceding bulleted list, representing the major debugging tools, are accessible by clicking on View in the menu bar. These debugging windows are generally used when Visual Basic enters break mode, which you can accomplish in numerous ways. Programmatically, you can enter break mode by issuing breakpoints, using **Stop** statements, or calling the **Assert** method of the **Debug** object. When Visual Basic encounters a **Stop** statement in code, it will enter break mode, if currently in run mode within the Visual Basic IDE. **Stop** statements are not recommended, because when erroneously left in a compiled executable, it will be treated as an **End** statement, resulting in complete termination of the running application. The preferred alternative to the **Stop** statement is the **Assert** method of the **Debug** object. This method receives a Boolean expression, conditionally instructing Visual Basic to enter break mode when the Boolean expression equals **False**. **Assert** is preferred because it is automatically stripped by the VB compiler when compiling an executable.

Graphically, you can enter or assign a breakpoint within the Visual Basic IDE, as seen in Figure 10.5. A breakpoint does not technically relate directly to any code statement; rather it is a setting or indicator of action to be performed. You can set breakpoints in four main ways. The first method, as seen in Figure 10.4, involves the Toggle Breakpoint button on the Debug toolbar. This sets the breakpoint status for the current line the cursor inhabits within the code window having the current focus. You can also apply a breakpoint to this same line by pressing F9, using the Debug menu item, or clicking in the left-hand margin of a code window next to the desired line. Any of these actions adds a round breakpoint marker in the left-hand margin. When Visual Basic encounters a breakpoint, **Stop** statement, or appropriately evaluated **Assert** method call, it enters break mode prior to executing the current statement. For example,

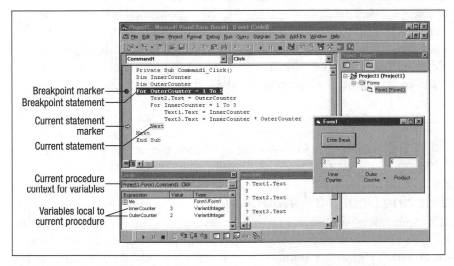

**Figure 10.5**     While in break mode, the Immediate window allows dynamic querying of variables and object properties.

in Figure 10.5, if the current statement was one line sooner, the value of **Text3.Text** (the Product shown in the Form1 dialog box) would still be 4. You can also issue breakpoints dynamically during run mode by using the key combination Ctrl+Break.

You cannot place explicitly set breakpoints on just any line of code. For example, a line of code cannot be the recipient of a breakpoint if it:

➤ Contains only comments

➤ Contains only line labels

➤ Contains only directives (such as **Dim**)

Analyzing the runtime modifications being made to variable data can often lead to the root of runtime and logical errors. Being able to see the value of variables while a program is executing lets you spot the exact moment an error is being induced. Use of the debugging windows is designed to facilitate the process of monitoring the data as the application is stepped through. For the remainder for this chapter, we will be focusing mainly on detecting runtime errors by using the Immediate, Locals, and Watch windows within the Visual Basic IDE.

# Checking Values By Using The Immediate Window

The Immediate window provides the ability to perform a number of different activities. If you want to evaluate expressions, invoke procedures currently within the scope, print debug information from the application, or assign values to variables and properties, the Immediate window supports these activities. This provides a wide range of possibilities for testing solutions, debugging procedures, and evaluating what-if scenarios without the need to compile or produce hard-code statements to generate the desired feedback during development.

 The exam may include a number of questions that require you to evaluate what will be printed in the Immediate window at a given point in the execution of code provided. Be fully aware of the support provided for printing to the Immediate window.

## *Printing Debug Information*

The Immediate window can provide a window for print information relating to debug status or custom messages concerning application execution. Printing information within the Immediate window is accomplished by using either **Debug.Print** within the application code, or by using **Print** typed directly into the Immediate window. Using **Debug.Print** allows dynamic information display without requiring Visual Basic to halt program execution. If break mode has already been entered, or actions need to be taken within break mode based on the information printed in the Immediate window, then use the **Print** statement directly within the Immediate window. As seen in Figure 10.5, you can use a question mark (?) as shorthand for the **Print** statement. You can use the **Print** statement to print variable values, property values, or assorted textual information.

### Changing Variable And Property Values

While in break mode, you can enter numerous types of statements into the Immediate window for evaluation. Included in the list of valid statements are value assignments for both variables and object properties. Assigning values within the Immediate window allows for testing the effects of these changes. This provides a lot of power over property and variable values, allowing modifications as if the result of an "act of God." Be careful to maintain the same scope considerations as if the statement were being encountered as the current statement lined up for execution in the code window.

### Testing Procedures

The Immediate window allows the execution of procedures and functions currently accessible within the scope of the current statement in the code window. Typing in a procedure or function, including parameters, will temporarily revert Visual Basic to run mode to execute the code, as if the statement were temporarily injected as the current statement. Scope issues continue to apply.

### Checking Error Descriptions

One unique use of the Immediate window is to issue an error statement. Using the code **error** *error_number* will result in a message box being issued with the information pertaining to the error raised, as if the error were actually generated and raised by the executing code. This can ease the research of information for unknown error numbers.

## Monitoring Values In The Locals Window

The Locals window is used to uniformly reveal the current values of all variables within the scope of the current procedure, form, or module. Through the process of code execution, the variables listed in the Locals window switch among the variables that remain within the listed scope. The Locals window allows you to change the values of the variables. To do so, merely click in the Value column of the desired variable, change the value, and move away from the box by using Tab, Enter, the up or down arrow keys, or by clicking somewhere else within the project to move focus. If the value modification is valid, it will take effect. If the modified value is invalid, the value will remain highlighted and active, and an error message will appear.

Note the special element listed first in the Expression column. This is a special module variable. For forms, this variable takes on the system variable of **ME**. Expanding this will reveal all the available properties of the **Form** object, including elements representing the active control on the form, and one entry for every constituent control on the form. The properties for the constituent controls are also available by continuing to drill down through the hierarchy.

In the upper right-hand corner of the Locals window is a button with ellipses, which opens up a small dialog box called the *Call Stack window*. You can also open this dialog box by clicking on the far right-most button on the Debug toolbar (or by typing Ctrl+L). The Call Stack window is used to reveal the order of currently executing procedures. As procedures make calls to other procedures or functions, these new procedures or functions are added to the list. Therefore, the bottom item in the list represents the most recent procedure call. As the procedures finish executing and return to the calling procedure, the concluded procedure disappears from the list. As you can see in Figure 10.6, the **Command1_OnClick** event handler is calling out to a procedure called **GoofyRules**. This procedure has merely taken on the task of performing the multiplication of the two counter variables, **InnerCounter** and **OuterCounter**,

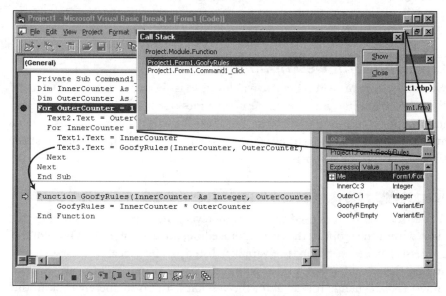

**Figure 10.6**    The Call Stack window provides a very useful way to track the chain of method calls.

previously handled inline by the **Command1_OnClick** event handler procedure, as seen earlier in Figure 10.5. The Call Stack window shows the two executing procedures in full **Project.Module.Function** notation. The Show button in the Call Stack window allows a very quick and convenient way of navigating directly to any procedure in the call stack, which can be quite useful at times as you try to backtrack through the code to track down the start of logic errors.

Take a close look at Figures 10.5 and 10.6. Do you notice the names used for the variables and the function used for the offloaded computational task? It is wise to follow standard naming conventions for variables and procedural names. Because the variables actually represent counters, having the word *counter* in the name of the variable is good, but adding a prefix to represent the data type is highly recommended. For example, a variable name of **intCounter1** might be more appropriate.

When naming procedures, a much less stringent naming convention exists. The primary concern is to use names that are unique, but highly functional, or indicative of their use. Granted, a procedure name of **GoofyRules** certainly meets the uniqueness characteristic, but fails miserably in the category of functionality. Conveying the fact that Goofy is better than Mickey can certainly be an acceptable acknowledgment of the "developer's prerogative," but it leaves far too much ambiguity as to the functionality of the procedure itself. In the case of this particular function, a name such as **FindProduct** might be more useful.

## Setting Watch Expressions Using The Watch Window

The Watch window is used to set and monitor what are referred to as *watch expressions*. These are either variables or expressions whose values can be monitored for changes. Adding a watch expression can be performed by right-clicking within the Watch window and choosing Add Watch. You can also choose Edit Watch or Delete Watch. After choosing Add Watch, a dialog box, as shown in Figure 10.7, will appear.

Creating a watch expression involves defining the expression definition, its context (for evaluation purposes), and the behavioral nature or type of the expression. The watch expression definition can be either a value or an actual expression. When defining a watch expression on a variable, the value of the variable will be monitored. When defining a watch expression as an actual

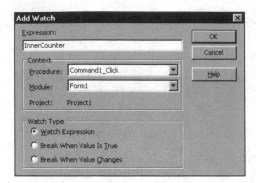

**Figure 10.7** Adding a watch expression includes establishing a definition, context, and watch type in the Add Watch dialog box.

expression, the Boolean value of the expression, that is, its status as being a true or a false expression, is monitored. Next, choose the context in which the watch expression will be evaluated, and module and procedure in which the value will be monitored. The drop-downs provide choices of All Procedures and All Modules, allowing for a large flexibility in opening or limiting the range in which the expression is monitored. This can be useful when duplicate variable names exist in different procedures or modules. Finally, choose a watch type:

➤ Watch Expression

➤ Break When Value Is True

➤ Break When Value Changes

> Review the standards for definition of scope. The exam will test your understanding of scope issues in light of using the watch expressions. The exam will ask some tricky questions that require you to pick the acceptable context value for a given watch expression.

Setting a watch expression to the watch type of Watch Expression instructs Visual Basic to simply monitor the value of the watch expression. As long as the context for the watch expression remains in the current scope, the value will be dynamically updated in the Watch window. Whenever the context, as defined for a particular watch expression, moves out of scope, the value assigned or displayed for that watch expression in the Watch window will show as **<Out of context>**.

Assigning a watch type of Break When Value Is True to a watch expression instructs Visual Basic to not only watch the value but to enter into break mode when the watch expression evaluates to **True**. This can be used with variables of Boolean type, but is more often used when the watch expression definition involves an expression. This is useful when trying to hunt down exactly at what point in your code a variable obtains a particular value that is known to be either invalid or undesired.

Choosing the last watch type value, Break When Value Changes, is, as the name implies, an instruction to Visual Basic to enter into break mode *anytime* the value of the watch expression changes. This choice is primarily limited to variables that change infrequently in value. You can use this setting to test for changes in a Boolean variable that signify a global module flag or setting.

After defining the assorted watch expressions, start the application; the result may look a little like what is shown in Figure 10.8. Notice that the top watch expression has a different icon. This watch expression was set up using the watch type of Break When Value Is True. Also notice the location of the current statement. Because the breakpoint was removed from the first line in the **Command_OnClick** event, the application ran uninterrupted until a watch expression forced the application into break mode. The watch expression, as shown in Figure 10.8, initiated break mode because the line *previous* to the current statement was completely executed, hence the value of the watch expression became **True**.

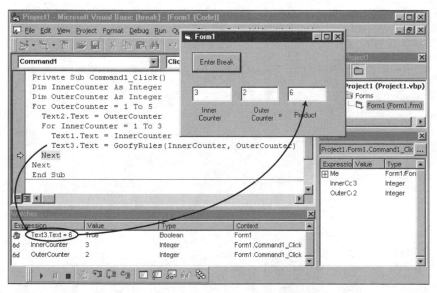

**Figure 10.8**    Break When Value Is True forces the application to stop on the statement *following* the line of code that forced the watch expression to evaluate to **True**.

Be sure to recognize that the current statement in an application in break mode has not been executed. This fact is important when evaluating the output of code entered into the Immediate window.

# Practice Questions

## Question 1

Visual Basic allows application to be compiled directly to native code. What are the benefits of doing so? [Check all that apply]

- ❑ a.  Speeding up application execution that performs numerous financial calculations

- ❑ b.  Speeding applications that modify or move large amounts of bytes within local memory

- ❑ c.  Speeding up applications that leverage a large number of subroutine calls, thereby increasing call stack utilization

- ❑ d.  Eliminating the need for the VB runtime DLL

- ❑ e.  Slightly increasing the number of compiling optimization choices

The correct answers are a and b. When an application performs numerous repetitive or complex nonstring calculations, such as those involving financial calculations and the **Currency** data type, compiling to native code can provide numerous performance improvements. Applications that perform operations involving a large amount of bytes or data stored in internal local memory also benefit from having been compiled to native, thereby passing a great deal of the reliance on the VB runtime DLL.

The overhead involved in setting up and breaking call stacks is handled about as efficiently by the p-code engine as by natively compiled code, therefore answer c is incorrect. Answer d is incorrect because the need for the VB runtime DLLs is not eliminated, but merely reduced greatly in some situations. Answer e is also incorrect, making this a trick question. Compiling to native code does not increase the number of optimization choices slightly; in fact, it provides all of the basic and advanced optimization choices.

# Question 2

> Which of the following choices are considered advanced compiler optimization options?
>
> ○ a.  Remove Safe Pentium FDIC Checks
>
> ○ b.  Favor Pentium Pro
>
> ○ c.  Allow No Aliasing
>
> ○ d.  Create Symbolic Debug Info
>
> ○ e.  None of the above

The correct answer is e. This is certainly a trick question, as several items are close, but still not correct. Answer a is close, but incorrect because the advanced optimization choice is to Remove Pentium FDIV, or floating point division checks, not FDIC checks as in your banking establishment. Favor Pentium Pro is a valid optimization option, but in the basic category. Answer c is incorrect because the correct advanced option is Assume No Aliasing, not Allow. In fact, allowing aliasing when setting this option is what can cause problems. Create Symbolic Debug Info is a complex option that involves providing debugging information for advanced application debugging, but it is not considered an advanced form of optimization for compiling.

# Question 3

> Which methods for setting or providing values for conditional compilation constants are supported by Visual Basic 6?
>
> ○ a.  Using the Command Line Parameter textbox on the Project Properties dialog box
>
> ○ b.  Using the Conditional Compilation Arguments textbox on the Project Properties dialog box
>
> ○ c.  Using the **/cmd** command-line parameter
>
> ○ d.  Using the **Const** directive
>
> ○ e.  Using the **#If...then** conditional directive

The correct answer is b. The three ways to supply values for conditional compiling constants are to:

➤ Use the Conditional Compilation Arguments textbox (answer b).

➤ Use the **/d** command-line parameter for VB6.EXE.

➤ Use the **#Const** conditional directive.

The Command Line Parameter textbox provided on the Make tab of the Project Properties dialog box is used to identify command-line parameters for use with the application, not VB6.EXE, therefore answer a is incorrect. The **/cmd** command line parameter is used to pass a string to the **command$** function, not to provide conditional compilation constants, therefore answer c is incorrect. Answer d is made incorrect because the **Const** directive must be used for declaring standard constants, not conditional compilation constants. Finally, answer is incorrect because the **#If...then** directives use conditional compilation directives, not supply values to them.

# Question 4

Which of the debugging tools provided by Visual Basic can be used to show a variable's value? [Check all that apply]

❑ a. Locals window

❑ b. Immediate window

❑ c. Debug window

❑ d. Call Stack window

❑ e. Watch window

The correct answers are a, b, and e. The Locals windows can reveal the value of variables that are local to the current scope of the next line of executing code. The Immediate window can be used to provide variable value information by using the **Print, ?,** or **Debug.Print** methods to print the values. The Watch window can be used to display the values of variables by creating watch expressions to monitor the values.

Answer c is incorrect, simply because no actual window is known as the Debug window. The Call Stack window is used only to display the current stack of executing procedures, therefore answer d is incorrect.

## Question 5

When in break mode, the Debug toolbar provides a number of buttons to allow quick navigation of the lines of executing code. Which "stepping" options does the Debug toolbar provide? [Check all that apply]

❑ a. Into

❑ b. Out

❑ c. Around

❑ d. Over

❑ e. Through

The correct answers are a, b, and d. The Debug toolbar provides the ability to:

➤ "Step Into" the lines of code, which allows complete, line-by-line walkthroughs.

➤ "Step Over" the procedure calls, which allows walking through code while jumping over the procedural calls.

➤ "Step Out" of procedures, which allows the walkthrough to finish executing the current procedure and then stepping out of run mode again.

Stepping around and stepping through are not valid code stepping options, therefore answers c and e are incorrect.

# Need To Know More?

The Mandlebrot Set International Ltd.: *Advanced Microsoft Visual Basic 6.0*. Microsoft Press, 1998. ISBN: 1572318937. This book contains very updated information on version six of Visual Basic. Chapters are included on components and Y2K issues, but the book is written moderately deep. Good book for the middle-of-the-pack developer in terms of overall experience.

For more information regarding the topics covered in this chapter, search the MSDN Library of Visual Studio 6.0 with the following phrases:

➤ Using the Debugging Windows

➤ Tips for Debugging

➤ Approaches to Debugging

➤ Using Conditional Compilation

➤ Understanding Optimization

# Distributing Applications

## Terms you'll need to understand:

✓ Internet Component Download
✓ CAB files
✓ Packages
✓ Information files
✓ DCOMCNFG
✓ CODEBASE
✓ VBR files
✓ Authenticode

## Techniques you'll need to master:

✓ Using the Package and Deployment Wizard to create a setup program that installs a distributed application, registers the COM components, and allows for uninstall
✓ Planning and implementing floppy- or compact disk-based deployment for a distributed application
✓ Planning and implementing Web-based deployment for a distributed application
✓ Planning and implementing network-based deployment for a distributed application
✓ Registering a component that implements DCOM
✓ Configuring DCOM on a client computer and on a server computer

# Distribution Components

Once your distributed application has been developed and tested, you must distribute it to your users. Fundamentally, this includes the acts of packaging the application and deploying it.

To *package* an application means creating a redistributable container that includes all the files necessary for the application to run properly and the instructions for placing the files into the proper directories on the computer on which it will run. To *deploy* the application means moving the package to a location where it can be easily installed on the destination computer. The bulk of this chapter will focus on the Package and Deployment Wizard that ships with Visual Studio. This tool performs both packaging and deployment for an application created in Visual Basic.

This topic is complicated somewhat by the fact that in a distributed application you may need to package and deploy applications that use Remote Automation or Distributed COM (DCOM) to communicate with ActiveX components installed on an NT server; these run in Microsoft Transaction Server (MTS). As a result, you'll need to know how to configure a client computer to use DCOM and how to package and deploy a component that will be used in this way.

# Packaging The Application

The *Package and Deployment Wizard* is the tool you'll use to create your distributable package. The wizard creates one or more compressed cabinet (CAB) files and optionally a setup EXE that a user can execute to install the application.

You can launch the wizard in three different ways: standalone from the Microsoft Visual Studio 6.0 Tools program group, as an add-in accessible through the Add-Ins menu, or through a command line interface using the program PDCMDLINE.EXE. By running it as an add-in, you can only create packages for the project currently loaded in VB.

After you launch the wizard you'll be prompted with the wizard's main window, as shown in Figure 11.1. After selecting a VB project file using the Browse button, click on the Package button to begin creating the package.

If you've not compiled the executable or DLL for your project, the wizard will prompt you to do so before it can continue. Once the project is compiled, the wizard presents up to three different package types that you can create: standard, Internet, and dependency files.

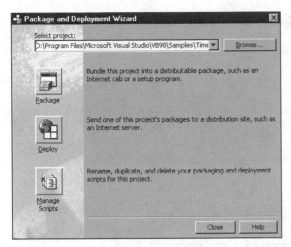

**Figure 11.1**    The Package and Deployment Wizard.

# Standard Setup Package

A *standard setup package* is one that you'll use to create a SETUP.EXE program to install the application, rather than having it downloaded through a browser.

As you walk through the wizard, you'll first be prompted for the location of the package. By default this is a directory called Package that is created directly beneath the directory that contains the VBP file for the project. However, you can also create the package directly on a network share or mapped drive.

Next, the list of files that will be distributed appears, as shown in Figure 11.2. This list will always contain the files shown in Table 11.1, in addition to any

| Table 11.1 | Files automatically included in a standard setup package. |
| --- | --- |
| **File** | **Description** |
| SETUP.EXE | The bootstrap EXE that is first executed when the application is installed. It loads the actual setup program and prepares the program to be installed. |
| SETUP1.EXE | The main setup program for the application. This is a VB executable that can be customized by using the template in the Wizards\PDWizard\Setup1 directory. For more information about customizing the setup program, see "The Setup Toolkit" in the *Visual Basic 6.0 Programmer's Guide*. |
| ST6UNST.EXE | The application-removal utility that allows users to remove your application from the Control Panel. |
| VB6 Runtime and OLE Automation | This includes all the runtime and support files for VB6. |
| VB6STKIT.DLL | Library that contains functions used by SETUP1.EXE. |

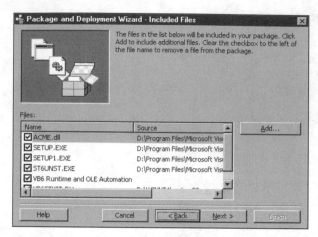

**Figure 11.2** Files to be included in the package.

components that your application is using. For each component a dependency file may exist; this specifies which other files must be distributed with the component. For example, all the ActiveX controls that ship with VB also include dependency files, so that if you redistribute them with your executable, the package will contain all the necessary files for their proper use.

> *Note: Without the proper dependency information the application may not work correctly when installed on a client computer. We'll discuss dependency files later in this chapter in the section "Dependency Files."*

At this point you can also add any other files that should be distributed. Typically this includes help files, utilities, INI files, or JET database files.

After the files are selected the wizard prompts for CAB options and size. In this dialog box you're able to specify whether the package should be created as a single CAB file or spread across multiple files. By choosing multiple files, you are given the option of choosing the disk size using the standard floppy disk sizes. This option has an impact on which deployment options are available when you go to deploy the application. If you choose a single CAB you will not be given the option of performing a floppy disk-based deployment. For this reason you should choose multiple files if you intend to deploy using floppy disks, even if your application can fit in a single CAB.

The next two screens in the wizard give you the opportunity to provide an installation title used by the setup program and the Start menu location of the application. These options do not affect functionality, but are helpful to the user when installing and running your application.

The final two screens deal with the location and properties of the files to be installed. The first provides a list of the application files to be installed and gives you the option of choosing the installation location. The options are shown in Table 11.2. You can also use these paths as the starting point and then add to them by entering the values in the dialog box.

The final wizard screen allows you to mark your files as shared files. This indicates that they can be used by other applications and should not automatically be removed when uninstalling the application. The operating system will keep a reference count for each of these DLLs and will increment it as new applications use the file or decrement it as they are uninstalled. When the reference count reaches zero, the user is prompted to remove the file completely.

The script that encapsulates all the choices made thus far can then be given a name and saved. The package will then be created in the package directory chosen earlier and will contain the CAB files, the SETUP.EXE program, and a file called SETUP.LST. The LST file is used by the setup program and contains the instructions regarding which files to install and where to install them. A Support directory is also created under the Package directory and includes uncompressed copies of all the files to be distributed. The two extra files in this directory you'll want to examine are the DDF and BAT files. The DDF file contains the instructions for rebuilding the CAB files; the BAT file contains the command to re-create the installation package from the command line.

| Table 11.2 | Installation locations. |
| --- | --- |
| **Location** | **Description** |
| $(AppPath) | The application installation directory as chosen by the user during the setup program. |
| $(WinSysPath) | The \Windows\System directory in Win9x or the \Winnt\System32 directory in Windows NT. |
| $(WinPath) | The \Windows directory in Win9x or the \Winnt directory in Windows NT. |
| $(CommonFiles) | The common files directory \Program Files\Common Files. |
| $(CommonFilesSys) | The common system files directory \Program Files\Common Files\System. |
| $(ProgramFiles) | The \Program Files directory. |
| $(MSDAOPath) | The location where the Microsoft Data Access Object components are stored. Normally you would not use this in your applications. |
| $(Font) | The \Windows\Fonts directory in Win9x or the \Winnt\Fonts directory in Windows NT. |

# Internet Setup Package

The *Internet setup package* is used primarily to package components that will be installed through a browser. These components can be ActiveX controls, ActiveX code components, DHTML applications, or ActiveX documents.

This package does not include a traditional setup program, but rather incorporates the setup information in a CAB file that is downloaded by the browser, unpacked, and installed. This process is called the *Internet Component Download* and is a feature of Internet Explorer (IE). You can see the files created by the wizard for this type of package in Table 11.3.

The CAB and HTM files are created in the Package directory, whereas the remaining files are placed in a Support directory beneath Package.

The most interesting file here is certainly the INF file, which contains the instructions for installing the component. Although space prohibits a complete discussion of the syntax of the INF, it is structured much like an INI file and contains sections for each of the files to be installed. For example, the section for an ActiveX control in the INF file might look like the following:

```
[DataControl.ocx]
file-win32-x86=thiscab
RegisterServer=yes
clsid={D87DD03E-5C9C-11D1-A019-006008EB5F25}
DestDir=
FileVersion=1,0,0,0
```

Note that name-value pairs in this example imply that the INF file can reference components that are not packaged in this CAB file or even components compiled for a specific platform. This allows the creation of a single INF file

| Table 11.3 | Internet package files. |
|---|---|
| **File Type** | **Description** |
| CAB | Compressed file that contains the component or components to be distributed (DLL or OCX files), directions on how to install the component, and—optionally—the support files that are required. |
| DDF | Known as a *Diamond Directive file*, this file contains the directions for building the CAB file. |
| HTM | Sample file created by the wizard that provides instructions for downloading the component using IE. |
| INF | Information file that specifies the files to be installed, their versions, and their locations. |

that can be used to install versions of the component on different platforms and packaged in different CAB files.

## Internet Component Download

As mentioned earlier, the Internet Component Download feature allows IE to uncompress and install ActiveX components directly from CAB files. It also provides security mechanisms to check that the component is from a known source and that it is safe to be used in a Web page.

To specify the component to be downloaded, the <**OBJECT**> tag is used in an HTML page. The sample HTM file created by the wizard will contain the appropriate tag for the component that was packaged. The <**OBJECT**> tag conveys three essential pieces of information to the browser: the name with which the component will be referenced, the GUID of the component, and the location where the component can be downloaded. Each of these pieces of information is conveyed through attributes of the tag. An example of an <**OBJECT**> tag follows:

```
<OBJECT ID="dcCustomerData"
CLASSID="CLSID:D87DD03E-5C9C-11D1-A019-006008EB5F25"
CODEBASE="DataControl.CAB#version=1,0,0,0">
</OBJECT>
```

The **ID** attribute specifies the name that code embedded within the Web page will use to reference the component. The **CLASSID** attribute defines the unique identifier (described in Chapter 4) assigned to the component at compile time. The **CODEBASE** attribute identifies the location and version of the package created by the Package and Deployment Wizard.

When IE parses an <**OBJECT**> tag such as this it performs the following steps:

1. Checks the Registry for the CLSID listed in the **CLASSID** attribute. If the component is not registered, it refers to the **CODEBASE** attribute to find the location of the installation package. If IE does find the CLSID, it compares the version of the component referred to in the Registry with the version in the **CODEBASE** to see if it is current and proceeds with the download if it is not.

2. Downloads and uncompresses the appropriate CAB file.

3. Processes the INF file associated with the CAB file.

4. Makes Registry settings, if appropriate, including those related to security (as we'll discuss shortly).

5. Checks to see whether all the necessary files or components are already installed as specified in the INF file. If they are, it checks to see whether the files or components are current. If they are current, IE makes no changes to them. If they are not current, IE replaces them with a new copy that it downloads and extracts from the information found in the INF file.

6. Installs and registers the component.

7. Activates the component so that it is ready for use in the browser.

In describing the process, you'll note that much depends on the **CODEBASE** attribute. This attribute controls the minimum version of the component required and the installation point for the component. In the previous example, the **CODEBASE** attribute read as follows:

```
CODEBASE="DataControl.CAB#version=1,0,0,0"
```

This specifies that version 1.0.0.0 or higher of the component is required and can be installed from the information in the DataControl.CAB file. It is essential that you increment this number in the HTML if you want to distribute a newer version of your component. The browser uses this number to determine whether to download the CAB file and read the INF file. This will be done automatically if you check the Auto Increment checkbox in the Project Properties dialog box (shown in Figure 11.3) before compiling and repackaging your component.

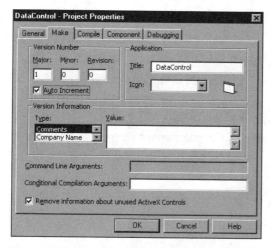

**Figure 11.3**   The Project Properties dialog box showing the Auto Increment option.

Checking Auto Increment is also pertinent to an application packaged using the standard package. If you do not increment the version number, the setup program will not overwrite the older version.

## *File Locations*

Using the standard setup package, all the files to be installed on the client machine are compiled into the CAB files and placed on the distribution media. With the Internet package you can specify that the support files are downloaded from a site other than where the component resides. The File Source dialog box shown in Figure 11.4 gives you the option of specifying your own URL for the file or the Microsoft site (**www.activex.microsoft.com/controls**) where the files are kept up to date.

All of this information is stored in the INF file created by the Package and Deployment Wizard. For example, by choosing the Microsoft site as the file source for the VB6 runtime files, the INF entry for the VB6 runtime DLL MSVBVM60.DLL is:

```
[msvbvm60.dll]
hook-msvbvm60.cab_Installer
FileVersion=6,0,81,76
[msvbvm60.cab_Installer]
file-win32-x86=http://activex.microsoft.com/controls/vb6/VBRun60.cab
run=%EXTRACT_DIR%\VBRun60.exe
```

One strategy that can be employed for intranet applications is to provide a site accessible on the local network where the support and runtime files can be stored. This allows the download to be faster and more secure, and gives your

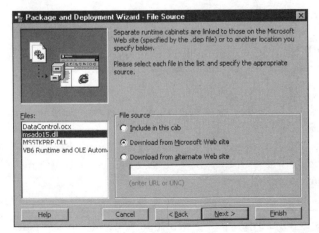

**Figure 11.4**    The File Source dialog box.

organization more control over the versions of these files that are installed. In addition, an Internet connection is not required.

> *Note: In either case, remember that these support and runtime files are only downloaded once for each client computer unless a component requires a later version.*

## Safety Issues

Users downloading components from a Web site are naturally wary of the effects these components may have on their computers. To alleviate these concerns, you can take three steps:

➤ Use digital signatures to ensure that the downloaded code is actually from a trusted author and that it has not been tampered with. This process uses a technology called *Authenticode*.

➤ Mark the component *safe for scripting* to ensure that the component does not harm the user's computer when it is used in code running within the browser. Note that this does not change the functionality of the component, but is a guarantee of sorts that a malevolent script using the component cannot erase or overwrite system files, insert unregulated information in the Registry, or perform other similar actions that could harm the computer.

➤ Mark the component *safe for initialization* to ensure that the component does not harm the user's computer when it is initialized with data by the HTML page. Like safe for scripting, this option is a non-binding contract that states that any data passed into the component cannot be used to harm the user's computer.

Authenticode uses the cryptographic technique of *public* and *private keys* to create a digital signature for a piece of software. Basically, this key pair allows data to be encrypted with a private key and decrypted by the public key. As a result, the public key, as its name implies, must be widely distributed, whereas the private key is kept secret.

When a component is digitally signed, a special number called a *hash* is encrypted with the private key and inserted in the file with the component. Once the component is downloaded, the browser decrypts and verifies the hash value using the public key. The browser can then be sure that the file was not tampered with during transmission.

In addition, the public key can be used to determine the identity of the author of the component. This is done by checking with the issuer of the key pair, provided with the public key, known as a *certificate authority*. The certificate authority then provides the identity of the author using its own private key. In this way IE can be sure that the component was authored by a verified source.

> *Note: This process does not fully protect a user's machine from malicious components. It only provides accountability.*

Digital signatures provide security for the transport and identification of components, whereas the safety options concern whether the component will be loaded by the browser. You can actually mark your component safe for initialization and scripting in two ways. The simplest method is to use the Safety Settings dialog box presented by the wizard and shown in Figure 11.5.

By marking the control safe using the wizard, instructions are added to the INF file (in the AddToRegistry section) to add Registry settings to the user's computer when the control is installed. IE checks these settings against the security settings of the browser when the component is initialized. If the settings do not allow unsafe components to be loaded or scripted, an error message will result.

The second method for marking the component safe is to implement the IObjectSafety interface in the component. This method, although more complicated, has the advantage of begin encapsulated into the component and so is not dependent on the method that is used to install the component. This topic is outside the scope of this book, but you can find more information in the "Need To Know More?" section at the end of the chapter.

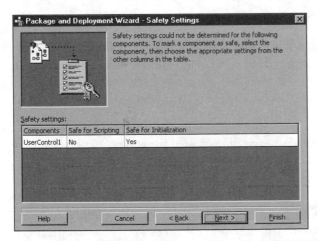

**Figure 11.5**   Marking the component safe for initialization and scripting.

### Licensing Components

In order to protect the investment of developers creating components, VB exposes an option on the Project Properties dialog box called "Requires License Key." When set, this option instructs the VB runtime engine to request a specific license key each time an instance of the component is created on a user's computer. If the component is downloaded over the Internet (as opposed to being compiled into an executable program), this license key will not be present.

As a result, to use licensed components over the Internet, the browser must know where to download the license key so that it may instantiate the component using the key. IE supports this by using a license manager object to download and apply the license. The license itself must be packaged in an LPK file that is created by the License Package Authoring Tool (\Tools\LPK_TOOL.EXE) that ships with VB.

The Package and Deployment Wizard will include code in the HTM file created by the wizard that shows the **<OBJECT>** tag required to use the license manager:

```
<OBJECT CLASSID="clsid:5220cb21-c88d-11cf-b347-00aa00a28331">
    <PARAM NAME="LPKPath" VALUE="LPKfilename.LPK">
</OBJECT>
```

 Even if an HTM file contains more than one component, the licenses for all components must be packaged in a single LPK file.

# Dependency Files

The final type of package that can be created is not actually a package, but simply a *dependency file* with a .DEP extension. This file lists all the runtime requirements of the project for which you are creating the package. This information is important for components that you create that may be used in other projects.

If a standard or Internet package is being created for an application that uses one of your components, the dependency file is read by the Package and Deployment Wizard to ascertain which support files must be included. In a standard setup package this information is then included in the SETUP.LST file; in an Internet package it is included in the INF file. If dependency information is missing, the wizard will display a dialog box and warn you that once installed, the application may not run correctly.

*Note: Dependency information is included for all components that ship with VB in either standalone DEP files or the VB6DEP.INI file.*

Generally, you should create a dependency file for any component that you create in VB that might be distributed with other applications. This wizard also includes an option for packaging the dependency information into a CAB file for deployment over the Web.

# Deploying The Application

The Package and Deployment Wizard can use three methods to deploy applications after they have been packaged: a folder, a floppy disk, or a Web site. You must choose one of the saved packages created by the packaging wizard by clicking on the Deploy button on the main screen.

## Folder Deployment

*Folder deployment* simply copies the contents of the Package directory (not including the Support subdirectory) to any location accessible by the computer running the wizard, including a local or network drive. Normally this option is useful for deploying the application to a share point on a file server.

Optionally, you can deploy to a local drive and then copy the contents to a CD-ROM for duplication and distribution.

## Floppy Deployment

*Floppy deployment* is only available if you had chosen to package the application using multiple CAB files in the packaging wizard. This option gives you the choice of formatting diskettes before copying the contents.

## Web-Based Deployment

*Web-based deployment* gives you the option of uploading the contents of the package to a URL on a Web server. This is especially convenient for components that will be used in HTML pages or IIS and DHTML applications created with VB.

Unlike the previous deployment options, this method provides dialog boxes that allow you to choose which files to upload to the Web server, including any files under the directory in which the project is located.

The final screen of the wizard shown in Figure 11.6 allows you to configure a Web Publishing Site. The site specifies the URL to upload to, the protocol to use (FTP or HTTP), and—for some packages—whether to install the package on the Web server after the upload is complete.

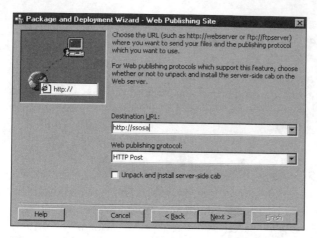

**Figure 11.6** Configuring Web-based deployment.

*Note: For the deployment to work using the HTTP protocol, the Web server must support this feature. Internet Information Server supports the feature using its Posting Acceptor.*

The wizard also gives you the option of saving this information so that it can be recalled the next time you wish to deploy a package.

# Distributed Application Issues

When developing distributed applications, you not only have to worry about packaging and deploying client executables and components, but also about components that are run on the server and called by your client application through Remote Automation or DCOM. In this section we'll address packaging and deployment issues related first to applications that use Remote Automation or DCOM and then those that use Microsoft Transaction Server (MTS). Finally, we'll discuss installing and configuring DCOM client and server computers.

## Applications Using Remote Automation Or DCOM

For these types of distributed applications the client calls a server component implemented as an executable and running on a different computer (often called a *remote server*). The primary difference between Remote Automation and DCOM applications is the remote transport used to communicate between the client and server (which is outside the scope of this book). The distribution issues related to these applications are distributing the remote server and configuring the client computers to use the remote server.

## *Packaging And Distributing The Remote Server*

To package and distribute the remote server, you use the Package and Deployment Wizard, as discussed earlier. The only difference is that you install the package once on a server computer, rather than on multiple clients. Normally the standard setup package is used to install the remote server on the computer on which it will be run.

However, before you compile the remote server you must click on the Remote Server Files checkbox on the Component tab of the Project Properties dialog box in VB. This option instructs VB to create VBR and TLB files when the project is compiled.

The VBR file contains Registry changes that must be made on the client computer in order to communicate with the remote server. The TLB file contains a type library that can be distributed to client computers that wish to use the remote server's interfaces.

## *Configuring The Client Computer*

In order for the client computer to be able to call a remote server, you must add the VBR to the package. Do so by adding the VBR files of any remote servers to the packaging wizard by clicking on the Add button on the Included Files dialog box. Even though a TLB file is also created, as discussed previously, distributing the TLB file is not required for compiled client applications to be able to communicate with the remote server.

After clicking on Next, a Remote Servers dialog box displays. This dialog box, shown in Figure 11.7, allows you to specify whether the remote server will be

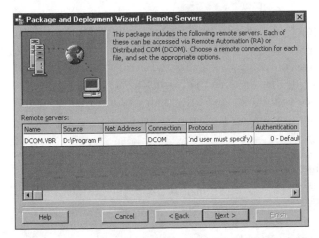

**Figure 11.7**    Setting the remote server properties in the packaging wizard.

called using Remote Automation or DCOM, the Net address (computer name) where the remote server will run, the network protocol that will be used (if Remote Automation is selected), and the authentication method.

When the setup package is installed on a client machine, it essentially runs the CLIREG32.EXE program to extract the information from the VBR file and insert it into the client's Registry. This utility is installed with Visual Studio; you'll find it in the \Visual Studio\Common\Tools\Clireg directory.

 You can also use this utility to manually register remote servers on a client computer. See Knowledge Base article Q155939 for more details.

# Applications Using MTS

The other class of distributed application is one that calls components running in MTS. These types of applications always use DCOM to communicate with in-process servers (DLLs) that are running in a process supplied by MTS. The distribution of these applications falls into the categories of configuring the server component and deploying the client application.

## *Packaging And Distributing The Server Component*

As with remote servers, the method for packaging and distributing the server component is the same as discussed earlier in the chapter. The difference lies in the fact that once the component is installed on the server, you must create and add the component to an MTS package. You can find the process for creating and configuring packages in Chapter 8.

Unlike working with Remote Automation or DCOM applications that do not use MTS, you do not have to create VBR and TLB files when compiling the server component. Likewise, the setup package for the client application should not contain any reference to the server components. If a local version of the server component is added to the Included Files dialog box of the packaging wizard, you should remove it before creating the package.

 If you accidentally install the server component on the client computer, be sure to remove any InprocServer32 and LocalServer32 keys from the server application's Registry entries on the client machine.

The task of configuring the client computer is handled through MTS itself.

### Configuring The Client Computer

MTS contains its own method of creating client setup programs for components that are part of an MTS package. Note that this method creates the necessary Registry entries to allow a client computer to communicate with all the components in the MTS package. To use this method follow these steps:

1. Run the Microsoft Management Console (MMC) snap-in for MTS.

2. Highlight the package you want to configure on the client computer.

3. Right-click on the package and click on Export.

4. Enter a path for the PAK file to be created.

When you click on Export, MTS will create a PAK file that includes information necessary to import the package on another server running MTS. However, for our purposes it also creates a Clients subdirectory where the PAK file was created. This directory contains an executable of the same name as the MTS package. You can now run this executable on a client computer to automatically configure the client to communicate with the MTS package.

> *Note: Do not run the client executable on the server computer. Doing so will put incorrect information in the server's Registry.*

## Installing And Configuring DCOM

In order for a client application to call a remote server using DCOM or a component running in MTS, the DCOM client files must be installed on the client computer. On Windows NT 4.0 the files are included as part of the base installation. However, on Windows 9x systems the DCOM files must be installed separately. The DCOM98 1.0 installation ships as a part of Visual Studio 6.0 and can be installed using the DCOM98.EXE program.

> *Note: This installation works on both Windows 95 and Windows 98, although user-level security must be enabled.*

When you are troubleshooting or implementing increased security, you'll need to configure the way in which a client or server computer uses DCOM. For this purpose, use the DCOMCNFG.EXE utility; because it is not installed in a program group, you must execute it using Start|Run. When you do so, three tabs display:

➤ **The Applications tab** Lists all the components that can be configured to use DCOM. In order for a component to appear in this list, it must have one of its CLSID in the list of CLSIDs under the HKEY_CLASSES_ROOT\AppID key in the Registry.

➤ **The Default Properties tab** Shown in Figure 11.8, this allows you to set the default communication properties for all the components on the computer.

➤ **The Default Security tab** Lets you set the default access, launch, and configuration permissions.

If you don't see your component in the list, it may be listed by its CLSID and not its English name (ProgID). To display it by a readable name, alter the Registry key HKEY_CLASSES_ROOT\AppID\ *{your CLSID}* and change the Default key that reads "value not set" to the ProgID. Then close and reopen DCOMCNFG.

To set the individual permissions for a component, select it from the list of applications on the Applications tab and click on Properties. These properties are stored as values in the AppID key for the CLSID of the component. The options that are presented and those you would set differ according to whether you are configuring the client computer or the server.

## Configuring A Server Computer

On the server computer the Properties dialog box will show four tabs. The server Properties dialog box for a component called MyTest.Math running in MTS is shown in Figure 11.9. Because it is a local server, you'll have the option of overriding the default security settings and the user context under which the

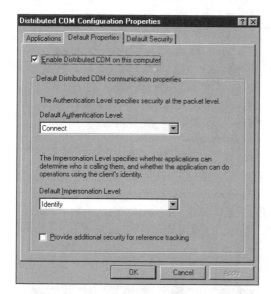

**Figure 11.8** Default DCOM communication properties.

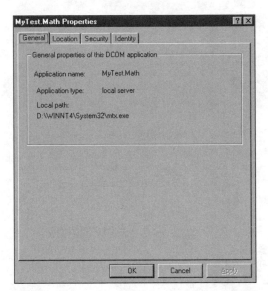

**Figure 11.9**    DCOMCNFG Properties dialog box for a server component running in MTS.

component should be run. MTS allows you to configure some of these values using its MMC snap-in.

### Configuring A Client Computer

You can also run DCOMCNFG on the client computer to configure DCOM. For components or servers that are called remotely, however, the Properties dialog box shows only two tabs instead of four.

The primary tab you'll be interested in on the client is the Location tab, which specifies the computer on which the component can be found. You can see the client dialog box from a Windows 98 computer using the same MyTest.Math component running in MTS in Figure 11.10.

Setting the remote computer name creates a RemoteServerName value under the AppID key for the CLSID of the component in the Registry.

# Managing Scripts

As you create packages or deploy them, the Package and Deployment Wizard automatically creates scripts so that you can re-create your actions. You can assign all of these scripts a name as you save them.

The Manage Scripts button at the bottom of the wizard allows you to copy, delete, rename, and duplicate any of the scripts. The scripts are classified into

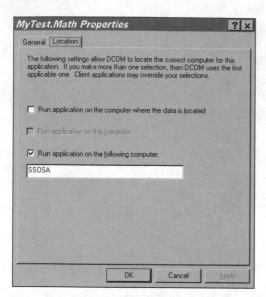

**Figure 11.10** DCOMCNFG Properties dialog box for a client component running in MTS.

Packaging Scripts and Deployment Scripts. Note that you can only view scripts in this dialog box for the project that is selected in the Select Project text box.

# Practice Questions

## Question 1

The Package and Deployment Wizard can be used to do all the following except:

○ a.  Create a setup program for a client application created in Visual Basic.

○ b.  Create a setup program that configures a client computer to use an MTS component.

○ c.  Deploy an application to a Web server.

○ d.  Create an installation package for use with the Internet Component Download feature of Internet Explorer.

The correct answer is b. The MTS snap-in provides an Export function that creates a client executable used to configure the client computer. The Package and Deployment Wizard can, however, create the installation package for the client application itself.

Answer a is incorrect because you can use the Standard setup package to create an executable install program. Answer c is incorrect because you can use Web-based deployment to deploy the setup package to a Web server via HTTP or FTP if the server supports it. Answer d is incorrect because the Internet setup package creates CAB files that IE can download, uncompress, and install.

## Question 2

Which syntax for using the **CODEBASE** attribute to download version 1.0 of MyComponent is correct?

Trick! question

○ a.  CODEBASE=MyComponent.cab#version=1.0.0.0

○ b.  CODEBASE=MyComponent.cab#1,0,0,0

○ c.  CODEBASE=MyComponent.cab#version=1,0,0,0

○ d.  CODEBASE=MyComponent.exe#version=1,0,0,0

Answer c is correct. To instruct IE to download a CAB file and check a specific version, you must use the **#version** syntax after the CAB file.

Answer a is incorrect because it uses periods rather than commas to separate the version numbers, whereas answer b leaves out the version identifier altogether. Answer d is incorrect because it is pointing to an executable file rather than a CAB file and the Package and Deployment Wizard only creates CAB files.

## Question 3

> Which is the best method for distributing a new version of an application created in VB to client computers?
>
> O a. Place the new version of the EXE into the Support directory and re-create the CAB files using the supplied DDF file.
>
> O b. Compile the new version of the EXE using the Auto Increment checkbox and re-create the setup package using a saved script file in the Package and Deployment Wizard.
>
> O c. Compile the new version of the EXE using the Remote Server Files checkbox and re-create the setup package using a saved script file in the Package and Deployment Wizard.
>
> O d. Place the new version of the EXE in the Package directory and rerun SETUP1.EXE to re-create the setup package.

The correct answer is b. The Auto Increment feature in the Project Properties dialog box is essential to allow the setup package to overwrite the older version of the executable on the client machine. By re-creating the setup package using a saved script, you also ensure that any new support files are installed on the client machine.

Although answer a can be done, it does not update the INF or LST files with the new version information (assuming Auto Increment was checked) and it does not account for possible new dependencies in the application (new referenced controls or components). Answer c is incorrect because the Remote Server Files checkbox creates a VBR file that is used to assist in installing client applications that use remote servers and is not related to versioning. Answer d is incorrect because the setup package cannot be re-created without running the Package and Deployment Wizard.

## Question 4

How would you manually edit the Registry of a client computer to specify that a component with a CLSID of 903268B7-5CA1-11D1-A019-006008EB5F25 be run on a remote server?

○ a.  Run the REGEDIT utility. Edit the key HKEY_CLASSES_ROOT\AppID\{903268B7-5CA1-11D1-A019-006008EB5F25}. Add a DCOMServerName string value and set it to the name of the server on which the component will run.

○ b.  Run the REGEDIT utility. Edit the key HKEY_CLASSES_ROOT\{903268B7-5CA1-11D1-A019-006008EB5F25}. Add a RemoteServerName string value and set it to the name of the server on which the component will run.

○ c.  Run the REGEDIT utility. Edit the key HKEY_CLASSES_ROOT\AppID\{903268B7-5CA1-11D1-A019-006008EB5F25}. Add a RemoteServerName string value and set it to the name of the server on which the component will run.

○ d.  Run the REGEDIT utility. Edit the key HKEY_LOCAL_MACHINE\AppID\{903268B7-5CA1-11D1-A019-006008EB5F25}. Add a RemoteServerName string value and set it to the name of the server on which the component will run.

The correct answer is c. In order for a component to use DCOM on a client computer, its CLSID must exist in the AppID key of HKEY_CLASSES_ROOT. It must then have a RemoteServerName string value that references the computer on which the server component will run.

Answer a is incorrect because it incorrectly identifies DCOMServerName as the value that points to the remote server. Answer b is incorrect because it does not include the AppID key under HKEY_CLASSES_ROOT. An entry for the component in this location does exist, but it is not used to specify the remote server name. Answer d is incorrect because it locates the key under HKEY_LOCAL_MACHINE rather than HKEY_CLASSES_ROOT.

## Question 5

> Which methods can be used to mark an ActiveX control as safe for scripting and initialization? [Check all correct answers]
>
> ❑ a.  Implement the IObjectSafety interface in the code of the control before compilation.
>
> ❑ b.  Add script in the HTM page to call the **SafeScript** and **SafeInitialize** properties of the control from the **window_onload** event.
>
> ❑ c.  Use the Package and Deployment Wizard.
>
> ❑ d.  Add a reference to an LPK file in the HTM file that downloads the control.

The correct answers are a and c. Remember that the packaging wizard, when creating an Internet package, gives you the option of specifying that the control is safe for initialization and scripting. This instructs the INF file to add Registry entries on the client computer that IE reads when the control is instantiated. Although this method forces you to choose these options for each package that uses the control, by implementing the IObjectSafety interface in the control before compilation, the safety features are always carried with the control.

Answer b is incorrect because no **SafeScript** or **SafeInitialize** properties exist. In any case, it would defeat the purpose if there were, because obviously the control would have to be scriptable and initialized before the code could be run. Answer d is incorrect because licensing is a separate issue and simply protects the control from being used by another developer.

## Question 6

> Which of the following is the best way to configure a client computer to use a component running in MTS on a remote server?
>
> ○ a.  Install the component on the client computer, delete it, and then manually edit the Registry.
>
> ○ b.  Install the type library on the client computer and use the CLIREG32.EXE utility to edit the Registry.
>
> ○ c.  Export the package in MTS and run the resulting client executable on the client computer.
>
> ○ d.  Run the DCOMCNFG utility to configure the Registry.

The correct answer is c. By exporting the MTS package from the MTS management console, a Clients directory is created that contains an executable of the same name as the MTS package. This executable can then be run on the client workstations to add the necessary Registry entries.

Answer a would actually work, but it is not the recommended method because it involves so much manual intervention. Answer b is incorrect because installing a type library on a client computer only allows development environments to read the interfaces and does not actually indicate where the component will be installed. Answer d is again partially correct because once the Registry of the client computer contains a reference to the component, you could use DCOMCNFG to redirect the calls to another server. Once again, however, this is not the best way to accomplish the task.

# Need To Know More?

 For the latest information about the Internet Component Download, see the Code Download Training Site at **support.microsoft. com/support/inetsdk/.** This site contains a section on Component Packaging/Code Download Resource in addition to the latest Knowledge Base articles relating to this technology.

 For more information on the Internet Component Download, see the Site Builder Workshop at **www.microsoft.com/workshop** and click on the Content & Component Delivery section in the table of contents.

 For a good overview of client-side security issues that relate to Authenticode, see the Signing and Marking ActiveX Controls white paper at **www.microsoft.com/workshop/components/ activex/signmark.asp.**

 Two particularly good Knowledge Base articles that you'll want to check out from Microsoft's support site at **support.microsoft. com/support** are Q186342, "HOWTO: Create a 3-Tier App using VB, MTS, and SQL Server" and Q161837, "HOWTO: Create a DCOM Client/Server App."

 Although out of the scope of this chapter, you can visit the RSA Data Security Web site at **www.rsa.com.** The founders of RSA developed the public key cryptosystem used in the Authenticode system employed by IE.

 Verisign is one of the companies used as a trusted third party or certificate authority. Their Web site at **www.verisign.com** allows you to test digital IDs for individual email use in addition to buying certificates used to digitally sign your code.

# Maintaining Distributed Applications

**12**

. . . . . . . . . . . . . . . . . . . . . . . . . . . . . . . . . . . . . .

## Terms you'll need to understand:

√ Load balancing

√ Static load balancing

√ Dynamic load balancing

√ Parallel deployment

√ Project compatibility

√ Binary compatibility

## Techniques you'll need to master:

√ Identifying techniques for deploying server components

√ Identifying techniques for implementing load balancing

√ Ensuring maintainability in a server component by using version compatibility

# Maintaining Your Application

Hopefully, the distributed applications you create with the tools and technologies discussed in this book will be successful. One measure of that success will be the volume of users and requests processed by the application. As user requests increase, however, concerns arise as to whether the application will be able to handle the increased load. To be ready for situations such as these, you need to be aware of the opportunities for deploying the application in different configurations and implementing load balancing to more efficiently use distributed components.

> *Note: Although out of the scope of this book, the main factor when determining whether the load on the server is unacceptable is user response time. This should be monitored frequently during peak and off-peak hours and compared on a regular basis. Only through careful monitoring will you be able to detect when you should consider the concepts covered in this chapter. The Windows NT Performance Monitor utility will also be able to log statistics such as processor utilization and network requests over time.*

In addition, requests will inevitably arise for increased functionality and subsequent releases of the software. As a result, you'll need to understand how to deploy new versions of distributed components without breaking existing clients.

# Deployment Issues

As demand for your application rises, the load on the middle-tier server running the MTS components will be particularly important to watch. Although MTS provides features such as *Just-In-Time (JIT) activation* and *thread management* to improve scalability on a single MTS server, it does not, as of release 2.0, support any kind of automatic load balancing to redirect component requests to multiple MTS servers. This capability will be a part of COM+ and included in the release of Windows 2000. In fact, COM+ will integrate many of the existing features of both MTS and *Microsoft Message Queue Server (MSMQ)* into the core COM services.

 For the exam, remember that MTS 2.0 does not automatically implement any form of load balancing or message queuing across multiple servers. In order to support copies of components running on multiple servers, the application must implement and use one of the schemes discussed in this chapter.

As a result of this increased demand, a time may come when the hardware of the server will become overloaded. The most common solution for this problem is to upgrade the hardware on the server, moving to a multiprocessor machine with more memory. However, because base clients using MTS components use DCOM to communicate, you can take advantage of DCOM's location transparency to implement a less expensive solution using multiple lower-level servers.

> *Note: Remember that* location transparency *refers to the fact that clients using COM components do not have to know where the actual component is loaded. The COM library takes care of the instantiation of the component whether it is in the same process, across processes, or even across the network.*

Basically, three standard approaches are used to deploy MTS components across multiple servers: parallel deployment, isolating critical components, and pipelining. Keep in mind that in most cases the components will be able to handle larger workloads if they are *stateless*. In other words, the component does not hold any state information for the client between calls to the component.

# Parallel Deployment

The simplest way to deploy components across multiple servers is to use *parallel deployment*. With this method, exact copies of the components (no recompilation is required) are installed on each server running MTS. The client applications then distribute their calls to the component based on one of the load-balancing schemes discussed later. Figure 12.1 shows the architecture of parallel deployment.

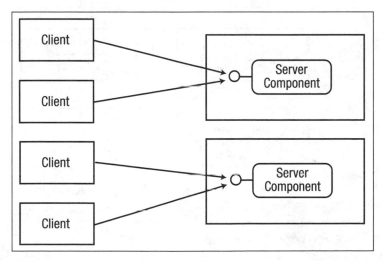

**Figure 12.1**  Parallel deployment.

Once the components are deployed, the clients must then be redirected to the appropriate server. As discussed in Chapter 11, a single Registry setting controls on which computer the component is created. Several methods exist for updating this information, including editing the Registry remotely and updating the Registry using an executable file or login script.

## Isolating Critical Components

Parallel deployment works well for applications that do not require synchronization or prioritization of requests from clients. For example, a typical *online transaction processing (OLTP)* application (such as a Web site that sells books) may take and fill requests from clients in any order without reference to specific clients. These applications can use parallel deployment because the copies of the components on parallel servers will not (and need not) prioritize the requests being made.

However, an application such as an electronic trading system must process buy and sell orders precisely as they are received. As a result, this type of application contains one or more bottleneck components that actually perform the important tasks, such as inserting the order in the database.

One method for dealing with applications that have bottlenecks is to isolate the components that are critical and run them on dedicated servers. In this way the maximum amount of computing power can be used to process the critical components as quickly as possible. You can also combine this technique with parallel deployment for those components that are not bottlenecks, as shown in Figure 12.2.

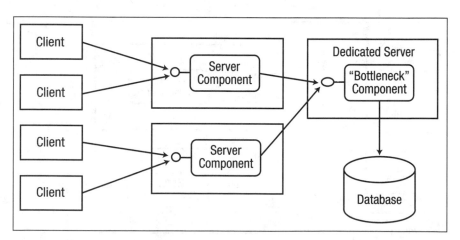

**Figure 12.2** Isolating critical components.

## Pipelining

Running critical components on dedicated servers will certainly have the effect of increasing throughput for those components. However, in some instances, this still does not provide enough of a performance gain because the critical component itself implements a multistep process that ties up server resources for an unacceptable period of time.

In cases like these it may be best to break down the critical component into multiple components, each of which implements a single step in the process and runs on a dedicated server. For example, a component that does a serialized insert into a database may perform the steps shown in Figure 12.3 that can be implemented as separate components.

Implementing these steps as components has the effect of allowing each component in the process to perform its assigned task, invoke the next component, and be ready to receive the next request. This has the overall effect of greater throughput and applies more processing power to the problem.

# Load Balancing

The previous section discussed techniques for the deployment of components; however, the issue of load balancing must also be addressed. In particular, *load balancing* refers to the methods used to determine which client applications use resources from which servers. Fundamentally, this can be accomplished through *static* load balancing or *dynamic* load balancing.

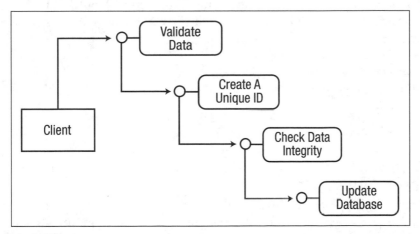

**Figure 12.3**   Pipelining.

# Static Load Balancing

One method of implementing load balancing is to permanently assign specific clients to specific servers. Because the assignments are not meant to change based on server load or network resources, this is called *static load balancing*. You can implement static load balancing in three basic ways: manipulating the Registry, keeping a central repository, and creating a referral component.

## *Registry Manipulation*

As mentioned earlier, it is possible to configure the user's Registry using a remote administration tool or login script. The advantage to this method is that at runtime no extra processing is required because the Registry already contains the appropriate server reference. The problem with this method is the difficulty encountered in the event you wish to assign a user to a different server.

## *Central Repository*

A more flexible approach is to keep an association of users to servers in a database table or file stored in a central location. This method is more flexible, because you can easily change the table or file to modify the distribution of users across servers. This method does require more processing by the client application because it must read the file or the table to find the appropriate server to access.

Once the information is read from the central location, you can use the **CreateObject** function to pass the server name to the COM library. For example, if a database table contains the name of the server APOLLO for use with a particular user's ID, a component called **ACME.Customers** would be called as follows:

```
Dim strServer as String
Dim objCust as ACME.Customer

'Function to retrieve the server name
strServer = GetServerName(strUserID)
Set objCust = CreateObject("ACME.Customer",strServer)
```

## *Referral Component*

The most flexible approach is to create a dedicated *referral component*. This method requires that you create a component that is passed in information such as user credentials, IP address, or machine name. The component then determines on which server to instantiate the component and actually returns a reference to that component on the remote server. This method requires more effort but is the most flexible, because it can grow to accommodate dynamic load balancing techniques, as we'll soon see. The referral component is usually deployed on a separate server referred to as a *routing server*.

# Dynamic Load Balancing

Although static load balancing is a good first step in distributing the work of a distributed application, and indeed is sufficient for most applications, it does have some drawbacks.

In situations where the load on the server is not predictable, a single server running components may still encounter resource problems when using static load balancing. Adjusting the allocation of clients to servers to avoid this problem would be a difficult and time-consuming task using the methods described previously.

To get around these issues you should consider implementing some form of *dynamic load balancing*. With this technique, the client is not statically assigned to a server; instead, the decision is deferred until the server component needs to be instantiated. The information required to make the decision normally consists of network load, network topology, or the usage pattern of the user. You can implement dynamic load balancing in two common ways:

## Referral Component

As mentioned previously, you can use a referral component to implement static load balancing. You can apply this same technique to dynamic load balancing by adding algorithms to the referral component to examine the appropriate statistics and make the assignment. Once again, the advantage of using a referral component is that it can grow along with your application and can be adjusted to support different forms of load balancing as user demand increases.

## Client Proxies

A second technique that can be implemented to perform dynamic load balancing is the use of *client-side proxies*. Using this technique, whenever a client invokes a method of a component, a customized proxy component residing on the client intercepts the call and reroutes it to the appropriate destination based on available statistics. This is referred to as *custom marshaling*. The problem with this method is that it requires a more in-depth understanding of COM, must be done using C or C++, and is not compatible with MTS.

> *Note: Although this technique is out of the scope of this book, you can read about the technical details in the "DCOM Architecture" white paper referred to in the "Need To Know More?" section at the end of the chapter.*

## Other Related Issues

As distributed applications become more common, the need for various forms of load balancing will become more important. Microsoft is addressing some of these concerns by introducing new services and products. Three of those that are not covered on the exam but relate to this topic are:

➤ **Windows Load Balancing Service (WLBS)** This product, recently acquired from another company, allows up to 32 NT Servers to appear as a single IP address to client machines and routes traffic to the appropriate server based on network load.

➤ **COM+** The new version of COM will also incorporate the ability to transparently implement load balancing of component calls based on a set of key network indicators. The technique used by COM+ will be based on the concept of a routing server discussed previously and will also address failover issues by rerouting method calls in the event the preferred server is unavailable.

➤ **MSMQ** You can use the message queue product to implement a form of load balancing because requests from clients can be sent to a message queue on a single server. Multiple servers running components can then pull from the queue, thereby reducing the load on any single server.

# Versioning

Another important aspect of maintaining a distributed application is the ability to add functionality to middle-tier components without breaking existing clients. This is an issue you must be aware of because the components running in the middle tier are COM objects on which the client program is relying.

One of the benefits of using COM to build component-based solutions is the fact that the client program is really only relying on the definitions of the middle-tier components and not their implementation. As a result, as long as the public interface of the component does not change, you can modify the implementation of the component without breaking programs already compiled and distributed to clients.

As we discussed in Chapter 4, each COM object that is compiled is assigned a GUID (called a CLSID) that identifies it, as are each of the interfaces implemented by the component (called an *IID* or *interface ID*). These unique identifiers are then compiled into the client program, from which time the GUIDs must not change or the client program will not function correctly.

When modifying a COM component that is already referenced by client programs, you must be sure that the GUIDs used by the component remain the

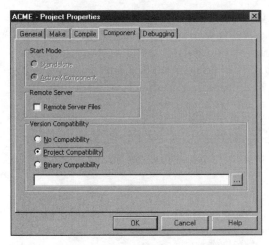

**Figure 12.4**   Compilation options.

same when you recompile it. To do this, you can set the Project Properties before compiling the project containing the component. The dialog box shown in Figure 12.4 is invoked from the Project|Project Properties menu.

In this dialog box you can set one of the three available options shown in Table 12.1.

| Table 12.1 | Compilation options. |
|---|---|
| **Option** | **Description** |
| No Compatibility | This option generates new type library information and GUIDs each time VB compiles the component. Existing clients will not be able to use this component. You should use this option to make a clean break with older versions of the component. |
| Project Compatibility | This option ensures that the type library information is maintained, but generates new GUIDs for interfaces in the component. This option is used when first developing a new component. By keeping the type library information the same, existing test projects will still be able to reference it. You would not use this option to release the component if you want to maintain compatibility with previous versions. When you select this option, the file box below it is enabled so that you can provide a path to the type library of the project. |
| Binary Compatibility | This option keeps all GUIDs intact, but will warn you if it detects that a class has changed. You can ignore the warning and reuse the GUIDs, but it may break existing clients. You should use this option when you have added interfaces or methods and want existing clients to continue to use the component. When you select this option, the file box below it is enabled so that you can provide a path to the type library of the project. |

Of course, choosing the Binary Compatibility option is only viable for classes whose signatures do not change. In other words, if you change the name, arguments, or return value of a single method within the class, you have broken compatibility and a new GUID should be generated. Visual Basic, however, does allow you to add methods and properties to the class and still maintain binary compatibility.

> *Note: Although this is technically against the rules of COM, Visual Basic does it in such a way that existing clients will not break.*

If changes are required, you should create a second interface in the component with the new signature and use binary compatibility. This technique allows new clients to use the new functionality without disrupting old clients. In fact, you can write code that can gracefully degrade from the second version of the interface to use functionality in the first.

For example, assume you have a component **ACME.Customer** that supports a **CheckCredit** method. The first version of this method takes a customer ID and purchase amount as arguments:

```
Public Function CheckCredit(ByVal CustID as Long, _
ByVal PurchaseAmount as Money) As Boolean
```

However, as time goes by you also want the method to authorize a credit card purchase. Obviously, adding an argument to the method will break compatibility. In this case you should create a **Customer2** class in the component that implements the existing Customer interface (using the **Implements** keyword) and then re-code the **CheckCredit** method, changing its signatures as required:

```
Public Function CheckCredit(ByVal CustID as Long, _
ByVal PurchaseAmount as Money, ByVal CCNumber as String) As Boolean
```

Code that you write in new client programs can then make calls to either the new or old version of the component by checking whether or not the new Customer2 interface is supported. You can see sample code that handles either interface in Listing 12.1.

## Listing 12.1   Using a secondary interface in a component.

```
Private Sub ProcessOrder(ByVal objCust As ACME.Customer, _
  CustID As Long, PurchaseAmount As Currency, _
  Optional CCNumber As String)
```

```
Dim flAns As Boolean
'Do other processing

'Check their credit
If TypeOf objCust Is ACME.Customer2 Then
    Dim lobj As ACME.Customer2
    Set lobj = objCust
    flAns = lobj.CheckCredit(CustID, PurchaseAmount, CCNumber)
Else
    'Degrade gracefully and do not pass the credit card
    flAns = objCust.CheckCredit(CustID, PurchaseAmount)
End If

End Sub
```

Notice that the **ProcessOrder** procedure takes an argument, **objCust**, of type **ACME.Customer**. This procedure will actually work for objects of type **ACME.Customer** and **ACME.Customer2** if the latter interface implements the former. Within the procedure you can then use the Visual Basic **TypeOf** statement to determine if the object supports the Customer2 interface. If so, it can safely call the new version of **CheckCredit**, passing it the credit card number as the third argument.

# Practice Questions

## Question 1

> To implement load balancing using MTS you need to:
>
> ○ a. Do nothing, MTS automatically supports load balancing.
>
> ○ b. Check the Load Balance checkbox in the MTS package properties.
>
> ○ c. Implement the ILoadBalance interface in your components.
>
> ○ d. MTS does not support load balancing.

The correct answer is d. MTS, as of release 2.0, does not support any form of load balancing. To implement load balancing you'll need to use one of the deployment and load balancing techniques discussed in the chapter. These include parallel deployment, isolation of critical components, and pipelining using static or dynamic load balancing.

Because MTS does not implement load balancing, answers a and b are obviously incorrect, because no graphical way exists to turn it on. Answer c is incorrect because there is no interface called ILoadBalance, although you could certainly create one to implement your load-balancing algorithms.

## Question 2

> If you want to add functionality to an existing and already deployed component while maintaining compatibility, what should you do when compiling the component in Visual Basic?
>
> ○ a. Use the Binary Compatibility option on the Project Properties dialog box.
>
> ○ b. Use the Project Compatibility option on the Project Properties dialog box.
>
> ○ c. You cannot maintain compatibility with components that are already deployed.
>
> ○ d. Nothing. Compatibility will be maintained automatically.

The correct answer is a. The Binary Compatibility option is used to direct the compiler to use the existing type library and GUIDs that were originally associated with the component. Remember that you also need to point the compiler to the appropriate type library (usually contained in the previous EXE or DLL) that is to be used as the reference version. You should only use this option if you do not change the definition of the classes in the component by changing data types or adding arguments. You may, however, add classes to the component or add methods to existing classes and still use this option. In order to create a new version of an existing class, one of your new classes can implement an existing class.

Answer b is incorrect because Project Compatibility is used only during development of a new component and does not ensure that your component contains the same GUIDs as a previously deployed component. Answer c is incorrect because you can in fact maintain compatibility as long as the class definition does not change and you use the Binary Compatibility option. Answer d is incorrect because Project Compatibility is the default, which is not sufficient to maintain compatibility with components that have been deployed.

## Question 3

What is the correct syntax to instantiate the COM object **ACME.Customer** on a remote server named APOLLO?

○ a.  Set obj = CreateObject("APOLLO","ACME.Customer").

○ b.  Set obj = APOLLO.CreateObject("ACME.Customer").

○ c.  Set obj = CreateObject("ACME.Customer","APOLLO").

○ d.  You cannot specify the server in VB code.

The correct answer is c. The name of the remote server is specified as the second argument to the **CreateObject** function. This is a new feature of Visual Basic 6 and is functionally equivalent to using the DCOMCNFG program to change the server or editing the Registry directly.

Answer a is incorrect because the arguments are switched; answer b is incorrect because APOLLO is not an object that contains methods, but rather the name of a server.

# Question 4

You have deployed a distributed application and after several months are now getting reports that response time is poor. The application uses MTS on a single server to host COM objects that implement business services. What can you do to address the problem? [Check all the apply]

- ❏ a. Deploy copies of the business objects on multiple MTS servers and use static load balancing.
- ❏ b. Add another processor and more RAM to the MTS server machine.
- ❏ c. Make sure object pooling is enabled on the MTS server.
- ❏ d. Enable the load-balancing support of the COM library using the Win32 API.

The correct answers are a and b. In this case, the problem is likely lack of resources on the server machine. To address this you could either boost the performance of the server by changing its hardware configuration (answer b), or use multiple lower-level servers to deploy copies of the components across multiple servers (answer a). In the case of answer a you would then also need to implement some form of load balancing so that client calls are spread across the servers.

Answer c is incorrect because MTS does not, as of release 2.0, support object pooling. Answer d is incorrect because the current version of COM does not intrinsically support load balancing. Some form of load balancing will be integrated into the COM+ services to be released with Windows 2000.

# Question 5

You determine that your application requires load balancing to decrease response times. Initially, you wish to assign users to use components on statically assigned servers. Which static load-balancing technique allows the most flexibility in the event that a more dynamic method of assignment is eventually required?

- ○ a. Referral component with a routing server
- ○ b. Central Repository using a relational table
- ○ c. Registry manipulation using CLIREG32.EXE
- ○ d. Pipelining

The correct answer is a. A referral component running on a dedicated routing server is the most flexible option since the algorithm used to assign the server can be changed without affecting the client computers. As a result you can move from a static to a dynamic load-balancing scheme more easily. The referral component requires more up-front design work and a dedicated server to run the component.

Answer b is incorrect because the central repository does not support dynamic load balancing because the assignments of users to servers is made in the table. Answer c is incorrect because manipulating the Registries of the client computers is time consuming and requires reconfiguring each client. Answer d is incorrect because pipelining is a technique used for deploying components and does not address load balancing.

# Question 6

You've created a component that processes customer orders and will be accessed remotely by Visual Basic clients. During development you wish to change the **CheckCredit** method to take an additional argument. Which project compatibility option should you choose when compiling your component? [Choose the best answer]

○ a. No Compatibility

○ b. Project Compatibility

○ c. Binary Compatibility

○ d. Interface Compatibility

The correct answer is b. The key to this question is taking note of the phrase "during development." Project Compatibility just ensures that any test projects created in VB will continue to work because the type library information is retained. If the component has not been deployed and referenced by compiled clients, you do not need to implement a new interface or use the Binary Compatibility option (answer c). Answer a may be perfectly acceptable if you have no test projects created (hence the trick) since this option will generate all new GUIDs for the project. Answer d is incorrect because there is no Interface Compatibility option available.

# Need To Know More?

 Pattison, Ted: *Programming Distributed Applications With COM and Microsoft Visual Basic 6.0.* Microsoft Press, 1998. ISBN: 1572319615. Chapter 5 contains an excellent discussion of compatibility issues when creating components in VB.

 For more information on the Windows Load Balancing Services (WLBS), see the Frequently Asked Questions on the Microsoft site at **www.microsoft.com/ntserver/ntserverenterprise/exec/ moreinfo/faq.asp**.

 You can also find good information on load-balancing techniques in the "DCOM Technical Overview" white paper in the MSDN library that ships with Visual Studio 6 or MSDN online at **msdn.microsoft.com**.

 A white paper containing a good overview of the entire architecture of distributed COM or DCOM called, not surprisingly, "DCOM Architecture," is located in the MSDN library on the MSDN Web site at **msdn.microsoft.com**.

# Sample Test

In this chapter, we provide pointers to help you develop a successful test-taking strategy, including how to choose proper answers, how to decode ambiguity, how to work within the Microsoft testing framework, how to decide what you need to memorize, and how to prepare for the test. At the end of the chapter, we include 57 questions on subject matter pertinent to Microsoft Exam 70-175, "Designing and Implementing Distributed Applications with Microsoft Visual Basic 6.0." Good luck!

# Questions, Questions, Questions

There should be no doubt in your mind that you are facing a test full of specific and pointed questions. If the version of the Visual Basic 6 Distributed exam that you take is fixed-length, it will include 71 questions, and you will be allotted 90 minutes to complete the exam. If it's an adaptive test (the software should tell you this as you begin the exam), it will consist of somewhere between 25 and 35 questions (on average) and take somewhere between 30 and 60 minutes.

Whichever type of test you take, for this exam, questions belong to one of five basic types:

➤ Multiple choice with a single answer

➤ Multiple choice with multiple answers

➤ Multipart with a single answer

➤ Multipart with multiple answers

➤ Simulations whereby you click a GUI screen capture to simulate using the Visual Basic 6 interface

Always take the time to read a question at least twice before selecting an answer, and you should always look for an Exhibit button as you examine each question. An *exhibit* is usually a screen capture of program output or GUI information that you must examine to analyze the question's contents and formulate an answer. The Exhibit button brings up graphics and charts used to help explain a question, provide additional data, or illustrate page layout or program behavior.

Not every question has only one answer; many questions require multiple answers. Therefore, you should read each question carefully, determine how many answers are necessary or possible, and look for additional hints or instructions when selecting answers. Such instructions often occur in brackets, immediately following the question itself (multiple-answer questions).

# Picking Proper Answers

Obviously, the only way to pass any exam is to select enough of the right answers to obtain a passing score. However, Microsoft's exams are not standardized like the SAT and GRE exams; they are far more diabolical and convoluted. In some cases, questions are strangely worded, and deciphering them can be a real challenge. In those cases, you may need to rely on answer-elimination skills. Almost always, at least one answer out of the possible choices for a question can be eliminated immediately because it matches one of these conditions:

➤ The answer does not apply to the situation.

➤ The answer describes a nonexistent issue, an invalid option, or an imaginary state.

➤ The answer may be eliminated because of information in the question itself.

After you eliminate all answers that are obviously wrong, you can apply your retained knowledge to eliminate further answers. Look for items that sound correct, but refer to actions, commands, or features that are not present or not available in the situation that the question describes.

If you're still faced with a blind guess among two or more potentially correct answers, reread the question. Try to picture how each of the possible remaining answers would alter the situation. Be especially sensitive to terminology; sometimes the choice of words ("remove" instead of "disable") can make the difference between a right answer and a wrong one.

Only when you've exhausted your ability to eliminate answers, but remain unclear about which of the remaining possibilities is correct should you guess at an answer. An unanswered question offers you no points, but guessing gives you at least some chance of getting a question right; just don't be too hasty when making a blind guess.

If you're taking a fixed-length test, you can wait until the last round of reviewing marked questions (just as you're about to run out of time or out of unanswered questions) before you start making guesses. If you're taking an adaptive test, you'll have to guess to move on to the next question if you can't figure out an answer some other way. Either way, guessing should be a last resort.

# Decoding Ambiguity

Microsoft exams have a reputation for including questions that can be difficult to interpret, confusing, or ambiguous. In our experience with numerous exams, we consider this reputation to be completely justified. The Microsoft exams are tough, and they're deliberately made that way.

The only way to beat Microsoft at its own game is to be prepared. You'll discover that many exam questions test your knowledge of things that are not directly related to the issue raised by a question. This means that the answers you must choose from, even incorrect ones, are just as much a part of the skill assessment as the question itself. If you don't know something about most aspects of Visual Basic 6, you may not be able to eliminate obviously wrong answers because they relate to a different area of Visual Basic than the one that's addressed by the question at hand. In other words, the more you know about the software, the easier it will be for you to tell right from wrong.

Questions often give away their answers, but you have to be Sherlock Holmes to see the clues. Often, subtle hints appear in the question text in such a way that they seem almost irrelevant to the situation. You must realize that each question is a test unto itself and that you need to inspect and successfully navigate each question to pass the exam. Look for small clues, such as the mention of times, group permissions and names, and configuration settings. Little things such as these can point to the right answer if properly understood; if missed, they can leave you facing a blind guess.

Another common difficulty with certification exams is vocabulary. Microsoft has an uncanny knack for naming some utilities and features entirely obviously in some cases and completely inanely in other instances. Be sure to brush up on the key terms presented at the beginning of each chapter. You may also want to read through the glossary at the end of this book the day before you take the test.

# Working Within The Framework

The test questions appear in random order, and many elements or issues that receive mention in one question may also crop up in other questions. It's not uncommon to find that an incorrect answer to one question is the correct answer to another question, or vice versa. Take the time to read every answer to each question, even if you recognize the correct answer to a question immediately. That extra reading may spark a memory, or remind you about a Visual Basic feature or function that helps you on another question elsewhere in the exam.

If you're taking a fixed-length test, you can revisit any question as many times as you like. If you're uncertain of the answer to a question, check the box that's provided to mark it for easy return later on. You should also mark questions you think may offer information that you can use to answer other questions. On fixed-length tests, we usually mark somewhere between 25 and 50 percent of the questions on exams we've taken. The testing software is designed to let you mark every question if you choose; use this framework to your advantage. Everything you'll want to see again should be marked; the testing software can then help you return to marked questions quickly and easily.

 For fixed-length tests, we strongly recommend that you first read through the entire test quickly, before getting caught up in answering individual questions. This will help to jog your memory as you review the potential answers and can help identify questions that you want to mark for easy access to their contents. It will also let you identify and mark the tricky questions for easy return

> as well. The key is to make a quick pass over the territory to begin with—so that you know what you're up against—and then to survey that territory more thoroughly on a second pass, when you can begin to answer all questions systematically and consistently.

If you're taking an adaptive test, and you see something in a question or one of the answers that jogs your memory on a topic, or that you feel you should record if the topic appears in another question, write it down on your piece of paper. Just because you can't go back to a question in an adaptive test doesn't mean you can't take notes on what you see early in the test, in hopes that it might help you later in the test.

> For adaptive tests, don't be afraid to take notes on what you see in various questions. Sometimes, what you record from one question, especially if it's not as familiar as it should be or reminds you of the name or use of some utility or interface details, can help you on other questions later on.

# Deciding What To Memorize

The amount of memorization you must undertake for an exam depends on how well you remember what you've read, and how well you know the software by heart. If you're a visual thinker and can see the drop-down menus and dialog boxes in your head, you won't need to memorize as much as someone who's less visually oriented. However, the exam will tax your ability to remember numerous new, existing, and related technologies that a Visual Basic developer will use. The bar has been raised on what a VB developer does, especially when creating distributed applications. The exam will test your ability to integrate SQL, MTS, COM, VB, DHTML, and ASP as needed and with the singular focus of producing applications in a very component-oriented manner. Be prepared to think on multiple levels, in sometimes abstract ways.

At a minimum, you'll want to memorize information about the following topics:

➤ ADO/RDO

➤ MTS

➤ COM components

➤ ActiveX projects (controls, documents, EXE, and DLL)

➤ SQL

If you work your way through this book while sitting at a machine with Visual Basic installed and try to manipulate the environment's features and functions as they're discussed throughout, you should have little or no difficulties mastering this material. Also, don't forget that The Cram Sheet at the front of the book is designed to capture the material that's most important to memorize; use this to guide your studies as well.

# Preparing For The Test

The best way to prepare for the test—after you've studied—is to take at least one practice exam. We've included one here in this chapter for that reason; the test questions are located in the pages that follow (and unlike the preceding chapters in this book, the answers don't follow the questions immediately; you'll have to flip to Chapter 14 to review the answers separately).

Give yourself 90 minutes to take the exam, and keep yourself on the honor system—don't look at earlier text in the book or jump ahead to the answer key. When your time is up or you've finished the questions, you can check your work in Chapter 14. Pay special attention to the explanations for the incorrect answers; these can also help to reinforce your knowledge of the material. Knowing how to recognize correct answers is good, but understanding why incorrect answers are wrong can be equally valuable.

# Taking The Test

Relax. Once you're sitting in front of the testing computer, there's nothing more you can do to increase your knowledge or preparation. Take a deep breath, stretch, and start reading that first question.

You don't need to rush, either. You have plenty of time to complete each question and to return to those questions that you skip or mark for return (if you're taking a fixed-length test). If you read a question twice and remain clueless, you can mark it if you're taking a fixed-length test; if you're taking an adaptive test, you'll have to guess and move on. Both easy and difficult questions are intermixed throughout the test in random order. If you're taking a fixed-length test, don't cheat yourself by spending too much time on a hard question early on in the test, thereby depriving yourself of the time you need to answer the questions at the end of the test. If you're taking an adaptive test, don't spend more than five minutes on any single question—if it takes you that long to get nowhere, it's time to guess and move on.

On a fixed-length test, you can read through the entire test, and before returning to marked questions for a second visit, you can figure out how much time you've got per question. As you answer each question, remove its mark. Continue to review the remaining marked questions until you run out of time or complete the test.

On an adaptive test, sct a maximum time limit for questions and watch your time on long or complex questions. If you hit your limit, it's time to guess and move on. Don't deprive yourself of the opportunity to see more questions by taking too long to puzzle over questions, unless you think you can figure out the answer. Otherwise, you're limiting your opportunities to pass.

That's it for pointers. Here are some questions for you to practice on.

## Question 1

A COM component that provides a method to process a customer order according to business rules would be defined in which service layer?

○ a. User services

○ b. Business services

○ c. Data services

○ d. None of the above

## Question 2

Which of the following are benefits of adopting a three-tier architecture? [Check all that apply]

❑ a. Business logic is more maintainable.

❑ b. Performance in the user interface increases.

❑ c. Components can be reused in multiple applications.

❑ d. Data integrity is maintained.

## Question 3

You've developed a COM component you'd like to share with other developers in the organization. How can you accomplish this?

○ a. Use Visual Modeler to publish the component.

○ b. Use Visual Component Manager to publish the component.

○ c. Use DCOMCNFG to publish the component.

○ d. Use the **&lt;OBJECT&gt;** tag to publish the component.

## Question 4

In what situation should you set the **CausesValidation** property on a control to **False**?

○ a. When you want the control to initiate the validation process of the previous control in the tab order

○ b. When you place code in the **Validate** event of the control

○ c. When the control will be used to provide user assistance

○ d. When you do not place code in the **Validate** event of the control

## Question 5

What is the value of the **Form1** form-level variable **strName** after the following code has been run?

```
Load Form1
Form1.strName = "Mays"
Form1.Show
Unload Form1
```

○ a. Mays.

○ b. Empty string.

○ c. Null.

○ d. Nothing. The variable is out of scope.

## Question 6

The Win32 API function is declared as follows:

```
Public Declare Function SetTimer Lib "user32" _
(ByVal hwnd As Long, ByVal nIDEvent As Long, _
ByVal uElapse As Long, _
ByVal lpTimerFunc As Long) As Long
```

What is the correct calling syntax if the timer should be given the ID of 1 and set to fire every 1,000 milliseconds with a callback procedure named **TimerProc**?

○ a.  SetTimer Me.hwnd, 1000, 1, AddressOf TimerProc

○ b.  SetTimer Me.hwnd, 1, 1000, TimerProc

○ c.  SetTimer Me.hwnd, 1000, 1, TimerProc

○ d.  SetTimer Me.hwnd, 1, 1000, AddressOf TimerProc

## Question 7

What type of binding does the VB compiler use with the following code segment?

```
Dim obj as ACME.Customer
Set obj = CreateObject("ACME.Customer")
```

○ a.  Late binding

○ b.  DispID binding

○ c.  vtable binding

○ d.  Either DispID binding or vtable binding

## Question 8

Which two methods are valid for creating controls dynamically at runtime?

❑ a.  Using the **Load** statement to add a control to an existing control array

❑ b.  Using the **Add** method of the **Controls** collection

❑ c.  Using the **Load** statement to create a control that is not referenced in the project

❑ d.  Using the **AddControl** method of the **Controls** collection

## Question 9

What is the value of **Err.Number** after the following code executes?

```
Dim x as Integer
On Error Resume Next
x = 1/0
If Err.Number = 13 Then
   MsgBox Err.Description
End If
```

○ a.  0

○ b.  13

○ c.  Null

○ d.  None of the above

## Question 10

Which of the following menu properties can be set at runtime? [Check all that apply]

❑ a.  **Checked**

❑ b.  **Visible**

❑ c.  **Shortcut**

❑ d.  **NegotiatePosition**

## Question 11

Which event of the **UserControl** object is used to save properties to persistent storage?

- ○ a. **ApplyChanges**
- ○ b. **ReadProperties**
- ○ c. **WriteProperties**
- ○ d. **InitializeProperties**

## Question 12

Which line of code allows you to access the **Visible** property provided by the container from code within a **UserControl** object?

- ○ a. **Ambient.Visible**
- ○ b. **Extender.Visible**
- ○ c. **Object.Visible**
- ○ d. **Me.Visible**

## Question 13

What is the syntax for declaring an event, **DataHasChanged**, that takes no arguments in a **UserControl** object?

- ○ a. **Declare Event DataHasChanged()**
- ○ b. **Event DataHasChanged()**
- ○ c. **Private Event DataHasChanged()**
- ○ d. **Public WithEvents DataHasChanged()**

# Question 14

You are designing a method in a component that returns an ADO recordset (**rs**), using a connection object (**cnSQL**) and a SQL string (**strSQL**). The recordset must be able to be updated by the client application without retaining a reference to the component. Which statement should be used to create the recordset?

○ a.  rs.Open strSQL, cnSQL, adOpenForwardOnly, adLockReadOnly

○ b.  rs.Open strSQL, cnSQL, adOpenStatic, adLockOptimistic

○ c.  rs.Open strSQL, cnSQL, adOpenStatic, adLockBatchOptimistic

○ d.  rs.Open strSQL, cnSQL, adOpenKeyset, adLockPessimistic

# Question 15

What are the tradeoffs involved in choosing a dynamic, server-side cursor when creating an ADO recordset with SQL Server?

○ a.  The cursor will consume fewer server resources, but will be able to reflect changes made to the recordset by other users.

○ b.  The cursor will consume more server resources, but will not be able to reflect changes made to the recordset by other users.

○ c.  The cursor will consume fewer server resources, but will not be able to reflect changes made to the recordset by other users.

○ d.  The cursor will consume more server resources, but will be able to reflect changes made to the recordset by other users.

# Question 16

Which ADO objects can be created independently? [Check all that apply]

❑ a.  **Command**

❑ b.  **Recordset**

❑ c.  **Field**

❑ d.  **Error**

## Question 17

What are the benefits of using stored procedures for data access?
[Check all that apply]

❑ a. Better performance.

❑ b. The database schema can be abstracted from the calling
program.

❑ c. Increased security.

❑ d. Portability between database platforms.

## Question 18

Which SQL statement would update the last name column in the
**Authors** table, changing its value to "Mays" for the author with an
ID of "123-45-6789"?

○ a. UPDATE Authors LName = 'Mays' WHERE au_id = '123-
45-6789'

○ b. UPDATE Authors WHERE au_id = '123-45-6789' SET
LName = 'Mays'

○ c. UPDATE Authors SET LName = 'Mays' WHERE au_id =
'123-45-6789'

○ d. UPDATE Authors SET LName = 'Mays' FOR au_id =
'123-45-6789'

## Question 19

Which cursor type and location is the most efficient for retrieving
a recordset and displaying it in an HTML table in an Active Server
Page (ASP) using SQL Server?

○ a. Client-side static cursor

○ b. Server-side forward-only cursor

○ c. Client-side keyset cursor

○ d. Server-side dynamic cursor

## Question 20

What two pieces of information are conveyed by the **CODEBASE** attribute of the **<OBJECT>** tag?

❑  a.   The ID of the component to be used in scripts in the Web page

❑  b.   The version of the component to be installed on the client computer

❑  c.   The location of the component to be downloaded

❑  d.   Data with which to initialize the component after downloading

## Question 21

You develop an ActiveX control to be used in your application. What steps should you take to ensure that the control can be downloaded and used safely by Internet Explorer? [Check all that apply]

❑  a.   Mark the control as safe for scripting and initialization.

❑  b.   Include a VBR file in the setup package.

❑  c.   Encrypt the SETUP.CAB file using a digital certificate.

❑  d.   Create a INF file to include in the CAB file.

# Question 22

What is the result of the following code if the insert into the **Orders** table fails? (Assume that **cnSQL** is a valid ADO **Connection** object.)

```
cnSQL.Execute "INSERT INTO Customers VALUES _
    ('Willie','Mays')
cnSQL.BeginTrans
sqlCommand = "UPDATE Products SET Quantity = _
    Quantity - 1 "
sqlCommand = sqlCommand + "WHERE prodid = 15"
cnSQL.Execute sqlCommand
cnSQL.Execute "INSERT INTO Orders VALUES _
    (15,1,'12/14/1998')"
cnSQL.CommitTrans
```

❍ a. The **Products** table is updated and the **Customers** insert succeeds.

❍ b. The update to the **Products** table is rolled back, but the **Customers** insert succeeds.

❍ c. The insert into the **Customers** table and update to the **Products** table are both rolled back.

❍ d. The update to the **Products** table succeeds and the **Customers** insert is rolled back.

# Question 23

Which method can you use to configure a client computer to run a component on a different remote server once the application has been installed?

❍ a. Use the **CODEBASE** attribute of the **<OBJECT>** tag.

❍ b. Use the Package and Deployment Wizard.

❍ c. Use the DCOMCNFG utility on the server computer.

❍ d. Use the DCOMCNFG utility on the client computer.

## Question 24

Which of the following statements regarding the Package and Deployment Wizard is false?

○ a.  It can create packages to be used in Web pages.

○ b.  It can deploy setup packages to a network drive.

○ c.  You can save scripts to rebuild your setup package.

○ d.  It can create a license-packaging file for your components.

## Question 25

When would you create a dependency file using the Package and Deployment Wizard?

○ a.  When the project can be distributed as a part of another project

○ b.  When the project is not included in the VB6DEP.INI file

○ c.  When the project is a component that will run on a remote server

○ d.  When the project will be distributed over the Internet

## Question 26

You have already deployed version 1.0 of a COM component that contains a **CheckCredit** method in an interface called ICustomer. The component is used by several VB client applications. You now discover that the data type for one of the arguments must be changed from **Integer** to **Long**. What must you do to fix the component without breaking the existing clients?

○ a.  Fix the method and recompile the component using Binary Compatibility.

○ b.  Fix the method and recompile the component using Project Compatibility.

○ c.  Create a new interface, ICustomer2, In the component and fix the method in the new interface. Recompile the component using Binary Compatibility.

○ d.  You cannot avoid breaking existing clients if you recompile the component.

## Question 27

In order for your distributed application to serve a large number of users, you determine that your business components in MTS will likely need to run on multiple servers. What methods can you use to implement this? [Check all that apply]

❑ a. Use parallel deployment to deploy copies of the components on multiple MTS servers.

❑ b. Use the MTS Load Balancing Services (MLBS) to dynamically load balance on multiple servers.

❑ c. Use pipelining to break down your components into discrete objects and deploy them on multiple MTS servers.

❑ d. Use the Load Balance checkbox in the Project Properties dialog box in VB.

## Question 28

When developing an ASP-based application, an important concept known as a *user session* retains the state information required to produce a single instance of application access. This concept is important because information stored within the **Session** object is maintained or accessible only during a session. A separate session is maintained for each user currently accessing an ASP application. During what action or event is the session established for the user?

○ a. When the first HTML page is accessed or requested

○ b. When the first ASP file is accessed or requested

○ c. When the script contained within the first ASP has completed all processing

○ d. After the user has successfully logged into the application

# Question 29

Which line(s) of VBScript could be added at positions [6] and [7] in the following code to properly allow modification of the second member of the array stored in the **Session** object?

```
[0] <% ' Contents in First.asp
[1] Dim MemberIDs (2)
[2] MemberIDs (1) = "234"
[3] MemberIDs (2) = "345"
[4] Session("MemberIDs") = MemberIDs %>
[5] <% ' Contents in Second.asp
[6]
[7]
[8] Session("MemberIDs") = SecondArray %>
```

○ a.  SecondArray = Session("MemberIDs")
       SecondArray (2) = "abc"

○ b.  SecondArray = Session("MemberIDs")(2)
       SecondArray = "abc"

○ c.  SecondArray = Session("MemberIDs")
       SecondArray (1) = "abc"

○ d.  Session("MemberIDs") (2) = "abc"

# Question 30

On your development system, you previously installed a Perl interpreter to allow the use of Perl script within your ASP files. After moving the application to the production server, your application runs great, except for the pages that used Perl script. What must be performed to correct the problem?

○ a.  Install a COM-based Perl to JavaScript translator.

○ b.  Nothing. IIS only supports VBScript and JavaScript within ASP pages.

○ c.  Install a Perl interpreter on the production server.

○ d.  Port the Perl script to an ECMAScript equivalent.

## Question 31

Where must **Session** or **Application** object variables be declared prior to use within an ASP file? [Check all that apply]

- ❑ a. In the **Application_OnStart** event found in the GLOBAL.ASA file.
- ❑ b. In the **Session_OnStart** event found in the GLOBAL.ASA file.
- ❑ c. At the beginning of the first page using the variable.
- ❑ d. It is not necessary to declare **Session** or **Application** object variables prior to use.

## Question 32

The built-in **Application** and **Session** objects are stored as implicit, dynamic collections. This means that a member of the object collection can be created dynamically the first time the collection is referenced in script. Which default collection of the **Session** or **Application** object is used when implicitly (without explicitly naming the collection in script) creating a member of the object collection?

- ○ a. **Contents** collection
- ○ b. **StaticObjects** collection
- ○ c. **Scope** collection
- ○ d. **Members** collection

## Question 33

Invoking the **Abandon** method of the **Session** built-in object will result in which of the following behaviors concerning ASP script?

- ○ a. Script on the same page continues to execute, without the **Session** object being accessible.
- ○ b. Any script after the **Abandon** method will not execute.
- ○ c. Script on the same page continues to execute, with the **Session** object continuing to be accessible.
- ○ d. None of the above.

## Question 34

During the **Session_OnEnd** event, which of the ASP built-in objects are available?

◯ a.  **Request**, **Response**, and **Server**

◯ b.  **Application** and **Session**

◯ c.  **Request** and **Response**

◯ d.  **Application**, **Session**, and **Server**

## Question 35

When trying to access a member within a **Request** object collection, failing to explicitly list the collection to be searched will result in which of the following occurring?

◯ a.  An error will occur.

◯ b.  The collections will be searched in order (**Cookies**, **ServerVariables**, **ClientCertificate**, **Form**, and **Querystring**), returning the first element found of the desired name.

◯ c.  The **Request** object will default to the **Form** collection.

◯ d.  All the collections will be searched, returning an array of the matching values found.

## Question 36

You want to create an application installation package, including registration of the necessary components. You want to have the ability to uninstall the application, as well as install the application from the Web. What tool should you use?

◯ a.  Setup Installation Guide

◯ b.  Package Export Wizard

◯ c.  Application Wizard

◯ d.  Package and Deployment Wizard

# Question 37

You are in the process of creating a newer version of a deployed application. When using the Package and Deployment Wizard, it is important that the resulting application properly updates the existing application version already installed on the client system. What step must be taken to ensure it is completed properly?

○ a. Change the version number for the project when prompted by the Package and Deployment Wizard.

○ b. Set the Version Compatibility setting of the project to No Compatibility.

○ c. Change the version number for the project on the Make tab of the Project Properties dialog box.

○ d. Enable automatic version control in the Project Properties dialog box.

# Question 38

You want to pass data from a database to the user interface in an n-tier distributed application. The application is broken into four layers, consisting of the database, data services objects, business objects, and the user interface elements, such as constituent controls on a Visual Basic application. What is the proper series of steps to maintain proper n-tier architecture design when attempting to feed or populate UI elements with data from the database?

○ a. Retrieve the data directly from the database by using ADO recordsets.

○ b. Use the data service objects to retrieve data from the database. Use business objects to retrieve data from the data service objects. Use the business objects to populate the UI elements with the data.

○ c. Use the data service objects to retrieve data from the database, and then to populate the UI elements.

○ d. Populate the business objects with data from the database. Populate the UI elements with data from the business objects.

# Question 39

When modeling or designing a unique characteristic of a piece of data, such as an **AddressID** for use in an **Address** table in a database, how should this be physically implemented in your component?

○ a.  Event

○ b.  User-defined data type

○ c.  Method

○ d.  Property

# Question 40

You recently purchased an ActiveX control from a third-party vendor on the Internet. After downloading and registering the control on your system, you do not find the control available in your toolbox when opening a Standard EXE project. What steps must be taken to make the third-party control available on your toolbox? [Check all that apply]

❏ a.  Right-click on the controls toolbox, choose Components, and find the control from the list provided on the Controls tab.

❏ b.  Choose Project|Components and find the component in the list of registered controls/components.

❏ c.  Choose Project|Components and use the Browse button to find the control on your system.

❏ d.  Choose Project|References and find the component in the list of registered controls/components.

# Question 41

You are creating a Web-based solution for a local company, and have decided to create an ActiveX document project. After several days of work, you decide that the only solution to a difficult problem encountered is to break the application into several **UserDocument** objects within your project. Being new to ActiveX document projects, you are unsure how to navigate between the documents from within the Visual Basic code. What method or methods can be used to accomplish this task? [Check all that apply]

❑ a. The **Navigate** method of the **WebBrowser** object

❑ b. The **NavigateTo** method of the **HyperLink** object

❑ c. The **NavigateTo** method of the **UserDocument** object

❑ d. The **Navigate** method of the **HyperLink** object

# Question 42

You have experience in creating COM components with Visual Basic 5, but with Visual Basic 6 the class modules have a new property with which you are unfamiliar. You know that you want either all your component methods to participate in a client's transaction, or none to participate. With this design goal in mind, what value should be chosen for the **MTSTransactionMode** property?

○ a. **UsesTransaction**

○ b. **RequiresTransaction**

○ c. **Supports Transactions**

○ d. **NotAnMTSObject**

## Question 43

In your Standard EXE project, you have created a global variable that you called **User**. Somewhere in your code, the variable takes on a value of "Goofy", which causes your application to behave, well—goofy. You have used the Add Watch dialog box to configure a new Watch variable, as shown in the exhibit (Figure 13.1). What changes, if any, need to be made to the Watch variable to enter break mode when the global variable obtains the value of "Goofy"? [Check all that apply]

❑ a. Change the Module Context to Form1.

❑ b. Change the Procedure Context to the procedure in which the variable is declared.

❑ c. Change the Watch Type to Break When Value Is True.

❑ d. No changes are necessary.

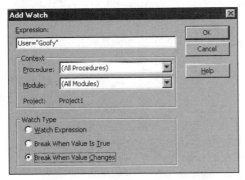

**Figure 13.1**   Exhibit for Question 43.

# Question 44

Due to the "feature creep" that has affected a recent development project undertaken by your small consulting company, it is necessary to add another developer to the project. Despite the fact that a proper scope document would have either eliminated or curtailed the unexpected "feature creep," you forge ahead and set up source code control for the development project, using Visual SourceSafe. You want to ensure that no code is added to the project that is not compilable, as intermediate builds are often made at unexpected times to satisfy the eccentric client. What must be done to ensure that no noncompilable code exists in the source code control database?

○ a. Compile the local projects on each developer workstation.

○ b. Run the auto-compile wizard to warn of the introduction of noncompilable code.

○ c. Schedule a nightly compile on the server housing the project database.

○ d. Allow simultaneous file checkouts within the project database.

# Question 45

After creating an ActiveX document project, you are preparing instructions for the client—as all good consultants do—explaining how to access the application. You remember that in Visual Basic 5, ActiveX documents could not be directly navigated to within the browser. What must be entered into Internet Explorer to allow the application to be accessed?

○ a. The HTML file containing the **CODEBASE** statement to link to the document

○ b. The ASP file that houses and instantiates the ActiveX document

○ c. The Automation server EXE created by the project

○ d. The VBD file generated for the application's initial document page

## Question 46

You have created several Watch variables to assist in debugging your application. When looking at the values for Watch variables configured with limited scopes, you notice an unusual value assigned to the variables when they are currently out of scope. What is that value?

○ a. <out of range>

○ b. <out of context>

○ c. <out of scope>

○ d. Null

## Question 47

You want to step through the code contained in your ActiveX Control project line by line when in break mode. How can this be accomplished?

○ a. Open a second instance of Visual Basic, start a Standard EXE project, and add an instance of the control to the project.

○ b. Compile the control, create a new Standard EXE project, and add a reference to the control.

○ c. Add a Standard EXE project to your project to create a project group. Add an instance of the control to a form in the added project and step through the code like normal.

○ d. Run the control project and choose the Step Through option on the debug toolbar.

## Question 48

Which of the following is required to configure a Windows 95/98 system to run a distributed application that uses components running within MTS on a remote system? [Check all that apply]

❑ a. Install the Microsoft Distributed Transaction Coordinator on the client system.

❑ b. Install DCOM support on the client system.

❑ c. Install MTS on the client system.

❑ d. Run the application installation executable.

# Question 49

After making significant changes to an ActiveX control, you determine that the control is no longer compatible with the most recently deployed version. What steps should be taken to ensure existing applications will not attempt to use the modified version?

○ a. Set the Version Compatibility option to Binary Compatibility.

○ b. Set the Version Compatibility option to Retain Compatibility.

○ c. Set the Version Compatibility option to No Compatibility.

○ d. Set the Version Compatibility option to Project Compatibility.

# Question 50

In your Visual Basic application, you are using RDO to retrieve data from a Microsoft SQL Server. You prefer to avoid having temporary stored procedures be generated on the server when using the **Execute** and **OpenResultset** methods. Which option should be used to accomplish this?

○ a. **rdFetchLongColumns**

○ b. **rdAsynchEnable**

○ c. **rdExecDirect**

○ d. **rdOpenKeySet**

# Question 51

You have decided to create a Visual Basic project that will be marked for unattended execution. With this option set, which of the following project scenarios would be a good match for unattended execution? [Check all that apply]

❏ a. ActiveX control

❏ b. ActiveX document

❏ c. ActiveX DLL project that requires some user interaction

❏ d. ActiveX EXE project that does not use any **Form** objects

# Question 52

If the following code is placed within your Visual Basic project, and the project is compiled on a 32-bit development platform, which code segment will not be included in the final compiled binary executable? [Check all that apply]

```
#If Win32 Then
    ' insert code segment A
#ElseIf Win16 Then
    ' insert code segment B
#Else
    ' insert code segment C
#End If
```

❑ a.  Code segment B.

❑ b.  Code segment A.

❑ c.  Code segment C.

❑ d.  No referenced segments will be included.

# Question 53

You have created an IIS application that uses multiple **WebClass** objects. You are unsure of the final destination of your application, therefore you cannot determine ahead of time what the URLs will be for the various Webitems within your application. What action can be followed to determine the proper URLs dynamically at runtime?

○ a.  Use the **URLEncode** method of the **Server** object.

○ b.  Check the **NameInURL** property of the **WebClass** object.

○ c.  Use the **URLFor** method of the **WebClass** object.

○ d.  Use the **HTMLEncode** method of the **Server** object.

## Question 54

Which segment of code should be added at line [1] to properly persist the data changed for an ActiveX DLL?

```
[1] ...
[2] PropBag.WriteProperty "InterestRate", _
    mIntRate, conDefRate
[3] End Sub
```

○ a. Private Sub Class_InitProperties(PropBag As PropertyBag)

○ b. Private Sub Class_ReadProperties(PropBag As PropertyBag)

○ c. Private Sub Class_WriteProperties(PropBag As PropertyBag)

○ d. Private Sub Class_Initialize(PropBag As PropertyBag)

## Question 55

You are preparing to implement a portion of your application design by creating a COM component. This component will provide objects to many different clients, and you especially need to have one instance of your component be able to supply objects to multiple clients. Which project type should you choose? [Check all that apply]

❑ a. ActiveX EXE with the **Instancing** property set to **SingleUse**

❑ b. ActiveX DLL

❑ c. ActiveX Document

❑ d. ActiveX EXE with the **Instancing** property set to **MultiUse**

# Question 56

You are developing a component with the intention to run within the MTS runtime environment. Your component performed multiple database connections within a particular method, with each action closely dependent on the success of the others. One of the database transactions is prone to failure. What provision should be coded into your component to account for the scenarios where this particular database procedure fails to complete properly?

○ a. Raise the **OnTransactionAbort** event of the **ObjectContext** object.

○ b. Invoke the **SetComplete** method of the **ObjectContext** object.

○ c. Invoke the **SetAbort** method of the **ObjectContext** object.

○ d. Raise the **OnTransactionCommit** event of the **ObjectContext** object.

## Question 57

You have just completed setting MTS up with role-based security. You create a role called "Dev" and have added the necessary users to the role. After applying the role to the components or component interfaces, as desired, you test out your solution. You find that the programmatic security you set up does not appear to be working. What should you change line 6 to so it will operate as intended?

```
[0] On Error GoTo HandleError
[1] Dim objCon As ObjectContext
[2] Set objCon = GetObjectContext()
[3] If objCon Is Nothing Then
[4]   Exit Function
[5] Else
[6]   If objCon.IsSecurityEnabled("Dev") Then
[7]     ' Perform privilege code
[8]   End If
[9] End If
```

○ a. **If objCon.IsSecurityEnabled() Then**

○ b. **If objCon.GetOriginalCaller = "Dev" Then**

○ c. **If objCon.IsCallerInRole("Dev") Then**

○ d. **If objCon.IsCallerInRole() Then**

**14**

# Answer Key

1. b
2. a, c
3. b
4. c
5. a
6. d
7. d
8. a, b
9. d
10. a, b
11. c
12. b
13. b
14. c
15. d

16. a, b
17. a, b, c
18. c
19. b
20. b, c
21. a, c
22. b
23. d
24. d
25. a
26. c
27. a, c
28. b
29. c
30. c

31. d
32. a
33. c
34. d
35. b
36. d
37. c
38. b
39. d
40. a, b
41. b
42. a
43. c
44. a
45. d

46. b
47. c
48. b, d
49. c
50. c
51. d
52. a, c
53. c
54. c
55. d
56. c
57. c

## Question 1

The correct answer is b. A COM component, like the one mentioned in the question, implements business logic that would be correctly placed in the Business Services layer. Answer a is incorrect because elements such as windows and Web pages make up User Services. Answer c is incorrect because components that modify the database directly are normally found in the Data Services layer, and no mention was made of accessing a database to process the customer order. Eventually, the information would most likely be placed into a database for persistent storage, but the processing of the customer order according to encapsulated business rules would not fall into the Data Services layer.

## Question 2

The correct answers are a and c. By splitting the application into three physical tiers, you are able to make changes in one of the tiers without necessarily affecting the others. This allows business logic implemented in components to be modified without affecting the clients. This directly increases the level of maintainability of the business logic. Part of standard three-tier architecture involves the encapsulation of business logic as components running within the middle or business tier. This provides the ability for components to be called from user interfaces written in multiple languages, allowing large-scale reuse of the components in multiple applications. Answer b is incorrect because implementing business logic in a remote component can increase response time as the call is made over the network. Answer d is incorrect because data integrity is maintained by the database regardless of the application architecture.

## Question 3

The correct answer is b. The Visual Component Manager is a utility that uses the Microsoft Repository to store information about components in a relational database. Other developers can then view published components and add them to their project. Answer a is incorrect because Visual Modeler is used to model applications, but not distributed components. Answer c is incorrect because DCOMCNFG is used to specify on which server to instantiate components, but is not used to publish them. Answer d is incorrect because the <OBJECT> tag is used to download and instantiate components on a Web page.

## Question 4

The correct answer is c. The **CausesValidation** property is by default set to **True** and causes the **Validate** event to fire for the control that had focus prior to the control with the property set. Normally, you would override the default when the control is used to provide user assistance such as showing a help file. In this way the user can get help, instead of being forced to re-enter data in the control. Answer a is incorrect; actually, the reverse is true. Answers b and d are incorrect because the **CausesValidation** property is not connected with the **Validate** event when referring to the same control.

# Question 5

The correct answer is a. VB does not actually deallocate the memory for module-level variables until the form is set to **Nothing**. Therefore, the value is retained and will remain set to the string "Mays" when it is reloaded.

Although it wasn't explicitly discussed in the book, this topic is important for understanding the fundamentals covered in the exam.

# Question 6

The correct answer is d. The key to this question is that the **AddressOf** operator must be used to pass the address of the procedure to use as the callback. In addition, the timer ID should be the second argument and the elapsed time is the third argument. Answers a and c confuse the second and third arguments and answer c also does not use the **AddressOf** operator. Answer b is correct, but it does not use the **AddressOf** operator.

# Question 7

The correct answer is d. Remember that DispID binding and vtable binding are both forms of early binding that allow the VB compiler to more efficiently make calls to COM objects. Which form of early binding is used is determined by how the **ACME.Customer** component has been implemented, as long as the VB code makes the explicit declaration in the **Dim** statement. VB will always use vtable binding if possible, because it is much faster than DispID binding.

# Question 8

The correct answers are a and b. The two methods in answers a and b can both be used; however, the first method can only be used to augment an existing control array on the form and so it is less flexible. The second method is new to VB6 and allows you to create both referenced and unreferenced controls by passing in the ProgID of the control to be created. Answer c is incorrect; the

**Load** statement is only used in conjunction with a control array. Answer d is incorrect because no **AddControl** member of the **Controls** collection exists.

## Question 9

The correct answer is d. When you use inline error handling as in the code sample, the value of the error is not cleared unless you call the **Err.Clear** method. Once **Clear** is called, the error number is reset to 0. Although this would appear to make the value of **Err.Number** equal to 13, this error number equates to a "Type Mismatch." The correct error number for a "Division by zero" error is 11. Answers a, b, and c are therefore incorrect.

## Question 10

The correct answers are a and b. Most of the menu properties can be set at either design time or runtime, but both the **Shortcut** and **NegotiatePosition** properties can only be set at design time.

This topic was not explicitly mentioned in the text of the book, but it is one of those topics that crosses over from the desktop exam and may appear on the distributed exam.

## Question 11

The correct answer is c. The **WriteProperties** event is called when the container destroys the instance of the control at design time. The event passes in a **PropertyBag** object that is used to encapsulate the properties that are passed in and out of the control. The **ApplyChanges** event in answer a is used by the **PropertyPage** object. Answer b is incorrect; the **ReadProperties** event is used to read the property values from persistent storage provided by the container. Answer d is incorrect because **InitializeProperties** is simply used to initialize properties at runtime.

## Question 12

The correct answer is b. The **Extender** object provides access to those extended properties provided by the container. These properties are normally those that the container needs to work with the control. Answer a is incorrect because you can get access to ambient properties, but only through the **AmbientChanged** event. Answer c is incorrect: The object reference can be used by code in the container to access a property of the same name as an extended property, but not from within the **UserControl**. Answer d is incorrect because the **Me** keyword is useful for referencing user-defined properties, but not extended properties.

## Question 13

The correct answer is b. To declare an event in **UserControl** object, you can simply use the **Event** keyword. You may also use the keyword **Public** in front of **Event** because the event must be public to be able to be seen from client applications. Answer c is incorrect because a **Private** event in an ActiveX control has no meaning and produces a syntax error. Answers a and d are incorrect because the **Declare** and **WithEvents** keywords are not used when declaring an event, although **WithEvents** is used when dimensioning an ActiveX component whose events you wish to use.

## Question 14

The correct answer is c. By creating a static cursor and using the **adLockBatchOptimistic** constant, you instruct ADO to create a disconnected recordset. This type of recordset can be updated without a valid connection and then passed back to a method in the component that calls the **UpdateBatch** method. Answer d would create an updateable recordset, but only if the database connection is maintained. Answers a and b are incorrect because they both specify lock types that would not allow updating.

## Question 15

The correct answer is d. Dynamic, server-side cursors are useful when you want to make sure you are able to see any changes made by other users. However, they generally do not perform as well because they require more activity on the part of the server to reflect those changes. The other answers simply offer the other combinations of these two tradeoffs.

## Question 16

The correct answers are a and b. The **Command, Recordset, and Connection** objects can be created independently of each other. This allows ADO to be flexible enough to create and associate these objects at a later time. The **Field** object is only available after a **Recordset** is created, and **Error** objects are dependent on the **Connection** object.

## Question 17

The correct answers are a, b, and c. The primary benefits of using stored procedures are better performance, because they are compiled and stored on the server; schema abstraction, because the calling program need not see the underlying database objects; and increased security, because permissions can usually be given only to the stored procedure without exposing the underlying tables. Answer d is incorrect because portability is usually an argument against using stored procedures. They are generally written in a variant of SQL that is specific to a database vendor.

## Question 18

The correct answer is c. To update a single row in a table, you must use a **WHERE** clause in the **UPDATE** statement that identifies the correct row. The **SET** clause identifies the column that is to be updated. Answer a is incorrect because it omits the **SET** clause. Answer b is incorrect because the **SET** and **WHERE** clauses are transposed. Answer d is incorrect; it does not use the **FOR** keyword in the **UPDATE** statement.

## Question 19

The correct answer is b. Usually the most efficient way to retrieve data that is going to be traversed and displayed quickly is to use the default forward-only server-side cursor with the lock type set to read only. Although this provides less functionality than the other options mentioned in the answers, scrollability and updateability are not required for this kind of operation.

## Question 20

The correct answers are b and c. The **CODEBASE** attribute of the <**OBJECT**> tag specifies the location of the component to download, as well as the version number. When the browser parses the Web page, it reads this information to determine whether to download and install the component using this information. Answer a is incorrect because the ID is specified as a separate attribute of the tag. Answer d is incorrect because data used to initialize the component can be provided by client-side script or <**PARAM**> tags.

## Question 21

The correct answers are a and c. Two primary issues should be addressed when you distribute binary components such as ActiveX controls on the Internet. The first issue is the safety of the component when run on the client machine. By marking the control safe for scripting and initialization, you are saying that scripts run using your control, or data that initializes the control, will not harm the user's computer. The second issue is accountability. By encrypting your control with a digital certificate from a trusted third party like VeriSign, your control is able to be traced to its source (you). Answer b is incorrect; a VBR file is used when creating a setup package for an application that accesses a component running on a remote server. Answer d is incorrect because an INF file is always created during an Internet setup package and does not address security issues.

## Question 22

The correct answer is b. The **BeginTrans** and **CommitTrans** methods of the ADO **Connection** object can be used to wrap data modification statements that must be executed as a single unit of work. If one of the statements after the **BeginTrans** and before the **CommitTrans** fails, then all the other statements will be rolled back. The insert into the **Customers** table is still committed because it was executed outside the scope of the transaction.

## Question 23

The correct answer is d. The DCOMCNFG utility can be used on the client computer to specify the remote server name. Answer a is incorrect; the **CODEBASE** attribute is used to specify the location of the component to install when used in a Web page and always installs the component locally. Answer b is incorrect, although the Package and Deployment Wizard can be used to include a VBR file that will configure the client application to use a remote component when the application is first installed. Answer c is incorrect because you run DCOMCNFG on the client and not on the server for this function.

## Question 24

The correct answer is d. The Package and Deployment Wizard can be used to create both standard and Internet setup packages, as well as save the scripts that create these packages. The deployment options include an option to place the setup package on a network drive. However, you must use the LPK_TOOL.EXE utility to create the license-packaging file (LPK) to distribute your licensed control on a Web page. If your control is licensed and an LPK file is not present, the control will not run in the browser.

## Question 25

The correct answer is a. Dependency files list all the runtime requirements of the project for which you are creating the package. This information is important for components that you create that are used in other projects. The resulting DEP file can then be read by the Package and Deployment Wizard to compile a list of all the support files needed. Answer b is incorrect because VB6DEP.INI contains dependency information for components that ship with VB. Answer c is incorrect, but VBR files are required and should be included in the setup package for a client application if your component will be instantiated on a remote server. Answer d is incorrect because the distribution method is irrelevant when dealing with dependency information.

## Question 26

The correct answer is c. Remember that if you change a method signature, you cannot use Binary Compatibility without creating a new interface within the component and retain compatibility. The new interface should implement the existing one and then recode all the members, making changes where appropriate. Existing clients will still be able to use the old interface, but new clients will be able to get a reference to the new interface. Answer a is incorrect because by fixing the method (changing its signature) you will be able to compile in Binary Compatibility if you ignore the warnings, but this will cause errors to occur when existing clients attempt to use the method. Answer b is incorrect because Project Compatibility creates new identifiers in the component, making it incompatible with previously released versions.

## Question 27

The correct answers are a and c. Parallel deployment and pipelining are two deployment techniques you can use to help alleviate the load on a single MTS server. Answer b is incorrect because MTS does not support any automatic load balancing. Answer d is incorrect because VB does not include any compilation options that reference load balancing.

## Question 28

The correct answer is b. Accessing or requesting any file with an .ASP extension that is found within the directory structure identified for the application will generate a user session, if one does not already exist. Initial invocation of the ASP ISAPI extension generates the user session, making the **Session** object available to the code within the requested ASP file. Answer a is incorrect because an HTML file with an .HTM or .HTML extension will not invoke the ASP extension, thus a session will not be generated. Answer c is incorrect because the **Session** object must be available to the server-side ASP script even for the first page requested. The **Session** object requires that a user session be established, thus the session must be created prior to the script in the requested file being initiated. Answer d is incorrect because ASP-based applications do not inherently require a unique form of application login. Accessing the server itself may require authentication, but not at the ASP application level.

## Question 29

The correct answer is c. In order to modify a member of an array stored within the **Session** object, the array must first be stored in a local variable. Once the modification has been made to the appropriate member of the local array, the modified array collection can then be stored back in the **Session** variable. Answer a is incorrect because the question asked to modify the second element in the array. Since arrays are zero-based, an index value of 2 would refer to the third element in the array. Answers b and d are incorrect because the **Session** object is stored as a collection. Attempting to access an indexed member of a **Session** variable, such as **Session("MemberIDs")(2)**, would access a member of the **Session("MemberIDs")** collection instead of a member of the array stored in the first member of the **Session** object collection.

## Question 30

The correct answer is c. IIS and ASP support any scripting language for which an interpreter has been properly installed on the Web server. Answers a, b, and d are incorrect because Perl or any other scripting language can be directly interpreted, without translation or porting, provided an interpreter has been installed.

## Question 31

The correct answer is d. Members of the **Application** or **Session** object collections do not need to be predefined or declared prior to using them in script. These objects are stored as dynamic collections, and members may be created "on the fly" within script simply by setting values to the collection member. Answers a, b, and c are incorrect because the dynamic nature of the **Application** and **Session** objects does not require any manner of member declaration prior to referencing the members in script.

## Question 32

The correct answer is a. The **Contents** collection is the default collection of the **Session** and **Application** built-in objects. Explicitly mentioning the collection name is not required. Answers c and d are additionally incorrect because the **Session** and **Application** objects do not expose collections with these names.

## Question 33

The correct answer is c. The **Abandon** method causes the **Session** object to be queued for deletion, but the object is not actually deleted until all script on the current page has completed execution. Answer a is incorrect because the **Session** object is initially queued for deletion, therefore it continues to be accessible.

## Question 34

The correct answer is d. During the **Session_OnEnd** event, only the **Application, Session,** and **Server** objects are available.

## Question 35

The correct answer is b. When attempting to access a member of a **Request** object collection without explicitly naming the collection to be searched, each collection is searched until a collection member of the desired name is found.

## Question 36

The correct answer is d. Visual Basic 6 introduces the Package and Deployment Wizard to allow the developer to package a project's files into one or more CAB files for deployment, deploy a packaged application to a desired media, and view or manipulate scripts generated during previous deployment or packaging sessions. The Package and Deployment Wizard can be used to create an installation program that can register components on a client system needed by the application. An application installed using this wizard will be registered with the client system's Add/Remove Programs applet in the Control Panel. This allows the application to be uninstalled from the client system conveniently. One of the available deployment methods provided by the Package and Deployment Wizard includes Web Publishing, allowing publishing of a package to a Web server for installation from the Web. Answer a is incorrect because Visual Basic 6 does not provide a utility called the Setup Installation Guide. Answer b is incorrect because the Package Export Wizard is provided by Microsoft Transaction Server to export MTS component packages. Answer c is incorrect because Visual Basic does not provide an Application Wizard utility.

## Question 37

The correct answer is c. Visual Basic provides the ability to set the Version Number of a project on the Make tab of the Project Properties dialog box. The version number is split into three parts: Major, Minor, and Revision. Changing one of the values that make up the version number will result in installation of the application, causing an update of any previous version of the application installed on the client system. Answer a is incorrect because the Package and Deployment Wizard does not provide the opportunity for the developer to provide or otherwise alter the version number entered on the Make tab of the Project Properties dialog box. Answer b is incorrect because the Version Compatibility setting for a project impacts the reassignment of identifiers for interfaces, type libraries, and/or components, but does not impact the application universally when updating an existing version. Answer d is incorrect because Visual Basic does not provide an automatic version control feature. Visual Basic does provide an auto-increment functionality that provides automatic version updating of the application between successive compilations.

## Question 38

The correct answer is b. To maintain n-tier architecture design in a distributed application consisting of four layers, data population in user controls should occur in a systematic order through neighboring layers. This means that data from a database is used to populate data service objects, which in turn populate business objects, which in turn are used to finally populate the controls in the user interface layer. Answer a is incorrect because retrieving data directly from a database would violate the separation of application services as defined by an n-tier architecture. Answer c is incorrect because data service objects reside in a non-neighboring layer to the user services tier. Answer d is incorrect because the data service objects would be bypassed, deviating from an n-tier architecture.

## Question 39

The correct answer is d. Unique characteristics of data that need to be exposed for use by client applications to manipulate, access, or otherwise modify should be implemented as properties of objects. Information designed to uniquely identify a collection of data that is combined with classes to create objects should be accessible as distinct attributes of the objects, and only a property allows such direct and distinct physical implementation. Answer a is incorrect because an event is an action that does not directly map to a unique attribute of an object, but rather indicates a certain state or condition regarding information that has been achieved. Answer b is incorrect because a user-defined data type does not, by itself, allow access to information stored within an instance of a variable defined with the data type. Answer c is incorrect because a method indicates a series of code statements to expose for invocation on demand by a client using the component, but does not inherently represent data used with a component.

## Question 40

The correct answers are a and b. Both choices will bring up the Components dialog box. The default tab for the Components dialog box is the Controls tab on which the list of all currently registered components can be found. Selecting the appropriate component from this list will make it available on the Controls toolbox. Answer c is incorrect because the Browse button is only used when the component has not been previously registered on the system, and the question stated that the control was already registered on the system. Answer d is incorrect because controls are not added using the References dialog box.

## Question 41

The correct answer is b. The **UserDocument** object has access to a **HyperLink** object. The **HyperLink** object has a method called **NavigateTo** that allows hyperlink-aware document host containers to initiate an HTTP request for the URL passed to the **NavigateTo** method. Answer a is incorrect because although the **WebBrowser** object provided by Internet Explorer through SHDOCVW.DLL does have a **Navigate** method, this method is not made available to **UserDocument** objects. Answer c is incorrect because the **NavigateTo** method is provided by the **HyperLink** object, not the **UserDocument** object. Answer d is incorrect because the method provided by the **HyperLink** object for issuing HTTP requests is named the **NavigateTo** method, rather than **Navigate**.

## Question 42

The correct answer is a. Setting the **MTSTransactionMode** property to **UsesTransaction** will result in the component's methods participating in client transactions, if they exist, and not utilizing transactions if the client does not have a transaction. Answer b is incorrect because the **RequiresTransaction** setting for the **MTSTransactionMode** class module property will cause component methods to participate in client transactions, but in the event that the client is not participating in a transaction, the component method invoked will cause a transaction to be created. Answer c is incorrect because **SupportsTransactions** is not a valid setting for the **MTSTransactionMode** property. **Supports Transactions** is the MTS package configuration setting equivalent of **UsesTransaction**. Answer d is incorrect because setting the **MTSTransactionMode** property to **NotAnMTSObject** will not allow the component to participate in transactions.

## Question 43

The correct answer is c. The Watch variable being configured as shown in Figure 13.1 needs to be set to Break When Value Is True. This setting will cause the project to enter break mode exactly when the value of the variable named **User** obtains the value of "Goofy", exactly as desired by the question. Answers a and b are incorrect; because it is a global variable, if the **User** variable is assigned the value of "Goofy" outside the scope defined by the context chosen, the project will not enter into break mode when desired. Answer d is incorrect because these settings will result in the project entering break mode whenever the value of **User** changes.

## Question 44

The correct answer is a. To ensure that only code that can be successfully compiled is inserted into the Visual SourceSafe database, you must compile the code prior to checking the modified code into Visual SourceSafe. Answer b is incorrect because VB and VSS do not provide an auto-compile wizard. Answer c is incorrect because a nightly compile of checked-in code does not address the question's concerns. Answer d is incorrect because it does not address checking in files, or compiling of checked-in code.

## Question 45

The correct answer is d. Navigating to an ActiveX document-based application is performed by navigating to a VBD file created for the initial **UserDocument** that defines the start of the application. Answer a is incorrect because beginning with Visual Basic 6, the **CODEBASE** information formerly provided by a corresponding HTML file is now embedded within the VBD file. Answer c is incorrect because the Automation server is not navigated to directly. Answer b is incorrect because an ASP file is used to house and instantiate DHTML applications, not ActiveX documents.

## Question 46

The correct answer is b. When a Watch variable being monitored is outside the current scope, the value shown for the variable is <out of context>.

## Question 47

The correct answer is c. When debugging an ActiveX control by adding an instance of the control to a **Form** object, within a Standard EXE project added to your ActiveX control project, entering break mode and stepping through the code line by line is supported, even when the code for the control is invoked. Answer a is incorrect because an ActiveX control is a form of in-process component. An instance of the control existing within one instance of Visual Basic will not be accessible to a project running within another instance. Answer b is incorrect because compiling the code and using the control in a Visual Basic project will not allow the control's code to be debugged. Answer d is incorrect because an ActiveX control project by itself cannot be run.

## Question 48

The correct answers are b and d. In order to run a distributed application using remote MTS components, the system must have DCOM support. On a Windows 95/98 system, DCOM support must be installed. After DCOM support is installed, running the application installation executable should register all the necessary remote components properly. Answer a is incorrect because MS-DTC is not inherently required for just using remote components when directly called. Answer c is incorrect because using an MTS component does not require—nor use—MTS on the client system, which would violate the requirement that the components are running remotely.

## Question 49

The correct answer is c. When attempting to establish a clean break from existing component versions, only setting the Version Compatibility option to No Compatibility, as opposed to any other value, will generate a clean set of GUID for the interfaces, components, and so on. All other settings will retain some degree of compatibility that will link the previous version of the control to the new version. Answer a is incorrect because setting the Version Compatibility option to Binary Compatibility will produce the exact opposite effect of the desired one. A complete degree of compatibility will be retained between the component versions. Answer b is incorrect because the Version Compatibility option does not have a Retain Compatibility setting. Answer d is incorrect because setting the Version Compatibility option to Project Compatibility will retain the same component class ID, resulting in the component remaining a compatible version of its predecessor.

## Question 50

The correct answer is c. The **rdExecDirect** option instructs RDO to use the **SQLExecDirect** function of the ODBC API. By using the **SQLExecDirect** function, the **SQLPrepare** step of the ODBC API is skipped, causing the preparation of temporary stored procedures to be skipped. Answer a is incorrect because it instructs RDO to download all the data for long binary and long character columns, but does not directly control the creation of temporary stored procedures. Answer b is incorrect because the RDO **rdAsyncEnable** option instructs the command to operate asynchronously. Answer d is incorrect because **rdOpenKeySet** is a cursor type constant that has no bearing on the mode of execution for the command.

Although it wasn't explicitly discussed in the book, this topic is important for understanding the fundamentals covered in the exam.

## Question 51

The correct answer is d. An application can be marked for unattended execution and must be designed without the user interface elements. ActiveX DLL or ActiveX EXE projects are therefore safe for setting to unattended execution, as long as they do not require user interface elements or user interaction, such as with **Form** objects. Answers a and b are incorrect because projects marked for unattended execution can't have **UserControl** or **UserDocument** objects added to them. These objects will gray out or be unavailable for adding once the projects are marked for unattended execution. Projects already containing one of these object types will have the option of unattended execution disabled in the Project Properties dialog box. Answer c is incorrect because it depends on user interaction; therefore it would require some manner of user interface element, which would be suppressed if set to unattended execution.

## Question 52

The correct answers are a and c. When evaluating the conditional compilation logic shown in the code segment for the question, Win32 and Win16 are compile constants used to determine the system platform on which the compiler is occurring. When compiling on a 16-bit Windows development platform, Win16 automatically evaluates **True**, whereas Win32 evaluates to **False**. The opposite is true when compiling on a 32-bit Windows development platform. In the question scenario, code segments B and C, mapping to answers a and c, will not be included when compiling on a 32-bit development environment, because Win32 will evaluate to **True**, causing only code segment A to be included. For this same reason, answers b and d are incorrect.

## Question 53

The correct answer is c. The **WebClass** object has a method, **URLFor**, that provides the current URL that represents a specified Webitem. When the final exact location of an IIS application is not known at development time, then the **URLFor** method may be necessary to determine and provide by code the proper URL for a specified Webitem. The **URLFor** method can take an event parameter, but simply passing the name of the Webitem to the **URLFor** method of the **WebClass** object in code suffices. This method is often used with the **Write** method of the **Response** object. Answer a is incorrect because the **URLEncode** method of the **Server** object is used to modify a provided URL to ensure that the characters that comprise the URL string do not contain characters that would invalidate or otherwise confuse a browser or Web server being asked to either request or respond to the invalid URL. Answer b is incorrect because the **NameInURL** property of the **WebClass** object determines the name of the ASP file that is auto-generated for the **WebClass** object. This ASP file is used to host the **WebClass** object. Answer d is incorrect because the **HTMLEncode** method of the **Server** object is used to modify character strings to apply HTML encoding to a string to allow the string to be evaluated by the client browser as properly formed HTML code.

## Question 54

The correct answer is c. The **WriteProperties** event is fired when the **PropertyChanged** method has been previously invoked to inform the application that information has changed that requires saving. The proper place to save or persist state information such as this is by using the **WriteProperty** method from within the **WriteProperties** event. Answer a is incorrect because the **InitProperties** event is fired only upon loading a component until information has been saved to the **PropertyBag** object, after which it will no longer fire. This event is involved in the process of setting up information, rather than saving changed information. Answer b is incorrect because the **ReadProperties** event is also dealing primarily with the reading of information for a component previously having been saved. Answer d is incorrect because the **Initialize** event deals with the start of a component, not the saving of information periodically throughout the life of a component.

## Question 55

The correct answer is d. In order to provide multiple objects to a single client from a single instance of your component, the **Instancing** property must be set to **MultiUse**. This is not enough, though, for the component must be out of process in order to allow multiple clients to create objects from just one instance of your component. This, therefore, requires an ActiveX EXE with the **Instancing** property set to **MultiUse**. Answer a is incorrect because if the **Instancing** property is set to **SingleUse** for an ActiveX EXE, multiple clients can create objects from a single component, *but* every object of a given class created starts a new instance of the component. Answer c is incorrect because ActiveX documents create single instances of visible components, therefore they cannot be shared among clients.

## Question 56

The correct answer is c. When a component is designed to run within the MTS environment and participate in transactions, the component must be designed to invoke the **SetAbort** and **SetComplete** methods of the **ObjectContext** object when necessary to signal that methods of the component have either completed successfully or failed. In the case of the scenario presented by the question, the **SetAbort** method would need to be fired. Answers a and d are incorrect because the **OnTransactionAbort** and **OnTransactionCommit** events fire in response to the **SetAbort** and **SetComplete** methods, respectively, having been fired. These events are available to ASP objects, allowing ASP pages to be transacted and therefore participate in MTS transactions. Answer b is incorrect because the scenario calls for a failure of the step to be provided for, not a successful completion, which would require that the **SetComplete** method be invoked.

## Question 57

The correct answer is c. The code listing indicates an attempt to check whether the direct caller of the component belongs to the recently defined and applied "Dev" role. If the client application or another object calling this object is running under the security context of an account that has been mapped to the "Dev" role, then only by using the **IsCallerInRole** method, passing the name of the role to be checked, will produce the desired programmatic security checks. In fact, line [6] as presented would produce an error, as the **IsSecurityEnabled** method does not expect an argument of any kind. Answer a is incorrect because the **IsSecurityEnabled** method only determines if security is established on the object, but does not provide any information about the role membership of the direct caller of the object. Answer b is incorrect because the **GetOriginalCaller** method does not exist. The **ObjectContext** object does have a **SecurityProperty** object that possesses a **GetOriginalCallerName** method, among others, but this does not check for role membership of the original caller.

# Glossary

**Active Server Page (ASP)**—Special variation of an HTML page that also contains server-side script that is executed on the server prior to sending the page to the client.

**ActiveX Data Objects (ADO)**—An object layer that provides simplified access to the OLE DB interfaces. ADO provides a flexible model that allows VB, VBScript, and VBA developers to communicate with a number of data providers.

**ADO Command object**—An object that encapsulates the properties of a command that is to be sent to a data provider. Typically, ADO **Command** objects are used to call stored procedures and statements that are to be reused.

**ADO Connection object**—An object that represents a connection to a data provider. The **Open** method is used to connect to the provider and send it a connection string.

**ADO Recordset object**—An object that represents a set of records returned by a data provider. Methods such as **MoveNext** and **MovePrevious** are used to scroll through the recordset. The functionality of the object depends on the cursor type used to create it.

**Ambient properties**—Properties exposed by the container of a control, but not implemented by the control itself. Ambient properties are used to assist the developer in placing and working with the control.

**Application object**—Built-in ASP object used to provide access to special variable collections that are universally accessible to all instances of a given ASP file in memory being processed.

**ApplyChanges event**—Event of the **PropertyPage** object that is fired when the developer applies changes to properties or clicks the OK button. It is used to set the values of the properties based on the user interface controls of the **PropertyPage** object.

**Archive operation**—Visual SourceSafe Administrator process available for removing or archiving portions of a VSS project. Also used to initiate moving a project from database to database.

**Assert method**—The **Debug** object provides an **Assert** method for programmatically inducing break mode.

**Authenticode**—A process using digital signatures and encryption that is used by Internet Explorer to determine the author of an ActiveX component.

**Binary Compatibility**—An option that can be set that instructs the VB compiler to use the same unique identifiers from previous builds, if possible. It allows clients compiled against previous builds to work with versions compiled with this option.

**Breakpoint**—A special setting configured sequentially within code to instruct the Visual Basic IDE to pause program execution and enter into break mode. Breakpoints can be issued by using the **Assert** method of the **Debug** object, using the **Stop** command, or by visually establishing a breakpoint by using the F9 key or clicking in the left margin of the code editor.

**Business Services**—A segment of the software that encapsulates the business logic and processes of a distributed application.

**Cabinet files**—Compressed files with a .CAB extension. These are frequently used to distributed ActiveX components through Web pages.

**Call Stack**—A special VB IDE debug window used during break mode to see the current hierarchy of invoked application methods.

**CanPropertyChange method**—Method of the **UserControl** object used to determine if a property can be changed. Often used when developing ActiveX controls that bind to data controls to check if a particular property is bound to read-only field.

**CausesValidation property**—Property available in VB for all standard and intrinsic controls. It is used to determine whether the **Validate** event is fired on the control that had focus prior to the control for which the property has been set.

**Class module**—Used as the foundation or starting point for creating COM components. Class modules can be used in many other types of Visual Basic projects, but when used in ActiveX DLL or EXE projects, they provide templates for creating new objects.

**CODEBASE**—Attribute of the **<OBJECT>** tag used to refer to ActiveX components in a Web page. Refers to the location and version of the component so that it may be downloaded if it does not already exist on the client computer.

**COM DLL**—Another name for an ActiveX DLL.

**COM EXE**—Another name for an ActiveX EXE.

**Compiler options/switches**—Settings provided by Visual Basic to alter the characteristics of the binary-compiled executable.

**Conceptual design**—A process used to determine the fundamental business problem to be solved by a piece of software. May include user interviews and requirements gathering.

**Conditional compiler constants**—Special constants used and evaluated only by conditional compilation directives. Defined with the **#CONST** command.

**Conditional compiler directives**—Special variations of the standard **If...then** statement pair used for conditional programming. **#If, #Else,** and **#End If** are used for directing the flow of compiling into native code, dictating which code segments are included in the binary executable and which are not.

**Constituent controls**—ActiveX or intrinsic controls that combine to make up the user interface of an ActiveX control written in VB. These controls are placed on the **UserControl** object at design time.

**Container**—When dealing with ActiveX controls it refers to the program that is hosting the control. Examples of containers include the Visual Basic IDE and Internet Explorer.

**Controls collection**—Collection of **Control** objects exposed by the **Form** object that represents all the controls on the form.

**Cursors**—Defines the functionality of a set of records accessed by a program (including whether they can be updated and how they can be navigated). Cursor types in ADO include Forward Only, Dynamic, Static, and Keyset.

**Data Services**—A segment of the software that provides the business services with the ability to retrieve, insert, update, and delete data.

**DataMembers collection**—A collection exposed by the **UserControl** object that represents the recordsets made available by an ActiveX control acting as a data source. Bound controls can bind to one of the available recordsets.

**DCOM**—Derivation of or enhancement to the Component Object Model that provides transparent support for component communication over disparate networks or between remote systems.

**DCOMCNFG**—A utility used to configure the properties of ActiveX components to allow the components to be called over a network. Properties include the remote server name and security settings.

**Declarative security**—Explicit assignment of security or authorization checking for a component or package within MTS by the MTS Administrator.

**DHTML application**—A type of application that produces a DLL for downloading by a Web client. The DLL intercepts and processes all user interactions and provides the necessary application logic for the HTML-based Web application.

**Disconnected recordsets**—A type of ADO recordset that allows updates to be made while the recordset is disconnected from the data provider. Modifications can later be sent to the data provider when a connection is re-established.

**Dynamic load balancing**—A method of implementing load balancing whereby clients are assigned to use components running on specific servers dynamically using statistics such as network topology or network load.

**Early binding**—Used to describe a method VB uses to set up calls to a COM object. Used when declaring the object with its assigned ProgID. Can take the form of DispID or vtable binding and is more efficient because the VB compiler can resolve the calls during compilation.

**GetDataMember event**—Event of the **UserControl** object that is fired when an ActiveX control acting as a data source receives a request for information about the recordsets that are exposed by the control.

**GetObjectContext**—An API provided by MTS for use by components in obtaining an object reference to a client's transaction.

**HelpContextID property**—Property of ActiveX and intrinsic controls used to display the appropriate topic within a help file when the user presses the F1 key.

**HelpFile property**—Property of the **App** object used to specify the name and location of the help file to be called when the user presses the F1 key.

**HTML Template file**—A file used by **WebClass** objects within IIS applications to provide an initial framework or guide for the HTML code to be returned to the client.

**HyperLink object**—Object available to the **UserDocument** object for providing HTTP request capabilities to the document.

**IIS application**—An IIS application is a type of project that produces a server-side DLL and ASP file. The DLL contains **WebClass** objects that are used to respond to event and user interaction initiated by the client.

**Immediate window**—Special VB IDE window used for debugging. This window allows variable and property values to be displayed or modified, methods to be invoked, and general code to be executed out of sequence.

**Implements keyword**—VB keyword used in class modules to implement an existing COM interface. Can be used to allow client programs to use interfaces interchangeably. Provides polymorphic behavior for COM interfaces created in VB.

**Information files**—Files with an .INF extension that contain all the information necessary for Internet Explorer to completely install software from a .CAB or .ZIP file.

**InitProperties event**—Event of the **UserControl** object that is fired by the container when the control is placed on a form in design mode. Used to initialize properties of the control.

**Inner join**—A type of join used to retrieve rows from multiple tables based on common column values, where each table participating in the join satisfies the join condition.

**Instancing property**—Dictates whether instances of the class can be created by other applications. This property is used to determine whether a class module is available for public instantiation or for use solely by internal, private code modules.

**Internet Component Download**—The term used to describe the process by which Internet Explorer uncompresses and installs ActiveX components contained in CAB or ZIP files.

**IsCallerInRole method**—A method of the **ObjectContext** object available in MTS-enabled components that is used to determine whether the direct caller of the object belongs to a specified role defined and applicable to the component invoking the method.

**IsSecurityEnabled method**—A method of the **ObjectContext** object available in MTS-enabled components that is used to determine whether declarative security or authorization checking is enabled for the component using the method.

**IUnknown**—The most basic COM interface inherited by all COM interfaces. Contains the **QueryInterface, AddRef,** and **Release** methods.

**KeyDown and KeyUp events**—Events of the **Form** object that are fired when the user presses or releases any key on the keyboard. Each passes in arguments that represent the **KeyCode** value that corresponds to a constant and the state of the Alt, Ctrl, and Shift keys.

**KeyPress event**—Event fired when the user presses any of the ANSI keys (printable characters). It passes in the ASCII key value that can be altered.

**KeyPreview**—Property of the **Form** object that is fired when any keystrokes are made on the form and before they are available to the control. Used in conjunction with the **KeyPreview** property of the form.

**Late binding**—Used to describe a method VB uses to set up calls to a COM object. Late binding is used when declaring the object with the **Object** keyword. It uses the Dispatch interface of the component and is less efficient, though more flexible, because the compiler cannot resolve calls during compilation.

**Load balancing**—Refers to techniques and algorithms used to determine which clients use components on which servers. Types of load balancing include static and dynamic load balancing.

**Locals window**—Special debugging window that displays the values of the currently executing line of code.

**Lock and Unlock methods**—Methods used by the ASP **Application** object to control application access to application variables.

**Logical design**—A process used to determine the architecture of the software. This primarily involves segmenting the application into User, Business, and Data services.

**LostFocus event**—Event available in VB for all standard and intrinsic controls. It is fired as focus moves from the control and cannot be used to stop the focus from moving.

**MTSTransactionMode property**—A new class module property introduced in VB6 to define the transactional behavior of components within the MTS environment.

**NavigateTo method**—Method of the **HyperLink** object used to navigate to and load a different document in to the browser.

**NextItem property**—**WebClass** object property used within IIS applications to define the next Webitem to be immediately sent to the client. Typically first set in the **Start** event of the **WebClass** object.

**ObjectContext object**—An interface provided by MTS to expose a reference or link to the transaction context of the client's transaction, if one exists.

**OLE DB**—A set of COM interfaces that define a standard way to connect to, retrieve, and manipulate data. This is the lynchpin in Microsoft's Universal Data Access strategy.

**OLE DB Provider**—A layer of software that implements the vendor-specific code necessary to communicate with a data provider. Analogous to ODBC drivers.

**OnTransactionAbort event**—Event made available to ASP in conjunction with participation in an MTS transaction. This event fires within the ASP when the transaction has been aborted by one or more components participating in the transaction.

**OnTransactionCommit event**—Event made available to ASP in conjunction with participation in an MTS transaction. This event fires within the ASP when the transaction has been committed by MTS.

**Optimistic locking**—A method of locking in which the record is not locked until the actual update occurs. This method ensures greater concurrency, but less consistency. Can be specified when creating an ADO **Recordset** object.

**Package**—The name given to the organization unit housing components running within the MTS environment. A package provides process boundary definition and security boundaries.

**Parallel deployment**—A method of deploying components in which exact copies of the components are deployed across multiple servers. Used to reduce the utilization of any particular server running components.

**Parent project**—The name given to topmost organization unit available for storing development projects within a Visual SourceSafe database.

**Pessimistic locking**—A method of locking in which the record is locked from when it is first edited to the time the actual update occurs. This method ensures greater consistency, but less concurrency. Can be specified when creating an ADO **Recordset** object.

**Physical design**—A process used to determine how the software will be implemented in terms of technology and hardware. A primary concern is whether single or multiple tiers will be used to deploy the application.

**Print method**—Used within the Immediate window to display information. Can be replaced with a question mark (?) as a shortcut. Can also be used as a method of the **Form** object, to print information onto the form.

**Programmatic security**—Use of assorted methods of the **ObjectContext** object, such as **IsCallerInRole** and **IsSecurityEnabled**, to apply security measures to component functionality.

**Project Compatibility**—An option that can be set that instructs the VB compiler to use the same type library information from previous builds. Does not allow clients compiled against previous builds to work with versions compiled with this option.

**Property Get function**—Defines the event-handling procedure or function for the read aspect of an object property

**Property Let function**—Defines the event-handling procedure or function for the write aspect of an object property for properties returned as a nonobject data type.

**Property Set function**—Defines the event-handling procedure or function for the write aspect of an object property for properties returned as an object data type.

**PropertyBag object**—A "black-box" object that is provided by the container to store and read properties for an ActiveX control created in VB. VB uses this object to instruct the container to save and retrieve properties when the control is initialized and destroyed.

**PropertyChanged method**—A method of the **PropertyBag** object used to notify **PropertyBag** that a property has changed, so the **WriteProperties** event will fire.

**ReadProperties event**—Event of a **UserControl** object that is fired when the control is created by the container and used to read properties from persistent storage.

**Request object**—Built-in ASP object used to retrieve information sent from the client, such as by submitting a form or appending to URLs.

**Response object**—Built-in ASP object used to send information to the client in the form of HTTP responses. The most common method is the **Write** method.

**Restore operation**—Visual SourceSafe Administrator operation used to add a previously archived project into a VSS database.

**Reverse-delta storage**—A highly efficient form of storage used by Visual SourceSafe in which only the changes to data are stored in a database, along with the most recent full copy of the data being stored. This allows for rapid reverting back to previous versions of a file or piece of data, while reducing the overall storage requirements to maintain data history.

**Role**—The name given to an abstract grouping of user accounts and/or NT groups used to limit access to components or packages within MTS

**Role membership folder**—A folder that exists in the MTS Explorer hierarchy for components and component interfaces that lists the defined roles applied to the component.

**SelectedControls collection**—A collection of **Control** objects used in a property page to refer to the instance of the ActiveX control that the developer selected before invoking the property page.

**SelectionChanged event**—Event of the **PropertyPage** object that is fired when the property page is opened; it is used to populate controls on the property page with property values from the control itself.

**Server object**—Built-in ASP object used to expose information, settings, or methods of a server-level application. For example, **CreateObject** is the most common method of the **Server** object.

**Session object**—Built-in ASP object used to stored variables that are accessible from any ASP within an individual user session.

**SetAbort method**—A method of the **ObjectContext** object used to notify MTS that the results of the calling object method are such that the transaction may not be completed.

**SetComplete method**—A method of the **ObjectContext** object used to notify MTS that the results of the calling object method are such that the transaction may be safely completed.

**Stack Overflow error**—An error that typically occurs when events in a VB program are called repeatedly until the memory is exhausted. This can occur if developers use the **LostFocus** event to validate data and keep the focus on a particular control.

**Static load balancing**—A method of implementing load balancing whereby clients are permanently assigned to use components running on specific servers.

**Stored procedures**—Database-specific code that resides on the database server and can be used to encapsulate SQL statements or flow of control syntax. They often provide good performance by being precompiled by the database server and may also abstract the database schema from calling programs.

**Transactional commit and rollback**—Methods of ensuring that data remains consistent in a relational database. Multiple SQL statements may be included in a single transaction that will not be written to disk until committed. Rollback is used to return the data to the state before the beginning of the transaction, in the event that one of the SQL statements fails.

**UpdateBatch method**—Method called when using an ADO disconnected recordset to send all modifications to the data provider.

**User Services**—A segment of the software that provides the user interface and interacts directly with the user. May include a graphical or programmatic interface.

**UserControl object**—The template used to create the user interface of an ActiveX control in VB. It provides the methods, properties, and events that allow the control to interact with the container of the control.

**UserDocument object**—The template used to create the user interface of an ActiveX document. It provides the methods, properties, and events that allow the document to interact with the container of the document.

**Validate event**—Event available in VB for all standard and intrinsic controls that can be used to validate the contents of the control and keep the focus on the control. It is preferable to using the **LostFocus** event.

**VBControlExtender**—A special VB object used to handle events for dynamically created controls that are not referenced by the project. It exposes a single event, **ObjectEvent**, that passes in an argument of type **EventInfo** that contains the event name and its parameters.

**VBD file**—File that is produced for an ActiveX document. This is the file that must be navigated to start or launch an ActiveX document in a browser.

**VBR file**—File that contains Registry settings that must be made on a client computer in order for it to use a remote server. It must be included in the setup package if the component is to be called across the network.

**Visual Component Manager**—Utility based on the Microsoft Repository used to publish components that can then be shared by developers across a company.

**Watch variable**—A special expression defined whose value can be displayed automatically in the Watch window during program execution. Can also be defined to force break mode.

**Watch window**—Special VB IDE debugging window used to display currently defined Watch variables during program execution.

**WebClass object**—A special COM object contained within IIS applications that can be instantiated by user interactions and requests.

**Webitem**—Object within an IIS application used by the **WebClass** object to send information to the client in the form of an HTTP response. Typically, Webitems are HTML template files included with the IIS application.

**WriteProperties event**—Event of the **UserControl** object that is fired when the control is destroyed by the container and used to store properties in persistent storage.

# Index

# R

# CERTIFIED CRAMMER SOCIETY

PHI SLAMMA CRAMMA

breed apart, a cut above the rest—a true professional. Highly skilled and superbly trained, certified IT professionals are unquestionably the world's most elite computer experts. In an effort to appropriately recognize this privileged crowd, The Coriolis Group is proud to introduce the Certified Crammer Society. If you are a certified IT professional, it is our pleasure to invite you to become a Certified Crammer Society member.

Membership is free to all certified professionals and benefits include a membership kit that contains your official membership card and official Certified Crammer Society blue denim ball cap emblazoned with the Certified Crammer Society crest—proudly displaying the Crammer motto "Phi Slamma Cramma"—and featuring a genuine leather bill. The kit also includes your password to the Certified Crammers-Only Web site containing monthly discreet messages designed to provide you with advance notification about certification testing information, special book excerpts, and inside industry news not found anywhere else; monthly Crammers-Only discounts on selected Coriolis titles; *Ask the Series Editor* Q and A column; cool contests with great prizes; and more.

## GUIDELINES FOR MEMBERSHIP

Registration is free to professionals certified in Microsoft, A+, or Oracle DBA.
Coming soon: Sun Java, Novell, and Cisco. Send or email your contact information and proof of your certification (test scores, membership card, or official letter) to:

Certified Crammer Society Membership Chairperson
**THE CORIOLIS GROUP, LLC**
14455 North Hayden Road, Suite 220, Scottsdale, Arizona 85260-6949
Fax: 602.483.0193 • Email: ccs@coriolis.com

---

## APPLICATION

Name: _____

Society Alias: _____

Choose a secret code name to correspond with us
and other Crammer Society members.
Please use no more than eight characters.

Address: _____

Email: _____

# CORIOLIS HELP CENTER

Here at The Coriolis Group, we strive to provide the finest customer service in the technical education industry. We're committed to helping you reach your certification goals by assisting you in the following areas.

## Talk to the Authors

We'd like to hear from you! Please refer to the "How to Use This Book" section in the "Introduction" of every Exam Cram guide for our authors' individual email addresses.

## Web Page Information

The Certification Insider Press Web page provides a host of valuable information that's only a click away. For information in the following areas, please visit us at:

**www.coriolis.com/cip/default.cfm**

- Titles and other products
- Book content updates
- Roadmap to Certification Success guide
- New Adaptive Testing changes
- New Exam Cram Live! seminars
- New Certified Crammer Society details
- Sample chapters and tables of contents
- Manuscript solicitation
- Special programs and events

## Contact Us by Email

Important addresses you may use to reach us at The Coriolis Group.

### eci@coriolis.com

To subscribe to our FREE, bi-monthly on-line newsletter, *Exam Cram Insider*. Keep up to date with the certification scene. Included in each *Insider* are certification articles, program updates, new exam information, hints and tips, sample chapters, and more.

### techsupport@coriolis.com

For technical questions and problems with CD-ROMs. Products broken, battered, or blown-up? Just need some installation advice? Contact us here.

### ccs@coriolis.com

To obtain membership information for the *Certified Crammer Society*, an exclusive club for the certified professional. Get in on members-only discounts, special information, expert advice, contests, cool prizes, and free stuff for the certified professional. Membership is FREE. Contact us and get enrolled today!

### cipq@coriolis.com

For book content questions and feedback about our titles, drop us a line. This is the good, the bad, and the questions address. Our customers are the best judges of our products. Let us know what you like, what we could do better, or what question you may have about any content. Testimonials are always welcome here, and if you send us a story about how an Exam Cram guide has helped you ace a test, we'll give you an official Certification Insider Press T-shirt.

### custserv@coriolis.com

For solutions to problems concerning an order for any of our products. Our staff will promptly and courteously address the problem. Taking the exams is difficult enough. We want to make acquiring our study guides as easy as possible.

## Book Orders & Shipping Information

### orders@coriolis.com

To place an order by email or to check on the status of an order already placed.

### coriolis.com/bookstore/default.cfm

To place an order through our online bookstore.

### 1.800.410.0192

To place an order by phone or to check on an order already placed.